The Used Book Lover's Guide
to the
Central States

Colorado, New Mexico, Arizona, Texas, Nevada
Utah, Montana, Idaho, Wyoming, Nebraska
Oklahoma, Kansas, North Dakota, South Dakota, Tennessee
Arkansas, Louisiana, Mississippi and Alabama

By
David S. and Susan Siegel

Book Hunter Press
PO Box 193
Yorktown Heights, NY 10598

The Used Book Lover's Guide To The Central States by David S. and Susan Siegel. © Copyright 1997. Book Hunter Press.

Printed and bound in the United States of America

Library of Congress Catalog Card Number: 96-096937

ISBN 0-9634112-6-8

Acknowledgments

We would like to thank the Arkansas Booksellers Association, the Guild of Arizona Antiquarian Booksellers, the Colorado Antiquarian Booksellers Association and the Mountains & Plains Booksellers Association for their membership directories.

Thanks also to the dealers who publish the following area guides: Book Buyer's Guide to New, Used and Antiquarian Bookstores in the Phoenix, AZ, Metropolitan Area, Used and Out-Of-Print Booksellers of the Greater Houston Area, the Used & Antiquarian Booksellers Directory for Albuquerque, NM, Santa Fe's Dealers in Antiquarian and Out-Of-Print Books, the Booksellers Guide of Southern Nevada, the Northern Nevada Antiquarian & Used Booksellers Guide, Tulsa Area Bookstores, the Northern Colorado & Southern Wyoming Used Book Buyer's Guide and the 1966 Directory of Boulder, CO booksellers.

Special thanks also to Robert W. Strain, David G. Nussbaum, Richard Wilcox, Donald Russell, Fred Smith and Allen J. Petersen for their help identifying dealers in their regions and to Alan and Susan Berkow who kept their eyes open for used book stores while traveling in the West.

Last but not least, we would like to thank the over 1,250 book dealers listed in this Guide who patiently answered our questionnaire, responded to our phone calls and chatted with us during our visits. Without their cooperation, this book would not have been possible.

Also Available From Book Hunter Press

The Used Book Lover's Guide to New England, a guide to over 750 used book dealers in Maine, New Hampshire, Vermont, Massachusetts, Connecticut and Rhode Island.

The Used Book Lover's Guide to the Mid-Atlantic States, a guide to over 900 used book dealers in New York, New Jersey, Pennsylvania and Delaware.

The Used Book Lover's Guide to the South Atlantic States, a guide to over 600 used book dealers in Maryland, Washington, DC, Virginia, North Carolina, South Carolina, Georgia and Florida.

The Used Book Lover's Guide to the Midwest, a guide to over 1,000 used book dealers in Ohio, Indiana, Illinois, Michigan, Wisconsin, Minnesota, Iowa, Missouri, Kentucky and West Virginia.

The Used Book Lover's Guide to the Pacific Coast States, a guide to over 1,350 used book dealers in California, Oregon, Washington, Alaska and Hawaii.

If you've found this book useful in your book hunting endeavors and would like to order copies of any of the other guides, you will find a convenient Order From at the back of this book. Or, you can call or write to us at:

Book Hunter Press
PO Box 193
Yorktown Heights, NY 10598
(914) 245-6608
Fax: (914) 245-2630

Table of Contents

List of Maps

4

Is It Possible?

It's difficult to believe.

Little did we know what we were getting ourselves into back in December, 1992 when we wrote the "Genesis" for T*he Used Book Lover's Guide to New England*, our very first guide.

What's even more difficult to believe is that here we are completing the series we once dreamt about – comprehensive guides to used book dealers in *ALL* 50 states. Our guides have indeed become the Baedekers to the American used book world.

Looking back, we weren't sure if our dream made any sense. Would people buy our book? Where there other bookaholics like us who planned vacation trips around the locations of used book stores? Would there be a second or third or even fourth volume?

And on a more practical level, would we be able to sell enough books to cover our costs and perhaps even turn a small profit?

Little did we know then what we were about to start. And little did we know that our fun "retirement" project would quickly mushroom into a full time business venture.

Charting the unknown, we decided to start out close to home following our New Englandd guide with one to the Mid-Atlantic States.Then, once we sensed we were on the right track, we continued down the Atlantic seaboard publishing a South Atlantic Guide and into American's heartland for a Midwest edition. Given it's large number of used book dealers, the Pacific Coast guide was the next logical addition to the series.

We then took a close look at the map and studied the 19 states we had not yet covered, what we discovered was several clusters of states, none of which had a large enough population base or a sufficient number of used book dealers to sustain a guide of its own. For that reason, we decided to combine these states into the single Central States guide.

Needless to say, scheduling visits to the shops in this vast a region has been a logistical challenge, not to mention an exhausting experience, both for us and for our car. But out of necessity, we've learned how to make the most effective use of our time on the road; while Susan chats with the owner double checking store hours, clarifying travel directions and asking about other dealers in the area David pokes around to see if he can find a hidden treasure for this own collection but mostly to find the right words to describe the shop to others. Usually, this does not take as much time as one might think as many shops have a lot in common. There are, of course, glorious exceptions, and if you've read any of our other guides, you'll have learned about these places in our "Comments."

Six guides. Fifty states. Six thousand dealers. And God know how many books. We've finally achieved our dream; Does this mean we're finished? Not quite.

Two years ago, before setting off for the Pacific Coast, we returned to New England to research a completely revised new edition. At periodic intervals, we plan to issue new editions for the other regions as well. And inbetween editions, we'll continue to make Annual Supplements available to our readers for a nominal charge.

For those of you who have asked us about Canada as a future protect, we smile and say that covering the USA has been a challenge enough for us – but – who knows.

David S. & Susan Siegel
September, 1996

How To Get The Most From This Guide

This guide is designed to help you find the books you're looking for, whether you visit used book shops in person or "browse" by mail or phone from the comfort of your home. It's also designed to help you access the collections of the three categories of used book dealers: open shop, by appointment and mail order.

Open shop dealers maintain regular store hours. Their collections can vary in size from less than a 1,000 to more than 100,000 books and can either be a general stock covering most subject categories or a specialized collection limited to one or more specialty areas.

By appointment or chance dealers generally, but not always, have smaller collections, frequently quite specialized. Many of these dealers maintain their collections in their home. By phoning these dealers in advance, avid book hunters can easily combine a trip to open shops as well as to by appointment dealers in the same region.

Mail order only dealers issue catalogs and/or sell to people on their mailing list or in response to written or phone inquiries.

Antique malls. A growing number of dealers in all three of the above categories also rent space in multi dealer antique malls and some malls have more than one dealer. The size and quality of these collections vary widely from a few hundred fairly common titles to interesting and unusual collections, sometimes as large as what we have seen in individual book shops. While we include antique malls where we knew there were used book dealers, we have not, on a systematic basis, researched the multitude of antique malls in the Central States.

How this book is organized.

Because we believe that the majority of our readers will be people who enjoy taking book hunting trips, we have organized this guide geographically by state, and for open shop and by appointment dealers, within each state by location. Mail order dealers are listed alphabetically at the end of each state chapter.

To help the reader locate specific dealers or locations, at the beginning of each state chapter we have included both an alphabetical listing of all the dealers in that state as well as a geographical listing by location.

Within each listing, we have tried to include the kinds of information about book sellers that we have found useful in our own travels.

• A description of the stock: are you likely to find the kind of book you are searching for in this shop? (When collections are a mix of new and used books, and/or hardcover and paperback, we have indicated the estimated percentage of the stock in each category, listing the largest category first.)

• The size of the collection: if the shop has a small collection, do you want to go out of your way to visit it?

• Detailed travel directions: how can you get to the shop?

• Special services: does the dealer issue a catalog? Accept want lists? Have a search service? Offer other services?

• Payment: will the dealer accept credit cards?

Perhaps the most unique feature of this guide is the *Comments* section that includes our personal observations about a shop. Based on actual visits to open shops in the region, our comments are designed not to endorse or criticize any of the establishments we visited but rather to place ourselves in the position of our readers and provide useful data or insights.

Also, if you're interested in locating books in very specific categories, you'll want to take a close look at the *Specialty Index* in the back of the book.

Note that the owner's name is included in each listing only when it is different from the name of the business.

Also, in the *Special Services* section, if the dealer issues a catalog, we generally have not listed "mail order" as a separate service.

Maps

The guide includes a series of 46 state, regional and city maps designed to assist readers plan book hunting safaris to open shops and by appointment dealers.

Only locations with dealers who have general collections are included on the maps: locations with open shops are shown in regular type while locations that only have by appointment dealers are in italics. Locations of "mostly paperback" shops are not included on the maps. (See "Paperbacks" below.) Note that the maps are not drawn to scale and are designed to be used in conjunction with actual road maps.

Comments

We are often asked, "Do you actually visit every dealer that appears in your books?" The answer, we must confess, is "No." To do so, would require far more time than one could possibly imagine and would make this book far too expensive.

We try instead to visit as many of the open shops with general collections (shops that we feel a majority of our readers are likely to be interested in) as possible. We do not normally visit specialty open shops, by appointment and mail order dealers or shops whose collection is predominately paperback. There are, of course, exceptions such as when a shop is either closed on the day that we are in the area or is too far off the route we have laid out for ourselves in order to make the most economical use of our travel time. For this reason we always welcome input from readers who may have personal knowledge of such shops so that we can share the information with other book lovers in future editions.

A few caveats and suggestions before you begin your book hunting safari.

Call ahead. Even when an open shop lists hours and days open, we advise a phone call ahead to be certain that the hours have not changed and that the establishment will indeed be open when you arrive.

Is there a difference between an "antiquarian" and a "used" book store? Yes and no. Many stores we visited call themselves antiquarian but their shelves contain a large stock of books published within the past ten or fifteen years. Likewise, we also found many pre 20th century books in "used" book stores. For that reason, we have used the term "antiquarian" with great caution and only when it was clear to us that the book seller dealt primarily in truly antiquarian books.

Used and Out-of-Print. Some used book purists also make a distinction between "used" books and "out-of-print" books, a distinction which, for the most part, we have avoided. Where appropriate, however, and in order to assist the book hunter, we have tried to indicate the relative vintage of the stock and whether the collection consists of reading copies of popular works or rare and unusual titles.

Paperbacks. The reader should also note that while we do not list shops that are exclusively paperback, we do include "mostly paperback" shops, although these stores are generally not described in great detail. While philosophically we agree with the seasoned book dealer we met in our travels who said, "Books are books and there's a place for people who love to read all kinds of books," because we believe that a majority of our readers are interested in hardcover volumes, we have tried to identify "mostly paperback" shops as a caveat to those who might prefer to shop elsewhere. In those instances where we did visit a "mostly paperback" shop, it was because, based on the initial information we had, we thought the percentage of hardcover volumes was greater than it turned out to be.

Size of the collection. In almost all instances, the information regarding the size of the collection comes directly from the owner. While we did not stop to do an actual count of each collection during our visits, in the few instances where the owner's estimate seemed to be exaggerated, we made note of our observation in the *Comments* section. Readers should note, however, that the number of volumes listed may include books in storage that are not readily accessible.

Readers should also note that with a few exceptions, only dealers who responded to our questionnaire or who we were able to contact by phone are included in the guide. If the dealer did not respond to our multiple inquiries, and if we could not personally verify that the dealer was still in business, the dealer was not listed.

And now to begin your search. Good luck and happy hunting.

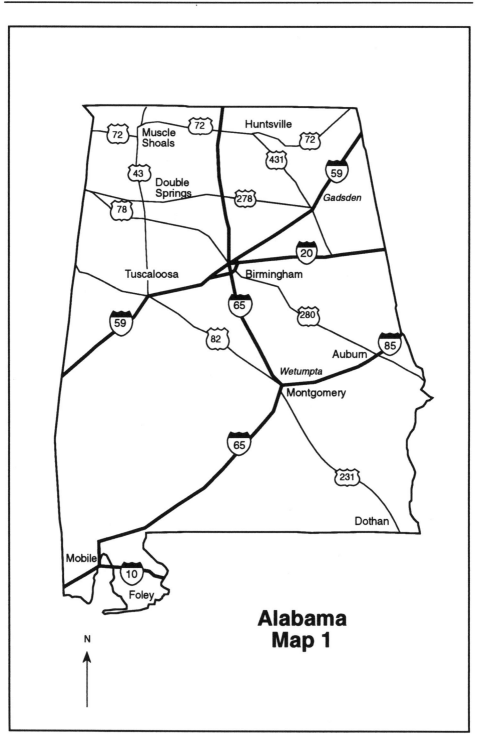

**Alabama
Map 1**

Alabama

Alphabetical Listing By Dealer

Alphabetical Listing By Location

Albertville

Golden Oldies Used Books   **Open Shop**
124 North Broad Street   35950   (205) 878-4966

Collection:	General stock of mostly paperback.
# of Vols:	8,000
Hours:	Sun 1-6. Mon, Thu, Fri, Sat 10-6.

Auburn

The Book Cellar   **Open Shop**
120 North College Street   36830   (334) 826-8830

Collection:	General stock of paperback and hardcover.
Specialties:	Literature; humanities; first editions.
Hours:	Mon-Sat 11-7.
Services:	Search service.
Travel:	Exit 51 off I-85. Follow signs to Auburn University, proceeding on College St.
Year Estab:	1994
Comments:	A student owned shop offering books, free coffee and chess boards. The stock is approximately 60% paperback.

Birmingham

Antique Art Exchange   **Open Shop**
3199 Cahaba Heights Road   35243   (205) 967-1700

Collection:	Specialty
Specialties:	Engravings; lithographs; plate books.
Hours:	Mon-Fri 11-5. Sat & Sun by appointment.
Services:	Appraisals, search service, mail order, accepts want lists.
Travel:	Hwy 280 exit off I-459. Proceed north on Hwy 280. Turn right at Cahaba Hts sign. At second light, turn right on Cahaba Hts Rd, then right at next light into industrial park. Shop is in building at dead end.
Owner:	Tom Phillips
Year Estab:	1993

Beachcomber Books   **Open Shop**
2805 Crescent Avenue   35209   (205) 879-2665

Collection:	General stock of paperback and hardcover.
# of Vols:	25,000
Hours:	Mon-Fri 11-6. Sat 11-3:30.
Services:	Search service, accepts want lists.
Travel:	In downtown Homewood. Oxmoor Rd exit off I-65. Proceed east on Oxmoor, then left on Crescent (first left after passing Our Lady of Sorrows Church). Shop is a few blocks ahead on right in a strip center.
Credit Cards:	Yes
Owner:	John LeVinge
Year Estab:	1991

Comments: The shop carries more paperbacks than hardcover volumes, but the hard-
                 cover books we saw were in good condition (most with dust jackets) and
                 reasonably priced. Most were of fairly recent vintage. The shop had a good
                 representation of modern fiction, science fiction and biography.

Books! By George   **Antique Mall**
At Hanna Antiques   (205) 323-6036
2424 7th Avenue South   35233   Fax: (205) 323-6014

Collection: General stock.
# of Vols: 22,000
Specialties: Civil War; Alabama; Southern Americana; fine bindings; maps.
Hours: Winter: Mon-Sat 10-5. Sun 1-5. Summer: Mon-Sat 10-5:30. Sun 1-5:30.
Services: Appraisals
Travel: At corner of 25th St.
Credit Cards: Yes
Owner: Frank W. George
Year Estab: 1981
Comments: Good quality, mostly serious titles. The books we saw were carefully
                 selected and in very good condition. If you're interested in the special-
                 ties listed above, you should enjoy a visit here. At the time of our visit,
                 the number of books on display was fewer than indicated above.

Highland Booksmith   **Open Shop**
2255 Highland Avenue   35205   (205) 939-3164

Collection: General stock of mostly used hardcover and paperback.
# of Vols: 60,000
Hours: Mon-Sat 10-6:30.
Services: Search service.
Travel: From I-65 northbound: 8th Ave exit. Proceed east on 8th Ave South to
                 23rd St, then right on 23rd St. Shop is about five blocks ahead at dead
                 end. From I-65 southbound: 4th Ave exit. Proceed east on 4th Ave to
                 23rd St, then right on 23rd St.
Credit Cards: Yes
Owner: Jake Reiss
Year Estab: 1990
Comments: A "Class Act. " The shop is neat, clean and comfortable to browse. The
                 books are attractively displayed on shelves carrying hand monogrammed
                 labels identifying the appropriate author or subject category. Most of
                 the books we saw were in very good condition. While there were some
                 paperbacks on display, they were out numbered by hardcover volumes,
                 a majority of which were of fairly recent vintage and unusual enough
                 to attract the true eclectic. Don't overlook several small rooms in the
                 rear of the shop, each devoted to a different subject area.

Reed Books   **Open Shop**
2323 1st Avenue North   35203   Fax: (205) 326-4468   (205) 326-4460
Collection: General stock and ephemera.

# of Vols:	50,000
Specialties:	Children's; humor; show business; poetry.
Hours:	Thu-Sat 10-5. Other times by appointment.
Services:	Search service.
Travel:	22nd St North exit off I-59. Proceed south on 22nd St, then left on 1st Avenue North. Shop is two blocks ahead on right.
Credit Cards:	Yes
Owner:	Jim Reed
Year Estab:	1980
Comments:	I would almost like to keep this shop a secret, at least until such time as I'm able to return to it and leisurely go through shelf after shelf selecting items to purchase. If you're a scholar searching for historical or scientific titles for research purposes, this shop is not likely to excite you. On the other hand, if, like me, you're a nostalgia buff and/or are interested in the shop's specialties, rush here before someone else beats you to it. Once you arrive, don't expect to find everything in its place. While that would make it easier for you to browse, that's not the owner's style so visiting here will be more of a challenge.

Vamp & Tramp Booksellers   **By Appointment**
1025 Montgomery Hwy, Ste 111   35216   (205) 979-9974
                                                            Fax: (205) 979-9886

Collection:	Specialty used and new.
# of Vols:	1,600
Specialties:	Mystery; southern fiction.
Services:	Search service, catalog, accepts want lists, mail order gift baskets for "readers" and "collectors."
Credit Cards:	Yes
Owner:	Vicky & Bill Stewart
Year Estab:	1995

Dothan

Red House Book Store   **Open Shop**
2013 South Oates Street 36301   (334) 792-1475

Collection:	General stock of mostly used paperback and hardcover.
# of Vols:	100,000
Hours:	Mon-Sat 10-6.
Travel:	From Hwy 231, take Business 231 which is S. Oates St.
Owner:	Margaret Jackson
Comments:	Stock is approximately 90% paperback. The owner operates a second shop in northern Alabama in Muscle Shoals (see below for comments on that shop).

Double Springs

Corner Bookstore   **Open Shop**
Highway 195 & Ingle Street   (205) 489-3534
Mailing address: PO Box 818 Double Springs 35553

Collection:	General stock of paperback and hardcover.
# of Vols:	10,000
Hours:	Mon-Fri, except closed Thu, 10-5. Sat 10-2.
Services:	Accepts want lists, mail order.
Travel:	On Hwy 195 in downtown, one mile south off Hwy 278.
Credit Cards:	Yes
Owner:	Glenda Rice
Year Estab:	1990
Comments:	Stock is approximately 55% paperback.

Foley

Verbatim Bookstore   **Open Shop**
311 North McKenzie   36535   (334) 943-2280
                                                         Fax: (334) 943-2280

Collection:	General stock of new and used.
# of Vols:	2,000 (used)
Specialties:	Aviation; Southern Americana.
Hours:	Mon-Fri 10-6. Sat 10-5.
Services:	Appraisals, search service, catalog (aviation), accepts want lists, book restoration.
Travel:	Located on Hwy 59, 2½ blocks north of Hwy 98.
Credit Cards:	Yes
Owner:	Douglas Barber
Year Estab:	1981
Comments:	Used stock is hardcover.

Gardendale

Book Basket   **Open Shop**
700 Main Street   35071   (205) 631-2503

Collection:	General stock of mostly paperback.
# of Vols:	20,000
Hours:	Mon-Fri 9-6. Sat 9-2.

Gadsden

Book Addiction   **By Appointment***
220 Wall Street 35904   (205) 442-4160

Collection:	General stock.
# of Vols:	19,000
Specialties:	Religion (Christianity); Alabama; fine bindings.

Services:	Appraisals, search service, accepts want lists, mail order.
Credit Cards:	Yes
Owner:	Ernie Seckel
Year Estab:	1990
Comments:	Open the third Saturday of every month from 9-2.*

Huntsville

Booklegger   **Open Shop**
4001 Holmes Avenue, NW   35816   (205) 895-0082

Collection:	General stock of hardcover, paperback and remainders.
# of Vols:	50,000 (hardcover)
Hours:	Mon-Sat 10-6. Sun 1-5.
Services:	Accepts want lists, mail order.
Travel:	Jordan exit off I-565. Proceed north on Jordan to Holmes. Shop is on southwest corner in a strip center.
Credit Cards:	Yes
Owner:	David Stone
Year Estab:	1976
Comments:	While this shop has a large selection of paperbacks, it also has an almost equally large collection of hardcover volumes in almost every subject area. Prices are exceedingly reasonable for books we have seen priced considerably higher elsewhere. We left the shop with a carton of books, several on our want list, and felt we had made a bargain purchase. The books vary in vintage and condition, and, as with similar shops, what you're likely to find at the time of your visit will of course depend on what the owner has purchased most recently. If I lived nearby, I would visit this shop often.

Bill Boulton   **Antique Mall**
At Railroad Station Antique Mall   Mall: (205) 533-6550
315 North Jefferson Street   Home: (205) 881-5021
Mailing address: 4003 Medford Drive Huntsville 35802

Collection:	Specialty
# of Vols:	1.000-1,500
Specialties:	Americana
Services:	Mail order.
Travel:	In center of downtown.

Penn Dilworth   **By Appointment**
1111 Beirne Avenue, NE   (205) 534-7244
Mailing address: PO Box 742 Huntsville 35804

Collection:	General stock and ephemera.
# of Vols:	4,000
Specialties:	Southern literature and history; black studies; modern first editions.
Services:	Accepts want lists, mail order.
Credit Cards:	Yes

Good Books   **By Appointment**
600 Beirne Avenue   (205) 533-6407
Mailing address: PO Box 2229 Huntsville 35801   Fax: (205) 533-6407

Collection:	General stock and ephemera.
# of Vols:	15,000+
Specialties:	Southern Americana; Civil War; rocketry; space; art; antiques; guns; hunting; fishing.
Services:	Appraisals, search service, catalog, accepts want lists.
Credit Cards:	No
Owner:	Kathy Wilson
Year Estab:	1993

Shaver's Bookstore   **Open Shop**
2362 Whitesburg Drive   35801   (205) 536-1604

Collection:	General stock of mostly new and used hardcover.
# of Vols:	50,000
Specialties:	Modern first editions; Southern Americana.
Hours:	Mon-Sat 9:30-5:30.
Services:	Appraisals, search service, accepts want lists, mail order.
Travel:	Memorial Pkwy exit off I-565. Proceed south on Memorial Pkwy to Bob Wallace, then left on Bob Wallace for one mile then right on Whitesburg. Shop is just ahead on right.
Credit Cards:	Yes
Owner:	John Shaver
Year Estab:	1987
Comments:	A mostly "new" bookshop with a sprinkling of used books and remainders, some scattered in among the new books and some standing alone in a section marked "collectibles." At the time of our visit, a sign outside the shop read: "Stephen King First Editions. "Perhaps that says it all.

Mobile

Entrekin Book Center   **Open Shop**
7730 Old Shell Road, #C   36608   (334) 634-0404

Collection:	General stock of new and used hardcover and paperback.
# of Vols:	30,000+
Hours:	Tue-Fri 10-6. Sat 10-5. Sun 1-5.
Services:	Appraisals, search service, accepts want lists, mail order.
Travel:	Airport Blvd exit off I-65 (or I-10). Proceed west on Airport for about seven miles, then right on Schillinger. At second light, turn right on Tanner Williams/Old Shell. Shop is 1/2 block ahead on left.
Credit Cards:	Yes
Owner:	Dee Entrekin
Year Estab:	1985
Comments:	With few exceptions, most of the used hardcover and paperback volumes we saw here were of more recent vintage. Attractively displayed,

the hardcover books were in good condition, most with dust jackets and mylar covers. At the time of our visit, the number of volumes on display appeared to be well below the number suggested above by the owner. Perhaps additional volumes are in storage.

Meg's Books & More   **Open Shop**
6950 Moffett Road   36618   (334) 649-0100

Collection: General stock of mostly paperback.
Hours: Mon-Fri 10-6. Sat 10-4.

My Book House   **Flea Market**
At Schillinger's Flea Market   (334) 666-7372
Schillinger Road
Mailing address: 1301 Azalea Road Mobile 36693

Collection: General stock of paperback and hardcover.
Hours: Sat & Sun 9-5.
Travel: Airport Rd exit off I-65. Proceed west on Airport Rd for about seven miles to Schillinger Rd. Right on Schillinger.
Owner: Kent Johnston

Montgomery

Book Nook   **Open Shop**
3453 Norman Bridge Road   36105   (334) 262-5229

Collection: General stock of mostly paperback.
Hours: Mon-Sat 9-6.

Curious Books   **Open Shop**
5054 Vaughn Road   36116   (334) 279-0700

Collection: General stock of new and used hardcover and paperback.
# of Vols: 15,000
Hours: Mon-Thu 10-7. Fri & Sat 10-9. Sun 12-6.
Services: Appraisals, search service, accepts want lists, mail order.
Travel: Exit 6 off I-85. Proceed south on East Blvd, then left at 5th light on Vaughn. Shop in first shopping center on right (Vaughn Plaza).
Credit Cards: Yes
Owner: Julian Godwin
Year Estab: 1983
Comments: Stock is approximately 65% used, 65% of which is hardcover.

Friends' Bookstore   **Open Shop**
245 High Street   36104   (334) 240-4993

Collection: General stock of paperback and hardcover.
Hours: Tue-Fri 12-5.
Travel: Northbound on I-85. Court St exit. Follow access road to McDonough. Left on McDonough and proceed to High St. Southbound on I-85.

Union St exit. Follow access road to McDonough. Right on McDonough and continue to High. Shop is located in the library.

Comments: Operated by Friends of the Public Library.

LHN Books By Appointment

616 Thorn Place   36106   Fax: (334) 264-1060   (334) 264-5858
E-mail: jnathan@mindspring.com

Collection: General stock of mostly hardcover.
# of Vols: 3,000+
Services: Appraisals, search service, accepts want lists, mail order.
Credit Cards: No
Owner: Lisa Harry Nathan
Year Estab: 1991

Trade 'n Books Open Shop

5145 Atlanta Highway   36109   (334) 277-0778

Collection: General stock of mostly paperback.
Hours: Mon-Sat 8:30-8.

Zelda's Books Open Shop

3058 Zelda Road   36106   (334) 272-2510

Collection: General stock of mostly paperback.
# of Vols: 30,000
Hours: Mon-Sat 10-6.

Muscle Shoals

Red House Books Open Shop

2105 Woodward Avenue   35661   (205) 383-3810

Collection: General stock mostly paperback.
# of Vols: 200,000+
Hours: Mon-Sat 10-6. Sun 12-5.
Services: Search service, accepts want lists, mail order.
Travel: Hwy 72 exit off I-65. Proceed west on Hwy 72 to Muscle Shoals where Woodward Ave is Hwy 72.
Credit Cards: Yes
Owner: Margaret Jackson
Year Estab: 1967
Comments: One may be initially discouraged by the preponderance of paperbacks here (over 90% of the store's stock). However, the shop does offer some hardcover volumes which may be of interest to collectors. We are not referring to the mostly forgotten best sellers of the 1930's and 1940's which fill several shelves but the occasional stand-out on a few of the shelves which the owner must have some knowledge of since these items were priced "at value."

Prattville

The Book Shelf   **Open Shop**
1122 South Memorial Drive   36067   (334) 361-9610

Collection: General stock of mostly paperback.
Hours: Mon-Fri 9-6. Sat 9:30-4.

Saraland

Book Rack   **Open Shop**
310 Shelton Beach Road   36571   (334) 675-6020

Collection: General stock of mostly paperback.
# of Vols: 25,000
Hours: Mon-Sat 9-5.

Tuscaloosa

Lodowick Adams, Bookseller   **Open Shop**
2021 8th Street   35401   (205) 345-9654
                                      E-mail: L.Adamsbk@intenet.mci.com

Collection: General stock of hardcover and paperback.
# of Vols: 6,000 (hardcover)
Hours: Mon-Fri 8-5.
Services: Appraisals, search service, mail order.
Travel: McFarland Blvd exit off I-20/59. Proceed west on McFarland to Uni-
                  versity Blvd exit. At end of exit ramp, turn right on University Blvd
                  (University Blvd South) and proceed to 21st Ave. Left on 21st Ave.
                  Shop is about three blocks ahead at corner of 8th Street.
Credit Cards: Yes
Owner: William H. Dobbs
Comments: A neat shop, small in size and in collection. The books we saw were in
                  good condition and covered many subject areas, although few were
                  covered in depth. While the shelves certainly contained quality titles,
                  unless your travels brings you to this part of Alabama, we're not sure a
                  special trip here is warranted.

Wetumpka

Wayne Mullins-Books   **By Appointment**
2337 Marshell Road   36092   (334) 567-4102

Collection: General stock of mostly paperback.
# of Vols: 5,000
Specialties: Mostly vintage mystery.
Services: Catalog, accepts want lists.
Credit Cards: No
Year Estab: 1991

Mail Order Dealers

Gibson's Books: Collectables   (205) 725-2558
3137 Old Highway 431   Ownes Cross Roads 35763
E-mail: gibsonb@interloc.com

Collection:	General stock.
# of Vols:	5,000
Specialties:	Women authors; American and British literature; performing arts; travel; adventure; history; first editions.
Services:	Search service, catalog, accepts want lists.
Credit Cards:	No
Owner:	Lonie Gibson & Kari Cook
Year Estab:	1990

Craig Legg Books   (205) 251-4665
1109 14th Avenue South   Birmingham 35205

Collection:	General stock of hardcover and paperback.
# of Vols:	5,000
Services:	Catalog, accepts want lists.
Credit Cards:	No
Year Estab:	1995

Randal R. Massey   (205) 664-9991
1509 Citation Terrace   Helena 35080   Fax: (205) 664-0532
E-mail: majorrm@aol.com

Collection:	Specialty
# of Vols:	6,000
Specialties:	English literature; European history.
Services:	Appraisals, accepts want lists, occasional catalog.
Credit Cards:	No
Year Estab:	1984

Gary Wayner, Bookseller   (205) 845-7828
1002 Glenn Boulevard, SW   Fort Payne 35967   Fax: (205) 845-2070
E-mail: gwayner@peop.tdsnet.com

Collection:	Specialty used and new.
# of Vols:	5,000
Specialties:	Natural history.
Services:	Search service, accepts want lists, catalog.
Credit Cards:	Yes
Year Estab:	1976

Arizona

Alphabetical Listing By Dealer

Alphabetical Listing By Location

Apache Junction

Apacheland Books   **Open Shop**
10402 East Apache Trail   85220   (602) 986-0538

Collection: General stock of mostly paperback.
Hours: Mon-Fri 10-5:30. Sat 10-5.

Aunties Attic Books & Crafts   **Open Shop**
11142 East Apache Trail   85220   (602) 986-2243

Collection: General stock of mostly paperback.
# of Vols: 1,000
Hours: Mon-Fri 8-5 but best to call ahead.

L & M Paperback Exchange   **Open Shop**
300 West Apache Trail, #117 & 118   85220   (602) 982-4325

Collection: General stock of mostly paperback.
# of Vols: 30,000
Hours: Mon-Sat 9-5.

Benson

Mary Ann's Mostly Books   **Open Shop**
150 West 5th Street   85602   (520) 586-2634

Collection: General stock of new and used paperback and hardcover.
# of Vols: 8,000 (used)
Hours: Tue-Fri 10-4, except Thu till 6. Sat 10-2.
Travel: Benson exit off I-10. Proceed on Hwy 80 (4th St) to Benson. Turn
                  south at Patagonia, then west on 5th.
Credit Cards: No
Owner: Mary Ann Steele
Year Estab: 1994
Comments: Used stock is 80% paperback.

The Paperback Recycler   **Open Shop**
251 West 4th Street, Bldg. #207   (520) 586-7970
Mailing address: PO Box 2091 Benson 85602

Collection: General stock of paperback and hardcover.
# of Vols: 18,000
Hours: Tue-Fri 10-4. Sat 10-2.
Services: Search service, accepts want lists.
Travel: Exit 303 (Benson) off I-10 eastbound from Tucson. Continue thru first
                  light (Ocotillo Rd). Shop is about 1/4 mile ahead on right.
Credit Cards: No
Owner: Lenore Kester
Year Estab: 1991
Comments: Stock is approximately 75% paperback.

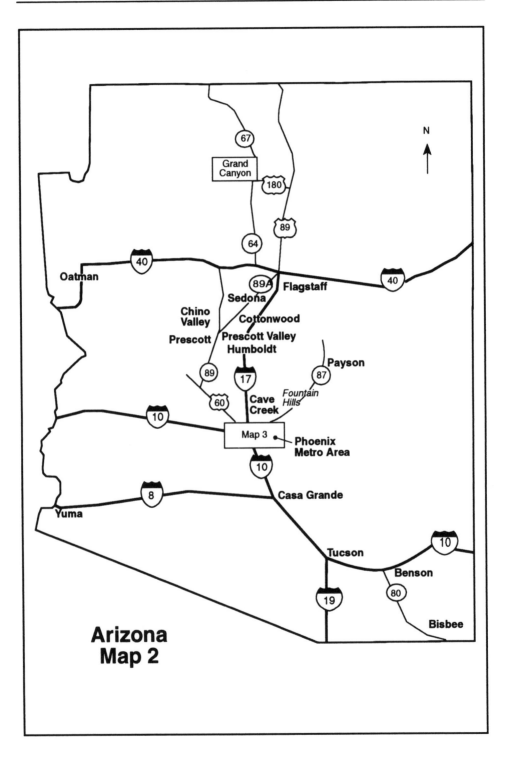

N

67
Grand
Canyon
180
89
64
40
Oatman
89A Flagstaff
Sedona
40
Chino
Valley   Cottonwood
Prescott   Prescott Valley
Humboldt
Payson
89   87
17
60   Fountain
Cave Hills
10   Creek
Map 3
Phoenix
Metro Area
10
8
Casa Grande
Yuma
10
Tucson
Benson
80
19
Bisbee

Arizona
Map 2

Bisbee

Atalanta's Music & Books   **Open Shop**
32 Main Street   (520) 432-9776
Mailing address: PO Box 317 Bisbee 85603

Collection:	General stock of used and new paperback and hardcover.
# of Vols:	15,000
Hours:	Daily 10-6.
Services:	Search service.
Travel:	Benson exit off I-10. Proceed south on Hwy 80 for about 45 miles to Bisbee Business District exit.
Credit Cards:	No
Owner:	Joan Werner
Year Estab:	1975
Comments:	Stock is approximately 75% used, 60% of which is paperback.

Eureka Books   **Open Shop**
18 Main Street   (520) 432-2472
Mailing address: PO Box 1873 Bisbee 85603

Collection:	General stock of hardcover and paperback.
# of Vols:	10,000
Specialties:	Railroads
Hours:	Daily 10-6.
Services:	Accepts want lists, catalog (railroads only), mail order.
Travel:	Located on Hwy 80 in Old Bisbee.
Credit Cards:	No
Owner:	Rick Schlak
Year Estab:	1993
Comments:	Stock is evenly divided between hardcover and paperback.

Bullhead City

Book Worm   **Open Shop**
809B Hancock Road   86442   (520) 763-2040

Collection:	General stock of mostly paperback.
# of Vols:	30,000
Hours:	Mon-Fri 9-5. Sat 10-2.

Fondren's Books   **Open Shop**
2350 South Miracle Mile, #240   86442   (520) 763-8383

Collection:	General stock of mostly paperback.
# of Vols:	4,500
Hours:	Mon-Sat 9:30-6. Sun 11-4. Closed second Sun of each month.

Carefree

Blue Bird Cafe and Books   **Open Shop**
7171 East Cave Creek Road   (602) 488-2611
Mailing address: Box 5210 Carefree 85377

Collection:	General stock of mostly new and some used paperbacks.
# of Vols:	6,000
Hours:	Daily 7am-7:30pm.

Casa Grande

K & L Antiques   **Open Shop**
315 North Florence Street   85222   (520) 258-5700
                                                     Fax: (520) 836-9436

Collection:	General stock.
# of Vols:	1,000
Hours:	Mon-Sat 9-5.
Services:	Appraisals, accepts want lists, search service, mail order.
Travel:	From I-10: Hwy 387 exit. Proceed south on Hwy 387 for about eight miles to "five corners." Go through light and proceed east on 2nd St. At second light, turn left on Florence. Shop is just ahead.
Owner:	Debrah & Gary Linscott
Comments:	Owners also sponsor book fairs under name Acorn Antique Guild.

Toonsa's Books   **Open Shop**
1145 East Florence Boulevard   85222   (520) 421-1044

Collection:	General stock of mostly paperback.
# of Vols:	9,000
Hours:	Mon-Sat 10-7, except Fri till 8. Sun 11:30-5:30.

Cave Creek

Book Barn   **Open Shop**
6140 East Cave Creek Road   (602) 488-9589
Mailing address: PO Box 4437 Cave Creek 85331

Collection:	General stock of mostly used paperback and hardcover.
# of Vols:	17,000
Hours:	Tue-Sat 10-5. Mon by chance.
Services:	Search service, accepts want lists.
Travel:	In downtown.
Owner:	Jim Zeno
Comments:	Stock is approximately 60% paperback.

Russ Todd Books   **By Appointment**
28605 North 63rd Street   85331   (602) 585-0070

Collection:	Specialty
# of Vols:	4,000

Specialties:	Western Americana; art (American).
Services:	Appraisals, accepts want lists, occasional catalog.
Credit Cards:	No
Year Estab:	1980

Chandler

Books Plus   **Open Shop**
1984 North Alma School Road   85224   (602) 821-2374
                                                                               Fax: (602) 894-5418

Collection:	General stock of new and mostly paperback used.
# of Vols:	15,000 (used)
Hours:	Mon-Fri 9-6:30. Sat 10-6. Sun 12-5.

Re-Read Bookstore   **Open Shop**
1076 West Chandler Boulevard, #112   85224   (602) 963-7117

Collection:	General stock of mostly paperback.
# of Vols:	25,000
Hours:	Mon, Tue, Sat 9-5. Wed-Fri 9-6.

Chino Valley

Page Turners   **Open Shop**
471-A North Highway 89   (520) 636-0061
Mailing address: 1010 Moon Shadow Chino Valley 86323

Collection:	General stock of paperback and hardcover.
# of Vols:	15,000
Specialties:	Biography; history.
Hours:	Tue-Fri 11-5. Sat 11-4.
Services:	Accepts want lists.
Travel:	Located on east side of Hwy 89 at Road 1 North.
Credit Cards:	No
Owner:	Sharon Duling Moehn
Year Estab:	1991
Comments:	Stock is approximately 65% paperback.

Coolidge

Bookstore   **Open Shop**
865 North Arizona Boulevard   85228   (520) 723-0378

Collection:	General stock of mostly paperback.
# of Vols:	2,000+
Hours:	Tue-Fri 9-5. Sat 9-3:30.

Cottonwood

A & W Graphics Books & Gifts   **Open Shop**
979 South Main   86326   (520) 634-2390
                                                        Fax: (520) 634-2390

Collection: General stock of mostly paperback used and new books.
# of Vols: 60,000
Hours: Mon-Fri 9-5:30. Sat 9-5.

Anchor Books   **Open Shop**
1431 East Highway 89A   86326   (520) 634-5658

Collection: General stock of paperback and hardcover.
Hours: Tue-Sat 10-5:30.
Owner: George & Joyce Thomson
Year Estab: 1980
Comments: Stock is approximately 75% paperback.

Flagstaff

Bookman's Used Books   **Open Shop**
1520 S. Riordan Ranch Road   86001   (520) 774-0005
                                            E-mail: bookman's@flagstaff.az.us

Collection: General stock of hardcover, paperback and remainders.
# of Vols: 250,000
Hours: Mon-Sat 9am-10pm. Sun 10-9.
Services: Appraisals, search service, accepts want lists, mail order.
Travel: Exit 195B (North Arizona Univ) off I-40. Proceed north on Milton Rd.
                  Turn right on Chambers and cross Riordan Ranch Rd into shopping
                  center parking lot.
Credit Cards: Yes
Owner: Robert Schlesinger
Year Estab: 1990
Comments: Normally, we become bit leery when entering a used book shop that
                  appears to have a supermarket like atmosphere. In this instance, how-
                  ever, we are pleased to report that, despite the number of paperbacks,
                  CDs, videos and magazines offered here, the store does have a solid
                  collection of hardcover volumes in most of the subject areas one gener-
                  ally seeks out in an establishment such as this. The books were in quite
                  good condition, were reasonably priced and ran the gamut from newer
                  items to some vintage material. We think a visit here would be a sound
                  investment.

Carriage House Antique Mall   **Antique Mall**
413 North San Francisco   86001   (602) 774-1337

Hours: Mon-Sat 10-5. Sun 11-4.
Travel: Exit 195B off I-40. East on Milton, which becomes Sitgreaves which
                  becomes Rte 66, then north on San Francisco. Mall is 4½ blocks ahead.

Dragon's Plunder   **Open Shop**
217 South San Francisco Street   86001   (602) 774-1708

Collection:	General stock of paperback and hardcover.
# of Vols:	10,000
Hours:	Winter: Mon-Sat 11-5. Summer: Mon-Sat 9-5:30.
Travel:	Exit 195B (North Arizona Univ) off I-40. Proceed north on Milton Rd, then right on Butler and left on San Francisco. Shop is on the corner.
Credit Cards:	No
Owner:	Rusty
Year Estab:	1987
Comments:	A small shop that uses every square inch it can to display books and a small selection of collectibles. If you're uncomfortable visiting shops where turning around in an aisle may be a chore or where books may not be as well organized as they could be, this may not be a shop for you. On the other hand, if you like vintage hardcover items, don't mind some of them being slightly worn, and know what is collectible and what is not, you could find a gem here. Oh yes, the shop also carries a fair number of paperbacks.

Starrlight Books   **Open Shop**
15 North Leroux   86001   (520) 774-6813

Collection:	General stock of hardcover and paperback.
# of Vols:	10,000
Specialties:	Grand Canyon; Southwest; Arizona; travel.
Hours:	Daily 10-7.
Services:	Accepts want lists, mail order.
Travel:	Exit 195B off I-40. Proceed north on Milton which becomes Santa Fe. Left on Leroux.
Credit Cards:	Yes
Owner:	Chuck Brown
Year Estab:	1994
Comments:	A relatively small shop with a mix of paperback (at the time of our visit, the back room was exclusively paperback science fiction) and both new and used hardcover items were intershelved. The hardcover volumes we saw were in mixed condition and mixed vintage. Nothing extraordinary.

Eric Stetson-Books   **Antique Mall**
2101 West Highway 66, # D6   86001   (520) 779-3597

Collection:	General stock.
# of Vols:	1,000+
Specialties:	Western Americana; Native Americans; southwest art; firearms; hunting; game animals.
Services:	Search service, accepts want lists, mail order.
Credit Cards:	Yes
Year Estab:	1995
Comments:	The dealer displays at several antique malls in the Flagstaff area. Call for a current list of the locations.

Fountain Hills

ESN Fine and Rare Books   **By Appointment**
15902 El Lago Boulevard   85268   (602) 837-6447

Collection: General stock.
# of Vols: 7,000
Specialties: Philosophy; history of science; art; archaeology; psychology; law; clas-
                   sical studies; Southwest Americana; fine press; limited editions.
Services: Appraisals, catalog, accepts want lists.
Credit Cards: No
Owner: Einer S. Nisula, Ph.D.
Year Estab: 1971

Glendale
(See Map 3, page 48)

A & G Books   **Open Shop**
15410 North 67th Avenue, #11-12   85306   (602) 486-2529

Collection: General stock of paperback and hardcover.
# of Vols: 30,000
Hours: Mon-Fri 10-7, except Thu till 7. Sat 10-5. Sun 12-4.
Travel: Glendale exit off I-17. Proceed west on Glendale to 67th Ave.
Credit Cards: Yes
Owner: Paul & Susan Goers
Year Estab: 1988
Comments: If there are 30,000 books in this store, at least 29,000 of them are paper-
                   back with perhaps 1,000 recent hardcover volumes (mostly fiction).

Coury House/Ed & Bette's Books   **Open Shop**
5802 West Palmaire   85301   (602) 435-1522

Collection: General stock.
Specialties: Electronics; radio and television; telephone; children's.
Hours: Tue-Sat 12:30-3:30.
Services: Appraisals, search service, accepts want lists.
Travel: Glendale exit off I-17. Proceed west on Glendale, north on 59th, then
                   east on Palmaire. Shop is on northwest corner of 58th and Palmaire.
Credit Cards: No
Year Estab: 1993

Now, Then & Always   **Antique Mall**
7021 North 57th Drive   85301   (602) 931-1116

Hours: Summer: Tue-Sat 11-5. Sun 1-4:30. Winter: Mon-Sat 11-5. Sun 1-4:30

Shady Nook Books & Antiques   **Open Shop**
5751 West Glendale Avenue   85301   (602) 939-1462

Collection: General stock.
# of Vols: 5,000

Specialties:	Children's, cookbooks; history; comics.
Hours:	Mon-Fri 9-6. Sat & Sun 10-5.
Services:	Accepts want lists.
Travel:	Glendale Ave exit off I-17. Proceed west on Glendale to 58th Ave.
Credit Cards:	Yes
Owner:	Glenda Lee Stanley
Year Estab:	1990
Comments:	Susan I argue (more than we should) when we're on the road and have to make difficult choices about which shops to visit and which we just can't fit into our tight schedule. A perfect example of one such argument occurred before visiting this shop which our earlier research indicated was a combination book/antique shop with a limited selection of books (including comics). "Why are we going here?" I would ask and Susan would reply, "You never know." In this instance, what I now know is that the shop offers a mix of antiques, collectibles and a few thousand books of little distinction. However, since the neighborhood is the home to several such shops, if you enjoy visiting antique/collectibles shops, you may as well visit here as anywhere else.

Stewart's Books   **Open Shop**
4726 West Olive   85302   (602) 931-5894

Collection:	General stock of paperback and hardcover.
# of Vols:	10,000
Hours:	Mon-Fri 9-5. Sat 10-5.
Travel:	Dunlap exit off I-17. Proceed west on Dunlap which becomes Olive. Shop is at 47th Ave in Ted's Plaza, a strip shopping center.
Credit Cards:	Yes
Owner:	John & Jaclyn Noel
Year Estab:	1982
Comments:	Unfortunately, this shop was closed when we arrived. Looking through the window we were able to view lots of paperbacks and a more limited selection of hardcover volumes, primarily on the side and rear walls. Many of the shelves were only half filled and some appeared to be empty.

Thomas Books   **Open Shop**
4425 West Olive, Ste. 168   85302   (602) 435-5055
                                                     Fax: (602) 435-5055

Collection:	Specialty. Mostly used.
# of Vols:	6,000
Specialties:	First editions; mystery; fantasy; horror; science fiction; Arkham House; Southwest Americana; literature; signed; limited editions.
Hours:	Mon-Thu 12-5. Fri & Sat 10-5.
Services:	Appraisals, search service, catalog, accepts want lists.
Travel:	Dunlap exit off I-17. Proceed west on Dunlap for two miles to 43rd Ave. Shop is inside Olive Square Shopping Center/Office Park on southwest corner of Olive (Dunlap) and 43rd Ave.

Credit Cards:	Yes
Owner:	Tom Miller
Year Estab:	1992
Comments:	Another reason why we advise our readers to "call ahead." Based on the earlier information we had, we arranged our itinerary to take advantage of the owner's 10am opening. Unfortunately, when we arrived, we discovered that the dealer had changed his hours and would not be open until noon. These things do happen. Looking through the shop's window, we saw a small, very neat establishment with books that appeared to be in very good condition. As one whose interests coincide with the dealer's specialties, I would, based on my limited observations, certainly encourage others to either stop here or contact the owner with a list of wants.

Yesterday's Memories   **Antique Mall**
At Antique Treasures   Mall: (602) 931-8049
7025 North 57th

Collection:	General stock.
# of Vols:	7,000
Hours:	Mon-Sat 11-5, except Thu till 8. Sun 1-4.
Travel:	Glendale Ave exit off I-17. Proceed west on Glendale to 57th Dr, then right on 57th.
Year Estab:	1987
Comments:	About four or five bookcases, if that many, located in an antique mall. The books were generally older, in mixed condition and not particularly exciting. Typical antique mall fare.

Humboldt

Roadrunner Floral   **Open Shop**
12880 Main Street   86329   (520) 632-7052

Collection:	General stock of hardcover and paperback.
# of Vols:	5,000
Hours:	Mon-Fri 9-4. Sat 9-1. Best of call ahead.
Travel:	Off Hwy 169.
Comments:	The stock is evenly divided between hardcover and paperback.

Lake Havasu City

Book Exchange   **Open Shop**
1761 McCulloch Boulevard   86403   (520) 453-4043

Collection:	General stock of mostly paperback.
# of Vols:	20,000
Hours:	Mon-Sat 9-5. Also Nov-Mar: Sun 10-2.

Litchfield Park

Bonita Porter Books   **Open Shop**
506 East Indian School Road   (602) 935-3643
Mailing address: PO Box 1765 Litchfield Park 85340

Collection:	Specialty
# of Vols:	10,000
Specialties:	Arizona; Southwest Americana; modern first editions.
Hours:	Tue-Sat 9:30-5.
Services:	Accepts want lists, occasional catalog.
Travel:	Litchfield Rd exit off I-10. Proceed north on Litchfield for about three miles, then east on Indian School Rd.
Credit Cards:	No
Year Estab:	1965

Mesa
(See Map 3, page 48)

The Book Rack   **Open Shop**
2665 East Broadway, B106   85204   (602) 649-3380

Collection:	General stock of paperback and hardcover.
# of Vols:	35,000
Hours:	Mon-Fri 10-6. Sat 10-5.
Travel:	Gilbert exit off Hwy 60. Proceed north on Gilbert, then right on Broadway. Shop is in Lindsey Marketplace shopping center.
Owner:	Suzie Coyle
Comments:	Stock is approximately 70% paperback.

Bookend   **Open Shop**
6024 East McKellips Road, #5   85215   (602) 396-3351

Collection:	General stock of mostly paperback.
# of Vols:	50,000
Hours:	Mon-Fri 8-5:30. Sat 9-5.

Bookman's Used Books   **Open Shop**
1056 South Country Club Drive   85210   (602) 835-0505
                                                                  Fax: (602) 835-0026

Collection:	General stock of hardcover, paperback and remainders.
# of Vols:	500,000
Hours:	Mon-Sat 9am-10pm. Sun 11-7.
Services:	Search service, accepts want lists, mail order.
Travel:	Country Club exit off Hwy 60. Proceed north on Country Club to Southern Ave. Shop is in shopping center at northwest corner.
Credit Cards:	Yes
Year Estab:	1993
Comments:	Although we visited this shop's sister store in Flagstaff (see above) earlier in our travels, we thought we would stop here as we enjoyed our

earlier visit. Similar to the Flagstaff location, paperbacks and hardcover books are shelved in close proximity to one another, and while paperbacks outnumber hardcover items, there are a sufficient number and variety of the latter to make a visit here worthwhile. Stronger in more popular subjects than in scholarly areas, the store nonetheless maintains a nice balance.

Encore Books   **Open Shop**
1316 South Gilbert Road, #D2   85204   (602) 813-0550

Collection:	General stock of mostly paperback.
# of Vols:	50,000 +
Hours:	Mon-Sat 10-7.

Mesa Bookshop   **Open Shop**
50 West Main Street   85201   (602) 835-0757
                                                         Fax: (602) 835-2279

Collection:	General stock of mostly hardcover.
# of Vols:	80,000
Specialties:	Art; automotive; literature.
Hours:	Mon-Fri 9-6. Sat 10-5.
Services:	Accepts want lists, mail order.
Travel:	Country Club exit off I-60. North on Country Club Dr then east on Main.
Credit Cards:	Yes
Owner:	Tim & Carla Jelinek
Year Estab:	1987
Comments:	We're always happy to report a winner. The books here are plentiful, the shop is easy to browse and the subject areas covered are extensive (We noted several shelves devoted to ornithology.) We would have trouble thinking of a subject that wasn't represented. Paperbacks are consigned to a small section at the rear of the shop. Well worth a visit.

Mesa Book Gallery   **Antique Mall**
At Mesa Antique Mart   Mall: (602) 813-1909
1455 South Stapley Drive 85204   Book Gallery: (602) 263-8353

Collection:	General stock.
Hours:	Mon-Sat 10-6, except Thu till 8. Sun 12:30-6.
Travel:	Stapley exit off Hwy 60. Proceed north on Stapley for about 1/2 block. Mall is on the right side.
Owner:	Tanya Fahey & Mike Riley
Comments:	Based on our visits to the two shops that supply books for display here (the Book Gallery and Al's Books, both in Phoenix, see below) we believe your visit to this satellite location will leave a good taste in your mouth.

Read It Again Books   **Open Shop**
4210 East Main Street, #13   85205   (602) 830-8990

Collection:	General stock of paperback and hardcover.

# of Vols:	30,000
Hours:	Daily 8-8.
Services:	Accepts want lists, mail order.
Travel:	Greenfield exit off Hwy 60 Proceed north on Greenfield to Main, left on Main. Shop is on north side of street in shopping center.
Credit Cards:	Yes
Owner:	Vernon O'Hagan
Year Estab:	1993
Comments:	A modest sized shop with some nice children's books as well as military titles. The rest of the items we saw were more of a general nature. If you're schedule is tight you might want to call ahead to determine if a particular title you're searching for is available.

Second Chance Bookstore   **Open Shop**
500 West Southern Avenue, #31   85210   (602) 898-3721

Collection:	General stock of mostly paperback.
# of Vols:	24,000
Hours:	Mon-Sat 10-6.

Oatman

Old & Rare Books   **Open Shop**
Old Route 66   (520) 768-5513
Mailing address: PO Box 64   Oatman 86433

Collection:	General stock.
# of Vols:	2,000
Hours:	Fri-Tue 11:30-5 but best to call ahead.
Travel:	One mile south of Oatman
Credit Cards:	No
Owner:	Willa Noble
Comments:	Stock is primarily pre 1940 publications. Oatman is a quaint old western mining town.

Page

DelVecchio's Books   **Open Shop**
43 6th Avenue   86040   (520) 645-9089

Collection:	General stock of mostly used paperback and some new books.
# of Vols:	6,000 (used)
Hours:	Mon-Sat 10-6.

Payson

Leaves of Autumn Books   **Open Shop**
518 West Main Street   (520) 474-3654
Mailing address: PO Box 440 Payson 85547   Fax: (520) 474-0310

Collection:	General stock of new and used hardcover and paperback.

# of Vols:	25,000
Specialties:	Religion, with special focus on Seventh Day Adventist.
Hours:	Mon-Thu 8-5. Fri 8-12.
Services:	Catalog
Travel:	From Hwy 87, at Payson, turn west at traffic light for Main St.
Credit Cards:	Yes
Owner:	Garwood & Eleanor Baybrook
Year Estab:	1969
Comments:	Stock is approximately 75% used, 70% of which is hardcover.

Viking Bookstore   **Open Shop**
405 East South Beeline Highway   85541   (520) 474-7081

Collection:	General stock of mostly used hardcover and paperback.
# of Vols:	20,000 (used)
Hours:	Mon-Sat 9-5. Sun 9-4.
Travel:	Located on Hwy 87.
Credit Cards:	No
Year Estab:	1992
Comments:	Stock is evenly divided between hardcover and paperback.

Peoria

Amric Book Store   **Open Shop**
9794 West Peoria Avenue   85345   602-977-8175

Collection:	General stock of mostly used paperback.
# of Vols:	10,000 (used)
Hours:	Mon-Sat 9-5.

Once Upon A Time   **Open Shop**
8433 West Peoria Avenue   85345   (602) 486-3148

Collection:	General stock of hardcover and paperback.
# of Vols:	20,000
Hours:	Mon-Sat 10-4.
Services:	Accepts want lists, mail order.
Travel:	Peoria Ave exit off I-17. Proceed west on Peoria. Shop is in a strip center.
Credit Cards:	No
Owner:	Joan Post
Year Estab:	1984
Comments:	Stock is approximately 65% paperback.

Paradise Book Store   **Open Shop**
9008 North 99th Avenue, #6   85345   (602) 974-1748

Collection:	General stock of mostly used and new paperback and hardcover.
# of Vols:	50,000
Specialties:	Black studies.
Hours:	Tue-Sat 10-6.

Travel:	Olive exit off 101 Loop. Proceed west on Olive to 99th Ave. Shop is in a small strip center.
Credit Cards:	Yes
Owner:	Roslyn Mercer
Year Estab:	1993
Comments:	Used stock is approximately 75% paperback.

Phoenix

ABC Affordable Books   Open Shop
740 East Glendale Avenue   85020   (602) 943-6472

Collection:	General stock of hardcover and paperback.
Hours:	Mon-Fri 10-6. Sat 10-4. Sun 12-4.
Travel:	At 7th St.
Comments:	A not-for-profit shop. Proceeds used to support local animal shelter.

Abydos Books   Open Shop
4727 North Central Avenue   85012   (602) 265-7647
                                                      Fax: (602) 265-7280

Collection:	General stock.
# of Vols:	10,000
Specialties:	Ancient and medieval history; philosophy; theology.
Hours:	Mon-Fri 9-6. Sat 9-5. Other times by appointment.
Services:	Search service, accepts want lists, mail order.
Travel:	Between Camelback and Indian School.
Credit Cards:	Yes
Owner:	Jim Doyle & Patricia Gross
Year Estab:	1991
Comments:	The owner (Ms. Gross) was formerly a partner in Alcuin Books.

Al's Bookstore   Open Shop
3744 East Indian School Road   85018   (602) 253-6922

Collection:	General stock of mostly hardcover.
# of Vols:	20,000
Specialties:	First editions; literature; mystery; science fiction; fine bindings; Southwest Americana; military; history; art; children's; automobiles.
Hours:	Mon-Sat 10-7. Sun 12-5.
Services:	Appraisals, search service, accepts want lists, mail order.
Travel:	Northbound on I-10: Hwy 143 exit. Proceed north on Hwy 143 to McDowell, then west on McDowell, right on 40th St and left on Indian School Rd. Southbound on I-10: Indian School exit. Proceed east on Indian School.
Credit Cards:	Yes
Owner:	Mike Riley & Tanya Fahey
Year Estab:	1967
Comments:	Note quite as large as the Book Gallery owned by the same partners (see below) but equal in quality and good taste. The books we saw here

(Phoenix)

were carefully selected, attractively displayed and should be tempting to most discriminating book people. Well worth a visit.

Alcuin Books   **Open Shop**
115 West Camelback Road   85013   (602) 279-3031

Collection:	General stock and ephemera.
# of Vols:	15,000
Specialties:	American and European history; Western Americana; military; Civil War; Revolutionary War; World War I & II; religion; philosophy; natural history; biblical studies.
Hours:	Mon-Fri 10-6. Sat 10-5. Other times by appointment.
Services:	Appraisals, search service, accepts want lists.
Travel:	Camelback Rd exit off I-17. Proceed east on Camelback.
Credit Cards:	Yes
Owner:	Richard Murian
Year Estab:	1991
Comments:	We're happy to note that the sign outside the shop that describes the store as selling "Fine, Limited and Out-of-Print Books" is accurate in the sense that the books we viewed were indeed, and for the most part, in very good condition, were mainly (but not exclusively) scholarly and had interesting if not always unusual titles. The display space is larger than initially apparent. A nice store to browse.

All About Books & Comics   **Open Shop**
517 East Camelback Road   85012   (602) 277-0757

Collection:	General stock of paperback and hardcover.
# of Vols:	10,000
Hours:	Mon-Fri 10:30-7. Sat 10-6. Sun 12-5.
Travel:	Camelback exit off I-10. Proceed east on Camelback Rd.
Credit Cards:	Yes
Year Estab:	1975
Comments:	While this shop is predominately comic oriented, it has a larger selection of paperbacks and hardcover books than is usually available in similar stores. Indeed, the hardcover volumes go well beyond the typical science fiction, fantasy titles into general fiction, history, entertainment, etc. Most of the hardcover books we saw were reading copies but there were some vintage items on the shelves. As the shop is on the same street as three other major dealers, and depending on what you're looking for, a stop here would not be out of your way, nor in our opinion, a waste of time.

The Bent Cover Bookstore   **Open Shop**
12428 North 28th Drive   85029   (602) 942-3778
                                                               E-mail: jpatton@primenet.com

Collection:	General stock of paperback and hardcover.

# of Vols:	500,000
Specialties:	Modern first editions; science fiction; mystery; westerns; cookbooks.
Hours:	Mon-Fri 10-9. Sat 10-6. Sun 12-6.
Services:	Search service, accepts want lists, mail order.
Travel:	Cactus Rd exit off I-17. Proceed west on Cactus for one block to 28th Dr, then north on 28th Dr. Shop is one block ahead on left in strip center.
Credit Cards:	Yes
Owner:	June & Jay Patton
Year Estab:	1986
Comments:	A large shop (three storefronts wide) with a collection that is at least 75% paperback. However, the hardcover volumes do deserve one's attention as, for the most part, they are in good condition and certainly represent the subjects listed above as specialties. Don't restrict yourself to a single section of the shop. When looking for mysteries, for example, first editions mysteries are located in one section while more vintage titles are elsewhere. The same pattern is true for other subject categories.

Bob & Faye's Bookstore   **Open Shop**
1827 East Indian School Road   85016   (602) 264-6698

Collection:	General stock of mostly paperback.
# of Vols:	200,000+
Hours:	Mon-Sat 10-5.
Travel:	One block east of Squaw Peak Pkwy (Hwy 51).
Comments:	Predominately paperbacks with a thousand or so hardcover volumes, mostly on the top shelves or in the back of the shop. If your schedule is tight, keep going.

Book Exchange Plus   **Open Shop**
2601 East Bell Road, #12   85032   (602) 867-9014   (602) 867-1018
                                                     E-mail: booksolid@aol.com

Collection:	General stock of paperback and hardcover.
Hours:	Mon-Fri 10-8. Sat 10-5.
Services:	Search service, accepts want lists.
Travel:	Bell Rd exit off I-17. Proceed east on Bell for five miles to 26th St. Shop is on southeast corner.
Credit Cards:	Yes
Owner:	Deborah Neckel
Year Estab:	1982
Comments:	Stock is approximately 75% paperback.

Book Gallery   **Open Shop**
169 West Camelback Road   85013   (602) 263-8353

Collection:	General stock.
# of Vols:	30,000
Specialties:	First editions; literature; mystery; science fiction; fine bindings; Southwest Americana; military; history; art; children's.

(Phoenix)

Hours:	Mon-Sat 10-7. Sun 12-5.
Services:	Appraisals, search service, accepts want lists, mail order.
Travel:	Camelback exit off I-17. Proceed east on Camelback to 3rd St.
Credit Cards:	Yes
Owner:	Tanya Fahey & Mike Riley
Year Estab:	1990
Comments:	One of the more pleasant aspects of our trips, particularly if it happens at the end of the day, is the discovery of an absolutely wonderful book shop. This establishment falls into that category. While the shop is not huge, it is filled with quality books of every kind. Shelf upon shelf abounds with titles that run the gamut from scholarly titles in many subjects (we were particularly impressed with two to three shelves dealing with exotic birds) to good literature, fine bindings, collectibles and everything in between. If your visit to Phoenix is limited and you're only able to visit a few dealers, make this one of your stops and include its sister shop (see Al's Bookstore above) as well.

Book Store   **Open Shop**
4230 North 7th Avenue   85013   (602) 279-3910

Collection:	General stock of paperback and hardcover.
# of Vols:	50,000+
Hours:	Mon-Sat 9-6. Sun 9-5.
Travel:	Two blocks north of Indian School.
Credit Cards:	No
Year Estab:	1976
Comments:	An interesting shop that in addition to offering paperbacks, an extensive collection of special interest magazines (mostly new and some fairly recent back issues) and comics also has some hardcover books. The hardcover volumes we saw were, for the most part, reading copies. However, if you have patience and are willing to spend a few extra minutes here, you might locate a more valuable find. We think we did. The books are not overpriced.

Booked Solid   **Open Shop**
15440 North 7th Street, #18   85022   (602) 504-8621

Collection:	General stock of mostly paperback.
# of Vols:	8,000
Hours:	Tue-Fri 10-6. Sat 10-5.

Books   **Open Shop**
9201 North 7th Avenue   85021   (602) 678-4576

Collection:	General stock of paperback and hardcover.
# of Vols:	125,000
Hours:	Mon-Fri 10-6:30. Sat 10-5. Sun 10-4.
Services:	Search service, accepts want lists, mail order.

Travel:	Dunlap exit off I-17. Proceed east on Dunlap to 7th Ave, north on 7th Ave. Shop is about two blocks ahead.
Credit Cards:	Yes
Owner:	Mary Anne Ramirez
Year Estab:	1989
Comments:	A large shop offering a large supply of paperbacks, back issues of magazines (e.g., *National Geographic*), comic books and mostly reading copies and/or ex library copies of hardcover books, a majority of which were fiction. We did see a section marked "first editions" but most of these were of recent vintage. Very inexpensive.

Books & More   Open Shop
5801 North 7th Street   85014   (602) 263-8665

Collection:	General stock of paperback and hardcover.
# of Vols:	1,000 (hardcover)
Hours:	Daily 10-6.
Travel:	Bethany Home Rd exit off I-10. Proceed east on Bethany Home to 7th Street then south on 7th. Shop is 1/2 block ahead.

By The Book, L. C.   Open Shop
1045 East Camelback Road   85014   Fax: (602) 596-1672   (602) 222-8806
E-mail: bybooklc@interloc.com

Collection:	General stock.
# of Vols:	40,000
Specialties:	Children's; illustrated; medicine; science; literature; history; China; Japan.
Hours:	Mon-Fri 10-6. Sat 10-5.
Services:	Appraisals, search service, accepts want lists, mail order.
Travel:	7th St exit off I-10. Proceed north on 7th St to Camelback then east on Camelback.
Credit Cards:	Yes
Owner:	Jim Manwarren & Sam Hessel
Year Estab:	1991
Comments:	A pleasant shop with a nice ambience. Easy to browse. Books were well cared for and nicely organized. The specialties listed above were represented in modest numbers. While we liked what we saw in terms of the condition of the books and recognize that books of this quality are not inexpensive, we did spot several volumes that we have seen elsewhere costing a bit less.

Central Christian Supply   Open Shop
3525 North Central Avenue   85012   (602) 266-3031

Collection:	Specialty new and used.
Specialties:	Religion
Hours:	Mon-Fri 9-6, except Thu till 7:30. Sat 9-5.
Travel:	Between Osborne and Indian School.

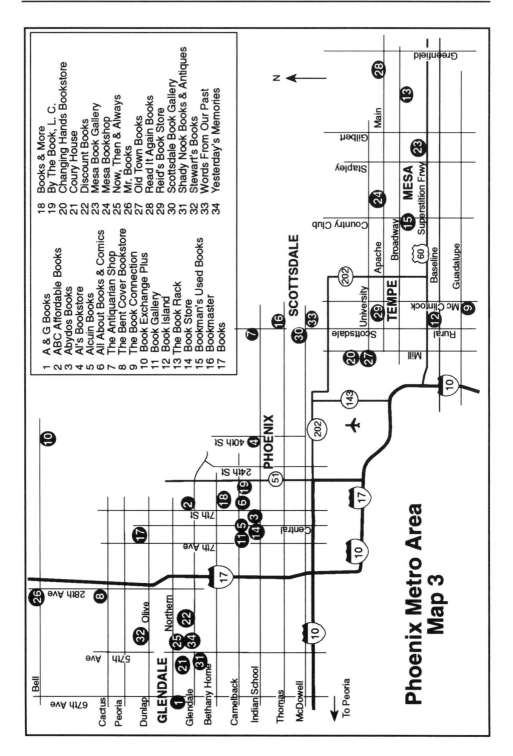

1   A & G Books
2   ABC Affordable Books
3   Abydos Books
4   Al's Bookstore
5   Alcuin Books
6   All About Books & Comics
7   The Antiquarian Shop
8   The Bent Cover Bookstore
9   The Book Connection
10 Book Exchange Plus
11 Book Gallery
12 Book Island
13 The Book Rack
14 Book Store
15 Bookman's Used Books
16 Bookmaster
17 Books

18 Books & More
19 By The Book, L. C.
20 Changing Hands Bookstore
21 Coury House
22 Discount Books
23 Mesa Book Gallery
24 Mesa Bookshop
25 Now, Then & Always
26 Mr. Books
27 Old Town Books
28 Read It Again Books
29 Reid's Book Store
30 Scottsdale Book Gallery
31 Shady Nook Books & Antiques
32 Stewart's Books
33 Words From Our Past
34 Yesterday's Memories

Phoenix Metro Area
Map 3

Discount Books   **Open Shop**
3650 West Glendale Avenue   85051   (602) 589-0188

Collection:	General stock of paperback and hardcover.
# of Vols:	75,000
Hours:	Daily, except closed Tue, 10-7.
Services:	Accepts want lists, mail order.
Travel:	At 35th Avenue, in Palm Glen Shopping Center.
Credit Cards:	Yes
Owner:	Chuck Brown
Year Estab:	1987
Comments:	Stock is approximately 75% paperback.

Five Quail Books - West   **By Appointment**
8540 North Central Avenue, #27   85020   (602) 861-0548

Collection:	Specialty books and ephemera.
# of Vols:	4,000
Specialties:	Grand Canyon; Colorado River and Plateau; Western Americana.
Services:	Appraisals, search service, catalog, accepts want lists.
Credit Cards:	No
Owner:	Dan Cassidy
Year Estab:	1995

John J. Ford, Jr.   **By Appointment**
PO Box 10317   85064   (602) 957-6443

Collection:	Specialty new and used.
Specialties:	Numismatics; Western Americana (regional & city directories from 1850-1900); credit reference books (Dun & Bradstreet, etc.).
Year Estab:	1961

Gifts Anon.   **Open Shop**
4524 North 7th Street   85014   (602) 277-5256

Collection:	Specialty. Mostly new and some used.
# of Vols:	4,000
Specialties:	Recovery; self care; alcoholism; eating disorders; addictions.
Hours:	Mon-Fri 9-7. Sat 9-5.
Services:	Catalog
Travel:	7th St exit off I-10. Proceed north on 7th St for about 2¾ miles.
Credit Cards:	Yes
Year Estab:	1977
Comments:	Stock is approximately 15% used, 70% of which is paperback.

Lost Dutchman Comics   **Open Shop**
5811 North 7th Street   85014   Fax: (602) 263-5249   (602) 263-5249
E-mail: ldcomics@netzone.com

Collection:	Specialty
Specialties:	Vintage paperbacks; movie and television related paperbacks..
Hours:	Daily 10-7.

(Phoenix)

Travel: Bethany Home Rd exit off I-17. Proceed east on Bethany to 7th St,
                   then south on 7th. Shop is one block ahead on right.
Credit Cards: Yes
Owner: R. Blake Shira
Year Estab: 1989

Mr. Books   **Open Shop**
2814 West Bell Road, #1495   85023   (602) 504-3766

Collection: General stock of hardcover and paperback.
Specialties: Pop-ups; science fiction (paperback).
Hours: Mon-Sat 10-9. Sun 11-5.
Travel: Bell Rd exit off I-17. Proceed west on Bell. Shop is just off exit, on
                   northwest corner, in Bell Canyon Pavilions shopping center.
Credit Cards: Yes
Owner: Mark Walters
Year Estab: 1990
Comments: A good sized shop. While a large majority of the stock is paperback,
                   we did see a significant number of hardcover volumes in many subject
                   areas, plus a few vintage books and some interesting titles "under
                   glass" to make this a worthwhile stop.

North Mountain Books   **Open Shop**
9226 North 7th Street   85020   (602) 997-1643

Collection: Specialty. Mostly used. (see comments)
# of Vols: 6,000
Specialties: Computers; electronics; construction; automotive; mathematics; sci-
                   ence; technology.
Hours: Mon-Fri 10-6. Sat 11-4.
Services: Accepts want lists, mail order.
Travel: Dunlap Ave exit off I-17. Proceed east on Dunlap, then north on 7th.
Credit Cards: Yes
Owner: Lawrence Jerome
Year Estab: 1982
Comments: Books are of recent vintage and of a practical nature as opposed to
                   "collectible" quality books of historical interest.

Paperback Paradise   **Open Shop**
1931A West Thunderbird Road   85023   (602) 993-5220

Collection: General stock of mostly paperback.
# of Vols: 30,000
Hours: Mon-Sat 10-6.

Royal Bookstore   **Open Shop**
2340 North 32nd Street   85008   (602) 955-8840

Collection: Specialty new and used books and magazines.

# of Vols:	10,000
Specialties:	Military; firearms.
Hours:	Mon-Sat 9-6.
Services:	Accepts want lists, mail order.
Travel:	On 32nd St between Thomas & McDowell.
Credit Cards:	Yes
Year Estab:	1963
Comments:	Stock is approximately 60% used.

Shannon's Book Trader   **Open Shop**
4428 North 19th Avenue   85015   (602) 264-5862

Collection:	General stock of mostly paperback.
# of Vols:	30,000
Hours:	Mon-Thu 10-6. Fri 10-7. Sat 10-5.

The Tattered Page   **Open Shop**
3329 East Bell Road, #7   85032   (602) 493-8680
                                                        Fax: (602) 493-8680

Collection:	General stock of mostly used paperback.
# of Vols:	25,000 (used)
Hours:	Mon-Fri 10-8. Sat 10-6.

Prescott

Anchor Books   **Open Shop**
1046 Willow Creek Road   86301   (520) 778-0629

Collection:	General stock of paperback and hardcover.
Hours:	Mon-Sat 10-5:30. Sun 11-4.
Travel:	I-17 to Hwy 69. Located in K-Mart Plaza.
Credit Cards:	No
Owner:	George & Joyce Thomson
Year Estab:	1980
Comments:	Stock is approximately 75% paperback.

Kea Books   **Antique Mall**
At Prescott Antique & Craft Market   Mall: (520) 445-7156
115 North Cortez   Home: (520) 717-1993
Mailing address: 2560 Sandia Drive Prescott 86301

Collection:	General stock.
# of Vols:	3,000
Specialties:	Arizona; Southwest Americana; visual arts; history; literature; aviation; mystery; nautical; metaphysics.
Hours:	Mon-Sat 10-5. Sun 12-5.
Travel:	Hwy 69 into town. Just off town square.
Owner:	Robert Kostuck
Year Estab:	1994

Charles Parkhurst Books   **By Appointment**
PO Box 10850   86304   (520) 776-9871
                                                          Fax: (520) 778-1075

Collection: General stock.
Specialties: Literature; modern first editions.
Services: Catalog
Credit Cards: Yes
Year Estab: 1988

Satisfied Mind Book Store   **Open Shop**
113 West Goodwin   86303   (520) 776-9766

Collection: General stock of new and used paperback and hardcover.
# of Vols: 20,000 (used)
Hours: Mon-Sat 9-6. Sun 12-4.
Services: Appraisals, search service, accepts want lists, mail order.
Travel: From Hwy 89 (Gurley St in Prescott), turn left on Cortez, then right on
                 Goodwin.
Credit Cards: Yes
Owner: Tom Brodersen
Year Estab: 1989
Comments: Stock is approximately 50% used, 60% of which is paperback.

Prescott Valley

Bookends   **Open Shop**
3040 Windsong, #106   86314   (520) 772-1868
                                                     E-mail: ajijic@aztec.asu.edu

Collection: General stock of paperback and hardcover.
# of Vols: 15,000
Hours: Mon-Sat 10-6.
Travel: From Hwy 69 in Prescott Valley, turn north on Windsong. Shop is in
                 Windsong Plaza.
Credit Cards: No
Owner: Bruce & Judy Taylor
Year Estab: 1996
Comments: Stock is approximately 75% paperback.

Books 'N' Things   **Open Shop**
8060 Frontage Road   (602) 772-1893
Mailing address: PO Box 26994 Prescott Valley 86312

Collection: General stock of hardcover and paperback.
# of Vols: 30,000
Hours: Mon-Fri 9-5. Sat 9-4.
Services: Appraisals, search service, accepts want lists, mail order.
Travel: Robert Rd exit off Hwy 89. Shop is just off exit on frontage road on
                 north side of highway.
Owner: Cheri Best

Year Estab: 1986
Comments: Stock is evenly divided between hardcover and paperback.

Merlin's Antiques & Furniture   **Antique Mall**
8196 Valley Road   (520) 772-9259

Hours: Mon-Sat 9:30-5:30. Sun 11-4.
Travel: From Hwy 69, turn north on Robert Rd, then west on Valley.

Safford

Twitchell's Books & Tea   **Open Shop**
425 Main Street 85546   (520) 428-3477

Collection: General stock of new and mostly paperback used.
Hours: Tue-Fri 10-5. Sat 10-3.

Scottsdale
(See Map 3, page 48)

The Antiquarian Shop   **Open Shop**
4246 North Scottsdale Road 85251   (602) 947-0535

Collection: General stock.
# of Vols: 5,000
Specialties: Antiquarian
Hours: Mon-Sat 11-5:30.
Services: Mail order.
Travel: Between Indian School and Camelback.
Credit Cards: Yes
Owner: George Chamberlin
Year Estab: 1963
Comments: In the course of our travels, we have visited several "truly antiquarian" book dealers and have usually been impressed by the age, condition and variety of the items offered for sale. This shop is no exception to that rule and would be equally at home in New York City, Boston or Chicago as at its current location in a suburb of Phoenix. The store is a pleasure to visit. In addition to 19th century (and perhaps earlier) volumes, the store also displays more popular first editions, i.e., Edgar Rice Burroughs titles. If you're planning to shop here, bring discriminating tastes and a healthy line of credit.

Book Exchange   **Open Shop**
4320 North Miller Road 85251   (602) 949-9507

Collection: General stock of mostly paperback.
# of Vols: 30,000
Hours: Mon-Fri 10-5:30. Sat 10-5.

Bookmaster   **Open Shop**
2949 North Scottsdale Road 85251   (602) 423-0501

Collection: General stock paperback and hardcover.

# of Vols:	500,000+
Hours:	Mon-Fri 9:30-7. Sat 9:30-6. Call for Sun hours.
Services:	Appraisals, accepts want lists, mail order.
Travel:	1/2 block north of Thomas Rd.
Credit Cards:	Yes
Owner:	Jim Cohen
Year Estab:	1990
Comments:	A large shop carrying a large selection of paperbacks and used magazines. The hardcover volumes, fewer in number, represented, at the time of our visit, approximately 10% of the total stock. Most of the titles we saw were in fairly good condition, were generally of more modern vintage and did not appear to be significantly unique, although when viewing a large number of volumes, one can never be certain that a real winner wasn't overlooked.

Guidon Books   **Open Shop**
7117 Main Street   85251   Fax: (602) 946-0521   (602) 945-8811
                                                   Web site: http://www.guidon.com

Collection:	Specialty new and used.
Specialties:	Civil War; Western Americana.
Hours:	Mon-Sat 10-5.
Services:	Appraisals, accepts want lists, mail order.
Credit Cards:	Yes
Owner:	Aaron L. & Ruth Kantor Cohen
Year Estab:	1964

Scottsdale Book Gallery   **Antique Mall**
At Antiques Super-Mall   Mall: (602) 874-2900
1900 North Scottsdale Road   85257   Book Gallery: (602) 263-8353

Collection:	General stock.
Travel:	One block north of McDowell, on west side of street.
Owner:	Tanya Fahey & Mike Riley
Comments:	Based on our visit to the two shops that supply the books for this display (the Book Gallery and Al's Bookstore, both in Phoenix) we believe your visit to this satellite location will leave a good taste in your mouth.

T. A. Swinford, Bookseller   **Open Shop**
7134 Main Street   85251   (602) 946-0022

Collection:	Specialty
# of Vols:	20,000
Specialties:	Western Americana.
Hours:	Mon-Sat 10-5.
Services:	Catalog
Travel:	One block south of intersection of Indian School Rd and Scottsdale Rd.
Credit Cards:	Yes
Year Estab:	1979

Words From Our Past   **Open Shop**
1017 North Scottsdale Road   85257   (602) 990-0492
                                                E-mail: KLTG77B @prodigy.com

Collection:	General stock of hardcover and paperback.
# of Vols:	65,000
Hours:	Mon-Fri 10-6. Sat 10-5. Sun 10-5 (Oct-Jun only).
Services:	Appraisals, search service, accepts want lists, mail order.
Travel:	Scottsdale Rd and Roosevelt.
Credit Cards:	Yes
Owner:	Katy Shannon
Year Estab:	1988
Comments:	A sign in the window reads "Rare, Out-Of-Print Book Search." Based on our visit to this shop where we saw a preponderance of paperbacks and approximately 5,000 hardcover volumes. We did see a few interesting hardcover titles but not in sufficient numbers to excite us.

Sedona

The Book Loft   **Open Shop**
175 Highway 179   (520) 282-5173
Mailing address: PO Box 2966 Sedona 86339

Collection:	General stock.
# of Vols:	10,000
Specialties:	Western Americana; children's; first editions; Native Americans.
Hours:	Daily 10-6, open till 7pm during summer.
Services:	Appraisals, search service, accepts want lists, mail order.
Travel:	Located at the intersection of Hwy 89A and Hwy 179 (the "Y").
Credit Cards:	Yes
Owner:	George & Noreen Ireland
Year Estab:	1984
Comments:	Located one flight up, the shop is small in size and therefore in selection but the books we saw were attractive, mostly in good condition and included quite a few first editions of merit. If you like mountain driving, native American crafts, your trip to Sedona should also include a visit to this shop.

Bradmar Books   **Open Shop**
2550 West State Route 89A   (520) 282-1736
Mailing address: 726 South 7th Street Cottonwood 86326

Collection:	General stock of hardcover and paperback.
# of Vols:	10,000+
Hours:	Mon-Sat 10-5:30.
Travel:	Hwy 179 exit off I-17. Proceed north on Hwy 179 to Hwy 89A, then left on Hwy 89A.
Credit Cards:	No
Owner:	Marilyn Manning
Year Estab:	1988

Comments: Unfortunately, this shop was not open on Sunday, the day our itinerary
                brought us to Sedona. We're advised by the owner that the stock is
                evenly divided between hardcover and paperback.

Sun City West

Bill The Bookie   **By Appointment**
13439 Shadow Hills Drive   85375   (602) 214-8365
                                                            Fax: (602) 214-8365

Collection: Specialty books and ephemera.
# of Vols: 10,000
Specialties: Cartoon and caricature; original cartoon art; boxing; baseball; journal-
                 ism.
Services: Search service, catalog, accepts want lists.
Credit Cards: No
Year Estab: 1986

Tempe
(See Map 3, page 48)

Bob & Faye's Family Book Store   **Open Shop**
2043 East University Drive   85281   (602) 966-2065

Collection: General stock of mostly paperback.
# of Vols: 100,00+
Hours: Mon-Sat 10-6.

The Book Connection   **Open Shop**
6434 South McClintock Drive   85283   (602) 820-2953

Collection: General stock of hardcover and paperback.
# of Vols: 35,000+
Specialties: Metaphysics; new age; self help; children's; science fiction.
Hours: Mon-Thu 10-7. Fri 10-9. Sat 10-6. Sun 1-6.
Services: Accepts want lists, mail order.
Travel: McClintock exit off Hwy 60. Proceed south on McClintock to Guadalupe
                 St. Shop is in Tempe Square Shopping Center.
Credit Cards: Yes
Owner: Diane Beatty & Barbara Furlone
Year Estab: 1994
Comments: Most of the books we saw were in good condition, of fairly recent
                 vintage and reasonably priced.

Book Island   **Open Shop**
1042 East Baseline Road   85283   (602) 820-8405

Collection: General stock of mostly hardcover.
# of Vols: 10,000
Hours: Mon-Sat 10-7. Sun 1-5.
Services: Search service, accepts want lists, mail order.

Travel:	Rural Rd exit off I-10. Proceed south on Rural to Baseline. Shop is in Lake Country Village center at northeast corner of Rural and Baseline.
Credit Cards:	No
Owner:	Karly Mapel
Year Estab:	1992
Comments:	We visited this shop on a Monday afternoon and were greeted by a gentleman (we assume the owner) who informed us that he did not wish to be listed in any guide. The only reason we could ascertain for his position was that he did not wish to be patronized by other dealers who would purchase books he would otherwise have available for his regular customers. At this point, we decided to leave the shop and can therefore offer little in terms of guidance for anyone who, after reading the above, still wishes to make a visit.

Books, Etc.   **Open Shop**
901 South Mill Avenue   85281   (602) 967-1111
                                                                            Fax: (602) 967-1145

Collection:	General stock of mostly new and specialty used paperbacks
Specialties:	Science fiction; mystery.
Hours:	Mon-Fri 9-9. Sat 9-8. Sun 10-6.
Credit Cards:	Yes
Owner:	John Wehr
Year Estab:	1978

Changing Hands Bookstore   **Open Shop**
414 South Mill Avenue, #109   85251   (602) 966-0203

Collection:	General stock new, used paperback and hardcover and remainders.
# of Vols:	10,000 (used)
Hours:	Mon-Thu 10-9. Fri & Sat 10-10. Sun 12-5.
Services:	Search service, accepts want lists, mail order.
Travel:	Mill Ave exit off Hwy 60 (Superstition Hwy). Proceed north on Mill.
Credit Cards:	Yes
Year Estab:	1974
Comments:	Primarily a "new" book shop with most of the used books located in a lower level. Most of the used books we saw were of fairly recent vintage with a few older volumes interspersed. While many subjects were represented and prices were quite reasonable, the size of the used collection is limited.

Delta Books   **Open Shop**
224 East Baseline Road   85282   (602) 831-0984

Collection:	General stock of mostly paperback.
Hours:	Mon-Fri 9-5. Other times by appointment.

Gamblers World   **Open Shop**
1938 East University   85281   (602) 968-2590

Collection:	Specialty. Mostly new.

# of Vols:	100 (used)
Specialties:	Gambling
Hours:	Mon 12-6. Tue-Sat 10-6.

Old Town Books   **Open Shop**
518 South Mill Avenue   85281   (602) 968-9881

Collection:	General stock mostly hardcover.
# of Vols:	8,000
Specialties:	Western Americana; Arizona; fishing.
Hours:	Mon-Sat 10-6. Sun 11-5.
Services:	Search service, mail order.
Travel:	Mill Ave exit off Hwy 60. Proceed north on Mill.
Credit Cards:	Yes
Owner:	Chris Smith
Year Estab:	1985
Comments:	A small, crowded shop offering a reasonable selection in the specialties listed above and a more limited selection of more general titles. The books were in mixed condition and of mixed vintage. If this is your area of speciality, drop in. Otherwise.....

Reid's New & Used Books   **Open Shop**
1250 East Apache Boulevard, #105   85281   (602) 894-3329
                                                     E-mail: reidsbks@aol.com

Collection:	General stock of paperback and hardcover.
# of Vols:	5,000
Hours:	Mon-Sat 12:30-10:30, except Wed 12-4. Call for Sun hours.
Travel:	Hwy 202 exit off I-10. Proceed east on Hwy 202 to Rural Rd , then right on Rural and left on Apache. Shop is in Dorsey Lane Shopping Center.
Credit Cards:	Yes
Owner:	Scott Krause
Year Estab:	1996
Comments:	A relatively new shop with more paperbacks and magazines (including some unusual types)) than hardcover volumes. Many of the hardcover books were of fairly recent vintage. Mostly reading copies.

Those Were The Days!   **Open Shop**
516 South Mill Avenue   85281   (602) 967-4729
                                                     Fax: (602) 967-1428

Collection:	Specialty used and new books and ephemera.
# of Vols:	50,000
Specialties:	Antiques and collecting; advertising; architecture; aviation; children's; cookbooks; art and illustration; Southwest Americana; Native Americana; medicine; natural history; photography; science; technology; transportation.
Hours:	Mon-Wed 9:30-6. Thu & Fri 9:30-9. Sat 10:30-9. Sun 12-5.
Services:	Mail order.
Travel:	I-17 to 1-10 then University exit off I-10. Proceed east on University then north on Mill.

Credit Cards: Yes
Year Estab: 1973
Comments: If you're a nostalgia buff you should enjoy a visit to this shop. In addition
                  to a large number of new publications celebrating yesteryear, the shop also
                  carries a modest number of older volumes in mixed condition that actually
                  date back to the late 19th and early 20th century.

Tombstone

Rose Tree Inn Books   **Open Shop**
116 4th Street   85638   (520) 457-3326

Collection: Specialty
# of Vols: 200-300
Specialties: Southwest Americana.
Hours: Daily 9-5.
Travel: At 4th and Toughnut, off Allen St.

Tucson

Baseball Books Only   **By Appointment**
5672 East Scarlet Street   85711   (520) 747-5394

Collection: Specialty. Mostly used and some new.
# of Vols: 9,000
Specialties: Baseball
Services: Search service, accepts want lists, mail order.
Owner: J.C. Percell
Year Estab: 1966

Beachcomber Book Shop   **Open Shop**
5763 West Potvin Lane   (520) 744-1619
Mailing address: PO Box 197 Cortaro 85652

Collection: Specialty
# of Vols: 25,000
Specialties: Military (20th century); aviation (20th century).
Hours: Mon-Fri 8-5. Sat & Sun by appointment.
Services: Appraisals, search service, accepts want lists, catalog.
Travel: Cortaro exit off I-10. Proceed north on east access road for two miles,
                  then right on Camino de Mannana Rd and left on Decker. Proceed for
                  3/4 of a mile and turn left at Beachcomber mailbox.
Credit Cards: Yes
Owner: Jim Thorvardson
Year Estab: 1956

Bertrand's Books   **Open Shop**
120 East Congress Street   85701   (520) 884-1899
                                                                    Fax: (520) 325-1694

Collection: General stock of paperback and hardcover.

# of Vols:	40,000
Specialties:	Science fiction; vintage paperbacks.
Hours:	Mon-Thu 10am-9pm. Fri & Sat 10am-11pm. Sun by appointment or chance.
Services:	Accepts want lists, mail order.
Travel:	Broadway exit off I-10. Proceed east on Broadway to 6th Ave, then left on 6th and left again on Congress. Shop is 1/2 block ahead on left.
Credit Cards:	Yes
Year Estab:	1994
Comments:	Located in the heart of downtown Tucson, the shop has more paperbacks than hardcover books. The hardcover volumes we saw were in generally good condition with a bit more representation in the specialties listed above. The majority of the titles were of fairly recent vintage. Worth a brief visit.

The Book Stop   **Open Shop**
2504 North Campbell Avenue   85719   (520) 326-6661

Collection:	General stock of paperback and hardcover.
# of Vols:	60,000
Hours:	Mon-Sat 10am-11pm. Sun 12-11pm.
Services:	Appraisals, search service, accepts want lists, mail order.
Travel:	Grant Rd exit off I-10. Proceed east on Grant Rd, then north on Campbell.
Credit Cards:	Yes
Owner:	Claire Fellows & Tina Bailey
Year Estab:	1968
Comments:	A good sized shop with hardcover items in mixed condition and of mixed vintage. The shelves were not always clearly labeled so one has to seek out subjects of interest. Many subjects were represented. Reasonably priced.

Booked Up   **Open Shop**
2828 North Stone Avenue   85705   (520) 622-8238

Collection:	General stock and ephemera.
# of Vols:	15,000
Hours:	Mon-Sat 10-6.
Services:	Accepts want lists, mail order.
Travel:	Grant exit off I-10. Proceed east on Grant, then left (north) on Stone. Shop is on right, about 40 yards north of Glen.
Credit Cards:	Yes
Owner:	Larry McMurtry
Year Estab:	1994
Comments:	Hardly as massive as the owner's Archer City, TX location but solid in terms of the books on hand. A good selection in history and literature. Certainly worth a visit. Reasonably priced.

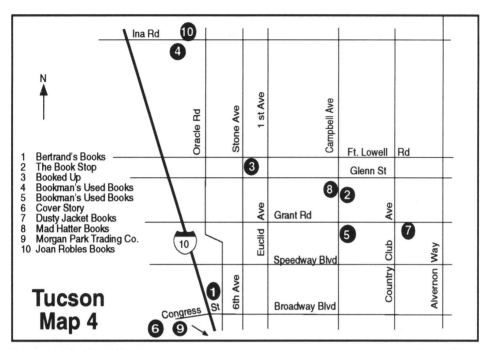

Tucson
Map 4

1 Bertrand's Books
2 The Book Stop
3 Booked Up
4 Bookman's Used Books
5 Bookman's Used Books
6 Cover Story
7 Dusty Jacket Books
8 Mad Hatter Books
9 Morgan Park Trading Co.
10 Joan Robles Books

Bookman's Used Books   **Open Shop**
1930 East Grant Road 85719   (520) 325-5767

Collection:	General stock of hardcover and paperback.
# of Vols:	750,000
Hours:	Daily 9am-10pm.
Services:	Accepts want lists.
Travel:	Grant Rd exit off I-10. Proceed east on Grant to Campbell. Shop is on the southeast corner.
Credit Cards:	Yes
Year Estab:	1987
Comments:	Slightly larger than the West Ina Road shop (see below).

Bookman's Used Books   **Open Shop**
3733 West Ina Road 85741   (520) 579-0303

Collection:	General stock of hardcover of paperback.
# of Vols:	120,000
Hours:	Daily 9am-10pm.
Services:	Search service, accepts want lists, mail order.
Travel:	Ina Rd exit off I-10. Proceed east on Ina to Thornydale. Shop is in North Pima Shopping Center.
Credit Cards:	Yes
Year Estab:	1992
	Somewhat smaller in size than the Bookman's we visited in Flagstaff or Mesa with the same general organization and atmosphere and almost the same selection of books and price patterns.

(Tucson)

Chosen Reflections   **Open Shop**
North La Cholla Blvd, Unit 166   (520) 297-0006
Mailing address: 7401 North La Cholla Blvd Tucson 85741

Collection:	Specialty
Specialties:	Magazines and ephemera.
Hours:	Mon-Fri 10-9. Sat 10-6. Sun 12-5.
Travel:	Ina Rd exit off I-10. Proceed east on Ina for three miles. Shop is at intersection of Ina and La Cholla in Foothills Mall.

Clues Unlimited   **Open Shop**
16 Broadway Village   85716   (520) 326-8533

Collection:	Specialty of mostly new and some used.
# of Vols:	Small used stock.
Specialties:	Mystery
Hours:	Mon-Fri 10-6. Sat 9-5.
Credit Cards:	Yes
Owner:	Christine Burke
Year Estab:	1986
Comments:	Used stock is primarily of collectible quality.

Cover Story   **Open Shop**
110 South Camino Seco   (520) 886-5364
Mailing address: PO Box 17833 Tucson 85731

Collection:	General stock of paperback and hardcover.
# of Vols:	70,000
Hours:	Mon-Sat 10-6. Sun 12-4. Other times by appointment.
Services:	Search service, accepts want lists.
Travel:	Houghton exit off I-10. Proceed north on Houghton to Spanish Trail, then left on Spanish Trail and right on Camino Seco. Shop is in Berkshire Village Shopping Center.
Credit Cards:	No
Year Estab:	1971
Comments:	Stock is approximately 75% paperback.

Dusty Jacket Books   **Antique Mall**
At The Antique Mall   Mall: (520) 326-3720
3130 East Grant   85732   Home: (520) 326-8520

Hours:	Mon-Sat 10-5:30. Sun 11-4:30.
Travel:	Southeast corner of Grant and Country Club.

Paul Gaudette: Books   **Open Shop**
2050 East 17th Street   85719   (520) 791-3868
                                                    Fax: (520) 791-9412

Collection:	Specialty used and new.
# of Vols:	100,000

Specialties:	Aviation; military; naval. (From World War I to present).
Hours:	Mon-Fri 8-4. Sat & Sun 8-1.
Services:	Catalog, accepts want lists.
Travel:	Broadway exit off I-10. Proceed east on Broadway to Plumber, south on Plumber, then west on 17th St.
Credit Cards:	Yes
Year Estab:	1960
Comments:	Stock is approximately 50% used.

Janus Books   **By Appointment**
PO Box 40787   85717   Fax: (520) 323-3351   (520) 881-8192
                                                        E-mail: janus@azstarnet.com

Collection:	Specialty
# of Vols:	2,500
Specialties:	Detective; mystery, suspense fiction; Sherlock Holmes. Also, related bibliography and criticism.
Services:	Catalog, accepts want lists.
Credit Cards:	Yes
Owner:	Michael S. Greenbaum
Year Estab:	1979

Mad Hatter Books   **Open Shop**
2729 North Campbell   85719   (520) 325-9474

Collection:	General stock of paperback and hardcover and records.
# of Vols:	10,000
Hours:	Mon-Sat 11-6:30.
Travel:	Grant exit off I-10. Proceed east on Grant, then north on Campbell. Shop is on west side, in strip center just before Glen.
Credit Cards:	No
Owner:	Larry Windham
Year Estab:	1978
Comments:	This shop is probably appropriately named, particularly if you're looking for a particular title and have a problem locating it here. Most of the middle section of the cluttered shop is devoted to LPs with the lower shelves of the bookcases lining the side walls stocked with paperbacks. If you don't mind getting a stiff neck, you'll see hardcover books along the top two shelves and in the rear of the shop (many dealing with nature). While you might find some winners here, you'll have to be very patient to do so. And, if you're interested, also among some of the shop's clutter, is a selection of used men's clothing (western style).

Morgan Park Trading Company   **Antique Mall**
At Unique Antique Mall   Mall: (520) 323-0319
5000 E. Speedway   E-mail: 73205,376@compuserve.com
Mailing address: 1555 North Arcadia Tucson 85712   Home: (520) 323-1709

Collection:	General stock.

(Tucson)

# of Vols:	1,500+
Specialties:	Mystery; children's; decorative arts.
Hours:	Mon-Sat 9-5. Sun 12-5.
Travel:	Kolb Rd exit off I-10. Proceed north on Kolb to Speedway, then west on Speedway.
Credit Cards:	Yes
Owner:	Beverly Furlow
Year Estab:	1973
Comments:	Additional stock is available for viewing on a by appointment basis.

Darlene D. Morris Antiques   **By Appointment**
5030 East Speedway   85712   (520) 577-6519

Collection:	Specialty
Specialties:	Antiques
Credit Cards:	Yes
Year Estab:	1976

Mostly Books   **Open Shop**
6208 East Speedway   85712   (520) 571-0110

Collection:	General stock of mostly paperback.
# of Vols:	60,000
Hours:	Mon-Fri 10-9. Sat 10-6. Sun 12-5.

Mary Odette Books   **By Appointment**
3831 North Cherry Creek Place   85749   (520) 749-2285

Collection:	Specialty new and used.
# of Vols:	2,000
Specialties:	Botanicals
Services:	Search service, accepts want lists, catalog.
Credit Cards:	No
Year Estab:	1994

M. Revak & Co   **Open Shop**
1440 North Stone Avenue   85705   Fax: (520) 624-8701   (520) 624-3445
                                                      E-mail: quid7@aol.com

Collection:	Specialty
# of Vols:	500
Specialties:	Law; art; Southwest Americana.
Hours:	Tue-Fri 10-4. Other times by appointment.
Services:	Appraisals, accepts want lists, catalog in planning stage.
Travel:	Speedway exit off I-10. Proceed east on Speedway to Stone, then left on Stone.
Credit Cards:	No
Owner:	Michael J. Green & Mary Beth Revak
Year Estab:	1990

Val D. Robbins
3450 North Drake Place   85749

By Appointment
(520) 749-8774

Collection:	General stock and ephemera.
# of Vols:	3,000
Services:	Appraisals, accepts want lists, mail order.
Credit Cards:	No
Year Estab:	1950

Joan Robles Books
At Haunted Bookshop
7211 North Northern
Mailing address: 5045 North Via Condesa Tucson 85718

Open Shop
Shop: (520) 297-4843
Home: (520) 884-1240

Collection:	General stock.
# of Vols:	6,000
Specialties:	Southwest Americana; children's.
Hours:	Mon-Sat 9-6. Sun 11-5.
Services:	Search service, accepts want lists, mail order.
Travel:	Ina exit off I-10. Proceed east on Ina to Oracle. Left on Oracle, then first left into shopping center. Shop is behind the stores in a separate building on the right.
Credit Cards:	Yes
Year Estab:	1976
Comments:	Located in an alcove of an otherwise "new" book store, the selection here, while offering some interesting titles, was limited in number. If you're looking for specific titles, we suggest a call to the owner as additional books can be viewed on a by appointment basis at the owner's home.

Ben Sackheim
5425 East Fort Lowell Road   85712

By Appointment
(520) 327-4285

Collection:	Specialty
# of Vols:	5,000+
Specialties:	20th century first editions; art.
Services:	Occasional catalog.
Credit Cards:	No
Year Estab:	1969

The Trail To Yesterday
PO Box 35905   85740

By Appointment
(520) 299-8517

Collection:	Specialty new and out-of-print.
# of Vols:	2,000
Specialties:	Arizona
Services:	Appraisals, catalog.
Credit Cards:	No
Owner:	Bob Pugh
Year Estab:	1981

Truepenny Books   **By Appointment**
2509 North Campbell Avenue   85719   Fax: (520) 323-6401   (520) 881-4822
                                                          E-mail: truepen@azstarnet.com

Collection:	General stock.
# of Vols:	5,000
Specialties:	Private press; books about books; illustrated; fine bindings.
Services:	Appraisals, search service, catalog, accepts want lists.
Credit Cards:	Yes
Owner:	William R. Laws
Year Estab:	1981

Gene Vinik, Books   **By Appointment**
2213 East Copper Street   85719   (520) 323-7188

Collection:	General stock.
# of Vols:	4,000-5,000
Year Estab:	1984

Yuma

Bandanna Books   **Open Shop**
395 South Main Street   85364   (520) 329-0417

Collection:	General stock of hardcover and ephemera and records.
# of Vols:	45,000
Specialties:	Southwest Americana.
Hours:	Tue-Sat 10-5. Closed August.
Services:	Search service, accepts want lists, mail order.
Travel:	Exit 2 off I-8. Follow Giss Pkwy to Main St. Shop is 1/2 mile ahead at corner of Giss Pkwy and Main St.
Owner:	Maggie Elmer
Year Estab:	1989
Comments:	The stock is approximately 70% hardcover.

G. W. Stuart Jr. Rare Books   **By Appointment**
204 Madison Avenue   85364   (520) 783-6742
                                                             Fax: (520) 783-9273

Collection:	Specialty
Specialties:	Early English and American literature; incunabula.
Services:	Appraisals, catalog.
Year Estab:	1966

Yuma's Book Gallery   **Open Shop**
2340 West 20th Street   85364   (520) 782-3747

Collection:	General stock of mostly paperback.
# of Vols:	100,000
Hours:	Tue-Fri 9:30-5. Sat 9:30-3.

A Booklover's Shop   (520) 881-8192
PO Box 43607 Tucson 85733

Collection:	Specialty
Specialties:	Santos; mission architecture; Hispanic New Mexico; Southwest fiction; pre-Vatican II literature; books on books.
Services:	Appraisals, accepts want lists.
Credit Cards:	No
Owner:	Bob Hershoff
Year Estab:	1988.
Comments:	Note: Telephone number is for messages only.

Beattie Book Company   (520) 896-3357
PO Box 5304 Oracle 85623   Fax: (520) 896-3356
                                                          E-mail: jbeattie@interloc.com

Collection:	Specialty
# of Vols:	1,000
Specialties:	Architecture and allied arts; medicine; archaeology.
Services:	Appraisals, catalog
Credit Cards:	Yes
Owner:	Jim Beattie
Year Estab:	1975
Comments:	From May-Sept can be reached at PO Box 739, Cape May, NJ 08204, (609) 886-5432.

Big Book Broker   (520) 881-5417
PO Box 91648 Tucson 85752

Collection:	Specialty
# of Vols:	100-200
Specialties:	Alcoholics Anonymous.
Services:	Appraisals
Credit Cards:	No
Year Estab:	1991

Broomfield Books   (602) 350-9115
1320 South Broadway Tempe 85212

Collection:	General stock.
# of Vols	2,000
Services:	Appraisals, lists, search service, accepts want lists.
Credit Cards:	Yes
Owner:	Eric Broomfield
Year Estab:	1990

The Dervish Brothers Books   (520) 326-7340
PO Box 43576 Tucson 85733

Collection:	Specialty
# of Vols:	8,000

Specialties: Central Asia;; Middle East; Sufism; Islam; Tibetan Buddhism; Gnosticism; metaphysics.
Services: Search service, accepts want lists, catalog.
Credit Cards: No
Owner: Dr. Khwaja Nuriya & Philip & Evelyn Boatnight

Duckett's Sporting Books   (602) 345-2698
1968 East Carson Drive Tempe 85282

Collection: Specialty new and used.
Specialties: Firearms; weapons; swords; trapping.
Services: Appraisals, search service, catalog, accepts want lists.
Credit Cards: No
Year Estab: 1989

Eborn Books   (602) 979-0707
PO Box 2093 Peoria 85380

Collection: Specialty used and new.
Specialties: Mormons
Services: Appraisals, search service, catalog.
Credit Cards: No
Owner: Bret & Cindy Eborn
Year Estab: 1988

Eliot Books   (520) 326-6486
PO Box 65136 Tucson 85728   Fax: (520) 326-6486
Collection: Specialty
Specialties: Modern first editions (fiction and non fiction); poetry; western; beat
                 generation.
Services: Catalog, accepts want lists.
Credit Cards: No
Owner: Walt Bartholomew
Year Estab: 1995

G. F. Armoury Books   (520) 747-9862
5718 East 34th Street Tucson 85711   E-mail: medieval@interloc.com

 Collection: Specialty new and used.
Specialties: Medieval and renaissance including heraldry, daily life, illumination,
                 arms and armor and costume.
Services: Search service, accepts want lists.
Credit Cards: Yes
Owner: William Taylor
Year Estab: 1986

Haidaway Books   (520) 828-3558
Box 9A, Bonita Route Klondyke 85643

Collection: General stock.
# of Vols: 5,000
Specialties: Children's; mystery; western

Services: Search service, catalog, accepts want lists.
Credit Cards: No
Owner: Lydia Markgraf
Year Estab: 1990

William R. Hecht (602) 948-2536
PO Box 67 Scottsdale 85252

Collection: Specialty
Specialties: Falconry; natural history; Americana.
Services: Catalog
Credit Cards: No
Year Estab: 1950

The Hide Bound Book (520) 744-2028
7130 North Camino de los Caballos Tucson 85743 Fax: (520) 744-9551

Collection: Specialty
# of Vols: 10,000
Specialties: Southwest Americana.
Services: Accepts want lists, occasional catalog.
Credit Cards: No
Owner: Richard King
Year Estab: 1982.

J. Juszyk Books (602) 977-8313
10326 West Griswold Road Peoria 85345 Fax: (602) 977-8313

Collection: Specialty new and used.
Specialties: Big game hunting; circus; mammals; zoos; hobbies.
Services: Search service, catalog, accepts want lists.
Credit Cards: No
Owner: Michael J. Juszyk
Year Estab: 1980

Natural History Books (520) 634-5016
PO Box 1004 Cottonwood 86326 Fax: (520) 634-1217

Collection: Specialty hardcover and paperback. Mostly used.
# of Vols: 55,000
Specialties: Earth and biological sciences.
Services: Catalog, accepts want lists.
Credit Cards: Yes
Owner: Donald E. Hahn
Year Estab: 1979

The Red Lancer (602) 964-9667
PO Box 8056 Mesa 85214 Fax: (602) 890-9495

Collection: Specialty
# of Vols: 2,000
Specialties: Military (19th & 20th Century).

Services: Appraisals, accepts want lists, catalog.
Credit Cards: Yes
Owner: Robin Bates
Year Estab: 1985

Carl Sciortino Militaria   (602) 585-5210
PO Box 13745 Scottsdale 85267

Collection: Specialty
# of Vols   5,000
Specialties: Military (US)
Services: Accepts want lists, catalog.
Credit Cards: No
Year Estab: 1990

Les Smith - Western Books   (602) 832-9373
PO Box 8094 Mesa 85214

Collection: Specialty
Specialties: Western Americana; cowboys; rodeo; Zane Grey; Will James.
Services: Search service, accepts want lists.
Credit Cards: No
Year Estab: 1985

Jerry Wentling   (520) 282-5433
386 Navahopi Road Sedona 86336

Collection: Specialty
# of Vols: 7,000
Specialties: Western Americana; gold rush.
Services: Accepts want lists.
Credit Cards: No
Year Estab: 1976

Gail Wilson Bookseller   (520) 622-7966
2733 West Pauley Place Tucson 85713

Collection: Specialty
Specialties: Illustrated; fine bindings; literature; folklore; fairy tales.
Year Estab: 1978

Ygor's Books   (602) 777-0827
PO Box 40212 Mesa 85274

Collection: Specialty
# of Vols: 1,500
Specialties: Horror; science fiction; fantasy; mystery. Primarily from 1875-1975.
Services: Search service, accepts want lists, catalog.
Credit Cards: No
Owner: Larry Hallock
Year Estab: 1993

Arkansas

Alphabetical Listing By Dealer

Alphabetical Listing By Location

Alexander

Partain's Antique Mall   **Antique Mall**
25014 Highway I-30   (501) 847-4978

Hours: Mon-Sat 9:30-5. Sun 1-5.
Travel: Eastbound on I-30: Exit 123. Westbound on I-30: Exit 26. Proceed on
                 access road along north side of interstate to mall.

Bella Vista

Antiques and Arts   **Open Shop**
At Hampton Place Shops   (501) 855-9600
3403 Bella Vista   72714

Collection: General stock.
# of Vols: 400+
Specialties: Children's; fine bindings; first editions; western Ozarks.
Hours: Mon-Sat 10-5.
Services: Appraisals, accepts want lists, mail order.
Travel: Bella Vista exit off Hwy 71. Shop is 3/4 mile ahead on left.
Credit Cards: Yes
Owner: Steve Whysel
Year Estab: 1994

Berryville

Antiques and Things Elderly   **Open Shop**
702 West Freeman   (501) 423-3775
Mailing address (Winter): 280 Palo Verde Lane Florence AZ 85232

Collection: Specialty
# of Vols: 1,200
Specialties: Children's; cookbooks; some non fiction.
Hours: Apr 15-Oct 30: Mon-Fri 10-4. Other times by appointment.
Services: Search service, catalog, accepts want lists.
Travel: Hwy 62 to Berryville. Turn on Freeman St. Shop is first house on left.
Credit Cards: No
Owner: Jean & Gordon Kennett
Year Estab: 1968

Clarksville

Roy's Trading Post   **Open Shop**
2900 West Main Street   72830   (501) 754-2544

Collection: General stock of mostly paperback and comics.
# of Vols: 20,000
Hours: Tue-Sat 9-4, except Fri till 5.

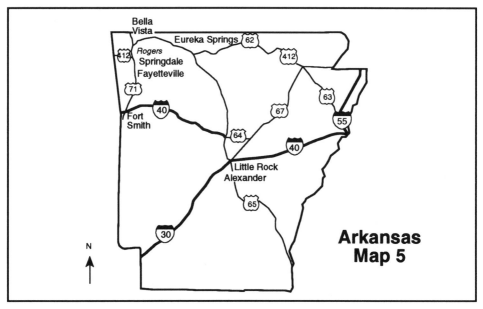

Bella Vista
Eureka Springs 62
Rogers
12
Springdale
Fayetteville
71
40
Fort Smith
63
67
64
55
40
Little Rock
Alexander
65
30
N

**Arkansas
Map 5**

El Dorado

Favorite Past Times   **Open Shop**
1003 North College Avenue   71730   (501) 863-8947

Collection: General stock of mostly paperback.
Hours: Mon-Fri, except closed Wed, 10-5. Sat 12-4.

Eureka Springs

Forgotten Treasures   **Open Shop**
53B-57 Spring Street   72632   (501) 253-9989

Collection: General stock.
# of Vols: 1,000-2,000
Hours: Mon-Sat 11-4.
Travel: From Hwy 62 (Business), turn north on Hwy 23. When Hwy 23 inter-
                  sects with Spring St, continue on Spring.
Owner: Marilyn Bromstad
Year Estab: 1976
Comments: Shop also sells antiques.

Fayetteville

Dickson Street Bookshop   **Open Shop**
325 West Dickson Street   72701   (501) 442-8182

Collection: General stock of mostly hardcover and ephemera.
# of Vols: 90,000
Hours: Mon-Sat 10-9. Sun 1-6.

Services:	Search service.
Travel:	Bus Hwy 71 exit off Hwy 71, then Dickson St exit off Bus Hwy 71. Proceed west on Dickson.
Credit Cards:	Yes
Owner:	Charles O'Donnell Choffel
Year Estab:	1978
Comments:	I hate it when Susan begins to drag and pull me out of a book store. Generally, this means that I've found my nirvana and am being lured away. This is how I felt as I left the Dickson Street Bookshop. It is truly a fabulous establishment with books in scholarly and technical areas as well as popular culture categorized in sub categories of sub categories. This is one of those establishments where you could spend hours if only your partner weren't reminding you about other obligations.

Fort Smith

Alpha Books & Comics   **Open Shop**
708 Garrison Avenue   72901   (501) 785-5642

Collection:	General stock of paperback, hardcover and comics.
# of Vols:	50,000
Hours:	Mon-Sat 10-5:30.
Travel:	Rogers Ave exit off I-540. Proceed west on Rogers for two to three miles. Take right fork to Garrison and continue west to 700 block.
Credit Cards:	Yes
Owner:	Michael Hightower
Year Estab:	1982
Comments:	The owner advised us that the stock consisted of 50,000 volumes. After visiting the shop, our observation would be 49,000 of the 50,000 volumes consisted of paperbacks, comics and magazines. Need we say more.

Book Shoppe   **Open Shop**
3120 Jenny Lind Road, #B   72903   (501) 783-3005

Collection:	General stock of mostly paperback.
# of Vols:	35,000
Hours:	Tue-Sat 10-5.

Johnston's Books   **Open Shop**
412 North 6th, Ste. A   (501) 783-5751
Mailing address: PO Box 1905 Fort Smith 72902

Collection:	General stock and ephemera.
Hours:	Mon-Fri 11-4. Other times by appointment.
Services:	Search service, accepts want lists, mail order.
Owner:	Mrs. Lou Johnston & John Johnston, Jr.
Year Estab:	1975
Comments:	When we attempted to visit this open shop dealer, we found a locked door and a note on the door indicating that UPS had attempted to make a delivery. A neighbor suggested that the proprietors might not keep

regular hours despite the information they provided us. If you're planning a visit, consider calling ahead.

Snooper's Barn Used Book Store   **Open Shop**
208 Towson Avenue   72901   (501) 783-7100

Collection:	General stock of hardcover and paperback.
# of Vols:	200,000
Hours:	Tue-Sat 10-5.
Travel:	Rogers Ave exit off I-540. Proceed west on Rogers, then left on Towson. Shop is 1½ blocks ahead on right.
Credit Cards:	Yes
Owner:	Lawrence Brandenburg
Year Estab:	1964
Comments:	Considering the fact that this book shop is the largest in town, quite possibly carrying the number of volumes indicated above (at least 35-40% of which were hardcover) we regret to say that a large percentage of the hardcover items we saw were in less than satisfactory condition. If you're looking for obscure titles, it is certainly possible that you might locate one or more here. However, the chance of your finding that volume in respectable enough condition "to bring home to mother" are odds that we would not take.

Hot Springs

Carole's Book Stop   **Open Shop**
7160 Central Avenue   71913   (501) 525-4033
413 Albert Pike   (501) 623-0772

Collection:	General stock of mostly paperback.
# of Vols:	50,000 (each)
Hours:	Mon-Sat 9-6.

Jacksonville

McIntire Rare Collectibles   **Open Shop**
27 Crestview Plaza   (501) 985-1663
Mailing address: PO Box 546 Jacksonville 72078

Collection:	Specialty
Specialties:	Civil War (ephemera only); numismatics.
Hours:	Mon-Fri 10-5.
Services:	Catalog, accepts, appraisals.
Travel:	Exit 9 off Hwy 167/67. Proceed east on Main St for 1½ blocks. Turn left into Crestview Plaza strip mall.
Credit Cards:	Yes
Owner:	Robert McIntire
Year Estab:	1971

Kingston

Page Books   **By Appointment**
HCR 65, Box 233   72742   (501) 861-5831

Collection:	Specialty
# of Vols:	6,000
Specialties:	Children's; illustrated.
Services:	Search service, catalog, accepts want lists.
Credit Cards:	Yes
Owner:	Maggie Page
Year Estab:	1990

Lakeview

Samadhi Metaphysical Literature   **By Appointment**
PO Box 170   72642   (501) 431-8830
                                                     Fax: (501) 431-5840

Collection:	Specialty
# of Vols:	1,000
Specialties:	Metaphysics; mysticism; hermetica; yoga; astrology; UFOs; psychic science.
Services:	Search service, catalog, accepts want lists.
Credit Cards:	No
Owner:	Dennis Whelan
Year Estab:	1970

Leslie

Books Plus   **Open Shop**
Main Street   72645   501-447-2219

Collection:	General stock of mostly paperback.
# of Vols:	9,000
Hours:	Mon-Sat 9-5.

Little Rock

The Books Inn   **Open Shop**
301 North Shackleford   72211   (501) 223-9587

Collection:	General stock of mostly paperback.
# of Vols:	17,000
Hours:	Tue-Sat 10-5. Sun 1-5.

The Book Store & Tobacco Row   **Open Shop**
7616 Asher Avenue   72204   (501) 562-1651

Collection:	General stock of paperback and hardcover.
# of Vols:	55,000

Hours:	Mon-Sat 8-6.
Travel:	Col. Glen exit off I-430. Proceed east on Col. Glen (which becomes Asher) for about two miles. Shop is located in a small shopping area.
Credit Cards:	No
Owner:	William Anderson
Year Estab:	1983
Comments:	Even if you arrive before the store opens, you may walk away with some books from the store's "freebie" display just outside the front door. (On the day we visited, some old encyclopedias were available.) In addition to offering a generous supply of worn paperbacks, the shop does carry several thousand hardcover volumes. Unfortunately, a large number of them were in less than satisfactory condition and several appeared to be water damaged. In addition to selling books, the shop also sells sports memorabilia and tobacco products.

Book Traders   **Open Shop**
5221 JFK Boulevard   North Little Rock 72116   (501) 753-8008

Collection:	General stock of paperback and hardcover.
# of Vols:	20,000
Hours:	Mon-Fri 10-7. Sat 10-5.
Travel:	Located on Hwy 107, just north of McCain, on the left in a small strip center.
Credit Cards:	Yes
Owner:	Ed & Jeri Myrick
Year Estab:	1994
Comments:	At the time of our visit, we were able to meet the new owners of an otherwise established shop. The majority of the books on hand were paperbacks but there was certainly a respectable selection of hardcover volumes, most of which appeared to be of a more recent vintage and in good condition. Little out of the ordinary. Our sense is that your chances of finding a rare or long lost title here are not high.

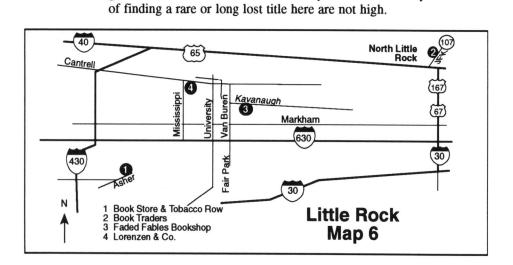

1 Book Store & Tobacco Row
2 Book Traders
3 Faded Fables Bookshop
4 Lorenzen & Co.

**Little Rock
Map 6**

Boutlette's Antiquarian Books   **By Appointment**
11724 Fairway Drive   72212   (501) 227-6060

Collection:	Specialty
# of Vols:	5,000
Specialties:	Fine bindings (17th-19th century); sets; fore-edge books.
Services:	Appraisals, catalog, accepts want lists.
Credit Cards:	Yes
Owner:	Arthur Boutlette
Year Estab:	1976

Faded Fables Bookshop   **Open Shop**
2919 Kavanaugh Boulevard   72205   (501) 664-4646

Collection:	General stock of hardcover and paperback.
# of Vols:	30,000
Specialties:	Arkansas; modern first editions.
Hours:	Mon-Fri 10-6. Sat 10-5.
Services:	Appraisals, search service, accepts want lists, mail order.
Travel:	Fairpark exit off I-630. Proceed north on Fairpark (which becomes Van Buren), then east on Kavanaugh. Shop is located at corner of Spruce St, on the right in Hillcrest Decorative Center, a small shopping area.
Credit Cards:	Yes
Owner:	Kathy & Paul Floyd
Year Estab:	1990
Comments:	Keep your eye out for this shop as it's easy to miss. Once you've found it, you should not be disappointed for while many of the books on hand are paperbacks and a number of the hardcover books are of the more common variety, we did see a number of unusual, collectible and truly antiquarian titles, plus some attractive sets, some historically important volumes and in one case, the remnants of a rare collection of books on magic and satanism. Certainly worth a visit.

The Little Book Store   **Open Shop**
1721 Main Street   North Little Rock 72114   (501) 753-7601

Collection:	General stock of mostly paperback.
Hours:	Mon-Sat 9-5:30. Longer hours in summer.

Lorenzen & Co.   **Open Shop**
7509 Cantrell Road   72207   (501) 663-8811

Collection:	General stock of mostly used hardcover and paperback.
# of Vols:	30,000
Specialties:	Arkansas; Civil War; literature.
Hours:	Mon-Sat 9-7. Sun 1-5.
Services:	Appraisals, search service, accepts want lists, mail order.
Travel:	Cantrell exit off Hwy 430. Proceed east to Mississippi. Shop is in the rear of the Tanglewood Shopping Center just east of Mississippi.
Owner:	Rod Lorenzen
Year Estab:	1976

Comments: A spacious shop that carries both new books and used hardcover and paperback volumes. Nicely organized, pleasant to browse and with well selected titles in the hardcover category. Several items caught our eye and depending upon your own taste, might intrigue you as well

Howard L. Norton   **By Appointment**
PO Box 22821   72221   (501) 223-4858

Collection:	Specialty
Specialties:	Civil War; Western Americana; documents; autographs.
Services:	Appraisals, mail order.
Year Estab:	1991

Rule's Fine Books   **Open Shop**
5823 Kavanaugh Street   (501) 664-1170
Mailing address: 218 King's Row Drive Little Rock 72207

Collection:	Specialty
# of Vols:	5,000-7,000
Specialties:	Fine bindings; sets; children's illustrated; travel.
Hours:	Tue-Sat 10-5.
Services:	Mail order.
Travel:	Cantrell exit off I-430. Proceed east on Cantrell to University, then left on University and right on Kavanaugh. Shop is one block ahead.
Owner:	Jim Rule
Comments:	The dealer also displays at Partain's Antique Mall in Alexander, AR and Market Central Antique Mall in Memphis, TN. (Note: the collection, as noted above, is divided between the three locations.)

Pine Bluff

Exchange Book Store   **Open Shop**
1610 Brentwood Drive   71601   (501) 536-9667

Collection:	General stock of mostly paperback.
# of Vols:	10,000
Hours:	Tue-Thu 9-5:30. Fri & Sat 10-5.

Rogers

Rock Bottom Used Book Shop   **Open Shop**
1709 South 8th Street   72756   (501) 621-0609

Collection:	General stock of mostly paperback.
# of Vols:	10,000
Hours:	Mon-Sat 11-8.

Trolley Line Books   **By Appointment**
522 South 4th Street   72756   (501) 621-9786

Collection:	General stock.
# of Vols:	2,500+
Specialties:	Southern writers; mystery.

Services: Appraisals, catalog, search service, accepts want lists.
Credit Cards: Yes
Owner: Myra Moran
Year Estab: 1986

Russellville

Books Unlimited   **Open Shop**
511 East 4th Street   72801   (501) 968-3545

Collection: General stock of mostly paperback.
# of Vols: 9,000
Hours: Mon-Fri 9:30-5:30. Sat 10-5.

Searcy

Bob Bethurem, Jr.   **By Appointment**
PO Box 354   72145   (501) 268-1890

Collection: Specialty books and ephemera.
# of Vols: 100 (books only)
Specialties: Arkansas history; railroads; Civil War.
Services: Accepts want lists.
Credit Cards: No
Year Estab: 1993

Springdale

Famous Hardware Antique Mall   **Antique Mall**
113 West Emma   72764   (501) 756-6650

Hours: Mon-Sat 10-5. Sun 1-5.
Travel: From Hwy 71 Business, turn east on Emma.
Comments: If you're addicted to antique malls, we would not wish to dissuade you
                 from visiting here. On the other hand, if your interest is limited to used
                 books, we do not believe you'll profit greatly from a stop here for
                 although the books on hand could well be of interest, in our judgment,
                 there weren't a sufficient number of them to warrant a special trip.

Texarkana

Books, Etc.   **Open Shop**
801 East Street   75502   (501) 772-0466

Collection: General stock of mostly paperback.
# of Vols: 40,000
Hours: Mon-Sat 8:30-6.

Texarkana Book Store   **Open Shop**
3232 North State Line Avenue   71854   (501) 774-8011

Collection: General stock of mostly paperback.
Hours: Mon, Tue, Thu, Fri 9:30-5:30. Wed 12-5. Sat 10-5.

Mail Order Dealers

The American Antiquary   (501) 442-3779
PO Box 1064 Fayetteville 72702   Fax: (501) 582-3779

Collection: General stock.
# of Vols: 500-1,000
Services: Occasional catalog, accepts want lists.
Owner: Tim Klinger
Year Estab: 1993

Richard Bynum, Bookseller   (501) 442-8422
927 Applebury Drive Fayetteville 72701

Collection: Specialty
# of Vols: 6,000
Specialties: Ancient history.
Services: Lists, search service, accepts want lists.
Year Estab: 1986

Douglas & Kathy George, Booksellers   (501) 246-2105
1508 Evans Street Arkadelphia 71923

Collection: General stock.
# of Vols: 1,000
Services: Search service, accepts want lists, catalog.
Year Estab: 1995

ReRead Books   (501) 224-1162
8 Secluded Point Little Rock 72210

Collection: Specialty
Specialties: American literature; Americana; Arkansas; signed books.
Services: Appraisals
Owner: Jeffrey L. Baskin
Year Estab: 1984
Comments: Also displays at Books Inn in Little Rock. See above.

South By Southwest Books   (501) 442-6385
PO Box 1561 Fayetteville 72702

Collection: Specialty
Specialties: Texas; Arkansas.
Services: Catalog, accepts want lists.
Owner: Dwain E. Manske
Year Estab: 1971

Yesterday's Books   (501) 623-6082
1115 Walnut Valley Road Hot Springs 71909

Collection: General stock.
# of Vols: 5,000
Services: Occasional catalog, accepts want lists.
Owner: Rose Edwards
Year Estab: 1976

Colorado

Alphabetical Listing By Dealer

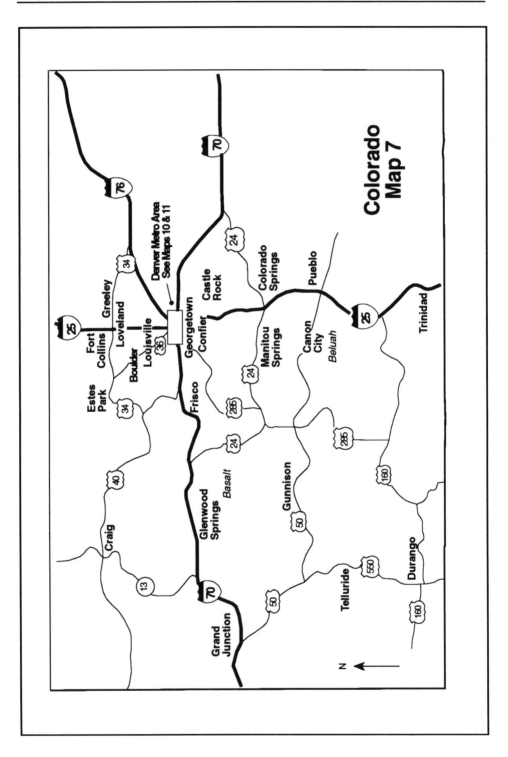

Colorado
Map 7

Alphabetical Listing By Location

Arvada
(See Map 11, page 120)

Black & Read   **Open Shop**
7821 Wadsworth Boulevard   80003   (303) 467-3236
                                                                    Fax: (303) 467-3269

Collection: General stock of paperback and hardcover.
# of Vols: 10,000
Hours: Mon-Sat 10-9. Sun 11-7.
Travel: Between 78th & 80th Streets. Proceeding north on Wadsworth, shop is
                  on left in Northridge Shopping Center.
Credit Cards: Yes
Owner: Danny Graul
Year Estab: 1991
Comments: A shop that caters to popular culture tastes. In addition to paperbacks
                  and hardcover books, the shop offers magazines, a closed section for
                  adult materials, magic games, LPs, vintage clothing, etc. We did see
                  some bound magazines that might fall into the collectible category for
                  some university but little else along those lines.

Grandfather Used Books   **Open Shop**
5612 Olde Wadsworth Boulevard   80002   (303) 420-7765
                                                            E-mail: dlech29@ios.orci.com

Collection: General stock of hardcover and paperback.
# of Vols: 10,000
Specialties: Fairy tales.
Hours: Tue-Sat 12-6.
Services: Search service, accepts want lists, catalog.
Travel: Wadsworth exit off I-70. Proceed north on Wadsworth for about two
                  blocks. "Olde" Wadsworth is two blocks to the west of the "new" road.
                  The shop is between 53rd and 57th Streets.
Credit Cards: No
Owner: Dick Lechman
Year Estab: 1994
Comments: Mea culpa. We scheduled a visit here on a Monday without double
                  checking the days and hours listed above.

Little Bookshop of Horrors   **Open Shop**
10380 Ralston Road   80004   (303) 425-1975

Collection: Specialty new and used.
Specialties: Science fiction; fantasy; horror; mystery; limited editions.
Hours: Tue-Sat 10:30-6.
Services: Occasional catalog, accepts want lists, mail order.
Travel: Kipling St exit off I-70. Proceed north on Kipling for two miles. Shop is
                  in Maplewood Village shopping center.
Credit Cards: Yes
Owner: Doug Lewis

Year Estab: 1990
Comments: Stock is approximately 40% used, 70% of which is paperback.

Pulp-N-Ink   **Open Shop**
9582 West 58th Avenue   80002   (303) 422-1169

Collection: General stock of paperback and hardcover.
# of Vols: 5,000-10,000
Hours: Mon-Fri 10-6:30. Sat 10-5.
Travel: Kipling exit off I-70. Proceed north on Kipling to 58th, then east on
              58th St to Independence. Shop is on southeast corner in Arvada Plaza.
Year Estab: 1995
Comments: Stock is evenly divided between paperback and hardcover.

Aurora
(See Map 11, page 120)

Book Outlet   **Open Shop**
14573 East Alameda Avenue   80012   (303) 366-2434

Collection: General stock of hardcover and paperback.
# of Vols: 20,000
Hours: Wed & Sat 10-4.
Travel: In a shopping center on northeast side of Alameda and Sable.
Comments: Operated by Friends of the Aurora Public Library.

Book World   **Open Shop**
2223 South Peoria Street   80014   (303) 695-1235

Collection: General stock hardcover and paperback.
# of Vols: 50,000
Specialties: Children's; military; cookbooks; literature; first editions; art.
Hours: Mon-Sat 10-6.
Services: Appraisals, search service, accepts want lists, mail order.
Travel: Iliff West exit off I-225. Proceed west on Iliff to Peoria. Shop is in Iliff
              Square Shopping Center at northwest corner of Iliff and Peoria.
Credit Cards: Yes
Owner: Josephine & Bob Benham
Year Estab: 1993
Comments: A very "pretty" store to visit with hardcover books attractively displayed
              and in quite good condition. If you have a special interest in Colorado,
              you'll even find some historically important reference works here (that is,
              if they haven't been sold by the time you arrive) With the exception of the
              shop's specialties, few areas are represented in great number.

H.C. Harris Bookman   **By Appointment**
1541 Clinton Street   80010   (303) 344-4742

Collection: Specialty
# of Vols: 8,000
Specialties: Judaica; Holocaust.

Services:	Accepts want lists, mail order.
Credit Cards:	No
Owner:	Herman Harris
Year Estab:	1992

Neighborhood Bookstore   **Open Shop**
16728 East Smoky Hill Road, #10A   80015   Fax: (303) 721-1774 (303) 766-9491
E-mail: nolbpc1@aol.com

Collection:	General stock of mostly paperback.
# of Vols:	40,000
Hours:	Mon-Fri 10-8. Sat 10-6. Sun 1-5.

Basalt

Backroad Books   **By Appointment**
2250 Emma Road   (970) 927-3428
Mailing address: PO Box 164 Basalt 81621

Collection:	General stock of hardcover and paperback and ephemera.
# of Vols:	30,000
Specialties:	Western Americana; biography; natural history; modern first editions; cookbooks.
Services:	Accepts want lists, mail order.
Credit Cards:	Yes
Owner:	Mary Lou Zordel
Year Estab:	1981
Comments:	Overnight accommodations for two in a refurbished pioneer cabin are free with a $200 book purchase. Reservations are a must.

Beulah

Barrie D. Watson, Bookseller   **By Appointment**
8760 Grand Avenue   81023   (800) 785-3136   (719) 485-3136
Fax: (719) 485-3838
E-mail: watsonbk@usa.net

Collection:	General stock.
# of Vols:	20,000
Specialties:	Falconry; hunting; fishing; Western Americana; law; World War II; American literature.
Services:	Appraisals, search service, catalog, accepts want lists.
Credit Cards:	Yes
Year Estab:	1968

Boulder

Abbey Road Books   **Open Shop**
813 Pearl Street   80302   (303) 939-8537

Collection:	General stock of hardcover and paperback.

(Boulder)

# of Vols:	10,000-15,000
Hours:	Mon-Sat 10-6. Sun 12-5.
Travel:	From Denver, Hwy 36 turns into 28th St. Proceed north on 28th, then left on Pearl.
Credit Cards:	Yes
Owner:	Ruth & Jeff Beard
Year Estab:	1992
Comments:	Most of the books we saw were in quite good condition. Many newer titles. Well organized and easy to browse. Good for a fast visit.

Acoma Books   **Open Shop**
2488 Baseline Road   (303) 494-3309
Mailing address: PO Box 366 Eldorado Springs 80025   Fax: (303) 494-3309

Collection:	General stock of hardcover and paperback.
# of Vols:	15,000
Specialties:	Scholarly; mathematics; physics; engineering; sciences; geology; astronomy.
Hours:	Mon-Sat 11-6. Sun 12-6. Extended summer hours.
Travel:	Baseline exit off Hwy 36. Proceed west on Baseline to Basemar Shopping Center.
Credit Cards:	No
Owner:	Lance & Gisell Rieker
Year Estab:	1992
Comments:	A good selection of books in the sciences, other scholarly areas and literature. Most of the books we saw were in good to excellent condition. Paperbacks play a very small role in this shop (mostly mystery titles). Generally speaking, quality books in a quality shop.

Aion Bookshop   **Open Shop**
1235 Pennsylvania Avenue   80302   (303) 443-5763
                                                      E-mail: aionbook@interloc.com

Collection:	General stock of hardcover and paperback.
# of Vols:	35,000
Hours:	Mon-Sat 10-7. Sun 12-6.
Services:	Appraisals, search service, accepts want lists, mail order.
Travel:	Baseline exit off Hwy 36. Proceed west on Baseline, north on Broadway, west on Pleasant St, left on 12th and left on Pennsylvania.
Credit Cards:	Yes
Owner:	Jim & Deborah Broaddus
Year Estab:	1987
Comments:	An interesting mix of scholarly titles (most on the main level) and more popular subjects (and paperbacks) on a lower level. The titles ran the gamut from recent publications to older volumes, including several sets. If it hasn't already been sold by the time you arrive, you could buy a 10 volume set of the works of Henrich Heine in the original German for only $1300.

Art Source International   **Open Shop**
1237 Pearl Street   80302   (303) 444-4080

Collection:	Specialty books and prints.
# of Vols:	10,000
Specialties:	Americana; Western Americana; geology; exploration.
Hours:	Mon-Sat 10-6. Sun 11-5.
Services:	Mail order.
Travel:	See Abbey Rd books above. Shop is in Pearl St pedestrian mall.
Credit Cards:	Yes
Owner:	George Karakehian
Year Estab:	1981

Authors & Artists   **Open Shop**
2539 Pearl Street   80302   Fax: (303) 444-3318   (303) 444-6131
                                              E-mail: aabooks@csd.net

Collection:	General stock.
# of Vols:	25,000
Specialties:	Modern first editions; signed and inscribed; native Americans; animals; ecology and environment; archaeology; anthropology; herbs; gardening; religion; mythology; occult.
Hours:	Mon, Wed, Fri 12-7. Other times by appointment.
Services:	Appraisals, search service, catalog, accepts want lists.
Travel:	See Abbey Road Books above. Shop is on right in a former residence.
Credit Cards:	Yes
Owner:	Shirley Bryant
Year Estab:	1995
Comments:	Several rooms of interesting titles, most of which were hardcover with some vintage paperbacks. While it would be easy for the casual browser to walk through this shop quickly, simply eyeing titles, it would equally be a mistake as the browser would likely pass up some items that could turn out to be just what he or she has been looking for. We suggest a more careful perusal before leaving. The shop also sells the works of local crafts people (the other half of the shop's name.)

Beat Book Shop   **Open Shop**
1713 Pearl Street   80302   (303) 444-7111
                                                        Fax: (303) 444-5322

Collection:	General stock of paperback and hardcover.
# of Vols:	1,500
Specialties:	Beat generation; counter culture; drugs; religion; biography; first editions.
Hours:	Sun-Tue 11-7. Wed-Sat 11-9.
Services:	Appraisals, catalog, accepts want lists.
Travel:	See Abbey Road Books above. Shop is at 17th & Pearl.
Credit Cards:	No
Owner:	Tom Peters
Year Estab:	1958

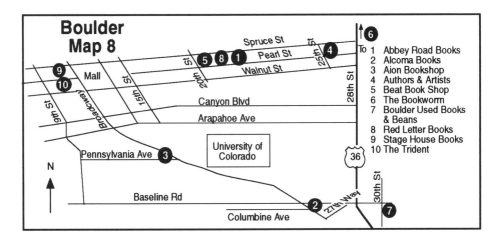

Boulder Map 8

Spruce St
Pearl St
Walnut St
Canyon Blvd
Arapahoe Ave
Pennsylvania Ave
Baseline Rd
Columbine Ave
Mall
University of Colorado
N

To 1 Abbey Road Books
2 Alcoma Books
3 Aion Bookshop
4 Authors & Artists
5 Beat Book Shop
6 The Bookworm
7 Boulder Used Books & Beans
8 Red Letter Books
9 Stage House Books
10 The Trident

The Bookworm   **Open Shop**
2850 Iris Avenue   80301   (303) 449-3765

Collection:	General stock of paperback and hardcover.
# of Vols:	200,000+
Hours:	Mon-Fri 10-6. Sat 10-5. Sun 12-5.
Travel:	I-25 becomes Hwy 36 which becomes 28th St. Continue on 28th St, then right into Diagonal Plaza (an inside shopping mall) which is just before Iris.
Credit Cards:	Yes
Owner:	Linda Peashka
Year Estab:	1984
Comments:	At first glance, all one sees upon entering this shop is row upon row of paperbacks. If you want to investigate further though, carry a long string as the shop is much larger than immediately apparent and the shop is a labyrinth of twists and turns. While the vast majority of the books on hand are indeed paperback, there are some hardcover volumes, as well as trade paperbacks, in several subject areas, most of which were recent best sellers. The store seems to do a brisk business but we doubt if many antiquarians are among the shop's customers

Boulder Used Books & Beans   **Open Shop**
671 30th Street   80303   (303) 443-8373

Collection:	General stock of paperback and hardcover.
# of Vols:	5,000+
Hours:	Mon-Sat 8-8.
Travel:	Baseline exit off Hwy 36. Proceed east on Baseline, then right on 30th St and immediate right into shopping center.
Year Estab:	1996
Comments:	A combination book shop/espresso bar in which the books match the quality of the refreshments, giving you all the more reason to stop for a cup of coffee. While the collection is general, there are enough titles

and variety in the non fiction categories to warrant a brief stop for the scholar and enough light reading (if the books can be put in that category) to make for a pleasant stop for the less erudite.

Empire Gallery Books and Art
7425 Empire Drive
Mailing address: PO Box 1725 Boulder 80306

By Appointment
(303) 499-9945

Collection:	General stock.
# of Vols:	40,000
Specialties:	First editions; maps.
Services:	Accepts want lists, mail order.
Credit Cards:	No
Owner:	Daniel Burns
Year Estab:	1981

The King's Market Bookshop
PO Box 709   80306

By Appointment
(888) 424-0059   (303) 447-0234
E-mail: robertwayne@kingsmarket.com

Collection:	General stock.
# of Vols:	20,000
Specialties:	Sailing; exploration; psychology; philosophy; Colorado.
Services:	Appraisals, search service, accepts want lists, catalog.
Credit Cards:	No
Owner:	Robert Wayne
Year Estab:	1966

Oak Knoll Fine Press Books

By Appointment
(303) 530-7567
E-mail: carolg@ix.netcom.com

Collection:	Specialty
Specialties:	Fine press books; books on books.
Services:	Search service, catalog.
Year Estab:	1995
Comments:	Partners with Oak Knoll Books in Newcastle, DE.

Red Letter Books
1737 Pearl Street   80302

Open Shop
(303) 938-1778

Collection:	General stock of paperback and hardcover.
# of Vols:	45,000
Specialties:	Eastern religion; psychology.
Hours:	Mon-Sat 10-9. Sun 12 5. Winter: Mon-Sat 10-7. Sun 12-5.
Travel:	See Abbey Road Books above.
Credit Cards:	Yes
Owner:	John Murray
Year Estab:	1991
Comments:	A mix of hardcover and paperback with an emphasis on the hardcover. Books in most subject areas in mixed condition. Quite reasonably priced. Worth a browse.

(Boulder)

Rue Morgue Mystery Bookshop
946 Pearl Street   80302

Open Shop
(303) 443-8346

Collection:	Specialty new and used.
# of Vols:	5,000-6,000 (used)
Specialties:	Mystery
Hours:	Mon-Sat 10-6. Sun 12-5.
Services:	Appraisals, catalog (new and used books are in separate catalogs).
Travel:	Canyon exit off Hwy 36. Proceed west on Canyon to 9th St, then north on 9th St for two blocks, then east on Pearl.
Credit Cards:	Yes
Owner:	Enid & Tom Schantz
Year Estab:	1970
Comments:	In our travels, we have visited a number of mystery book shops that carry both new and used books. In terms of the selection of used books, particularly of vintage hardcover titles, this shop is close to the top.

Stage House Books
1039 Pearl Street   80302

Open Shop
(303) 447-1433
Fax: (303) 447-0441

Collection:	General stock of hardcover and paperback and prints.
# of Vols:	75,000
Hours:	Daily 10-8.
Services:	Appraisals, accepts want lists, mail order.
Travel:	See Rue Morgue Bookshop above. Turn east on Pearl to 11th.
Credit Cards:	Yes
Owner:	Richard Schwarz
Year Estab:	1970
Comments:	An interesting shop with some interesting titles. Well organized although without some assistance from the staff, it may take you some time to find what you're looking for. At the time of our visit, most non fiction subjects were on the first level with fiction on a balcony surrounding the shop. While the shop does carry paperbacks, hardcover books in mixed condition predominate. Worth a visit.

The Trident
940 Pearl Street   80302

Open Shop
(303) 443-3133

Collection:	General stock of used paperback and hardcover and remainders.
# of Vols:	5,000-8,000
Hours:	Daily 10am-11pm.
Travel:	See Rue Morgue Bookshop above.
Credit Cards:	Yes
Owner:	Allen Rice, book store manager
Year Estab:	1983

Comments: A better than average book store/coffee shop combo with a nice selec-
                 tion of both hardcover volumes and paperbacks in mixed condition.
                 The shop's location, just off the pedestrian mall, makes for a pleasant
                 visit, even if you don't make a purchase.

Mary Williams Fine Arts   **Open Shop**
2116 Pearl Street, Unit C   80302   (303) 938-1588

Collection: Specialty
Specialties: Botanical magazines by Samuel Curtis.
Hours: Mon-Fri 10-6. Sat 10-5.

Word is Out Women's Bookstore   **Open Shop**
1731 15th Street   80302   (303) 449-1415

Collection: Specialty new and used.
# of Vols: 300 (used)
Specialties: Women's lesbian and gay.
Hours: Tue-Sat 10-6. Sun 12-5.

Broomfield
(See Map 11, page 120)

Books & Things   **By Appointment**
3461 West 144th Avenue   80020   (303) 465-1684

Collection: General stock.
# of Vols: 100,000
Specialties: Children's
Services: Mail order.
Owner: Vic Gammel
Year Estab: 1993

Paperbacks, Etc.   **Open Shop**
300 Nickel Street, #10   80020   (303) 466-0155

Collection: General stock of mostly paperback.
# of Vols: 25,000
Hours: Mon-Fri 9:30-6. Sat 9:30-5.

Canon City

Cheryl's Book Nook   **Open Shop**
404 Main Street   81212   (719) 275-4964

Collection: General stock of mostly paperback.
Hours: Tue-Sat 9:30-5.

Paragon Caffe & Booksellers   **Open Shop**
112 South 5th Street   81212   (719) 275-8575

Collection: General stock of hardcover and paperback.
# of Vols: 7,000

Hours:	Mon-Sat 9-5.
Travel:	5th St exit off Hwy 50 (which is Royal Gorge Blvd in Canon City). Proceed north on 5th St. Shop is 1/2 block ahead.
Credit Cards:	Yes
Year Estab:	1992
Comments:	Stock is approximately 70% hardcover.

Castle Rock

Country Palace   **Open Shop**
400 Third Street   80104   (303) 688-6775

Collection:	General stock.
# of Vols:	1,000-3,000
Hours:	Mon-Sat 10-6.
Travel:	Castle Rock exit off I-25. From east side of I-25, proceed on Wilcox to Third St, then east on Third.
Credit Cards:	Yes
Year Estab:	1966

Hooked On Books   **Open Shop**
112 South Wilcox   80104   (303) 688-1186

Collection:	General stock of mostly used paperback and some new.
# of Vols:	20,000 (used)
Hours:	Mon-Thu 9:39-7. Fri 9:30-6. Sat 9:30-5. Sun 11-4.

Colorado Springs

Aamstar Books   **Open Shop**
333 North Tejon   80903   (719) 520-0696
                                                                  Fax: (719) 520-0696

Collection:	General stock and ephemera.
# of Vols:	5,000
Specialties:	Railroads; Western Americana; children's.
Hours:	Mon-Sat 10-6. Sun 10-2.
Services:	Appraisals, search service, accepts want lists, mail order.
Travel:	Bijou exit off I-25. Proceed east on Bijou, then north (left) on Cascade and right on Boulder for one block.
Credit Cards:	Yes
Owner:	Jim Ciletti
Year Estab:	1992
Comments:	A nice selection of both antiquarian and used books of good quality. The areas identified above as specialties are well represented. Definitely worth a visit if you're in town.

Ashgrove Heirloom Books   **By Appointment**
1123 Martin Drive   80915   (719) 574-7975

Collection:	Specialty new and used.

# of Vols:	5,000
Specialties:	Modern first editions; Western Americana; signed.
Services:	Catalog, accepts want lists.
Credit Cards:	No
Owner:	Chuck Walch
Year Estab:	1994

Beth Anne's Book Corner
2204 East Pikes Peak Avenue   80909

Open Shop
(719) 471-7545

Collection:	General stock of mostly paperback.
# of Vols:	50,000
Hours:	Mon-Sat 10-6.
Travel:	Near Memorial Park. In a small strip center.
Comments:	If you're looking for romance, you'll find a plentiful supply here, along with paperback mysteries, sci fi, etc. As we walked to the rear of the shop, we saw an entire back wall filled with sagging book shelves overwhelmed by the weight of hardcover volumes — mostly reading copies of recent vintage.

Billions of Books
4741 North Carefree Circle   80917

Open Shop
(719) 380-1655

Collection:	General stock of paperback and hardcover.
# of Vols:	50,000
Hours:	Mon-Sat 10-6. Sun 12-5.
Travel:	From Academy, turn east on North Carefree Circle and continue for one mile. Shop is in shopping center between Ostenbluff and Constitution.
Comments:	Stock is approximately 65% paperback.

The Book Home
119 East Dale Street   80903

Open Shop
(719) 634-5885

Collection:	General stock of mostly used hardcover.
# of Vols:	50,000
Specialties:	Natural sciences; geology.
Hours:	Mon-Fri 9-5.
Services:	Search service, accepts want lists, occasional catalog.
Travel:	Northbound on I-25: Bijou exit. Proceed east on Bijou, north on Cascade and east on Dale for 1½ blocks. Southbound on I-25: Uintah exit. Proceed east on Uintah, south on Cascade and left on Dale. Shop is between Tejon and Nevada on south side.
Credit Cards:	No
Year Estab:	1942

Book Sleuth
2501 West Colorado Avenue   80904

Open Shop
(719) 632-2727

Collection:	Specialty new and used.
# of Vols:	12,000
Specialties:	Mystery

Hours:	Mon-Sat 10:30-5:30.
Services:	Hwy 24 exit off I-25. Proceed west on Hwy 24 for about four miles to Old Colorado City, then right on 26th St and right again on Colorado.
Credit Cards:	Yes
Owner:	Helen C. Randal
Year Estab:	1982
Comments:	Stock is approximately 30% used.

The Bookman   **Open Shop**
3163 West Colorado Avenue   80904   (719) 636-0055
                                                                      Fax: (719) 632-8484

Collection:	General stock of hardcover and paperback.
# of Vols:	110,000
Specialties:	Local history; regional interest..
Hours:	Daily 10am-9 pm, except open at 9am in summer and Christmas season.
Services:	Accepts want lists.
Travel:	Hwy 24 exit off I-25. Proceed west on Hwy 24 then north on 31st St for one block, then west on Colorado Ave. Shop is just ahead on left in Red Rock Canyon Shopping Center.
Credit Cards:	Yes
Owner:	Eric Verlo
Year Estab:	1990
Comments:	A good sized shop with a mix of hardcover books and paperbacks. The majority of the hardcover items we saw were in reasonably good condition. If you search diligently, and if the titles you're searching for are of a fairly recent vintage, your search could be successful.

Books For You   **Open Shop**
1737 South 8th Street   80906   (719) 630-0502

Collection:	General stock of paperback and hardcover.
# of Vols:	48,000
Hours:	Mon-Fri 10-6. Sat 10-5. Hours may vary in winter.
Travel:	Exit 141 off I-25. Proceed west on Hwy 24 to 8th St, then south on 8th Street for 1½ miles to Cheyenne Center. Shop is on the left.
Credit Cards:	Yes
Owner:	Gretchen Goldberg
Year Estab:	1989
Comments:	Stock is approximately 80% paperback.

Carefree Books & Espresso   **Open Shop**
3377 North Academy Boulevard   80917   (719) 573-6020

Collection:	General stock of mostly paperback.
Hours:	Mon-Fri 7-5:30. Sat 8-5.

Circle B Books   **Open Shop**
3111 North Hancock   80907   (719) 577-9879

Collection:	General stock of mostly paperback.
Hours:	Mon-Thu 10-6. Fri 9:30-4. Sun 1-4.

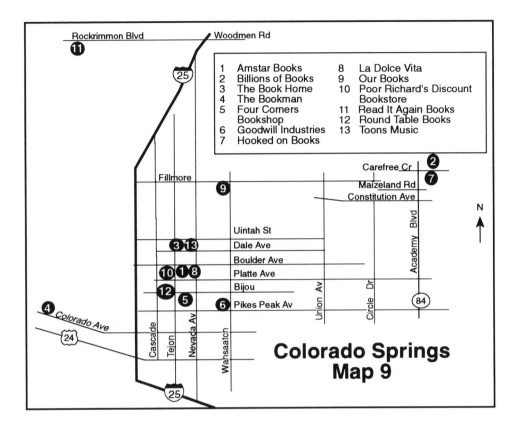

Colorado Springs
Map 9

1 Amstar Books
2 Billions of Books
3 The Book Home
4 The Bookman
5 Four Corners Bookshop
6 Goodwill Industries
7 Hooked on Books
8 La Dolce Vita
9 Our Books
10 Poor Richard's Discount Bookstore
11 Read It Again Books
12 Round Table Books
13 Toons Music

Four Corners Bookshop   **Open Shop**
119 East Bijou Street   80903   (719) 635-4514

Collection:	General stock of mostly used hardcover and remainders.
# of Vols:	150,000+
Hours:	Daily 9:30-7.
Travel:	Bijou exit off I-25. Proceed east on Bijou for two blocks which becomes Kiowa. Turn left on Nevada and left again on Bijou.
Credit Cards:	Yes
Owner:	Jerry Best
Year Estab:	1990
Comments:	We're always impressed by the attractive appearance of colorful remainders on display at shops like this. Seeing nice volumes that have, for one reason or another, not sold at list price and are being offered at substantial discounts makes us wonder about the strange world of publishing. At any rate, there are almost as many "genuine" used books on the shelves of this shop as there are remainders and the selection of both is extensive enough, and the store is well organized enough, to make it an interesting stop except for the most elite antiquarian.

(Colorado Springs)

Goodwill Industries   **Open Shop**
324 East Pikes Peak Avenue   (719) 635-1215

Collection: General stock of paperback and hardcover.
Hours: Daily 9-6.
Travel: At northwest corner of Wahsatch and Pikes Pike.

Hooked on Books   **Open Shop**
3918 Maizeland Road   80909   (719) 596-1621

Collection: General stock of used and new paperback and hardcover.
# of Vols: 300,000
Hours: Mon-Sat 10-6, except Fri till 8.
Travel: Northbound on I-25: Academy exit. Go north on Academy for about 10
                    miles. Right on Maizeland. Southbound on I-25: Academy exit. South on
                    Academy for 7½ miles. Left on Maizeland. Shop is in shopping center.
Credit Cards: Yes
Owner: Mary Francis Young
Year Estab: 1982
Comments: This establishment advertises itself as the "largest used book store in
                    Colorado." We don't know if any of the other dealers we list who have
                    large collections have challenged this statement, and we're really not
                    sure it would matter much. For, as Susan reminds me, large does not
                    always translate into quality. We did see a huge number of books here,
                    both hardcover and paperback, and the majority of the books were in
                    good condition. In most areas, however, paperbacks outnumber hard-
                    cover books, which is not to say that we did not spot several scarce
                    items which should make a stop here part of your itinerary, that is,
                    unless your tastes are very specialized.

La Dolce Vita   **Open Shop**
333 North Tejon   80903   (719) 632-1369

Collection: General stock of new and used hardcover and paperback.
# of Vols: 10,000
Hours: Mon-Sat 9am-10pm. Sun 12-3.
Credit Cards: Yes
Owner: Mary Francis Young & Jim Ciletti
Year Estab: 1996
Comments: An attractive book shop/coffee house that advertises itself as a "liter-
                    ary salon." The majority of the used books we saw were in good to very
                    good condition and appeared to be of more recent vintage. One of the
                    few combination book shop/coffee houses we have visited that had a
                    better than average selection of books.

Monarch Magazine Exchange   **Open Shop**
2214 East Platte Avenue   80909   (719) 473-2524

Collection: Specialty used and new.

Specialties:	Magazines (mostly popular, e.g., *Penthouse, Playboy*).
Hours:	Mon-Sat 11-10.
Travel:	Between Union and Circle.
Owner:	Mark Ford
Year Estab:	1961
Comments:	Shop also sells paperbacks.

Our Books   Open Shop
2224 North Wahsatch Avenue   80907   (719) 633-7484

Collection:	General stock of hardcover and paperback.
# of Vols:	30,000
Hours:	Mon-Fri 10:30-5:30. Sat 10:30-3:30.
Services:	Search service, accepts want lists.
Travel:	Fillmore exit off I-25. Proceed east on Fillmore, south on Nevada, east on Jackson, south on Wahsatch. Shop is just ahead, on right, in Bon Shopping Center.
Credit Cards:	No
Owner:	Jack Vawser
Year Estab:	1988
Comments:	A "paperbacks down the middle/hardcovers on the side and rear walls" type shop. In addition to a mixed selection of recent hardcover titles, we noted several older volumes, some sets and a few items that might be viewed as "hard-to-find." Reasonably priced.

Poor Richard's Discount Bookstore   Open Shop
320 North Tejon   80903   (719) 578-0012

Collection:	General stock of hardcover and paperback and remainders.
# of Vols:	75,000
Hours:	Daily 10-8.
Credit Cards:	Yes
Owner:	Richard Skorman
Year Estab:	1978
Comments:	Similar to another shop in town that also carries a large selection of remainders, although this shop probably has a greater proportion of used books. The shop's depth, both in physical space and in subject areas covered, provides lots of opportunity for browsing but if you're in a hurry, it's not difficult to locate the section/s you may be looking for.

Read It Again Books   Open Shop
205 West Rockrimmon Boulevard   80919   (719) 548-1440

Collection:	General stock of paperback and hardcover.
# of Vols:	60,000+
Hours:	Mon-Fri 10-6:30. Sat 10-5:30.
Services:	Accepts want lists, mail order.
Travel:	Woodmen exit off I-25. Proceed west on Woodmen for about 2½ miles. (Stay on Woodmen which becomes Rockrimmon after second light.) Shop is at corner of Rockrimmon and Delmonico in shopping center.

(Colorado Springs)

Credit Cards:	Yes
Owner:	Leah Setzer
Year Estab:	1990
Comments:	Almost two stores in one. One room housing a collection of hardcover books, including some labeled "collectible," is limited in size, but is the equivalent of many small "hardcover only" book shops. A second room is devoted mainly to paperbacks, with a sprinkling of some hardcover volumes, including some sets and classics.

Round Table Books   **Open Shop**
32 East Bijou   80903   (719) 578-5044

Collection:	General stock.
# of Vols:	5,000
Specialties:	Colorado
Hours:	Mon-Sat 10-5:30.
Services:	Appraisals, search service, catalog, accepts want lists.
Travel:	Bijou St exit off I-25. Left on Nevada then left on Bijou. Shop is two blocks ahead.
Credit Cards:	Yes
Owner:	Bill Porter
Year Estab:	1993
Comments:	While small in size, the quality of the books in this shop deserve attention. We saw titles in almost every area of interest, from scholarly to the more mundane and in almost every case the volumes represented hard-to-find titles that should be of interest to serious book people. Reasonably priced.

Toons Music   **Open Shop**
802 North Nevada   80903   Fax:(719) 632-8484   (719) 632-8410
                                         E-mail: crank@affront.com

Collection:	General stock of paperback and hardcover.
# of Vols:	45,000
Specialties:	Vintage paperbacks; magazines.
Hours:	Tue-Thu 11-9. Fri, Sat, Mon 11-midnight. Sun 12-6.
Travel:	Uintah exit off I-25. Proceed east on Uintah, then south at third light onto Nevada. Shop is three blocks ahead. Look for a brightly colored former service station.
Credit Cards:	Yes
Owner:	Eric Verlo
Year Estab:	1990
Comments:	Think psychedelic and you'll have no trouble locating this shop which occupies the site of a former gas station; once you arrive you'll see what we mean. In addition to selling LPs, CDs, cassettes, comics and an assortment of other equally intellectually challenging items, the shop does carry a modest selection of hardcover books and paperbacks ranging from literature to the performing arts to new age.

Commerce City

Bible Discount   **Open Shop**
6896 Highway 2   80022   (303) 287-7777

Collection:	Specialty new and used paperback and hardcover.
# of Vols:	30,000
Specialties:	Religion (Christianity)
Hours:	Mon-Sat 9-6.
Services:	Accepts want lists, mail order.
Travel:	Vasquez exit off I-70. North on Vasquez to Hwy 2, then east on Hwy 2.
Credit Cards:	Yes
Year Estab:	1976
Comments:	Stock is approximately 50% used, 70% of which is paperback.

Confier

Mountain Books   **Open Shop**
26001A Main Street   80433   (303) 838-4096

Collection:	General stock of paperback and hardcover.
# of Vols:	23,000
Hours:	Mon-Fri 9-7. Sat & Sun 10-5.
Services:	Accepts want lists, mail order.
Travel:	On Hwy 285.
Credit Cards:	Yes
Owner:	Jesse McKean
Year Estab:	1987
Comments:	Stock is approximately 70% paperback.

Craig

The Used Book Store   **Open Shop**
390 Rose Street   81625   (970) 824-7378

Collection:	General stock of hardcover and paperback.
# of Vols:	14,000+
Hours:	Mon-Sat 11-5. Sun 12-5.
Travel:	At 4th St, just off eastbound Hwy 40 or one block south of westbound Hwy 40.
Owner:	Al Romano
Year Estab:	1993
Comments:	Stock is evenly divided between hardcover and paperback.

Denver

Abracadabra (Antiquarian) Bookshop   **Open Shop**
32 South Broadway   80211   (303) 733-5700
                                                    E-mail: abrabks@abrabks.com

Collection:	General stock and ephemera.

# of Vols:	80,000
Specialties:	Colorado; Western Americana; literary first editions; children's illustrated; prints; maps; mountaineering; geology; military; Civil War; Americana.
Hours:	Mon-Fri 8-6. Sat 9-4.
Services:	Search service, catalog, accepts want lists.
Travel:	From downtown, proceed south on Broadway. From I-25 and Broadway, proceed north on Lincoln to Ellsworth, then left on Ellsworth and left on Broadway.
Credit Cards:	Yes
Owner:	Alan Culpin
Year Estab:	1976
Comments:	A very nice place to visit, well organized, and with an excellent selection of titles. There were very few subject areas that were not represented in strength. The books we saw were in generally good to very good condition, including those that fit into the antiquarian category. Our only caveat is that (and we recognize that we can't always to experts in this subject) a number of the volumes we saw appeared to be priced a bit higher than similar volumes in similar condition seen elsewhere.

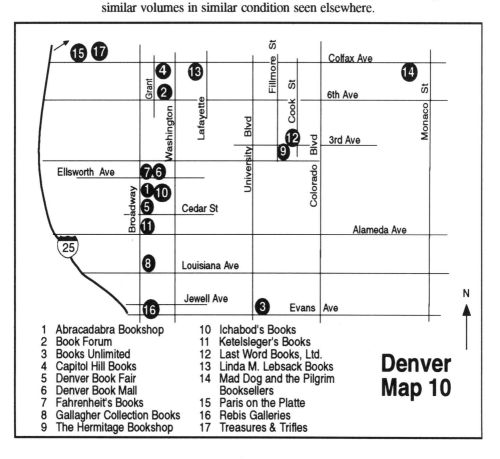

1 Abracadabra Bookshop
2 Book Forum
3 Books Unlimited
4 Capitol Hill Books
5 Denver Book Fair
6 Denver Book Mall
7 Fahrenheit's Books
8 Gallagher Collection Books
9 The Hermitage Bookshop
10 Ichabod's Books
11 Ketelsleger's Books
12 Last Word Books, Ltd.
13 Linda M. Lebsack Books
14 Mad Dog and the Pilgrim Booksellers
15 Paris on the Platte
16 Rebis Galleries
17 Treasures & Trifles

Denver Map 10

Alpha By Title   **By Appointment**
PO Box 9702   80209   (303) 722-1922

Collection:	Specialty
Specialties:	Cookbooks; children's; vintage paperbacks.
Owner:	Lee Morris
Comments:	Also displays at the Denver Book Mall. See below.

Already Read Books   **Open Shop**
7501 East Iliff Avenue   80231   (303) 752-2633

Collection:	General stock of mostly paperback.
# of Vols:	10,000
Hours:	Mon-Sat 10-6. Sun 12-5.

Book Forum   **Open Shop**
709 East 6th Avenue   80203   (303) 837-9069

Collection:	General stock.
# of Vols:	30,000
Specialties:	History
Hours:	Mon-Sat 12-5.
Travel:	6th Ave exit off I-25. Proceed east on 6th. Shop is between Washington and Clarkson.
Credit Cards:	No
Owner:	Tim Jepson
Year Estab:	1979
Comments:	Despite the sometimes narrow aisles and the books on the floor surrounding each shelf, we still found ourselves impressed by the number and scope of the hardcover volumes in this crowded shop. Most subjects were covered and in reasonable depth. A majority of the books were older volumes and in mixed condition. We spotted some winners and hope you're as fortunate.

The Book Garden   **Open Shop**
2625 East 12th Avenue   80206   (303) 399-2004
                                                      Fax: (303) 399-6167

Collection:	Specialty. Mostly new and some used.
Specialties:	Lesbian; women's studies.
Hours:	Daily 10-6, except Thu till 8.

Books etc.   **Open Shop**
878 East 88th Avenue   80229   (303) 288-2499

Collection:	General stock of mostly paperback.
Hours:	Mon-Sat 8-5.

Books Unlimited   **Open Shop**
2070 South University   80210   (303) 744-7180
                                                      (303) 744-0279

Collection:	General stock of hardcover and paperback.

(Denver)

# of Vols:	70,000
Specialties:	History; art; literature; performing arts; natural history.
Hours:	Mon-Sat 10-6. Sun 12-5.
Services:	Accepts want lists.
Travel:	University exit off I-25. Proceed south on University for three blocks.
Credit Cards:	Yes
Owner:	Joseph, Barbara & Owen Tierney
Year Estab:	1988
Comments:	A local lifestyles publication has designated this shop "The Best Used Book Store in Denver." The shop certainly has a respectable stock with far more hardcover volumes than we had anticipated. While the majority of the hardcover books were of more recent vintage, some would meet the test of "antiquarian" and a few would qualify as rare and/or collectible. Most were in good condition. All in all, a shop worth visiting.

Capitol Hill Books   **Open Shop**
300 East Colfax Avenue   80203   (303) 837-0700
                                                         Fax: (303) 860-7126

Collection:	General stock of hardcover and paperback.
# of Vols:	70,000
Hours:	Winter: Daily 10-6. Summer: Daily 9-7.
Services:	Accepts want lists, mail order.
Travel:	At intersection of Colfax and Grant across from State Capitol.
Credit Cards:	Yes
Owner:	Valarie Abney
Year Estab:	1979
Comments:	A corner shop with a reasonably large collection of hardcover and paperback volumes in mixed condition and of mixed vintage. Once you know where the books in your areas of interest are, it should not require too long for you to determine whether or not you'll make a purchase.

Category Six Books   **Open Shop**
1029 East 11th Avenue   80218   (303) 832-6263

Collection:	Specialty. Mostly new and some used.
# of Vols:	2,000
Specialties:	Homosexuality (male)
Hours:	Mon-Fri 10-6. Sat & Sun 11-5.
Credit Cards:	Yes
Owner:	Jim Schneider
Year Estab:	1981

Celebration Books   **By Appointment**
3617 Meade Street   80211   (303) 480-5193
                                                 E-mail: celebooklh@aol.com

Collection:	General stock of used and new.

# of Vols:	5,000
Specialties:	Books on books; reference books for the trade and collectors.
Services:	Appraisals, search service, catalog, accepts want lists, book store consultations and workshops.
Credit Cards:	Yes
Owner:	Lois Harvey
Year Estab:	1995
Comments:	Also displays at the Denver Book Mall (see below). The dealer owned a used book store in Denver for 16 years.

Colorado's Psychic Center   **Open Shop**
7352 North Washington Street   80229   (303) 289-1117

Collection:	Specialty. Mostly new.
Specialties:	Metaphysics
Hours:	Mon-Sat 10-7. Sun 1-6.

Denver Book Fair   **Open Shop**
44 South Broadway   80209   (303) 777-9946

Collection:	General stock of paperback and hardcover.
# of Vols:	75,000
Specialties:	Magazines
Hours:	Mon-Fri 10-7. Sat 10-6. Sun 12-5.
Services:	Accepts want lists, mail order.
Travel:	Hwy 6 exit off I-25. Proceed east on Hwy 6 to Broadway, then south on Broadway. Shop is about eight blocks ahead on east side of street.
Credit Cards:	Yes
Owner:	Jerry Robinette
Year Estab:	1973
Comments:	A shop that, in addition to selling used older hardcover volumes, also carries back issues of magazines, paperbacks and a special room for "adult" literature. If it was not on the same street as several other book dealers, we would not suggest a special trip.

Denver Book Mall   **Open Shop**
32 Broadway   80203   (303) 733-3808

Collection:	General stock.
Hours:	Mon-Sat 10-6. Sun 11-4.
Services:	Appraisals, search service, accepts want lists.
Travel:	Broadway/Lincoln exit off I-25. Proceed north on Lincoln, then left on First and left on Broadway.
Credit Cards:	Yes
Year Estab:	1994
Comments:	We've said it before but sometimes the truth needs to be repeated. A good group shop is always a pleasure to visit because the dealers (32 in this shop at the time of our visit) are likely to put their best foot (books) forward. This provides the browser with a wide selection of worthwhile titles. This shop was no exception to the above rule.

(Denver)

Fahrenheit's Books   **Open Shop**
38 Broadway   80203   (303) 744-1043

Collection:	General stock of hardcover and paperback.
# of Vols:	30,000
Specialties:	Metaphysics
Hours:	Mon-Fri, except closed Tue, 11-7. Sat 11-6. Sun 12-5.
Services:	Accepts want lists.
Travel:	See Denver Book Mall above.
Credit Cards:	Yes
Owner:	William Montague
Comments:	A mixed bag of mostly hardcover books with a fair supply of paperbacks. Most of the books we saw were in average to slightly better than average condition. While the shop was not very large, there was enough of a selection to make a visit here pay off, particularly as the shop is so close to several other dealers.

Gallagher Collection Books & Antiques   **Antique Mall**
At the Antique Guild   Mall: (303) 722-3358
1298 South Broadway   80210   Home: (303) 756-5821

Collection:	General stock.
# of Vols:	2,500 (See Comments)
Specialties:	Western Americana; children's; fine bindings.
Travel:	At Louisiana Ave.
Owner:	Don Gallagher
Year Estab:	1994
Comments:	For subject areas not on display, contact the dealer at his home number.

The Hermitage Bookshop   **Open Shop**
290 Fillmore Street   80206   (303) 388-6811
                                               Fax: (303) 388-6853

Collection:	General stock.
# of Vols:	10,000
Specialties:	Western Americana; books on books; women's studies; fine press.
Hours:	Mon-Fri 10-5:30. Sat 10-5. Sun 11-4.
Services:	Appraisals, search service, catalog, accepts want lists.
Travel:	Sixth Ave exit off I-25. Proceed east on Sixth Ave for several miles, then right on Fillmore. Shop is three blocks ahead at southeast corner of Third Ave and Fillmore in the Cherry Creek North shopping area.
Credit Cards:	Yes
Owner:	Robert Topp
Year Estab:	1972
Comments:	An absolutely must stop if you're visiting Denver. Located in an upscale shopping district one level below ground, the shop is spacious and the books, in fine to very fine condition, are attractively displayed.

The collection is strong in literature and scholarly titles with more than its share of antiquarian volumes. We also saw some attractive sets. Reasonably priced considering the quality of its stock.

Ichabod's Books   **Open Shop**
2 South Broadway   80209   (303) 778-7579

Collection:	General stock of hardcover and paperback and records.
# of Vols:	100,000
Hours:	Mon-Fri 10-7. Sat 10-6. Sun 11-5.
Services:	Accepts want lists, mail order.
Travel:	Broadway exit off I-25. Proceed north on Lincoln to Ellsworth, then west on Ellsworth. Shop is at corner of Ellsworth and Broadway.
Credit Cards:	Yes
Owner:	Kathleen & David Gomendi
Year Estab:	1993
Comments:	A fun place to visit, especially if you're lucky enough to arrive on one of the days the owner is in her clown costume. This is one of the very few combination used book stores/coffee shops that has an extensive collection of books in every category. The books were nicely priced and exceedingly well organized. While we were not able to spot any "long sought after" titles, we did see a large enough collection of hardcover books to enable us to walk out with a few; if we had more room in our car, we could have bought more

ISIS   **Open Shop**
5701 East Colfax Avenue   80220   (303) 321-0867

Collection:	Specialty. Mostly new.
# of Vols:	1,000 (used)
Specialties:	Metaphysics
Hours:	Mon-Thu 10-7. Fri & Sat 10-6. Sun 12-5.

Ketelsleger's Books   **Open Shop**
200 South Broadway   80209   (303) 722-5382

Collection:	General stock of hardcover and paperback.
# of Vols:	30,000
Specialties:	History; modern first editions.
Hours:	Mon-Sat 11-7. Sun 12-5.
Services:	Appraisals, search service, accepts want lists.
Travel:	Hwy 6 to Broadway, then south on Broadway for eight blocks to Cedar.
Credit Cards:	Yes
Owner:	Jeff Ketelsleger
Year Estab:	1994
Comments:	A modest sized shop with a mix of hardcover and paperback titles. Nicely organized and easy to browse. Most of the hardcover volumes we saw were in good to better condition with many worth a second look. Moderately priced.

(Denver)

Last Word Books, Ltd.   **Open Shop**
165 Cook Street, #303   80206   Fax: (303) 333-0277   (303) 333-0260
                                         E-mail: lastword@dimensional.com

Collection:	General stock.
# of Vols:	5,000
Hours:	Mon-Fri 8-5. Best to call to confirm.
Services:	Search service, accepts want lists, catalog in planning stage.
Travel:	From the south: Colorado exit off I-25. Proceed north on Colorado to 1st Ave, then left on 1st Ave and right on Cook. Shop is in an office building between 1st and 2nd Aves.
Owner:	Connie Freeman
Year Estab:	1996

Linda M. Lebsack Books   **Open Shop**
1228 East Colfax Avenue   80218   (303) 832-7190

Collection:	General stock and ephemera.
# of Vols:	10,000
Specialties:	Art (American); exhibition catalogs; Western Americana; Colorado; railroads.
Hours:	Mon-Fri, except closed Wed, 11-5. Sat 11-2 or by appointment.
Services:	Catalog, accepts want lists.
Travel:	Twelve blocks east of the State Capitol.
Credit Cards:	Yes
Owner:	Linda M. Lebsack
Year Estab:	1989
Comments:	We have seen neater looking shops during our travels but if you're looking for books and/or ephemera dealing with Colorado, other western states, Native Americans, cowboys and the like, there's a very good chance you might find the volume you're looking for here as the shop does maintain a good collection in these areas.

Mad Dog and the Pilgrim Booksellers   **Open Shop**
5926 East Colfax Avenue   80220   Fax: (303) 329-8011   (303) 329-8011
                                         E-mail: maddogbk@aol.com

Collection:	General stock of mostly hardcover.
# of Vols:	20,000
Specialties:	Children's; fiction; military; foreign languages; biography.
Hours:	Tue-Sat 11-5. Other times by appointment.
Services:	Appraisals, search service, accepts want lists, mail order, book repair.
Travel:	From the north: Colorado Blvd exit off I-70. Proceed south on Colorado to East Colfax, then east on Colfax to Jersey St.
Credit Cards:	Yes
Owner:	Lynda Z. German & Polly E. Hinds
Year Estab:	1990

Comments:	Picture yourself lost in time visiting a used book shop of yore. The shop (or should we say shops as there are two distinct storefronts separated by two other shops) is owned and operated by two gracious ladies who are more than happy to show you around and offer you a cup of coffee. The books we saw were a mix of vintages with an emphasis on older volumes (always a plus for those of us who are into such materials) and lots of interesting titles not typically seen. A bit crowded, but if you find a treasure, that aspect of browsing shouldn't bother you.

Magazine City   Open Shop
200 East 13th Avenue   80203   (303) 861-8249

Collection:	Specialty new and used.
Specialties:	Magazines
Hours:	Mon-Fri 10-6. Sat & Sun 11-5.
Travel:	One block south of the State Capitol.
Credit Cards:	Yes
Owner:	Warren Gross
Year Estab:	1992
Comments:	Stock is approximately 40% used with emphasis on popular magazines.

Metaphysical Book Store   Open Shop
2178 South Colorado Boulevard   80222   (303) 758-9113

Collection:	Specialty used and new hardcover and paperback.
Specialties:	Metaphysics
Hours:	Mon-Fri 10-5. Sat & Sun 11-5.
Travel:	Northbound on I-25: First Colorado exit. Proceed south on Colorado.
Owner:	Cheryl Coke Felts
Year Estab:	1972
Comments:	Stock is approximately 75% used, 75% of which is hardcover.

Murder By The Book   Open Shop
1574 South Pearl Street   80210   (303) 871-9401

Collection:	Specialty used and new.
Specialties:	Mystery
Hours:	Tue-Fri 11-6. Sat 10-5. Sun: holiday season and summers.
Services:	Accepts want lists, mail order.
Travel:	Washington St exit off I-25. Proceed south on Washington, west on Louisiana and south on Pearl.
Credit Cards:	Yes
Owner:	Shirley Beaird & Donna Mangum
Year Estab:	1981
Comments:	Stock is approximately 65% used, half of which is hardcover.

Old Algonquin Book Store   By Appointment
PO Box 18514   80218   (303) 766-1526

Collection:	General stock.
Specialties:	Fiction; mystery; history.

(Denver)

Credit Cards:	Yes
Owner:	John Dunning
Year Estab:	1984

The Old Map Gallery   Open Shop
1746 Blake Street   80202   (303) 296-7725

Collection:	Specialty
Specialties:	Maps
Hours:	Mon-Sat 10-5:30.
Services:	Appraisals, accepts want lists, catalog.
Travel:	Exit 212C off I-25. Proceed south on 20th St to Blake, then right on Blake.
Credit Cards:	Yes
Owner:	Paul Mahoney
Year Estab:	1991

Paperback Shack   Open Shop
3100 South Sheridan Boulevard   80227   (303) 922-7831

Collection:	General stock of mostly used paperback.
# of Vols:	42,000 (used)
Hours:	Mon-Fri 10-7. Sat 10-5. Sun 12-5.

Paris on the Platte   Open Shop
1553 Platte Street, #102   80202   (303) 455-2451

Collection:	General stock of used and new paperback and hardcover.
# of Vols:	10,000-15,000
Specialties:	Beatnik poetry; fine art.
Hours:	Mon-Thu 4pm-midnight. Fri & Sat 4pm-1am. Sun 7pm-midnight.
Services:	Accepts want lists.
Travel:	23rd Ave exit off I-25. Proceed northwest on 23rd Ave which becomes Platte St. Shop is 1/2 block passed first light on left.
Credit Cards:	Yes
Owner:	Jeff & Faye Maguire
Year Estab:	1986
Comments:	A combination coffee house/book store. Stock is approximately 65% used, 65% of which is paperback.

Park Hill Cooperative Book Store   Open Shop
4620 East 23rd Avenue   80207   (303) 355-8508

Collection:	General stock of mostly paperback used and new books.
# of Vols:	10,000 (used)
Hours:	Mon-Fri 10-6. Sat 10-5. Sun 12-4.
Comments:	A not-for-profit shop operated primarily by volunteers.

PS Books   Open Shop
3100 South Sheridan Boulevard   80227   (303) 922-7831

Collection:	General stock of mostly paperback used and new books.
Hours:	Mon-Fri 10-7. Sat 10-5. Sun 12-5.

Rebis Galleries   **Open Shop**
1930 South Broadway   80210   303-698-1841

Collection:	General stock of hardcover and paperback.
# of Vols:	20,000
Hours:	Daily 11:30-6.
Services:	Search service, accepts want lists, mail order.
Travel:	Two blocks north of Evans.
Credit Cards:	No
Owner:	Kristen Claussen & Ken DeBacker
Year Estab:	1994
Comments:	The hardcover volumes in this somewhat crowded shop represent a mix of vintages and condition. The books we saw did not appear to be exceptional in terms of desirability but since our visit here took place at the end of the day, we might well have missed a worthwhile selection or two. The rear portion of the shop was devoted to an art gallery.

Treasures & Trifles   **Open Shop**
8350 Washington Street   80229   (303) 288-8011

Collection:	General stock of mostly hardcover.
# of Vols:	7,000
Hours:	Tue-Fri 1-5. Sat 10-5.
Travel:	Exit 219 off I-25. Proceed east on 84th Ave to Washington, then south on Washington for 1/2 block.
Credit Cards:	No
Year Estab:	1973

Dillon

The Book Nook
130 Main, #5   970-468-5446
Mailing address: PO Box 1813 Dillon 80435   Fax: (303) 468-5446

Collection:	General stock of mostly paperback used and new.
# of Vols:	1,000 (used)
Hours:	Mon-Sat 10-6. Some seasonal variation.

Durango

The Bookcase   **Open Shop**
601 East Second Avenue   81301   (970) 247-3776

Collection:	General stock of paperback and hardcover and ephemera.
# of Vols:	20,000
Specialties:	Western Americana; anthropology; archaeology; history; railroads.
Hours:	Mon-Sat 9:30-5. Extended hours during summer.
Services:	Search service, accepts want lists, mail order.
Credit Cards:	Yes
Year Estab:	1984
Comments:	Stock is approximately 75% paperback.

Southwest Book Trader   **Open Shop**
175 East 5th Street   81301   (970) 247-8479

Collection:	General stock of hardcover and paperback and ephemera.
# of Vols:	50,000
Specialties:	Western Americana; archaeology; anthropology; Southwest Americana.
Hours:	Summer: Mon-Sun 9:30-7. Winter Mon-Sat 9:30-5.
Services:	Accepts want lists, mail order.
Travel:	Downtown, one block east of train station.
Credit Cards:	Yes
Owner:	George Hassan
Year Estab:	1980
Comments:	Stock is approximately 70% paperback.

Englewood
(See Map 11, page 120)

Colorado Carbooks   **Open Shop**
5138 South Broadway   80110   (303) 762-8595

Collection:	Speciality. Mostly new and some used.
Specialties:	Automobiles and motorcycles.
Hours:	Mon-Fri 10-7. Sat 9-4.

Colorado Pioneer Books   **Open Shop**
4755 South Broadway   80110   (303) 789-0379

Collection:	Specialty
# of Vols:	10,000
Specialties:	Western Americana.
Hours:	Tue-Fri 10-5. Sat 10-4.
Services:	Accepts want lists, mail order.
Travel:	Broadway exit off I-25. Proceed south on Broadway for about five miles.
Credit Cards:	Yes
Owner:	Dan Larson
Year Estab:	1983

Horizon Books   **Open Shop**
3438 South Broadway   80110   (303) 789-0305

Collection:	Specialty
# of Vols:	20,000
Specialties:	Religion (Christianity)
Hours:	Mon-Sat 10-5.
Services:	Appraisals, accepts want lists, mail order.
Travel:	Hampden Ave exit off I-25. East on Hampden then north on Broadway.
Credit Cards:	Yes
Owner:	Eddie Cook
Year Estab:	1995

Neighborhood Bookstore   **Open Shop**
8200 South Quebec Street, #A11   80112   (303) 721-7882

Collection:	General stock of mostly paperback.
# of Vols:	25,000
Hours:	Mon-Fri 10-8. Sat 10-6. Sun 1-5.

Willow Creek Books   **Open Shop**
8100 South Akron, Ste. 310   80112   (800) 891-7530   (303) 790-7530
                                                     Fax: (303) 790-7530
                                               E-mail: dacolb@aol.com

Collection:	General stock of mostly used.
# of Vols:	40,000
Specialties:	Western Americana; children's illustrated; mystery; modern fiction; poetry; art; photography.
Hours:	Mon-Fri 11:30-6. Sat 10-6. Sun by appointment.
Services:	Appraisals, search service, accepts want lists, mail order.
Travel:	County Line Rd exit off I-25. Proceed west on County Line for three blocks, then north on Akron. Shop is about 500 yards ahead in Highland Park office complex.
Credit Cards:	Yes
Owner:	Don & Nancy Colberg
Year Estab:	1989
Comments:	Some dealers are worth driving a few miles out of one's way to visit. Even though this shop is not in the center of Denver, it is well worth taking the time to visit. If you have any interest at all in the specialties listed above you'll find row upon row of titles to peruse. The books we viewed were in excellent condition, priced reasonably and the shop is easy to browse.

Estes Park

Fine Old Books   **Open Shop**
120 East Riverside   (970) 586-6384
Mailing address: PO Box 3928 Estes Park 80517

Collection:	General stock of hardcover and paperback.
# of Vols:	10,000
Hours:	Summer: Daily, except closed Tue, 10:30-5:30. Winter: Wed-Sun 11-5.
Services:	Search service, accepts want lists, mail order.
Travel:	Elkhorn Ave exit off Hwy 34. West on Elkhorn and left on Riverside.
Credit Cards:	Yes
Owner:	Dan & Louise Smith
Year Estab:	1992
Comments:	At the risk of sounding like a travel guide, should you visit Estes Park to view the beautiful scenery or the Stanley Hotel (of *The Shinning* fame) you may also want to drop in on this shop where you'll find mostly older volumes shelved in Dewey Decimal format and selling at resort area prices. Plenty of oldies but goodies.

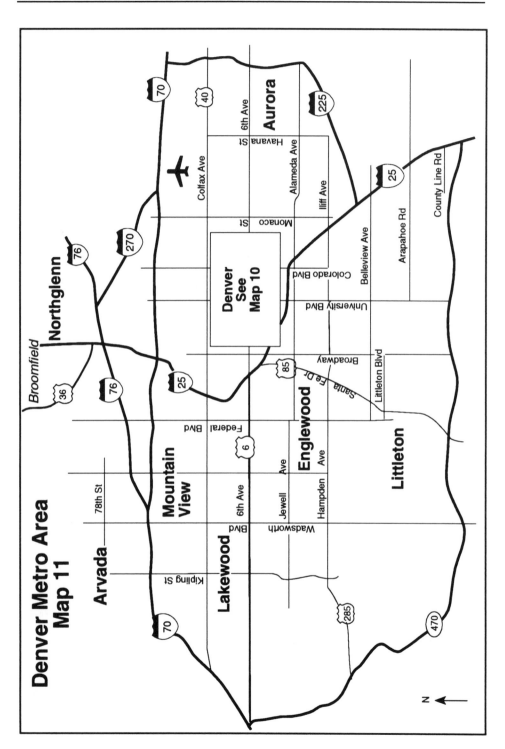

Evergreen

Bonaventura Books   **By Appointment**
PO Box 2709   80437   (303) 674-4830

Collection:	Specialty
# of Vols:	2,000
Specialties:	Western Americana.
Services:	Accepts want lists, catalog.
Credit Cards:	No
Owner:	Ann Johnston
Year Estab:	1985

Haunted Bookshop   **Open Shop**
4602 South Plettner Lane   80439   (303) 670-4240

Collection:	General stock of mostly paperback.
# of Vols:	12,000
Hours:	Mon-Sat 10-5. Summer only: Sun 12-5 and later opening on Mon.

Fort Collins

Book Rack   **Open Shop**
2020 South College Avenue, #2A   80525   (970) 484-7898

Collection:	General stock of mostly paperback.
# of Vols:	30,000
Hours:	Mon-Sat 10-6. Sun 12-4.
Travel:	Prospect exit off I-25. Proceed west on Prospect to College, then south on College. Shop is about three blocks ahead in a strip center.
Credit Cards:	Yes
Year Estab:	1977
Comments:	We stopped here, noted the stock was 99.5% paperback and moved on.

Eclectic Reader   **By Appointment**
2724 West Mulberry Street   80521   (970) 493-7933

Collection:	General stock of hardcover and paperback.
# of Vols:	5,000
Services:	Search service, accepts want lists, mail order.
Credit Cards:	No
Owner:	Cynthia Manuel
Year Estab:	1983
Comments:	Stock is approximately 70% hardcover.

Happenstance   **Open Shop**
201 South College   80524   (970) 493-1668

Collection:	General stock.
# of Vols:	8,000
Specialties:	Children's; mostly non fiction.
Hours:	Tue-Sun 10-6.

Services:	Accepts want lists.
Travel:	On Hwy 287, six blocks north of Hwy 14.
Credit Cards:	Yes
Owner:	Tom Rowland
Year Estab:	1995

The Novel Novel Bookstore   **Open Shop**
2721 South College Avenue, #6   80525   (970) 225-6314

Collection:	General stock of paperback and hardcover.
# of Vols:	15,000
Hours:	Mon-Thu 10-6. Fri 10-8. Sat 10-6. Sun 11-5.
Services:	Search service, accepts want lists, mail order.
Travel:	Northbound on I-25: Harmony exit off I-25. Proceed west on Harmony Rd for four miles, then north on College. Shop is about 1¾ miles ahead on left in Thunderbird Plaza. Southbound on I-25: Prospect exit. Proceed west on Prospect, then south on College.
Credit Cards:	Yes
Owner:	Larry Hulse, Bryan Thompson, M.H. Thompson
Year Estab:	1993
Comments:	A mix of mostly paperbacks with a couple of thousand hardcover volumes in mixed condition. Inexpensive and not particularly unusual.

Old Corner Book Shop   **Open Shop**
216 Linden Street   80524   (970) 484-6186

Collection:	General stock of hardcover and paperback.
# of Vols:	30,000
Specialties:	Western Americana; history; classics; children's.
Hours:	Mon-Sat 10-6. Sun 12-4.
Services:	Search service.
Travel:	Mulberry/Hwy 14 exit off I-25. Proceed west on Mulberry, right on Riverside for 1/2 mile than left on Linden.
Credit Cards:	Yes
Owner:	Jane B. Tester
Year Estab:	1970
Comments:	While we don't generally like to make comparisons, if you're passing through Fort Collins and have time for only one stop, make this it. Although the shop is small, the selection of hardcover volumes is nice and offers a balanced mix of older volumes (including some nice sets) and more recent items.

Paperback Heaven   **Open Shop**
109 East Stuart Street   80525   (970) 224-9044

Collection:	General stock of mostly paperback.
# of Vols:	14,000
Hours:	Mon-Sat 11-6.

Frisco

Frisco Books   **Open Shop**
220 Main Street   80443   (970) 668-5399

Collection:	General stock of new and used paperback and hardcover.
# of Vols:	8,000
Hours:	Mon-Sat 10-6. Sun 12-3.
Comments:	Approximately 20% of the stock is used, 75% of which is paperback.

Georgetown

Powder Cache Antiques   **Open Shop**
612 6th Street   (303) 569-2848
Mailing address: PO Box 984 Georgetown 80444

Collection:	General stock and ephemera.
# of Vols:	3,000
Specialties:	Mining; geology; technology; Colorado.
Hours:	Daily 10-5.
Services:	Appraisals, accepts want lists, mail order.
Travel:	Exit 228 off I-70. Follow signs to downtown. Shop is across from Information Center.
Credit Cards:	Yes
Owner:	Leo Stambaugh
Year Estab:	1986
Comments:	The shop also features a mining museum.

Glenwood Springs

Glenwood Books & Collectables   **Open Shop**
At King Mall, 720 Grand Avenue   81601   (970) 928-8825
                                       E-mail: huntbook@interloc.com

Collection:	General stock of hardcover and paperback and ephemera.
# of Vols:	10,000
Specialties:	Hunting; fishing; Western Americana.
Hours:	Mon-Sat 10:30-6. Sun 11-4.
Services:	Appraisals, search service, catalog, accepts want lists.
Travel:	Proceeding south on Hwy 82 (towards Aspen), cross Colorado River bridge (Hwy 82 becomes Grand Ave) and look for the first parking space. Shop is at foot of bridge.
Credit Cards:	Yes
Owner:	Michael & Seraina McCarty
Year Estab:	1995
Comments:	A small shop with a limited collection of nice books, most of which are in good condition. While an attempt is made to cover many areas of interest, the size of the shop limits the selection in any one category. This does not mean you would not enjoy a stop here.

Golden

Sundance Used Books   **By Appointment**
18579 West 60th Avenue   80403   (303) 278-9389
                                                          Fax: (303) 273-5825

Collection:	Specialty
# of Vols:	500
Specialties:	Western Americana.
Services:	Catalog in planning stage, search service, accepts want lists.
Credit Cards:	No
Owner:	Sylvia Franklin
Year Estab:	1996

Granby

Aspen Antiquarian   **By Appointment**
PO Box 889   80446   (970) 627-3159
                                                          Fax: (970) 627-3037

Collection:	Specialty
Specialties:	15th-19th century books; maps; color plate books.
Services:	Appraisals, search service.
Owner:	Joyce Lee
Year Estab:	1972
Comments:	When not in the United States, the dealer can be contacted in England via fax: 0181 651 4920.

Grand Junction

Author's Gallery Bookstore   **Open Shop**
537 Main Street   81501   (800) 890-4198   (970) 241-3696

Collection:	General stock of hardcover and paperback.
# of Vols:	20,000+
Hours:	Mon 9:30-5. Tue-Sat 9:30-6. Sun 11-4.
Services:	Search service, accepts want lists.
Travel:	Horizon Dr exit off I-70. Proceed south on Horizon to 12th St, then left on 12th to Main and right on Main. Shop is just passed 6th St in downtown shopping park.
Credit Cards:	No
Owner:	Edward & Sassy Dutton
Year Estab:	1992
Comments:	We like a shop that shows it priorities. The hardcover books take up most of the front half of this shop with paperbacks in the rear. The hardcover items we saw were a mix of vintages, some older volumes, a few sets, some more common items and a fair number of one (or two) of a kind titles.

Better Books & Teaching Aids   **Open Shop**
953 North Avenue   81501   (970) 245-2227

Collection: General stock of mostly paperback.
Hours: Mon-Sat 10-5:30.

Comics Odyssey   **Open Shop**
337 North Avenue   81501   (970) 241-0288

Collection: General stock of paperback used and comics.
Hours: Mon-Sat 10-5:30.
Comments: Approximately half the stock consists of used books, 80% of which are paperback.

Imagination Unlimited   **Open Shop**
1000 North Fifth Street   81501   (970) 243-2962

Collection: General stock of mostly paperback.
Hours: Mon-Fri 9-5.

Twice Upon a Time Book Shop   **Open Shop**
2692 Highway 50, #N   81503   (970) 242-3911

Collection: General stock of hardcover and paperback.
# of Vols: 10,000
Specialties: Western Colorado.
Hours: Mon-Sat 10-6.
Services: Search service, accepts want lists, mail order.
Travel: On south side of Grand Junction, one mile south of Colorado River bridge, in Orchard Mesa Shopping Center.
Credit Cards: Yes
Owner: Jean & Ross Transmeier
Year Estab: 1995
Comments: The hardcover volumes we saw were in mixed to good condition with some emphasis on regionalism. In addition to a selection of vintage fiction, the remaining volumes were a mix of mostly fiction titles with a smattering (anywhere from 1/2 to 1½ shelves) of the typical entertainment, sports, humor, etc. titles.

Greeley

Book Rack   **Open Shop**
1400 8th Avenue   80631   (970) 356-8961

Collection: General stock of mostly paperback.
Hours: Mon-Sat 10-6. Sun 12-5.

Mt. Falcon Books   **Open Shop**
926 9th Avenue   80631   (970) 356-9211

Collection: General stock of paperback and hardcover.
# of Vols: 20,000
Hours: Mon-Fri 10-5. Sat 10-3:30.

Services:	Appraisals, search service, accepts want lists, mail order.
Travel:	8th Ave exit off Hwy 85. If southbound, turn right on 8th Ave; if northbound turn left. Then turn west on 10th St, then north on 9th Ave.
Credit Cards:	Yes
Owner:	Suzy Ellis
Year Estab:	1979
Comments:	Stock is approximately 65% paperback.

Gunnison

Book Worm Bookstore   **Open Shop**
211 North Main Street   81230   (970) 641-3693
                                                                 Fax: (970) 641-3955

Collection:	General stock of mostly new and some used hardcover.
# of Vols:	1,000 (used)
Specialties:	Western Americana; hunting; fishing; children's.
Hours:	Mon-Fri 9-5. Sat 9-4.
Services:	Accepts want lists.
Travel:	1½ blocks north of Hwy 50 in center of town.
Credit Cards:	Yes
Owner:	Stuart & Marcia Duncan
Year Estab:	1983

Heritage Used & New Books   **Open Shop**
111 East Georgia   81230   (970) 641-2074

Collection:	General stock of mostly used books.
# of Vols:	5,000
Specialties:	Cookbooks; biography; history.
Hours:	Mon-Fri 10:30-5:30. Sat 12-4.
Services:	Accepts want lists, mail order.
Travel:	From Hwy 50, turn north on Hwy 135 (Main St), then right on Georgia.
Owner:	Norman S. Hatchell
Year Estab:	1990
Comments:	Stock is evenly divided between hardcover and paperback.

Kittredge

Chessler Books   **Open Shop**
26030 Highway 74   (303) 670-0093
Mailing address: PO Box 399 Kittredge 80457   Fax: (303) 670-9727
                                             Out of state mail order only: (800) 654-8502

Collection:	Specialty new and used books and ephemera.
# of Vols:	20,000
Specialties:	Mountaineering; polar; travel; exploration; caving; skiing; maps.
Hours:	Mon-Sat 8-5:30.
Services:	Catalog
Travel:	Exit 251 or 252 off I-70. Follow Hwy 74 to store.

Credit Cards:	Yes
Owner:	Michael Chessler
Year Estab:	1984
Comments:	Stock is approximately 50% used.

Lafayette

Alexandrian Library   **By Appointment**
595 East Sutton Circle   80026   (303) 665-7821

Collection:	Specialty
# of Vols:	1,500
Specialties:	Philosophy; religion.
Services:	Appraisals, accepts want lists, mail order.
Owner:	Julian Alexander
Year Estab:	1988

Lakewood
(See Map 11, page 120)

Corner Cupboard Books   **Open Shop**
At Antique Mall of Lakewood   Mall: (303) 238-6940
9635 West Colfax Ave   Home: (303) 674-9113
Mailing address: PO Box 3221 Evergreen 80437   Fax: (303) 674-9113

Collection:	General stock.
Specialties:	Antiques and collectibles; children's; children's series; Colorado; Western Americana; cookbooks; fiction (pre-1960).
Hours:	Mon-Sat 9-6. Sun 11-5.
Services:	Search service, accepts want lists, mail order.
Travel:	Kipling exit off I-70. Proceed south on Kipling to Colfax, then east on Colfax for two blocks. From I-25: Sixth Ave West or Colfax West exit.
Credit Cards:	Yes
Owner:	Toni Dunrud
Year Estab:	1991

Dog-Eared Books   **Open Shop**
1916 South Kipling Street   80227   (303) 763-8865

Collection:	General stock of mostly paperback.
# of Vols:	2,800
Hours:	Mon-Fri 10-7. Sat 10-5.

My Friends' Books   **Open Shop**
1545 Quail Street   80215   (303) 274-2755

Collection:	General stock of new and used paperback and hardcover.
# of Vols:	4,000 (used)
Hours:	Mon-Sat 10-6. Sun 12-5.
Comments:	Used stock is approximately 75% paperback.

Rosemary's Baby   **Open Shop**
1428 South Wadsworth Boulevard   80232   (303) 986-8799

Collection:	General stock of paperback and hardcover.
# of Vols:	7,000
Hours:	Mon-Sat 9:30-6. Sun 9:30-2:30.
Travel:	Wadsworth exit off Hwy 6. Proceed south on Wadsworth for about 20 blocks. Shop is on the left in a small strip center.
Owner:	Rosemary Barr
Year Estab:	1992
Comments:	A rather small shop with a limited collection of mostly paperbacks and some hardcover volumes, the majority of which were of recent vintage. Inexpensive, but not a great deal to offer.

Littleton
(See Map 11, page 120)

Aberdeen Bookstore   **Open Shop**
1360-H West Littleton Boulevard   80120   (303) 795-1890
                                                           Fax: (303) 795-1890

Collection:	General stock of mostly used hardcover.
# of Vols:	35,000
Specialties:	World War II; military.
Hours:	Mon-Sat 11-5. Sun 12-4.
Services:	Catalog, accepts want lists.
Travel:	Santa Fe exit off I-25. Proceed south on Santa Fe, then left on Littleton Blvd. Shop is on right in Littleton Plaza.
Credit Cards:	Yes
Owner:	Tom Petteys
Year Estab:	1992
Comments:	A neat shop with a very good collection of both scholarly and literary hardcover volumes in good to excellent condition. Quite strong in the specialties listed above. Worth a visit if you're in the area.

Paperback   **Open Shop**
1500 West Littleton Boulevard   80120   (303) 797-2243

Collection:	General stock of mostly paperback.
Hours:	Mon-Sat 10-5:30.

Longmont

The Used Book Store   **Open Shop**
1126 Francis Street   80501   (303) 772-3475

Collection:	General stock of mostly paperback.
# of Vols:	30,000
Hours:	Mon-Fri 10-5. Sat 10-4.

Louisville

Beebo's Used Books   **Open Shop**
925 Spruce Street   80027   (303) 666-4919

Collection:	General stock of paperback and hardcover.
# of Vols:	28,000
Hours:	Tue-Sat 10-6.
Services:	Search service, accepts want lists, mail order.
Travel:	1/2 block from Main.
Credit Cards:	No
Owner:	H.Y. Domaratz & M.L. Hoffman
Year Estab:	1984
Comments:	Stock is approximately 70% paperback.

Loveland

The Book Rack of Loveland   **Open Shop**
138 East 29th Street   80538   (970) 667-0118

Collection:	General stock of mostly paperback.
# of Vols:	30,000+
Hours:	Mon-Sat 10-6.

Footnote Book Store   **Open Shop**
257A East 29th Street   80538   (970) 663-2738

Collection:	General stock of used and new paperback and hardcover.
# of Vols:	17,000 (used)
Hours:	Mon-Sat 9-6. Sun 11-5.
Services:	From I-25, proceed west on Hwy 34, then turn north on Hwy 287 and proceed to 29th St. Shop is just after 29th St, on right, in Orchards Shopping Center.
Credit Cards:	Yes
Owner:	Rita Stricklin
Year Estab:	1980
Comments:	Considering the size of this shop (not too large) and the fact that half of the shop consists of new books, the selection of used books is rather limited with the emphasis on children's titles (mostly paperback) and a very modest selection of hardcover volumes in mixed condition and of mixed vintage.

The Haven   **Open Shop**
1528 North Lincoln   80538   (970) 203-1232

Collection:	Specialty new and used paperbacks.
# of Vols:	500-1,000
Specialties:	Science fiction; fantasy.
Hours:	Call for hours.

Loveland Book Exchange
119 East 4th Street   80537

Open Shop
(970) 635-0788
E-mail: bookmtn@ezlink.com

Collection:	General stock of paperback and hardcover.
# of Vols:	30,000+
Hours:	Mon-Sat 10-6.
Services:	Search service, accepts want lists, on-line catalog.
Travel:	4th St exit off Hwy 287. Proceed west on 4th St for 1/2 block.
Credit Cards:	Yes
Owner:	Phil & Mary Mueller
Year Estab:	1993
Comments:	A kind dealer who was nice enough to open early for us. The hardcover portion of the collection consisted of a mix of newer and vintage materials. Since the dealer is on-line, if there's a particular title you're looking for, you may want to send an e-mail message or check the dealer's web page and save yourself a journey.

Manitou Springs

AHH Firefly Antiques
727 Manitou Avenue   80829

Open Shop
(719) 685-5509

Collection:	General stock of mostly hardcover.
# of Vols:	3,000
Hours:	Mon-Sat 11-5.
Travel:	Manitou exit off Hwy 24. Proceed west on Manitou Ave.
Credit Cards:	Yes
Owner:	Chris Lee
Year Estab:	1986

Monument

Covered Treasures Bookstore
105 Second Street   80132

Open Shop
(719) 481-2665

Collection:	General stock of new and mostly paperback used.
# of Vols:	1,000 (used)
Hours:	Mon-Fri 9-6. Sat 9-4. Sun 12-4.

Mountain View
(Map 11, page 120)

Brownstone Bookstore
5430 West 44th Avenue   80212

Open Shop
(303) 424-5839

Collection:	General stock of mostly used hardcover and paperback.
# of Vols:	10,000
Hours:	Tue-Thu 11-6. Fri 11-7. Sat 10-6. Sun 11-4.
Travel:	Sheridan Ave exit off I-70. Proceed south on Sheridan to 44th Ave, then west on 44th Ave. Shop is across from Lakeside Mall.

Credit Cards:	No
Year Estab:	1994
Comments:	Stock is evenly divided between paperback and hardcover.

Northglenn
(See Map 11, page 120)

Brock's Used Books   **Open Shop**
609 Garland Drive   80233   (303) 252-7481

Collection:	General stock of paperback and hardcover.
# of Vols:	12,000
Hours:	Mon 9-7. Tue 9-5:30. Wed 9-5:30. Thu 9-1. Fri 11-7. Sat 12-5. Closed approximately 1/2 hour for lunch, usually between 1-2.
Travel:	104th exit off I-25. Proceed east on 104th to Washington then north on Washington and left on Garland into shopping center.
Credit Cards:	No
Year Estab:	1991
Comments:	Stock is approximately 65% paperback fiction and 35% hardcover non fiction.

Norwood

Bear Paw Books & Gifts   **Open Shop**
1611 Grand Avenue   81423   (970) 327-4266

Collection:	General stock of new and mostly used paperback.
# of Vols:	15,000
Hours:	Mon-Sat 10-7. Sun 10-5.
Comments:	Stock is approximately 50% used, 80% of which is paperback.

Parker

The Book Scene   **Open Shop**
10441 South Parker Road   80134   (303) 840-8056

Collection:	General stock of mostly paperback.
# of Vols:	10,000
Hours:	Mon-Fri 11-6. Sat 10-4.

Pueblo

Bargain Books   **Open Shop**
600 East Abriendo   81004   (719) 543-5101

Collection:	General stock of mostly paperback.
# of Vols:	100,000
Hours:	Mon-Sat 10-5:30.
Travel:	Abriendo exit off I-25. Shop is the second building on the right immediately after the first traffic light coming off exit.
Credit Cards:	No

Owner:	Nancy Catalano
Year Estab:	1968
Comments:	99,500 or so paperbacks and perhaps 500 or so old hardcover volumes of very little distinction. If you're interested in old issues of magazines (e.g., lapidary, hunting, sex) you may want to consider a visit.

Millet & Simpson Booksellers   Open Shop
224 South Union Avenue   81003   (719) 542-4462

Collection:	General stock and ephemera.
# of Vols:	15,000
Specialties:	History; Western Americana; biography; cookbooks.
Hours:	Tue-Fri 11-5. Sat 11-3.
Services:	Appraisals, search service, catalog, accepts what lists, minor book repairs.
Travel:	See Tumbleweed Books below. Continue on Union for about 3½ blocks.
Credit Cards:	Yes
Owner:	Leland S. Millet & Ronald C. Simpson
Year Estab:	1977
Comments:	We arrived at this shop about 15 minutes after the announced opening time and found the shop closed and the following message posted in the window:

> *OPEN most days about 9 or 10. Occasionally as early as 7.*
> *But some days as late as 12 or 1.*
> *WE CLOSE about 5:30 or 6. Occasionally about 4 or 5.*
> *But sometimes as late as 11 or 12.*
> *SOMEDAYS or afternoons we aren't here at all.*
> *And lately I've been here just about all the time.*
> *EXCEPT when I'm someplace else.*

Because the view inside the shop through the front window suggested that the shop stocked quality books, we left for an early lunch and returned about half an hour later to find the shop open. Our window observations turned out to be accurate. While the shop was not huge, the books on hand were indeed quality titles and in good condition. If you're visiting Pueblo and are only able to make one stop, this is where it should be, but call ahead to be sure the shop is open.

Pace's Book Exchange   Open Shop
122 South Union   81003

Collection:	General stock of paperback and hardcover.
# of Vols:	2,000+
Hours:	Mon-Fri 12:30-2:30.
Comments:	A shop that is, we assume, based on a sign in the window, run by volunteers for the support of a local charity. Looking through the window, we saw at least two full bookcases of older hardcover volumes as well as an ample supply of paperbacks. If you're in the area and have time, you might want to make a quick visit.

Tumbleweed Books   **Open Shop**
687 South Union Avenue   81004   (719) 544-3420

Collection:	General stock of hardcover and paperback.
# of Vols:	8,000
Hours:	Mon-Sat 10:30-5:30.
Services:	Accepts want lists, mail order.
Travel:	Abriendo exit off I-25. Proceed north on Abriendo to Union, then east on Union. Shop is just ahead on left (parking lot is across the street.)
Credit Cards:	No
Owner:	Phyllis Fairchild
Year Estab:	1982
Comments:	A mix of hardcover and paperback books. Most of the hardcover volumes we saw were older and looked it. However, there were some items that would be of interest to real book people, e.g., a copy of Ginsberg's *Kaddish* under glass.

Ridgeway

Cimarron Books & Coffeehouse   **Open Shop**
380 West Sherman   81432   (970) 626-5858

Collection:	General stock of mostly new.
# of Vols:	150+ (used)
Hours:	Mon-Fri 7:30-6. Sat & Sun 8:30-4.

Salida

All Booked Up   **Open Shop**
134 East 1st Street   81201   (719) 539-2344

Collection:	General stock of mostly used paperback.
# of Vols:	2,000 (used)
Hours:	Mon-Sat, except closed Wed, 11-5:30.

Steamboat Springs

Books & Booty   **Open Shop**
732 Lincoln Avenue, 2nd Fl   (970) 870-8448
Mailing address: PO Box 771003 Steamboat Springs 80477

Collection:	General stock of mostly paperback.
Hours:	Mon-Sat 10-6. Sun 10-5.

Telluride

Colorado Bookman   **Antique Mall**
At Telluride Antique Market   Mall: (970) 728-4323
Pacific Avenue   Home: (970) 626-5936
Mailing address: Box 470 Ridgeway 81432

Collection:	General stock and ephemera.

# of Vols:	600+
Specialties:	Western Americana; Native Americans; photography.
Hours:	Daily 10-6.
Owner:	Terre Bucknam
Comments:	Additional stock is available for viewing on a by appointment basis.

Thornton

Books Etc   **Open Shop**
878 East 88th Avenue   80229   (303) 288-2499

Collection:	General stock of mostly paperback.
# of Vols:	60,000
Hours:	Mon-Sat 8-5.

Trinidad

Bob's Books   **Open Shop**
249 North Commercial   (719) 846-4273
Mailing address: PO Box 722 Trinidad 81082

Collection:	General stock new and used paperback and hardcover.
# of Vols:	6,000
Hours:	Mon-Sat 9:30-12 and 1:30-5. Best to call ahead.
Travel:	See Mountain Branch Bookshop below.
Owner:	Bob Arko
Year Estab:	1991
Comments:	Stock is approximately 50% used, 50% of which is paperback.

Mountain Branch Bookshop   **Open Shop**
269 North Commercial Street   81082   (719) 846-6781

Collection:	General stock of mostly used hardcover.
# of Vols:	20,000
Hours:	Mon-Fri 10-6. Holidays and summer: open most evenings and weekends.
Services:	Appraisals, mail order.
Travel:	Exit 13B off I-25. Proceed north on Main St to Commercial, then left on Commercial. Shop is about two blocks ahead.
Credit Cards:	No
Owner:	Steve Jacobs
Year Estab:	1989
Comments:	A small store but with a nice selection of hardcover books, many of which fall into the vintage category, and priced, we believe, most reasonably. We were advised that an additional 500 or so boxes of books would be shelved and on display by the time this book was in print. We made a couple of purchases here and hope our readers are as fortunate as we feel we were.

Westminster

Jeff Jeremias Fine Arts   **By Appointment**
12120 Melody Drive   80234   (303) 450-6598

Collection: Specialty
# of Vols: 3,000
Specialties: Western Americana; Americana.
Services: Accepts want lists.
Credit Cards: No
Year Estab: 1990

Wheat Ridge

The Book Stop   **Open Shop**
10840 West 44th Avenue   80033   (303) 425-4960

Collection: General stock of mostly paperback.
# of Vols: 100,000
Hours: Tue-Sat 10-6.

Mail Order Dealers

Ace Zerblonski Books   (719) 634-3941
1419 North Royer Colorado Springs 80907

Collection:	General stock of mostly hardcover.
# of Vols:	5,000
Services:	Catalog, accepts want lists.
Owner:	Malcolm McCollum
Year Estab:	1993

Angling & Hunting Book Source   (303) 444-3388
1270 26th Street Boulder 80302

Collection:	Specialty
# of Vols:	1,000
Specialties:	Angling; hunting.
Services:	Catalog
Credit Cards:	No
Owner:	John B. Kline
Year Estab:	1990

Bella Luna Books   (800) 497-4717
PO Box 260425 Highlands Ranch 80163   Fax: (303) 791-7342
                                                E-mail: bellalun@aol.com

Collection:	General stock.
# of Vols:	40,000
Specialties:	Modern first editions; literature; mystery; illustrated.
Services:	Catalog, accepts want lists.
Credit Cards:	Yes
Owner:	Tony Delcaro & Pam Moser
Year Estab:	1993

Beyond Old Books   (303) 776-2109
803 Vivian Street Longmont 80501

Collection:	General stock.
# of Vols:	5,000-10,000
Services:	Appraisals, accepts want lists.
Credit Cards:	Yes
Owner:	Todd & Norma Ewalt
Year Estab:	1986

Book Quarry   (970) 962-9110
6410 North County Road 27 Loveland 80538   E-mail: bkquarry@interloc.com

Collection:	General stock.
# of Vols:	9,000
Specialties:	Natural history.
Owner:	Janet Keup
Year Estab:	1991

Bookfinders West and East (303) 861-4988
PO Box 18281 Denver 80218

Collection:	General stock.
# of Vols:	2,500
Specialties:	Far East history; literature.
Services:	Search service, occasional lists, accepts want lists.
Credit Cards:	No
Owner:	Robert Wang & Mary Dodge
Year Estab:	1994

Britton Booksellers (719) 630 2122
2110 Lockhaven Drive Colorado Springs 80909

E-mail: ourbooks@interloc.com

Collection:	Specialty
# of Vols:	10,000
Specialties:	Technical; reference; textbooks.
Services:	Subject catalogs.
Credit Cards:	Yes
Owner:	John & Linda Britton
Year Estab:	1986

Carolyn's Cookbooks (303) 781-8482
PO Box 36372 Denver 80236 Fax: (303) 781-8482

Collection:	Specialty
# of Vols:	2,000
Specialties:	Cookbooks
Services:	Catalog
Credit Cards:	Yes
Owner:	Carolyn George
Comments:	Also displays at the Denver Book Mall.

Lucy Colville Books (719) 636-1209
24 Park Avenue Colorado Springs 80906

Collection:	General stock.
# of Vols:	10,000
Services:	Accept want lists.
Credit Cards:	No
Year Estab:	1989
Comments:	Collection may also be viewed by appointment.

Gold Hill Books (303) 651-2985
PO Box 1523 Longmont 80502

Collection:	Specialty new and used.
# of Vols:	60,000
Specialties:	Geology; mining.
Services:	Appraisals, search service, catalog.
Owner:	Mark A. Steen

Green Toad, Books   (303) 494-4023
3150 Endicott Drive Boulder 80303

Collection:	Specialty. Mostly hardcover.
# of Vols:	50,000
Specialties:	Science fiction; mystery; modern literary first editions; history; biography; Australia; South Pacific.
Services:	Appraisals, search service, accepts want lists, catalog.
Credit Cards:	Yes
Owner:	Robert Alvis
Year Estab:	1980

Patricia Grego   (303) 722-1636
636 South Logan Denver 80209

Collection:	General stock.
# of Vols:	10,000
Services:	Accepts want lists.
Credit Cards:	Yes
Year Estab:	1988

The Large Print Book   (800) 305-2743   (303) 721-7511
PO Box 5375 Englewood 80155   Fax: (303) 721-7512

Collection:	Specialty
# of Vols:	1,000
Specialties:	Large print books in all subject areas.
Services:	Catalog
Credit Cards:	Yes
Owner:	Marian Haugh
Year Estab:	1995
Comments:	Also displays at Denver Book Mall.

Major Allen's Books   (303) 451-6376
10643 Sperry Street Northglenn 80234   (888) 451-6376
                                                           E-mail: bobadco@aol.com

Collection:	Specialty new and used.
# of Vols:	2,000
Specialties:	Civil War.
Services:	Accepts want lists, search service, catalog.
Owner:	Judy & Bob Huddleston
Year Estab:	1996.

Bernard A. Margolis Books   (719) 495-4379
10640 Hungate Road Colorado Springs 80908

Collection:	Specialty
# of Vols:#	5,000
Specialties:	Western Americana; the Shakers.
Services:	Appraisals, search service, accepts want lists, occasional catalog.
Year Estab:	1971

Mining the West (303) 569-2818
PO Box 1035 Georgetown 80444

Collection:	Specialty
# of Vols:	3,000
Specialties:	Western Americana; mining.
Services:	Search service, accepts want lists, catalog.
Owner:	Jeanne Waligroski
Year Estab:	1990

Northwind Books - International (719) 495-0532
13275 Frank Road Black Forest 80908 Fax: (719) 495-0532

Collection:	Specialty
# of Vols:	3,000
Specialties:	Natural history; sports; Western Americana.
Services:	Appraisals, search service, accepts want lists.
Credit Cards:	No
Owner:	A.J. Peterson
Year Estab:	1988

Platte River Books (303) 973-2221
PO Box 620982 Littleton 80162 E-mail: platribk@interloc.com

Collection:	Specialty
# of Vols:	3,000
Specialties:	Western Americana; railroads; natural history.
Services:	Search service, accepts want lists.
Credit Cards:	Yes
Owner:	Susan & Charles Pattison
Year Estab:	1993

Ed Rogers Books (719) 539-4113
PO Box 455 Poncha Springs 81242 Fax: (719) 539-4542

Collection:	Specialty
# of Vols:	5,000
Specialties:	Geological sciences.
Services:	Appraisals, accepts want lists, catalog.
Year Estab:	1991

Jim Rooney-Books (719) 275-3915
1717 Colorado Avenue Canon City 81212 Fax: (719) 275-0497
E-mail: 71572.1107@compuserve.com

Collection:	Specialty
# of Vols:	6,000
Specialties:	Western Americana; guns; hunting.
Services:	Search service, accepts want lists, inventory list is available on disk.
Credit Cards:	No
Year Estab:	1971

Ken Vincent, Bookseller   (970) 835-3393
PO Box 32 Eckert 81418

Collection: Specialty
# of Vols: 2,500
Specialties: Western Americana.
Services: Appraisals, accepts want lists, mail order, book binding.
Credit Cards: No
Year Estab: 1978

Hey folks, we're closing the store now. Would you like to buy that book?

Idaho

Alphabetical Listing By Dealer

Alphabetical Listing By Location

Boise

Bargain Books   **Open Shop**
6864 Glenwood Street   83703   (208) 853-9600

Collection: General stock of mostly used paperback and hardcover.
# of Vols: 25,000 (used)
Hours: Mon-Sat 10-6. Sun 1-5.
Travel: Near Hawks Stadium at intersection of State and Glenwood.
Credit Cards: Yes
Year Estab: 1988
Comments: Stock is approximately 60% paperback.

Boise Books & Search   **Open Shop**
4210 Emerald Street   (208) 345-8670
Mailing address: PO Box 6638 Boise 83707

Collection: General stock.
# of Vols: 35,000
Specialties: Western Americana; hunting; fishing; photography; literature.
Hours: Tue-Sat 9:30-6.
Services: Appraisals, search service, accepts want lists, catalog.
Travel: Vista St exit off I-84. Proceed north on Vista, west on Overland, north
                    on Roosevelt and west on Emerald. Shop is just ahead.
Credit Cards: Yes
Owner: Chuck Mary
Year Estab: 1986

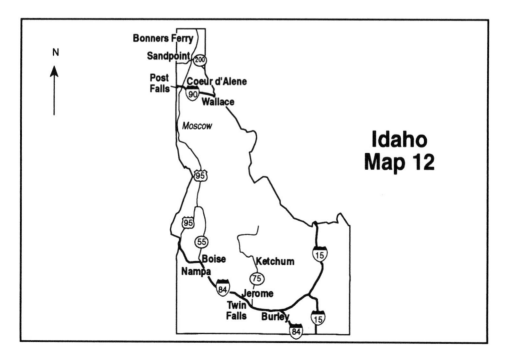

Hyde Park Book Store
1507 North 13th Street   83702

Open Shop
(208) 338-1152

Collection:	General stock of hardcover and paperback.
# of Vols:	100,000
Hours:	Mon-Sat 9:30-6. Other times by appointment.
Services:	Appraisals, search service, accepts want lists.
Travel:	Proceed on 13th St towards mountains.
Credit Cards:	Yes
Owner:	Russell & Rita Barnes
Year Estab:	1982
Comments:	Stock is approximately 75% hardcover.

New Mythology Comics & Science Fiction
1725 Broadway Avenue   83706

Open Shop
(208) 344-6744

Collection:	Specialty. Mostly paperback.
# of Vols:	100+
Specialties:	Science fiction.
Hours:	Mon-Sat, except closed Tue, 11-6. Sun 12-6.

Parnassus Books
218 North 9th Street
Mailing address: PO Box 1115 Boise 83701

Open Shop
(208) 344-7560

Collection:	General stock.
# of Vols:	30,000-40,000
Specialties:	Modern fiction; literary criticism; history; Western Americana.
Hours:	Mon-Fri 11-5:30. Sat 11-5.
Services:	Appraisals, search service, accepts want lists, mail order.
Travel:	Vista exit off I-80. Proceed north on Vista to downtown where Vista becomes Capitol Blvd. Continue on Capitol to Bannock. Left on Bannock, then left on North 9th.
Credit Cards:	Yes
Owner:	Judith Gardner
Year Estab:	1983

Rainbow Books
1310 West State Street   83702

Open Shop
(208) 336-2230

Collection:	General stock of mostly paperback.
# of Vols:	25,000
Hours:	Mon-Sat 10:30-5:30.

James R. Spencer Books
PO Box 9017   83707

By Appointment
Fax: (208) 322-7205   (208) 322-7120
Orders only: (800) 788-8354
E-mail: 70662.3504@compuserve.com

Collection:	General stock.
# of Vols:	2,000

Specialties:	Mormons; occult; religion.
Services:	Search service, catalog, accepts want lists.
Credit Cards:	Yes
Year Estab:	1994

Phil White Books & Collectibles   **Antique Mall**
At Collectors Choice Too   Mall: (208) 336-3170
5284 Franklin Road
Mailing address: 14099 Lakeshore Drive Nampa 83686

Collection:	Specialty books and ephemera.
# of Vols:	3,000
Specialties:	Hunting; fishing; Western Americana; western fiction.
Hours:	Mon-Sat 10-6. Sun 12-6.
Travel:	Exit 52 off I-84. Proceed north on Orchard St for two miles to Franklin. Shop is in Franklin Shopping Center.
Credit Cards:	Yes
Year Estab:	1985

Bonners Ferry

Bonners Books   **Open Shop**
7195 Main Street   (208) 267-2622
Mailing address: PO Box 1141 Bonners Ferry 83805

Collection:	General stock of mostly used hardcover and paperback.
# of Vols:	11,000 (used)
Hours:	Mon-Thu 9-5. Fri 9-5:30. Sat 10-5.
Credit Cards:	Yes
Owner:	John & Shaela O'Connor
Year Estab:	1986
Comments:	Used stock is evenly divided between hardcover and paperback.

Burley

Lost But Found Books   **Open Shop**
1332 Albion Avenue 83318   (208) 678-1368

Collection:	General stock of paperback and hardcover.
# of Vols:	7,500
Hours:	Mon-Sat 7:30-6, except Fri till 10.
Travel:	Exit 208 off I-84. South on Overland, left on Main, right on Albion.
Owner:	Dave Long
Year Estab:	1996
Comments:	Stock is approximately 65% paperback.

Coeur d'Alene

The Bookery   **Open Shop**
211½ Sherman Avenue 83814   (208) 765-3028

Collection:	General stock of mostly hardcover.

# of Vols:	37,000
Hours:	Mon-Sat 11-5. Sun 12-4.
Services:	Appraisals, search service, accepts want lists.
Travel:	Downtown, across from the plaza.
Credit Cards:	Yes
Owner:	Mike Winderman
Year Estab:	1992

Browsers Book Store   **Open Shop**
2145 North Government Way, #2   83814   (208) 667-3964
                                              E-mail: jrhiller@interloc.com

Collection:	General stock of hardcover and paperback.
# of Vols:	20,000
Hours:	Mon-Sat 12-5.
Services:	Search service, accepts want lists.
Travel:	Hwy 95 exit off I-90. Go north on Hwy 95 for one block to Apple Way, then east on Apple and south on Government Way. Shop is just ahead.
Owner:	John R. Hiller
Year Estab:	1986
Comments:	Stock is approximately 60% hardcover.

George Nolan Books   **Open Shop**
118 North 2nd Street   83814   (208) 667-2222

Collection:	General stock.
# of Vols:	17,000
Hours:	Mon-Sat 10:30-5.
Travel:	Any exit off I-90. Proceed downtown. Shop is between Lakeside & Sherman.
Credit Cards:	Yes
Year Estab:	1984

Jerome

Rose Antique Mall   **Antique Mall**
130 East Main   (208) 324-2918

Hours:	Tue-Sat 10-5.

Frontier Antiques   **Antique Mall**
149 West Main   (208) 324-1127

Hours:	Tue-Sat 10-5. Mon by chance.

Ketchum

Iconoclast Books   **Open Shop**
131 4th Street West   (208) 726-1564
Mailing address: PO Box 806 Ketchum 83340   E-mail: inconocla@interloc.com

Collection:	General stock of hardcover and paperback.
# of Vols:	25,000

Specialties:	Idaho; literature; movies.
Hours:	Mon-Sat 10-6. Sun 11-4.
Services:	Search service.
Travel:	Two blocks off Main St.
Credit Cards:	Yes
Owner:	Gary Hunt
Year Estab:	1993
Comments:	Stock is evenly divided between hardcover and paperback.

Lewiston

...and BOOKS, too!   **Open Shop**
1037 21st Street 83501   (208) 746-7120

| *Collection:* | General stock of mostly paperback. |
| *Hours:* | Mon-Fri 10-6. Sat 10-5. |

Meridian

Pages Plus   **Open Shop**
52 East State Avenue 83642   (208) 888-7557

Collection:	General stock of mostly paperback.
# of Vols:	10,000
Hours:	Mon-Fri 9-6.

Moscow

Meyer & Meyer Bookseller   **By Appointment**
307 South Main Street, Ste 4 83843   Fax: (208) 882-3353   (208) 882-3353
E-mail: meyerbks@interloc.com

Collection:	General stock of mostly hardcover.
# of Vols:	5,000
Services:	Appraisals, search service, accepts want lists, mail order.
Credit Cards:	No
Owner:	David Meyer
Year Estab:	1991

Twice Sold Tales   **Open Shop**
220 West Third 83843   Fax: (208) 882-8781   (208) 882-8781
E-mail: ewegner@pullman.com

Collection:	General stock of mostly paperback.
# of Vols:	50,000
Hours:	Mon-Sat 11-6.

Mountain Home

John Hiler - Fine Books   **By Appointment**
PO Box 688 83647   Fax: (208) 587-5416   (208) 587-9871

| *Collection:* | Specialty books and ephemera. |

# of Vols:	2,000
Specialties:	Fly fishing; Western Americana; Idaho; William Caxton.
Services:	Appraisals, search service, accepts want lists, mail order.
Credit Cards:	Yes
Year Estab:	1970

Nampa

Book Exchange   **Open Shop**
205 15th Avenue South   83651   (208) 465-0327

Collection:	General stock of mostly paperback.
# of Vols:	100,000
Hours:	Mon-Sat 10-6. Sun 1-5.

Twice Sold Tales   **Open Shop**
1215 1st Street South   83651   (208) 467-3329

Collection:	General stock of hardcover and paperback and ephemera.
# of Vols:	100,000
Specialties:	Children's; magazines.
Hours:	Mon-Sat 10-5:30.
Services:	Accepts want lists, mail order.
Credit Cards:	Yes
Owner:	Gretchen Gardner
Year Estab:	1990
Comments:	Stock is approximately 50% hardcover.

The Yesteryear Shoppe   **Open Shop**
1211 First Street South   (208) 467-3581
Mailing address: PO Box 797 Nampa 83653

Collection:	General stock of mostly hardcover and ephemera.
# of Vols:	150,000
Specialties:	Western Americana; literature; children's; hunting; fishing; illustrated; travel; exploration.
Hours:	Mon-Sat 11-5:30.
Services:	Appraisals, search service, catalog, accepts want lists.
Travel:	In downtown, approximately one mile south of I-84.
Credit Cards:	Yes
Owner:	David C. & Stephan Gonzales
Year Estab:	1974

Orofino

Page-Turner Books   **Open Shop**
804 Riverside Avenue   (208) 476-3801
Mailing address: PO Box 133   Orofino 83544

Collection:	General stock of mostly paperback.
# of Vols:	9,000
Hours:	Mon-Sat 9:30-5:30.

Pocatello

Bookmark   **Open Shop**
1128 North Main Street   83204   (208) 232-0550

Collection:	General stock of mostly paperback.
# of Vols:	5,000 (hardcover)
Hours:	Mon-Sat 10-6.

Post Falls

Saint Vincent Books & More   **Open Shop**
205 West Seltice Way   83854   (208) 773-6836

Collection:	General stock of paperback and hardcover.
# of Vols:	3,000+
Hours:	Mon-Sat 9-5.
Travel:	Spokane St exit off I-90.
Comments:	Not-for-profit store. All books are donated.

Sandpoint

The Book Gallery   **Open Shop**
402 Poplar Street   83864   (208) 263-0178
                                                                   Fax: (208) 263-0178

Collection:	General stock of hardcover and paperback.
# of Vols:	30,000
Specialties:	Regional authors and history; cookbooks; how-to; Native Americans; metaphysics; crafts; sports (outdoors).
Hours:	Mon-Sat 10-6. Sun 11-4.
Services:	Search service, accepts want lists.
Travel:	Located in 5th St Mall, one half block east of Hwy 95 (5th St).
Credit Cards:	Yes
Owner:	Joel Mack & Barbara Forman
Year Estab:	1994
Comments:	Stock is approximately 50% hardcover.

Book Trader II   **Open Shop**
216 North 1st Avenue   83864   (208) 263-1041

Collection:	General stock of mostly used paperback used and new.
Hours:	Mon-Sat 9:30-5:30.

Books At Foster's Crossing   **Open Shop**
504 Oak Street   83864   (208) 263-7620

Collection:	General stock of hardcover and paperback.
# of Vols:	25,000
Hours:	Mon-Sat 9:30-5:30. Sun 11-4.
Owner:	Bill & Jan Temple

Year Estab: 1985
Comments: Stock is evenly divided between hardcover and paperback.

Twin Falls

Book Territory   **By Appointment**
PO Box 1718   83303   (208) 733-1962

Collection: General stock.
# of Vols: 10,000
Specialties: Idaho; Western Americana; Caxton Press.
Services: Accepts want lists, mail order.
Credit Cards: No
Owner: Art Selin
Year Estab: 1991
Comments: Also displays at Frontier Antiques in Jerome. See above.

Snow's Antiques   **Antique Mall**
136 Main Avenue North   (208) 736-7292

Hours: Mon-Sat 10-5.

Wallace

RC's Book Barter   **Open Shop**
520 Cedar Street   83873   (208) 556-2821

Collection: General stock of mostly used paperback and hardcover.
# of Vols: 30,000
Hours: Mem Day-Labor Day: Daily 10-5. Remainder of year: Mon-Sat 10-5.
Services: Accepts want lists, mail order.
Travel: Exit 61 off I-90. Follow "Historical Route" to town. Left on Cedar.
                   Shop is just ahead on right.
Credit Cards: Yes
Owner: Ruth Carole Hayman
Year Estab: 1978
Comments: Stock is evenly divided between hardcover and paperback.

Mail Order Dealers

Bee's Book Been   (208) 733-3819
1535 Princeton   Twin Falls   83301

Collection: General stock.
# of Vols: 8,000
Services: Search service, accepts want lists.
Credit Cards: No
Owner: Bee Stewart
Year Estab: 1991
Comments: Also displays at antique malls in Jerome and Twin Falls. See above.

Kansas

Alphabetical Listing By Dealer

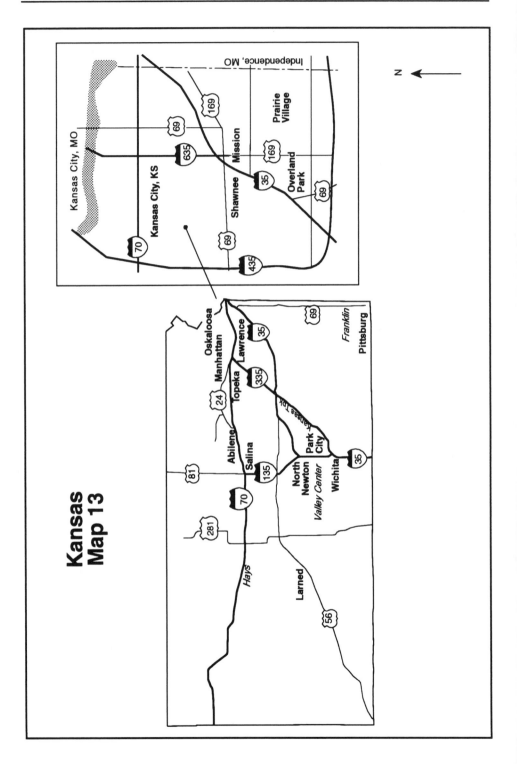

Kansas
Map 13

Alphabetical Listing By Location

Abilene

Book Rack   **Open Shop**
306 North Buckeye Avenue   67410   (913) 263-1707

Collection:	General stock of paperback and hardcover.
# of Vols:	10,000-15,000
Hours:	Tue-Sat 10-5.
Travel:	Abilene exit off I-70. Proceed south on North Buckeye (Hwy 15). Shop is on west side of street, just before second light.
Credit Cards:	No
Year Estab:	1983
Comments:	Stock is approximately 75% paperback.

Chanute

Barb's Book Exchange   **Open Shop**
116 East Main Street   66720   (316) 431-2827

Collection:	General stock of mostly paperback.
Hours:	Mon-Sat 10-6.

Colby

Twice Sold Tales   **Open Shop**
140 East 4th Street   67701   (913) 462-8387

Collection:	General stock of mostly paperback.
Hours:	Mon-Fri 10-5:30. Sat 10-4.

Franklin

Rust & Dust Antiques & Books   **By Appointment**
2nd and Grapevine   (316) 347-4390
Mailing address: PO Box 5304 Franklin 66735   Fax: (316) 347-4890

Collection:	General stock.
# of Vols:	5,000
Specialties:	Harold Bell Wright; children's series.
Services:	Search service, accepts want lists, mail order.
Credit Cards:	No
Owner:	Carol Doss
Year Estab:	1983

Garden City

Paperback Book Nook   **Open Shop**
1808½ East Kansas Avenue   67846   (316) 275-2210

Collection:	General stock of mostly paperback.
Hours:	Mon-Sat 10-5:30.

Hays

J.A.S. Books   **By Appointment**
PO Box 61 67601   (913) 628-3924
                                          E-mail: jstegman@dailynews.net

Collection:	General stock of hardcover and paperback.
Services:	Search service, catalog.
Credit Cards:	No
Owner:	Judy Stegman
Year Estab:	1996
Comments:	Stock is approximately 80% hardcover.

Hutchinson

Steve's Paperbacks   **Open Shop**
14 East 2nd Avenue   67501   (316) 662-6656

Collection:	General stock of mostly paperback.
Hours:	Mon-Sat 10-5:30.

Junction City

Book & Comic Exchange   **Open Shop**
1016 North Washington Street   66441   (913) 238-1100

Collection:	General stock of mostly paperback.
# of Vols:	30,000
Hours:	Mon-Fri 10:30-7. Sat 10:30-6. Sun 1-5.

Larned

Noah's Ark New & Old Books   **Open Shop**
423 Broadway Street 67550   (316) 285-2801

Collection:	General stock of mostly hardcover used and new.
# of Vols:	3,000+ (used)
Specialties:	Religion (Christianity).
Hours:	Mon-Sat 10-5:30.
Travel:	On Hwy 56.
Credit Cards:	No
Owner:	Charles Phemister
Year Estab:	1978
Comments:	Stock is approximately 65% used, most of which is hardcover.

Lawrence

The Chapman   **Open Shop**
731 New Hampshire   66044   (913) 841-0550

Collection:	General stock.
# of Vols:	2,000

Hours:	Tue-Sat 12-6.
Travel:	Between 7th & 8th Streets.
Credit Cards:	Yes
Owner:	C.M. Chapman
Comments:	A small shop that seems to sell "stuff" that mom or grandma used to have around the house (clothing, bric a brac, etc.) and that also carries some older used books, not necessarily collectibles, but then one can never tell what treasure may have arrived shortly after our departure.

Dean's Books   **Open Shop**
1115 Massachusetts Street   66044   (913) 842-0216

Collection:	General stock of mostly paperback.
# of Vols:	10,000
Hours:	Mon-Fri 10-6. Sat 10-5.

Dusty Bookshelf   **Open Shop**
708 Massachusetts Avenue   66044   (913) 749-4643

Collection:	General stock of hardcover and paperback.
# of Vols:	35,000
Hours:	Mon-Sat 10-8. Sun 1-5.
Travel:	See J. Hood, Booksellers below.
Owner:	Diane Meredith
Year Estab:	1996
Comments:	Not yet open at the time of our visit to Lawrence, we were advised by the owner that this new shop would be similar to its sister shop in Manhattan (see below). The owner anticipates that the stock here will be evenly divided between hardcover and paperback.

J. Hood, Booksellers   **Open Shop**
1401 Massachusetts   66044   Fax: (913) 594-3386   (913) 841-4644
                                                                     E-mail: jhoodbks@interloc.com

Collection:	General stock of mostly hardcover.
# of Vols:	65,000
Specialties:	Scholarly; medieval studies; philosophy; literary criticism; psychology; art history.
Hours:	Mon-Sat 11-5. Sun 1-5.
Services:	Mail order.
Travel:	East Lawrence exit off I-70. Proceed south towards Lawrence. After crossing bridge, turn left on 6th and proceed one block, then right on Massachusetts. Continue on Massachusetts to 14th St.
Credit Cards:	Yes
Year Estab:	1974
Comments:	If your interests are in the more scholarly topics, you should find this shop a bonanza. It's organization, the quality of its books (both in terms of condition and unusual titles) and the scope of its collection should make this a "must" stop. Don't look for bargains in terms of prices, but then again, you get what you pay for.

Lonesome Prairie Books   **Antique Mall**
At Quantrill's Antique Mall   Mall: (913) 842-6616
811 New Hampshire Street   Home: (816) 822-9588
Mailing address: 625 East 63rd Terrace Kansas City, MO 64110

Collection:	General stock.
# of Vols:	2,500
Hours:	Daily 10-5:30.
Travel:	Exit 204 (East Lawrence) off I-70. Follow signs to downtown outlet mall. At mall, continue straight for two blocks.
.Owner:	Richard Park & Greg Huff
Year Estab:	1995
Comments:	At the time of our visit three used book dealers were displaying (in close proximity to each other) in this mall; two of the dealers had open shops elsewhere and one (Lonesome Prairie Books) displayed here exclusively. As the mall is just a short distance from three other dealers in town, making a stop here is economically feasible.

Vagabound Bookman   **Open Shop**
1113 Massachusetts 66044   (913) 842-2665
                                                             (800) 318-2665

Collection:	General stock.
# of Vols:	12,000
Specialties:	Harold Bell Wright; Gene Stratton Porter; Will James; Gladys Taber.
Hours:	Mon-Sat 10-6. Sun 1-5.
Services:	Appraisals, accepts want lists, mail order.
Travel:	See J. Hood, Booksellers above.
Owner:	Howard Hartog
Year Estab:	1985
Comments:	If you're into the popular culture of days gone by, or the world of nostalgia, you could find just what you're looking for here as the shop has a strong collection of older volumes in these subject areas. The books we saw were in mixed condition and prices varied depending on what one might view as rarity and/or desirability.

Leavenworth

Book Barn   **Open Shop**
410 Delaware Street 66048   (913) 682-6518

Collection:	General stock mostly paperback.
# of Vols:	40,000
Hours:	Mon-Sat 10-5:30, except Thu till 8.

Book Exchange   **Open Shop**
2920F South 4th Street 66048   (913) 682-7721

Collection:	General stock of mostly paperback.
# of Vols:	35,000
Hours:	Mon-Sat 10-8. Sun 12-5.

Services:	Search service, accepts want lists.
Travel:	Highway 7 becomes 4th St in Leavenworth.
Credit Cards:	No
Year Estab:	1987
Comments:	A mostly paperback shop with a couple of hundred hardcover books scattered throughout. Clean, neat, but with a limited selection.

Manhattan

Dusty Bookshelf   **Open Shop**
700 North Manhattan Avenue   66502   (913) 539-2839

Collection:	General stock of paperback and hardcover.
# of Vols:	60,000
Hours:	Mon-Fri 10-8. Sat 10-6. Sun 1-5.
Travel:	Bluemont Ave exit off Hwy 24. Proceed west on Bluemont, then south on Manhattan.
Owner:	Diane Meredith
Comments:	Quite close to the Kansas State University campus with many of its books reflecting college tastes. The stock of hardcover books (most in good condition and with dust jackets), while attractive, is far outnumbered by paperbacks. The shop is spacious and easy to browse and should not require too long a visit. Prices were most reasonable.

Mission

Billie Miller Books, Limited   **Open Shop**
6104 Johnson Drive   66202   (913) 362-1779
                                                         E-mail: billiebk@interloc.com

Collection:	General stock of hardcover and paperback.
# of Vols:	36,000
Specialties:	Rivers; steamboating; folklore; storytelling.
Hours:	Mon-Sat 10-9. Sun 1-6.
Services:	Search service.
Travel:	Southbound on I-35: Lamar Ave exit. Proceed south on Lamar, then east on Johnson Dr for 1½ blocks. Northbound on I-35: Johnson Dr exit. Proceed east on Johnson for about three miles.
Credit Cards:	Yes
Owner:	Richard & Susan Wilcox
Year Estab:	1992
Comments:	A quality bookstore. The books on display represented all subject areas, with many quality and unusual titles available at quite reasonable prices. The front part of the shop contains a charming room dedicated to the shop's namesake, a book lover who inspired her nephew's (the shop's current owner) current vocation. We would be surprised if you did not spot several titles of interest here.

Books Plus   **Open Shop**
6516 Martway   66202   (913) 384-2787

Collection:	General stock of new and used.
Hours:	Mon-Sat 10-6.
Comments:	Used stock (approximately 25% of total stock) is primarily paperback.

North Newton

Book ReViews   **Open Shop**
2505 Main   67117   (316) 283-3442

Collection:	General stock of hardcover and paperback.
# of Vols:	3,000+
Hours:	Mon-Fri 9-5, except Thu till 7. Sat 9-1.
Services:	Accepts want lists, mail order.
Travel:	Bethel College exit off I-35. Proceed south on Hwy 15 (which becomes Main St) to North Newton. Shop is at corner of 24th St.
Owner:	Ruth Unrau
Year Estab:	1989
Comments:	Stock is approximately 65% hardcover.

Oskaloosa

The Book Barn   **Open Shop**

Collection:	General stock of ex library books.
Hours:	Saturdays
Comments:	A mystery shop for our readers to "check out." We've been assured (by City Hall) that a book "shop" does operate in Oskaloosa on Saturdays. Unfortunately, the "shop" has no phone and no one seems quite sure of the owner's name. So, if you're in the area and feel adventuresome, you might want to check this location out and let us know what you find.

Overland Park

A. Friendly's Books   **Open Shop**
7947 Santa Fe Drive   66204   913-599-6977

Collection:	General stock of mostly hardcover.
# of Vols:	40,000+
Specialties:	Modern first editions.
Hours:	Mon-Fri 10-7. Sat 10-5. Call for Sun hours.
Services:	Search service, mail order, accepts want lists.
Travel:	Metcalf Ave exit off I-35. Proceed south on Metcalf to 80th St, then west on 80th for four blocks. Shop is at intersection of 80th and Santa Fe.
Credit Cards:	Yes
Owner:	Robert & Diane Meyers
Year Estab:	1994
Comments:	We visited this establishment shortly before its move to the above address and saw a neat, well organized shop with carefully selected volumes. For

the most part, hardcover and paperback volumes were shelved together. A majority of the hardcover items sported dust jackets and were priced in a manner reflective of their good condition. More collectible items (including some signed volumes and first editions) were shelved behind glass. With a few exceptions, we didn't spot too many older volumes.

The Book Nook for Cooks, Ltd.   **Open Shop**
6917 West 76th Street, Ste 104   66204   (913) 385-1996

Collection:	Specialty new and used.
Specialties:	Cookbooks; nutrition; health books.
Hours:	Call for hours.
Travel:	Metcalf exit off I-435. Proceed north on Metcalf to 76th St, then east on 76th St. Shop is in an office building.
Owner:	Maxene Bogmol
Year Estab:	1995

The Cook's Books   **Open Shop**
9071 Metcalf   66212   (913) 383-0333
     Fax: (913) 383-0144

Collection:	Specialty new and used.
Specialties:	Cookbooks
Hours:	Mon-Sat 10-6.
Services:	Accepts want lists, mail order.
Travel:	I-70 to I-435 south to Metcalf exit.
Credit Cards:	Yes
Owner:	Juanita Copeland
Year Estab:	1993
Comments:	Stock is evenly divided between new and used.

Read It Again Books   **Open Shop**
8832 West 95th Street   66212   (913) 648-5065

Collection:	General stock of paperback and hardcover.
# of Vols:	40,000
Hours:	Mon-Fri 10-8. Sat 9-6. Sun 1-5.
Travel:	Hwy 69 exit off I-435. Proceed north on Hwy 69, then 95th St exit off Hwy 69, Proceed east on 95th St for about one mile. Shop is at northwest corner of 95th St and Antioch in a shopping center.
Credit Cards:	Yes
Owner:	Kevin Powell & Wayne Vanderpol
Year Estab:	1994
Comments:	Stock is approximately 70% paperback.

Read It Again Books   **Open Shop**
7316 West 80th Street   66212   (913) 385-2424

Collection:	General stock of paperback and hardcover.
# of Vols:	100,000

Hours:	Mon-Fri 9-7. Sat 9-6. Sun 1-5.
Travel:	Metcalf Ave exit off I-435. Proceed north on Metcalf to 80th St, then left on 80th for three blocks.
Credit Cards:	Yes
Owner:	Kevin Powell & Wayne Vanderpol
Year Estab:	1995
Comments:	Stock is approximately 70% paperback.

Park City

Park City Antique Mall   **Antique Mall**
6227 North Broadway   67219   (316) 744-2025

Hours:	Mon-Sat 9:30-7. Sun 1-6.
Travel:	61st St exit off I-135. Proceed west on 61st to Broadway.

Pittsburg

Mostly Books   **Open Shop**
111 East 6th   66762   Fax: (316) 231-0999   (316) 231-0999
                                         E-mail: mostlybk@pitton.com

Collection:	General stock and ephemera.
# of Vols:	50,000
Specialties:	Western Americana; Kansas; literature.
Hours:	Mon-Sat 9-6. Sun 3-7. Other times by appointment.
Travel:	From Hwy 69, take Bus Hwy 69 to downtown, then turn east on 6th.
Credit Cards:	Yes
Owner:	Roger & Janet O'Connor
Year Estab:	1976
Comments:	If you're a traveling book person, try to visit this shop before the scouts descend on it. And when you arrive, don't satisfy yourself by looking only at the books in the main display area; in addition to a second room, you might ask if you can browse the "books in the vault," a large former fur vault. We were most impressed by both the quality and quantity of the fine titles we saw here, particularly in the specialties cited above. We hesitate to mention certain unusual sets and/or single volumes that, despite our wide travels, we have not seen elsewhere, for fear that when our gentle reader visits, those treasures might be gone.

Prairie Village

Mission Road Antique Mall   **Antique Mall**
4101 West 83rd Street   66208   (913) 341-7577

Hours:	Mon-Sat 10-7. Sun 12-6.
Travel:	Roe Blvd exit off I-435. Proceed north on Roe, then east on 83rd. From I-35 southbound: Mission Rd exit. Proceed south on Mission to 83rd.

Salina

Budget Book Store   **Open Shop**
106 South Santa Fe Avenue   67401   (913) 823-6282
                                                  E-mail: bksma@aol.com

Collection:	General stock of paperback and hardcover.
Hours:	Mon-Sat 8:30-5.
Services:	Accepts want lists.
Travel:	9th St exit off I-70. Proceed south on 9th St for 2½ miles, then east on Iron St and south on Santa Fe. Shop is just ahead on west side of street.
Credit Cards:	Yes
Owner:	Alfred K. Mattson
Year Estab:	1987
Comments:	Located in the downtown business district, this establishment attempts to maintain a balance between hardcover and paperback titles with the balance weighted in favor of the latter. One bookcase containing older hardcover items (not in the best condition) was labeled "Rare Items" and elsewhere paperbacks and hardcover volumes were intershelved with most of the hardcover items of a more recent variety. Not a place that you're likely to find a rare first edition but one that no doubt meets the reading needs of the community it serves.

Pat's Book Nook-Old and New   **Open Shop**
135 South 4th   67401   (913) 823-6577

Collection:	General stock of paperback and hardcover.
# of Vols:	25,000-30,000
Hours:	Tue-Sat 9-5.
Travel:	9th St exit off I-70. Proceed south on 9th to Iron, then east on Iron to 4th and south on 4th. Shop is 1/2 block ahead.
Credit Cards:	No
Owner:	Pat R. Chalmers
Year Estab:	1977
Comments:	While this shop does carry a couple hundred hardcover titles in its inventory, the vast majority of the books we saw during our visit were of the paperback variety. No problem if this is your cup of tea.

Shawnee Mission

All Booked Up   **By Appointment**
5123 Rainbow Boulevard   66205   (913) 362-4918

Collection:	General stock.
# of Vols:	2,000+
Specialties:	Americana
Services:	Accepts want lists, mail order.
Owner:	Bettie & Ted Swiontek
Comments:	Also displays at Mission Road Antique Mall in Prairie Village. See above.

Topeka

Antique Plaza   **Antique Mall**
2935 SW Topeka Boulevard   (913) 267-7411

Hours: Mon-Sat 10-5:30. Sun 12-5.
Travel: Topeka Blvd exit off I-470. Proceed north on Topeka.

Dean's Books   **Open Shop**
1426 South Kansas Avenue   66612   (913) 357-4708

Collection: General stock of paperback and hardcover.
# of Vols: 50,000
Specialties: Magazines
Hours: Mon-Fri 10-5:30. Sat 10-5.
Travel: 10th St exit off I-70. Proceed west on 10th St then south on Kansas.
Credit Cards: No
Owner: Tom Allen
Year Estab: 1973
Comments: Stock is approximately 80% paperback.

Friend's Booktique   **Open Shop**
1601 SW 10th Avenue, Ste. 102   66604   (913) 231-0595

Collection: General stock of paperback and hardcover.
Hours: Mon-Fri 12-4. Sat 10-12.
Travel: At 10th and Washburn, across from the public library.
Comments: Operated by the Friends of the Public Library.

The Kansan Relics & Old Books   **Open Shop**
3308 West 6th   66606   (913) 233-8232

Collection: General stock.
# of Vols: 2,000-3,000
Specialties: Kansas
Hours: Mon-Sat 8-5.
Services: Appraisals, accepts want lists.
Travel: Gage exit off I-470. Proceed south on Gage, then east on 6th.
Credit Cards: No
Owner: Joe Zimmer
Year Estab: 1985
Comments: Shop also sells antiques.

Rogers & Rogers Books & More   **Open Shop**
2705 NW Topeka Boulevard   66617   (913) 232-2383
                                                        E-mail: kansanns@interloc.com

Collection: General stock of paperback and hardcover.
# of Vols: 80,000
Hours: Mon-Sat 10-7.

Services:	Search service, accepts want lists.
Travel:	North Topeka Blvd exit off Hwy 24. Proceed north on Topeka for 1½ blocks. Shop is on west side of street in an old fire station.
Credit Cards:	No
Owner:	Ann Martin
Year Estab:	1995
Comments:	Stock is approximately 60% paperback. Approximately 50% of the stock is on display at the shop.

Lloyd Zimmer   **By Appointment**
3001 Munson   66604   (913) 235-9689

Collection:	General stock.
# of Vols:	6,000
Specialties:	Kansas; Americana.
Services:	Appraisals, lists, mail order.
Year Estab:	1992
Comments:	Also displays at Antique Plaza in Topeka. See above.

Valley Center

Chuck Potter Books   **By Appointment**
6 High Point Road   67147   (316) 755-0638

Collection:	General stock.
# of Vols:	1,500-2,000
Credit Cards:	No
Year Estab:	1994
Comments:	Also displays at Park City Antique Mall in Park City. See above.

Wichita

Al's Old & New Book Store   **Open Shop**
1710 West Douglas Avenue   67203   (316) 264-8763

Collection:	General stock of mostly hardcover.
# of Vols:	30,000-40,000
Specialties:	Children's; cookbooks.
Hours:	Mon-Sat 10-5.
Travel:	Seneca exit off Hwy 54. Proceed north on Seneca then west on Douglas.
Owner:	Helen Woodard
Year Estab:	1958
Comments:	If you like old books, both fiction and non fiction, in reasonably good condition, you'll enjoy visiting this shop. The collection is large, well organized and we hope (for the sake of its owner) that a change of landlord does not necessitate a move which would be no small task considering the number of volumes involved. While there are some paperbacks here, the hardcover collection could well conceal some rare or difficult to find titles. Lots of children's books, including an ample selection of children's series titles.

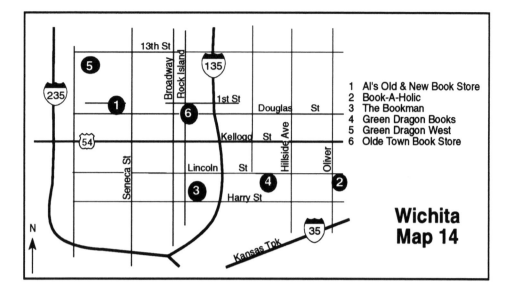

1 Al's Old & New Book Store
2 Book-A-Holic
3 The Bookman
4 Green Dragon Books
5 Green Dragon West
6 Olde Town Book Store

**Wichita
Map 14**

Book Mark
2073 North West Street   67203

Open Shop
(316) 943-9323

Collection: General stock of mostly paperback.
# of Vols: 16,000
Hours: Mon-Fri 10-6. Sat 10-4.

Book-A-Holic
924 South Oliver   67218

Open Shop
(316) 684-2600

Collection: General stock of paperback and hardcover.
# of Vols: 75,000
Hours: Mon-Fri 10-7. Sat 10-6. Sun 12-5.
Services: Search service, accepts want lists, mail order.
Travel: Kellogg exit off I-35. Proceed west on Kellogg, then left on Oliver.
                 Shop is located in the Parklane Shopping Center.
Credit Cards: Yes
Year Estab: 1992
Comments: While the shop is heavily weighted towards paperback titles, one can
                 find a smattering of hardcover fiction (mainly on the top shelves) and a
                 larger number of non fiction hardcover volumes in the rear in the shop.
                 Prices appear on stick on labels affixed to the front cover of each book.

The Bookman
322 East Harry   67211

Open Shop
(316) 267-7444

Collection: General stock of paperback and hardcover.
# of Vols: 50,000
Hours: Mon-Sat 8:30-5:30, except till 5 on Sat.
Travel: Harry exit off I-35. Proceed west on Harry. Shop is just before Broadway.
Credit Cards: No

Owner:	Richard Hill
Year Estab:	1979
Comments:	On the plus side, this shop opens early. While the majority of the books we saw were paperback, there were a substantial number of hardcover volumes, mostly in mixed condition and a few in poor condition. Lots of older titles, some classics, some obscure. One can even purchase some "girlie magazines" here. 'Nuff said.

Eighth Day Books   **Open Shop**
3700 East Douglas Avenue, #40   67208   (316) 683-9446

Collection:	General stock of mostly paperback.
# of Vols:	30,000
Hours:	Mon-Sat 10-6.

Green Dragon Books   **Open Shop**
2730 Boulevard Plaza   67211   (316) 681-0746

Collection:	General stock of hardcover and paperback.
# of Vols:	45,000
Specialties:	Art; history; aviation; Western Americana.
Hours:	Mon-Fri 10-5:30. Sat 10-5.
Travel:	Lincoln exit off I-35. Proceed east three blocks, then right on Boulevard Plaza. (Look for shopping center sign.) Kellogg exit off I-35. Proceed west on Kellogg to Hillside, then south on Hillside and west on Lincoln to the Boulevard Shopping Center.
Credit Cards:	Yes
Owner:	Charles R. & Larue Basom
Year Estab:	1975
Comments:	Another of those shops that every true book person wishes was in his or her neighborhood so they could browse on a more frequent basis. The collection here is large enough to satisfy most tastes yet the layout of the shop is such that the book lover can browse at an easy pace. While the shop does offer some paperbacks, the quality and quantity of the hardcover books in most categories and the fair prices make this a shop a pleasure to visit. At the time of our visit, the owner had just opened up a second shop in Wichita, the Green Dragon West (see below).

Green Dragon West   **Open Shop**
2411 West 13th Street   67203   (316) 943-1711

Collection:	General stock.
# of Vols:	10,000-12,500
Specialties:	Books on books; art; transportation; illustrated; limited editions.
Hours:	Tue-Sat 10-5:30.
Services:	Search service, mail order.
Travel:	13th Street exit off I-135. Proceed west on 13th St. Shop is in Indian Hills Shopping Center between Meridian and West.
Credit Cards:	Yes
Owner:	Charles R. & Larue Basom

Year Estab: 1996
Comments: Owned by the same proprietors of Green Dragon Books, this shop offers many of the same pluses, minus the paperback selection, and with a stronger emphasis on non fiction. The stock is a bit smaller in size but matching the quality of its sister store.

Olde Towne Book Store
835 East 1st Street 67202

Open Shop
(316) 265-0077

Collection: General stock of paperback and hardcover.
# of Vols: 25,000
Hours: Mon-Thu & Sat 10-6. Fri 10-8. Sun 1-5.
Travel: Kellogg exit off I-35. Proceed west on Kellogg then right Washington and left on 1st St.
Credit Cards: No
Owner: Donna Greenman
Year Estab: 1993
Comments: Stock is approximately 75% paperback.

Watermark West Rare Books
149 North Broadway   67202

By Appointment
(316) 263-3007

Collection: Specialty
# of Vols: 10,000
Specialties: Western Americana; 20th century British and American literature.
Services: Search service, catalog.
Credit Cards: Yes
Owner: Philip McComish
Year Estab: 1984

Yesterday's Antiques & Gifts
535 North Woodlawn   67208

Open Shop
(316) 684-1900

Collection: General stock.
# of Vols: 100+
Hours: Mon-Fri 10-6. Sat 10-5.
Travel: Between Central and 13th St.

A.C. Houston, Bookman
(913) 841-6811

309 Tallgrass Court Lawrence 66049

Collection:	General stock.
# of Vols:	17,000
Credit Cards:	No
Year Estab:	1987

Jayhawker Special Collections
(913) 843-0790

PO Box 67 Lawrence 66044

Collection:	Specialty
# of Vols:	10,000
Specialties:	Western Americana; Kansas.
Services:	Search service, accepts want lists.
Credit Cards:	Yes
Owner:	Dean Schaake
Comments:	Also displays at Quantrill's Antique Mall in Lawrence. See above.

Killing Time in Kansas
(913) 897-7916
Fax: (913) 469-8708

14033 Hayes Overland Park 66221

Collection:	Specialty
Specialties:	Mystery first editions; military; history; fiction.
Services:	Appraisals, search service, catalog, accepts want lists.
Credit Cards:	No
Owner:	Shari Berl & Bruce Bikson
Year Estab:	1994

Plains Bookman
(913) 776-2400

PO Box 1167 Manhattan 66505

Collection:	Specialty
# of Vols:	15,000
Specialties:	Non fiction.
Services:	Catalog, accepts want lists.
Credit Cards:	No
Owner:	J.P. Dennis Riordan
Year Estab:	1994

Steven D. Roberts
(316) 685-8926
Fax: (316) 683-2751
E-mail: gstc93b@prodigy.com

PO Box 8556 Wichita 67208

Collection:	Specialty
# of Vols:	8,000-10,000
Specialties:	Modern literature; science fiction; horror; Western Americana.
Services:	Appraisals, occasional catalog, accepts want lists, search service.
Credit Cards:	No
Year Estab:	1993

Shadow's Sanctum   (316) 263-2270
711 West 13th Street, #7 Wichita 67203

Collection:	Specialty
# of Vols:	3,000
Specialties:	Science fiction; pulps (original and reprints); vintage paperbacks.
Owner:	Ivan Snell
Year Estab:	1979

Werner Books   (316) 729-0010
PO Box 75292 Wichita 67275

Collection:	General stock.
# of Vols:	1,500
Services:	Accepts want lists.
Credit Cards:	No
Owner:	Irene Werner
Year Estab:	1988

Window Seat Books   (913) 384-3558
6001 West 67th Street Overland Park 66202   (913) 384-3558
                                  E-mail: windowst@interloc.com

Collection:	General stock and ephemera.
# of Vols:	3,000
Specialties:	Agriculture; farming; back to the land; national parks.
Services:	Search service, catalog, accepts want lists.
Credit Cards:	No
Owner:	Kelly & Mary Jo Johnston
Year Estab:	1994

Louisiana

Alphabetical Listing By Dealer

Alphabetical Listing By Location

Baton Rouge

Book Exchange   **Open Shop**
216 South 19th Street   70806   (504) 387-4871
Mailing address:

Collection:	General stock of mostly paperback.
# of Vols:	10,000
Hours:	Mon-Sat 9-5:30.

Book Trader   **Open Shop**
11830 Coursey Boulevard   70816   (504) 295-0356

Collection:	General stock of mostly paperback.
# of Vols:	45,000
Hours:	Tue-Fri 10-6. Sat 10-4.

The Book Warehouse of Baton Rogue   **Open Shop**
9596 Florida Boulevard   70815   (504) 925-9505

Collection:	General stock of remainders and used paperback and hardcover.
# of Vols:	75,000
Hours:	Mon-Sat 9-8. Sun 12-6.
Travel:	Airline exit off I-12. Proceed north on Airline to Florida Blvd, then east on Florida. Shop is in Broadmoor Shopping Center.
Credit Cards:	Yes
Owner:	Gerald Pahres
Year Estab:	1987
Comments:	A very spacious shop with lots of paperbacks and remainders but a very modest collection of used hardcover items, most of which were, in our humble judgment, hardly deserving of a special trip.

Caliban's Books   **Open Shop**
3615 Perkins Road   70808   (504) 383-2665
                                                    E-mail: calibans@interloc.com

Collection:	General stock of mostly used hardcover and paperback.
# of Vols:	75,000
Specialties:	Louisiana; Southern Americana.
Hours:	Daily 7am-11pm.
Services:	Appraisals, search service, accepts want lists.
Travel:	Acadian Thwy exit off I-10. Proceed south on Acadian for about one block, then left on Perkins Rd and then an almost immediate left into shopping center.
Credit Cards:	Yes
Owner:	Philip Hackney, Barry Hough, Alton Schwartzkopf, Brad Lewis
Year Estab:	1992
Comments:	A bi-level shop with a combination of paperbacks and hardcover volumes, mostly of a more recent vintage, plus a cafe. We also saw some vintage paperbacks and a some other older items in our wanderings through the shop. The few titles we looked at more carefully were, we felt, priced a

trifle higher than similar volumes in similar condition seen elsewhere. There are, nonetheless, enough books on hand, with some perhaps not easily found elsewhere, to warrant a brief visit.

Taylor Clark Gallery   Open Shop
2623 Government Street   70806   (504) 383-4929

Collection:	Specialty
Specialties:	Audubon; color plates books (19th century); natural history.
Hours:	Mon-Fri 9:30-5:30. Sat 11-3. Other times by appointment.
Services:	Appraisals, accepts want lists, catalog.
Travel:	Government St exit off I-10. Proceed east on Government St for about one mile.
Credit Cards:	Yes
Owner:	Taylor Clark
Year Estab:	1946

Confederate States Military Antiques   Open Shop
2905 Government Street   70806   (504) 387-5044

Collection:	Specialty
# of Vols:	Limited
Specialties:	Civil War.
Hours:	Tue-Sat 10-5.

Cottonwood Books   Open Shop
3054 Perkins Road   70808   (504) 343-1266

Collection:	General stock of new and used, mostly hardcover.
# of Vols:	25,000
Hours:	Mon-Fri 10-6. Sat 10-5.
Services:	Appraisals, search service.
Travel:	See Caliban's Books above. Turn right on Perkins.
Credit Cards:	Yes
Owner:	Daniel Plaisance
Year Estab:	1978
Comments:	Stock is approximately 50% used, 75% of which is hardcover.

River City Books   Antique Mall
At West Moreland Antique Gallery   (504) 383-1003
3374 Government Street   70806

Collection:	General stock.
# of Vols:	15,000
Specialties:	Southern Americana; Civil War.
Hours:	Daily 10-6, except Thu till 9.
Services:	Appraisals, search service, accepts want lists, mail order.
Travel:	Acadian exit off I-10. Proceed north on Acadian to Government. Mall is in shopping center on southwest corner of Acadian and Government.
Credit Cards:	Yes

Owner:	Jim Taylor
Year Estab:	1986
Comments:	A good example of why one should not trust first impressions. Located in the corner of an antique mall, the books here are far more extensive in number, and certainly a step above in terms of quality, than most of the used book "booths" in antique malls.

Covington

Covington Book Exchange   **Open Shop**
1200 Business Hwy 190, #19   70433   (504) 892-5440

Collection:	General stock of mostly paperback.
# of Vols:	30,000
Hours:	Mon-Sat 10-5.

Ferriday

Baker's Book Bug   **Open Shop**
6384 Highway 84 East   71334   (318) 757-8324

Collection:	General stock of paperback and hardcover.
# of Vols:	10,000
Hours:	Tue-Sat 10-5.
Travel:	On Hwy 84, about two miles south of Ferriday.
Year Estab:	1990
Comments:	Stock is approximately 75% paperback.

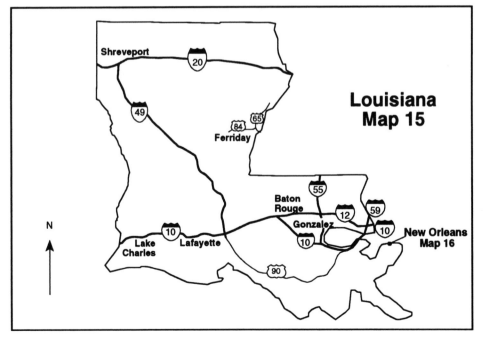

Gonzales

Liz's Book Rack   **Open Shop**
1505 North Burnside Avenue   70737   (504) 644-6671

Collection: General stock of paperback and hardcover.
# of Vols: 10,000
Hours: Mon-Fri 9:30-6. Sat 9:30-5.
Travel: Gonzales exit off I-10. Proceed east on Hwy 30, then turn left on Burnside.
Credit Cards: Yes
Owner: Debbie Hawley
Year Estab: 1988
Comments: Stock is approximately 60% paperback.

Gretna
(See Map 16, page 178)

Bayou Books   **Open Shop**
1005 Monroe Street   70053   (504) 368-1171

Collection: General stock of new and used hardcover and paperback.
# of Vols: 17,000+
Specialties: Louisiana
Hours: Mon-Fri 10-5.
Services: Appraisals, search service, accepts want lists.
Travel: Crescent City connection (bridge crossing Mississippi River) to Gen.
                   DeGaulle Dr west. Exit on Monroe St. Turn right at end of exit ramp.
                   Shop is on corner of Gen DeGaulle (Burmaster) and Monroe.
Credit Cards: Yes
Owner: Milburn & Nancy Calhoun
Year Estab: 1961
Comments: Prior to our trip, we were advised by the owners that the shop opened at
                   8:30am. However, when we arrived at 8:15am, we found a sign in the
                   window indicating that the shop opened at 10am. So much for the
                   consistency of hours–and yet another reason why we advise our read-
                   ers to "call ahead," especially if the shop is out of the way.

Lafayette

Alexander Books   **Open Shop**
2001 West Congress   70506   (318) 234-2096

Collection: General stock of hardcover and paperback.
# of Vols: 50,000
Hours: Tue-Fri 10-6. Sat 10-5. Sun 1-5.
Services: Search service, accepts want lists.
Travel: Hwy 82 exit off I-10. Proceed south on Hwy 82 to West Congress, then
                   right on Congress. Shop is just ahead on left.
Credit Cards: Yes
Owner: Barbara Alexander

Year Estab: 1989
Comments: Stock is evenly divided between hardcover and paperback. Those in the know speak well of this shop.

Lake Charles

Second Hand Prose   **Open Shop**
223 South Ryan Street   70601   (318) 439-4115

Collection: General stock of paperback and hardcover.
# of Vols: 50,000
Hours: Mon-Sat 10-6.
Travel: Ryan St exit off I-10. Proceed south on Ryan, then right on South Ryan.
Credit Cards: No
Year Estab: 1976
Comments: Stock is approximately 75% paperback.

Leesville

Marthas's Half Priced Used Books   **Open Shop**
209 North 3rd   71446   (318) 238-0104

Collection: General stock of mostly paperback.
Hours: Tue-Sat 10-5.

Mandeville

Cover to Cover Bookstore   **Open Shop**
1852 N. Causeway Approach   70471   (504) 626-4783
             Fax: (504) 6264750

Collection: General stock of mostly paperback.
Hours: Mon-Sat 10-6:30. Sun 12-5.

Metairie
(See Map 16, page 178)

Book Haven of New Orleans   **Open Shop**
238 Metairie Road   70005   Fax: (504) 828-4240   (504) 828-4242
           E-mail: bookhavn@accesscom.net

Collection: General stock of mostly hardcover.
# of Vols: 6,500
Specialties: Modern first editions; religion (scholarly); history; Southern Americana; Louisiana.
Hours: Mon-Fri 10-6. Sat 10-5.
Services: Appraisals, search service, catalog, accepts want lists.
Travel: Metairie Rd exit off I-10. If westbound, turn left at light, go under I-10 and continue on Metairie Rd. If eastbound, turn right on Metairie. Shop is about six blocks ahead on left.
Credit Cards: Yes

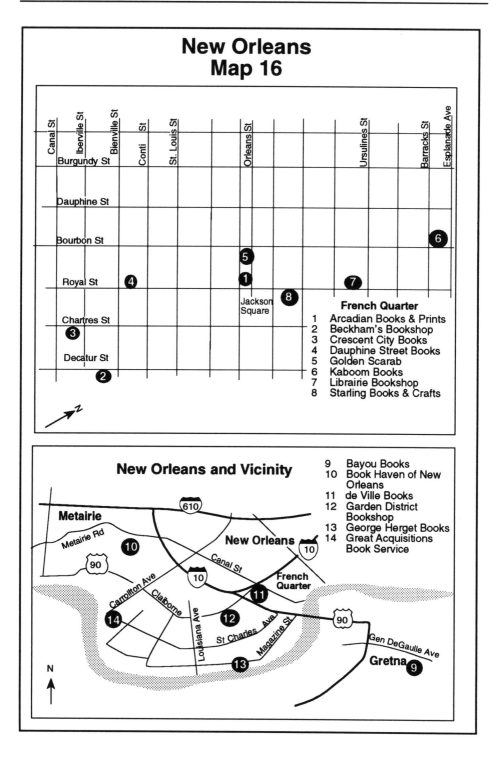

New Orleans
Map 16

French Quarter

1 Arcadian Books & Prints
2 Beckham's Bookshop
3 Crescent City Books
4 Dauphine Street Books
5 Golden Scarab
6 Kaboom Books
7 Librairie Bookshop
8 Starling Books & Crafts

New Orleans and Vicinity

9 Bayou Books
10 Book Haven of New Orleans
11 de Ville Books
12 Garden District Bookshop
13 George Herget Books
14 Great Acquisitions Book Service

Owner:	Samuel A. Nugent
Year Estab:	1994
Comments:	The pluses include a shop that displays its books in an attractive fashion offering the visitor plenty of room for comfortable browsing. Many of the books had mylar covered dust jackets and, in our opinion, were priced a trifle higher than similar books in the same condition seen elsewhere. While the selection was limited in size, the quality and collectibility of many of titles was quite respectable.

New Orleans

Antique Book Gallery   **Open Shop**
811 Royal Street   70116   (504) 524-6918

Collection:	Specialty
# of Vols:	2,000+
Specialties:	Children's; illustrated; first editions.
Hours:	Mon-Sat 10-5. Sun 12-5.
Services:	Appraisals, accepts want lists, mail order.
Travel:	Between St. Ann & Dumaine Streets.
Credit Cards:	Yes
Owner:	Ben Scheel
Year Estab:	1976

Arcadian Books & Prints   **Open Shop**
714 Orleans Street   70116   (504) 523-4138

Collection:	General stock of hardcover and paperback and ephemera.
# of Vols:	15,000+
Specialties:	French language books.
Hours:	Mon-Sat 10:30-6:30. Sun 12-5.
Services:	Accepts want lists, mail order
Travel:	In the French Quarter, between Royal and Bourbon Streets.
Credit Cards:	Yes
Owner:	Russell Desmond
Year Estab:	1981
Comments:	If this shop had more space, browsing would be a lot easier. As it is, the shop is small, the shelves are crowded and the limited aisle space makes it extremely difficult to view the books comfortably. The above notwithstanding, the books we saw were certainly worthy of note. If you're visiting New Orleans, we suggest you stop here when you're still energetic.

Beckham's Bookshop   **Open Shop**
228 Decatur Street   70130   (504) 522-9875

Collection:	General stock of mostly hardcover and records.
# of Vols:	70,000
Specialties:	Regional
Hours:	Daily 10-6.
Travel:	In the French Quarter between Iberville and Bienville Streets.

(New Orleans)

Credit Cards:	Yes
Owner:	Carey C. Beckham & Alton L. Cook
Year Estab:	1967
Comments:	A very nice bi-level shop with a healthy selection of books in almost every category, from "old novels" to scholarly titles, and a handy map of the store to help you locate the subjects you're looking for. Most reasonably priced.

Centuries Old Maps & Prints   **Open Shop**
517 St. Louis Street   70130   (504) 568-9491

Collection:	Specialty
Specialties:	Antique maps and prints.
Hours:	Mon-Sat 10:30-6. Sun 11-6.
Travel:	In the French Quarter, between Chartres & Decatur Streets.

Crescent City Books   **Open Shop**
204 Chartres Street   70130   (800) 546-4013   (504) 524-4997
                                                            Fax: 5045589729
                                                            E-mail: ccbks@aol.com

Collection:	General stock.
# of Vols:	20,000
Specialties:	History; scholarly; ancient history; Middle Ages; literary criticism; art monographs; university press; fine bindings.
Hours:	Daily 10-6, except Thu-Sat till 9.
Services:	Search service, catalog, accepts want lists.
Travel:	In the French Quarter, one block in from Canal at corner of Chartres and Iberville Streets.
Credit Cards:	Yes
Owner:	J. Phillips & G.P. Hurst
Year Estab:	1991
Comments:	A bi-level shop that houses an extensive collection of quality books in almost every subject area. The stock here could well satisfy scholars in many areas of research.

Dauphine Street Books   **Open Shop**
410 Dauphine Street   70112   (504) 529-2333

Collection:	General stock of hardcover and paperback.
# of Vols:	20,000+
Specialties:	Modern literature; local history; jazz; black studies.
Hours:	Thu-Mon 11-7.
Services:	Accepts want lists, mail order.
Travel:	In the French Quarter, between Conti and St. Louis Streets.
Credit Cards:	Yes
Owner:	Steve Lacy
Year Estab:	1971

Comments: Another shop with good books that suffers from narrow aisles and cramped space. Try to visit on a cool day when you're able to view the titles comfortably and chances are you'll find something of interest as the quality of what we saw was quite good.

de Ville Books   **Open Shop**
344 Carondelet   70130   Fax: (504) 525-5264   (504) 525-1846
                                                                   E-mail: devilleb@interloc.com

Collection: General stock of mostly new books.
# of Vols: 15,000+
Specialties: Louisiana
Hours: Mon-Fri 9:30-5:30.
Services: Appraisals, search service, accepts want lists, mail order.
Travel: In Central Business District, between Poydras and Canal, five blocks from Superdome.
Credit Cards: Yes
Owner: David Brewington
Year Estab: 1976
Comments: Primarily a new book store, the shop has a separate small room displaying a limited selection of used hardcover books. Fiction and non fiction titles were shelved together. More valuable used books were shelved behind glass in the shop's main display area.

Faulkner House Books   **Open Shop**
624 Pirate's Alley   70116   (504) 524-2940

Collection: Specialty
# of Vols: 7,500
Specialties: Modern first editions; southern authors; William Faulkner; local and regional history.
Hours: Daily 10-6.
Services: Appraisals, accepts want lists, mail order.
Travel: In the French Quarter, just off Jackson Square. (Note: facing the cathedral, the left alley.)
Credit Cards: Yes
Owner: Joe DeSalvo
Year Estab: 1990

Garden District Bookshop   **Open Shop**
2727 Prytania   70130   (504) 895-2266

Collection: General stock of mostly new books.
# of Vols: 400-500 (used)
Specialties: New Orleans; Louisiana; southern authors.
Hours: Mon-Sat 10-6. Sun 11-4.
Services: Search service, accepts want lists.
Travel: St Charles Ave exit off I-10. Proceed on St Charles to 4th St, then left on 4th and right on Prytania.

(New Orleans)

Credit Cards:	Yes
Owner:	Britton Trice
Year Estab:	1978

George Herget Books
3109 Magazine Street   70115

Open Shop
(504) 891-5595

Collection:	General stock of hardcover and paperback.
# of Vols:	50,000+
Specialties:	Music; regional.
Hours:	Mon-Sat 10-6. Sun by appointment.
Travel:	In Garden District, between 8th & 9th Avenues.
Credit Cards:	Yes
Owner:	Jean Nosich
Year Estab:	1982
Comments:	If you and/or your traveling companion/s enjoy antiquing, you'll have every opportunity to indulge that pleasure when visiting this dealer as the store is located in the midst of the city's "antique row." The shop has a healthy selection of books in the specialties listed above but its general stock is nothing to sneeze at. The condition of the books we saw was good to very good with some exceptions (some of the older books had seen better days.) Not a shop for recent best sellers, but a good choice if you're looking for older volumes of merit.

Golden Scarab
736 Orleans Street   70116

Open Shop
(504) 529-4520

Collection:	General stock of mostly hardcover and ephemera.
# of Vols:	10,000
Hours:	Wed-Mon 11-7.
Travel:	In the French Quarter, between Bourbon and Royal Streets.
Credit Cards:	Yes
Owner:	Richard Lewis & Greg Null
Year Estab:	1993

Great Acquisitions Book Service
8200 Hampson Street, #311   70118

Open Shop
(504) 861-8707
Fax: (504) 866-8007

Collection:	General stock.
# of Vols:	6,000
Specialties:	Louisiana literature and history; art; modern literature.
Hours:	Mon-Fri 10-4. Other times by appointment.
Services:	Appraisals, search service, accepts want lists, catalog.
Travel:	Carrollton exit off I-10. Proceed south on Carrollton to Maple, then right on Maple to Dante and left on Hampson. Shop is at intersection of Hampson and River Rd in an office building.
Credit Cards:	No

Owner:	Joseph Cohen
Year Estab:	1992
Comments:	The permanent sign on the door to this shop indicates a 10am opening. However, on the day of our visit, when we arrived at 10am, we found a second, temporary sign, indicating that the dealer would return at 11am along with a permanent typed note explaining that as a "one man operation" the owner sometimes found it necessary to close during his regularly posted hours and apologizing in advance if this caused the visitor any inconvenience. Since this was the second time that morning that we had been greeted by locked doors, and since both locations were a distance from downtown, we'll let our gentle readers guess how we felt and why we so often advise our readers to "call ahead," especially if their destinations are somewhat out of the way.

House of Art Books   **By Appointment**
806 Perdido, Rm 302   70112   (504) 522-7043
Fax: (504) 522-7043

Collection:	Specialty new and used.
# of Vols:	3,500
Specialties:	Art; photography; architecture; beat generation.
Services:	Catalog
Credit Cards:	No
Owner:	Edwin J. Blair
Year Estab:	1991
Comments:	Stock is approximately 40% used.

Kaboom Books   **Open Shop**
901 Barracks Street   70116   (504) 529-5780

Collection:	General stock of hardcover and paperback.
# of Vols:	25,000-30,000
Hours:	Thu-Mon 11-7.
Travel:	In the French Quarter at corner of Bourbon Street.
Comments:	Although not overly large, the shop is spacious enough so that the visitor can comfortably browse the collection. Also, because of its location several blocks from the heart of the French Quarter, browsers will probably find the shop less crowded and its stock less picked over than the other used book shops in the Quarter. The shop offers a good selection of titles in most subject areas and is a shop we would certainly add to our list of places we would want to visit again.

Librairie Bookshop   **Open Shop**
823 Chartres Street   70116   (504) 525-4837

Collection:	General stock of mostly hardcover and ephemera.
# of Vols:	70,000
Hours:	Daily 10-8.
Travel:	In the French Quarter, near Jackson Square.
Credit Cards:	Yes

(New Orleans)

Owner:	Carey C. Beckham & Alton L. Cook
Year Estab:	1967
Comments:	A smaller version of Beckham's Bookshop (see above) owned by the same dealers. The books here, while worth a browse, are hardly as impressive as those in its sister shop. Most of what we saw were in average to good condition representing a mix of time spans. A majority of the books were non fiction and most of the fiction titles we saw appeared to be reading copies.

Old Children's Books   **Open Shop**
734 Royal Street   70116   (504) 525-3655
                                                              Fax: (504) 522-2567

Collection:	Specialty
# of Vols:	3,000
Specialties:	Children's
Hours:	Mon-Sat 10-1.
Services:	Accepts want lists, mail order.
Travel:	In the French Quarter, seven blocks from Canal St. Ring bell for entry.
Credit Cards:	No
Owner:	Henry Weiss
Year Estab:	1973

Starling Books & Crafts   **Open Shop**
1022 Royal Street   70116   (504) 595-6777

Collection:	General stock.
# of Vols:	1,000
Specialties:	Modern first editions; occult; local interest.
Hours:	Thu-Mon 11-7.
Services:	Catalog, accepts want lists.
Travel:	Esplanade Ave exit off I-10. Proceed south on Esplanade for 10 blocks to Royal. Right on Royal. Shop is 3½ blocks ahead.
Credit Cards:	Yes
Owner:	Jan Spacek & Claudia Williams
Year Estab:	1995

Shreveport

Books - D & B Russell   **Open Shop**
129 Kings Highway   71104   Fax: (318) 868-1403   (318) 865-5198
                                             E-mail: russells@interloc.com

Collection:	General stock.
# of Vols:	10,000
Specialties:	Louisiana; east Texas; southern Arkansas; trans-Mississippi; Civil War.
Hours:	Mon-Fri 10-6. Sat 9-6. Other times by appointment.
Services:	Appraisals, search service.

Travel:	From I-20, exit at I-49 south, then Kings Hwy exit off I-49. Proceed east (left) on Kings Hwy for about 1.3 miles. Shop is between Centenary and Alexander. From I-49 north, exit at Kings Hwy and follow above.
Credit Cards:	Yes
Owner:	Donald A. & Elizabeth Russell
Year Estab:	1992
Comments:	Although not particularly large, this shop offers "a little bit of every-thing," including a nice selection of regional history, general fiction, cookbooks and children's books. The books we saw were in generally good condition and quite reasonably priced

C & B Bookstore   **Open Shop**
3816 Linwood Avenue   71103   (318) 631-0393

Collection:	General stock of hardcover and paperback.
# of Vols:	3,000-5,000
Hours:	Tue-Fri 10-5. Sat 10-3.
Services:	Accepts want lists.
Travel:	Linwood exit off I-20. Proceed south on Linwood. Shop is across from cemetery.
Credit Cards:	No
Owner:	Calvin & Betty Douglas
Year Estab:	1993
Comments:	Stock is approximately 70% hardcover.

Slidell

The Book Sack   **Open Shop**
1234 Bayou Lane   70460   (504) 649-6136

Collection:	General stock of mostly paperback.
Hours:	Tue-Sat 10-5.

Sulphur

Second Hand Prose   **Open Shop**
209 Roddam Street   70663   (318) 528-9004

Collection:	General stock of mostly paperback.
# of Vols:	15,000+
Hours:	Tue & Wed 10-5. Thu & Fri 1-5. Sat 10-2.

McLaughlin's Used Books   **Open Shop**
512 Terry Parkway   70056   (504) 367-3754

Collection:	General stock of mostly paperback.
# of Vols:	25,000
Hours:	Mon-Sat 10-6. Sun 1-5.

Mail Order Dealers

Peter Chocheles   (504) 885-4832
4624 Wade Drive   Metairie 70003

Collection:	Specialty
# of Vols:	500
Specialties:	Modern Library firsts.
Services:	Appraisals, catalog, accepts want lists.
Credit Cards:	No
Year Estab:	1986

Hollis The Bookseller   (504) 926-6191
PO Box 41044   Baton Rouge 70835

Collection:	General stock.
# of Vols:	8,000
Services:	Accepts want lists.
Owner:	Hollis Fulton
Year Estab:	1989
Comments:	Books are also on display at the Book Warehouse in Baton Rouge (see above), Petit Jean Antiques on Druscilla Street in Baton Rouge and the Romantique Antique Shop in Denham Springs.

Hughes Books   (504) 948-2427
PO Box 840237   New Orleans 7018   E-mail: hughesbook@aol.com

Collection:	Specialty
# of Vols:	2,000
Specialties:	Civil War; Southern Americana; Western Americana.
Services:	Appraisals, accepts want lists, catalog.
Credit Cards:	No
Owner:	Bill Grady
Year Estab:	1992
Comments:	Collection may also be viewed by appointment.

Red River Books   (318) 929-7520
Drawer RB   Blanchard 71009

Collection:	General stock.
# of Vols:	8,000
Specialties:	Louisiana
Services:	Accepts want lists, occasional lists.
Credit Cards:	Yes
Owner:	Eugene Spruell
Year Estab:	1976

Mississippi

Alphabetical Listing By Dealer

Alphabetical Listing By Location

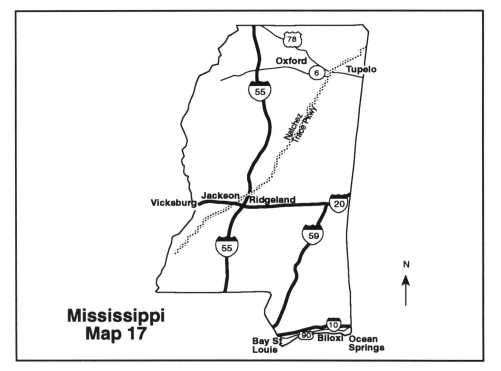

Mississippi Map 17

Bay Saint Louis

Bookends   **Open Shop**
111 Highway 90   39520   (601) 467-9623
Fax: (601) 467-9623

Collection:	General stock of new and used hardcover and paperback.
# of Vols:	3,000 (used)
Hours:	Mon-Sat 10-5:30.
Travel:	Westbound on I-10: Exit 13. Eastbound on I-10: Exit 2. Proceed east on Hwy 90.
Credit Cards:	Yes
Owner:	Susan Daigre
Year Estab:	1987
Comments:	Used stock is about evenly divided between hardcover and paperback.

Old Books And Curiosities   **Open Shop**
126 Main Street   39520   (601) 467-9791

Collection:	General stock.
# of Vols:	4,000+
Hours:	Mon-Sun, except closed Tue, 10:30-5.
Services:	Accepts want lists, mail order.
Travel:	Exit 13 off I-10. Proceed south on Hwy 603 (which becomes Nicholson Ave after crossing Hwy 90) for about seven miles. Left on Beach Blvd and proceed for about 2½ miles. Then left on Main St.
Credit Cards:	Yes
Owner:	Nancy Blancé

Biloxi

Spanish Trail Books   **Open Shop**
781 Vieux Marche   39530   (601) 435-1144

Collection:	General stock of hardcover and paperback and ephemera.
# of Vols:	44,000
Specialties:	First editions; Civil War; Americana; Mississippi.
Hours:	Mon-Fri 11-5. Weekends by chance or appointment.
Services:	Appraisals, search service, occasional catalog, accepts want lists, mail order.
Travel:	Exit 46A (I-110) exit off I-10, then exit 1A (downtown) off I-110. Turn left on G.E. Ohr St and proceed three blocks to Vieux Marche Mall.
Credit Cards:	Yes
Owner:	Patricia & William Hutter
Year Estab:	1970
Comments:	Some new books, some paperbacks and a very nice selection of used hardcover items. Strong in the specialties listed above as well as in other more general subject areas. Clean, neat, well organized and reasonably priced. Almost all the books we saw were in very good condition.

Hattiesburg

Books Etc   **Open Shop**
2107 Oak Grove Road   39402   (601) 261-5310

Collection: General stock of mostly paperback.
Hours: Mon-Fri 9-5. Sat 9-2.

Jackson

Choctow Books   **Open Shop**
926 North Street   39202   (601) 352-7281

Collection: General stock.
# of Vols: 50,000
Specialties: History; Civil War; Southern literature; Southern Americana.
Hours: Mon-Sat 9-5.
Services: Appraisals, search service, accepts want lists, mail order.
Travel: Exit 96C (Fortification St) off I-55. Proceed west on Fortification.
                  After Jefferson St, take left on North St. Shop is fourth building on left.
Credit Cards: Yes
Owner: Fred Smith
Year Estab: 1982
Comments: This is the type of shop I wouldn't mind being stranded in for an extended
                  period of time. In addition to the books in the shop's specialties which are
                  represented in healthy numbers, there are several separate rooms devoted
                  to more general subjects. We saw a number of titles by long forgotten
                  authors rarely seen elsewhere. Prices are reasonable. Organization is top
                  notch. If you haven't yet guessed, this is a place we highly recommend.

Lemuria Bookstore   **Open Shop**
4465 I-55N, 202 Banner Hall   39206   (601) 366-7619
                                                               Fax: (601) 366-7784

Collection: Specialty used and general stock of new books.
# of Vols: 1,000 (used)
Specialties: First editions, with emphasis on modern literary firsts..
Hours: Mon-Sat 10-7. Sun 1-5.
Services: Occasional catalog.
Travel: Just off exit 100 off I-55.
Credit Cards: Yes
Year Estab: 1976
Comments: Primarily a new book store with a specialized collection of used books.

Ocean Springs

The Book Hound   **By Appointment**
3706 Point Clear Drive   (601) 875-4807
Mailing address: PO Box 292 Ocean Springs 39566   Fax: (601) 8754807

Collection: Specialty

# of Vols:	1,000
Specialties:	Modern first editions; classic literature first editions; children's illustrated; signed; limited editions.
Services:	Accepts want lists, mail order.
Owner:	John Comunelli
Year Estab:	1992

Favorites: Book, Art Etc   **Open Shop**
1209 Government Street   39564   (601) 875-0082

Collection:	General stock new and used paperback and hardcover.
# of Vols:	2,000 (used)
Hours:	Mon-Fri 10:30-6. Sat 10-5.
Travel:	From I-10 eastbound: Washington Ave exit. Proceed south on Washington over Ft Bayou bridge, through Hwy 90 intersection and over railroad tracks. At blinking light, turn left on Government St. Shop is 2½ blocks ahead.
Credit Cards:	Yes
Owner:	Marilyn Lunceford
Year Estab:	1993
Comments:	Used stock is approximately 55% paperback.

Oxford

Off Square Books   **Open Shop**
1110 Van Buren Avenue   38655   (601) 236-2267

Collection:	General stock of remainders and used.
# of Vols:	1,200 (used)
Hours:	Mon-Sat 9-6. Sun 12-5.
Travel:	North Lamar exit off Hwy 6. Proceed north on North Lamar to Courthouse Square. Shop is just off the square.
Credit Cards:	Yes
Owner:	Richard Howarth
Year Estab:	1993
Comments:	Used stock is a mix of hardcover and paperback.

Purvis

Janet's Books and More   **Open Shop**
107 Shelby Speights Drive   39475   (601) 794-5080

Collection:	General stock of mostly paperback.
# of Vols:	7,000
Hours:	Mon-Fri 9-4. Sat 9-12.

Ridgeland

The Bookshelf   **Open Shop**
637 Highway 51 South, Ste AA   39157   (601) 853-9225

Collection:	General stock of paperback and hardcover.

# of Vols:	7,000
Hours:	Mon-Sat. 10-5:30.
Travel:	On Highway 51 in a small strip center.
Credit Cards:	Yes
Owner:	Lisa Perry
Year Estab:	1992
Comments:	Stock is approximately 75% paperback.

Tupelo

Book Rack   **Open Shop**
West Main Shopping Center, West Main Street   (601) 844-5707
Mailing address: 101 Industrial Road North, #D Tupelo 38801

Collection: General stock of mostly paperback.
Hours: Mon-Sat 9:30-6.

The Cottage Bookshop   **Open Shop**
214 North Madison   38801   (601) 844-1553
                                              E-mail: cotbooks@interloc.com

Collection:	General stock.
# of Vols:	14,000
Specialties:	Mississippi authors (especially Faulkner and Welty); southern authors.
Hours:	Mon-Sat 10-5.
Services:	Appraisals, search service, catalog, accepts want lists.
Travel:	From Hwy 45: Main St exit. Proceed west on Main to Madison, then north on Madison for 1/2 block. From Hwy 78, Hwy 45 exit and proceed as above. From Hwy 6, follow directions from Hwy 45.
Credit Cards:	Yes
Owner:	N. Kenneth Nail
Year Estab:	1984
Comments:	Located appropriately enough in a modest sized cottage in which several rooms display quality titles (mostly fiction) with a heavy emphasis on both southern literature and Welsh writers. Other subjects are represented in less depth. The books we saw were in generally very good condition and were reasonably priced.

Wise Owl Book Store   **Open Shop**
2301 West Main Street   38801   (601) 842-6500

Collection: General stock of mostly paperback.
Hours: Mon-Sat 9-5:30.

Vicksburg

Yesterday's Treasures   **Antique Mall**
1400 Washington Street   39180   (601) 638-6213
                                                          Fax: (601) 636-4502

Collection: General stock.

# of Vols:	2,500-3,000
Specialties:	History; local interest; children's.
Hours:	Mon-Sat 10-5.
Services:	Accepts want lists.
Travel:	Clay St exit off I-20. Shop is located in an antique mall in downtown mall area.
Credit Cards:	Yes
Year Estab:	1990

Mail Order Dealers

Book Search Service   (800) 258-9802
206 Pebble Lane   Clinton 39056   (601) 924-7816

Collection:	Specialty. Primarily used hardcover.
# of Vols:	1,200+
Specialties:	Hymnology; church music; worship and liturgy; music history and literature.
Services:	Appraisals, search service, catalog, accepts want lists.
Credit Cards:	No
Owner:	Lewis Oswalt
Comments:	Collection may also be viewed by appointment.

Gulf Coast Books   (601) 872-6220
PO Box 1251   Ocean Springs 39566   Fax: (601) 872-6220
       E-mail: bookhunter@aol.com

Collection:	General stock (fiction only).
# of Vols:	1,500
Specialties:	Mystery
Services:	Appraisals, accepts want lists, catalog.
Credit Cards:	No
Owner:	James Wright
Year Estab:	1985
Comments:	Collection may also be viewed by appointment.

Nouveau Rare Books   (601) 956-9950
PO Box 12471 Jackson 39236   Fax: (601) 984-6620
       E-mail: silbrman@aol.com

Collection:	Specialty
# of Vols:	5,600
Specialties:	Modern literature.
Services:	Catalog
Credit Cards:	Yes
Owner:	Steve Silberman
Year Estab:	1980

C. Clayton Thompson, Bookseller

20 Jay Drive   Gulfport 39503

(601) 831-4097
Fax: (601) 831-4097
E-mail: Greatbooks@aol.com

Collection:	Specialty. Mostly used.
Specialties:	Civil War; military; signed modern first editions; Americana; some children's.
Services:	Appraisals, catalog, accepts want lists.
Credit Cards:	Yes
Year Estab:	1991
Comments:	Collection may also be viewed by appointment.

Tristero Bookseller

(601) 856-5209

PO Box 220   Ridgeland 39158

Collection:	General stock of used and new.
# of Vols:	3,000
Specialties:	Southern literature.
Services:	Catalog, accepts want lists.
Credit Cards:	No
Owner:	Floyd & Bean Sulser
Year Estab:	1990
Comments:	Stock is approximately 75% used.

Montana

Alphabetical Listing By Dealer

Alphabetical Listing By Location

Alberton

Montana Valley Book Store   **Open Shop**
512 Railroad Avenue   (406) 722-4950
Mailing address: PO Box 152 Alberton 59820

Collection:	General stock of hardcover and paperback.
# of Vols:	100,000
Hours:	Daily 8-7.
Services:	Accepts want lists.
Travel:	Exit 75 or 77 off I-90 and follow signs to Alberton. Shop is on main street in center of town.
Credit Cards:	Yes
Owner:	Keren Ranney
Year Estab:	1978
Comments:	Stock is approximately 75% hardcover.

Anaconda

Old Book Shoppe   **Open Shop**
101 Main Street 59711   (406) 563-7962

Collection:	General stock of mostly paperback.
# of Vols:	37,000
Hours:	Tue-Fri 10-7. Sat & Mon 10-5. Sun 12-5.

Big Sky

Moose Rack Books   **Open Shop**
48025 Gallatin Road 59716   (406) 995-4521

Collection:	Specialty. Mostly new and some used hardcover.
# of Vols:	50-100 (used)
Specialties:	Western Americana (including first editions).
Hours:	Winter & Summer: Daily 9-6. Fall & Spring: Daily 10-5:30.

Bigfork

Bay Books & Prints   **Open Shop**
Grand Street   (406) 837-4646
Mailing address: PO Box 426 Bigfork 59911

Collection:	Specialty new and used.
# of Vols:	10,000
Specialties:	Western Americana; fur trade; Native Americans; Charles Russell.
Hours:	May 1-Oct 1: Daily 9-5. Oct 2- Apr 30: By appointment.
Services:	Appraisals, mail order.
Travel:	From Missoula, take Hwy 93 north to Somers, then Hwy 35 to Bigfork.
Credit Cards:	Yes
Owner:	O'Neil Jones
Year Estab:	1964
Comments:	Stock is evenly divided between new and used.

Bob Borcherdt
PO Box 556   59911

By Appointment
(406) 837-6660

Collection:	Specialty books and ephemera.
Specialties:	Western Americana; Montana; fur trade; guns; hunting.
Hours:	May-Oct only. (See Comments)
Services:	Appraisals, search service, accepts want lists, mail order.
Credit Cards:	No
Year Estab:	1977
Comments:	See Boulder City, NV for owner's winter address.

Billings

Barjon's Books

Open Shop

2718 Third Avenue North   59101   (800) 788-4318   (406) 252-4398

Collection:	Specialty. Mostly new books.
Specialties:	Metaphysics; holistic health; psychology; religion.
Hours:	Mon-Sat 9:30-5:30.

The Book Cellar
1120 16th Street West   59102

Open Shop
(406) 248-4284

Collection:	General stock of paperback and hardcover.
# of Vols:	10,000
Hours:	Mon-Fri 10-5:30. Sat 10-5.
Travel:	King Ave exit off I-90. Proceed west on King Ave to 24th St, then right on Grand Ave and right on 16th St.
Credit Cards:	Yes
Owner:	Larry Kennedy
Year Estab:	1990
Comments:	Stock is approximately 75% paperback.

Book Cottage
811 16th Street West   59102

Open Shop
(406) 254-2051

Collection:	General stock of mostly paperback.
Hours:	Tue-Fri 10:30-5:30. Sat 10-4:30.

Book Place
2814 1st Avenue North   59101

Open Shop
(406) 256-3500

Collection:	General stock of mostly hardcover.
# of Vols:	40,000
Hours:	Mon-Sat 11-5.
Travel:	27th St exit off I-90. Proceed north on 27th St to 1st Ave North then west on 1st Ave. Shop is 1½ blocks ahead.
Credit Cards:	Yes
Owner:	Larry Kennedy
Year Estab:	1994

The Book Shelf   **Open Shop**
113 North 30th Street   59101   (406) 248-1850

Collection:	General stock of mostly paperback.
Hours:	Mon-Sat 10-6. Sun 12-4.

Bookworm West   **Open Shop**
3405 Central Avenue   59102   (406) 652-1166

Collection:	General stock of mostly paperback.
Hours:	Mon-Sat 10-6. Sun 12-4.
Travel:	King Ave west exit off I-90. Proceed west on King to 32nd St, then right on 32nd and left on Central. Continue to 34th St.

The Broken Diamond Books   **Open Shop**
2710 2nd Avenue North   59101   (406) 259-3440

Collection:	General stock of hardcover and paperback and prints.
# of Vols:	5,000-10,000
Specialties:	Modern American first editions; Western Americana; Yellowstone National Park; photography.
Hours:	Mon-Sat 10-5:30. Other times by appointment.
Services:	Appraisals, search service, accepts want lists, mail order.
Travel:	27th St (City Center) exit off I-90. Proceed north on 27th St to 1st Ave, then left on 1st Ave for one block, right on 28th St and right again on 2nd Ave.
Credit Cards:	Yes
Owner:	Frederick Longan
Year Estab:	1980's
Comments:	Stock is approximately 70% hardcover.

Stop & Swap Bookshop   **Open Shop**
520 Wicks Lane   59105   (406) 248-5159

Collection:	General stock of mostly paperback.
# of Vols:	30,000
Hours:	Mon-Sat 10-5:30.

Bozeman

Vargo's Jazz City and Books   **Open Shop**
1 East Main Street   (406) 587-5383
Mailing address: PO Box 966 Bozeman 59771

Collection:	General stock of new and used hardcover and paperback.
Hours:	Mon-Sat 10-5:30. Sun 12-5.
Travel:	In downtown, at corner of Main and Tracy.
Credit Cards:	Yes
Owner:	Francis Vargo
Year Estab:	1984

Butte

The Book Exchange   **Open Shop**
3100 Harrison Avenue   59701   (406) 494-7788
                                                          Fax: (406) 494-5778

Collection:	General stock of used and new paperback and hardcover.
# of Vols:	10,000
Hours:	Mon-Fri 11-9. Sat 10-6. Sun 12-5.
Travel:	City Center exit off I-90. Proceed south on Harrison Ave. Shop is about two blocks ahead, on left, in Butte Plaza Mall.
Credit Cards:	Yes
Year Estab:	1979
Comments:	Stock is approximately 75% paperback.

Henry's Used Books   **Open Shop**
2071 Harrison Avenue   59701   (406) 782-2644

Collection:	General stock of mostly paperback.
Hours:	Daily 12-9.

Second Edition Used Books   **Open Shop**
129 West Broadway   59701   (406) 723-5108

Collection:	General stock of mostly hardcover and some ephemera.
# of Vols:	20,000
Specialties:	Montana; Western Americana; children's; mining; geology.
Hours:	Mon-Sat 10-5:30.
Services:	Appraisals, search service, accepts want lists, mail order.
Travel:	Montana St exit off I-15 or I-90. Proceed north (up hill) to Broadway. Right on Broadway.
Credit Cards:	No
Owner:	Kathleen Finch
Year Estab:	1986

Darby

The Booksmiths   **Open Shop**
201 North Main   (406) 821-3167
Mailing address: PO Box 1011 Darby 59829

Collection:	General stock of paperback and hardcover.
# of Vols:	40,000
Hours:	Mon-Sat 10-6.
Services:	Appraisals, search service, accepts want lists, mail order.
Travel:	In downtown, on west side of Hwy 93.
Credit Cards:	Yes
Owner:	Marvin F. Smith
Year Estab:	1989
Comments:	Stock is approximately 70% paperback.

Great Falls

Jim Combs Books   **By Appointment**
417 27th Street, NW   59404   (406) 761-3320

Collection:	Specialty books and ephemera.
Specialties:	Montana; C.M. Russell; Western Americana; hunting; fishing.
Services:	Appraisals, search service, accepts want lists, mail order.
Credit Cards:	No

Fireside Books   **Open Shop**
614 Central   59401   (406) 771-1522
                                                    Fax: (406) 771-1522

Collection:	General stock.
# of Vols:	10,000
Specialties:	Western Americana.
Hours:	10-5:30 Mon-Fri 10-5:30. Sat 12-5.
Services:	Appraisals, search service, accepts want lists.
Travel:	Great Falls exit off I-15. Shop is in old downtown.
Credit Cards:	Yes
Owner:	Niel Hebertson
Year Estab:	1993

Havre

Big Sky Books   **Open Shop**
301 Third Ave   (406) 265-5750
Mailing address: PO Box 1770 Havre 59501

Collection:	General stock of mostly used paperback and hardcover.
# of Vols:	25,000 (used)
Hours:	Mon-Sat 10:30-6.
Comments:	Used stock is approximately 80% paperback.

Helena

Gene Allen, Books   **By Appointment**
1011 University   59601   (406) 443-6475

Collection:	Specialty *
# of Vols:	2,000
Specialties:	Montana; Western Americana; sports; early western photographs.
Services:	Occasional catalog.
Credit Cards:	No
Owner:	Gene & Bev Allen
Year Estab:	1989
*Comments:**	Also has a small general stock.

Aunt Bonnie's Books
419 North Main   59601

Open Shop
(406) 443-3093

Collection:	General stock of used hardcover and paperback and new books.
# of Vols:	10,000
Hours:	Mon-Sat 10-5.
Travel:	Northbound on I-15: Capitol exit. Proceed west on Prospect, left on Montana, right on 11th and left on Last Chance Gulch (Main St).
Credit Cards:	Yes
Owner:	Mary Fagan
Year Estab:	1975
Comments:	Stock is approximately 65% used and used stock is evenly divided between hardcover and paperback.

Book Heaven
103 East 6th Avenue   59601

Open Shop
(406) 449-2879

Collection:	General stock of paperback and hardcover.
# of Vols:	30,000-40,000
Hours:	Mon-Sat 11-6.
Travel:	Capital exit of I-15. Proceed west on Prospect, left on Montana, right on 11th, left on Lawrence and right on 6th.
Credit Cards:	Yes
Owner:	Suzanne McHugh
Year Estab:	1994
Comments:	Stock is approximately 65% paperback.

Golden Hill Antiquarian
4250 Eagle Bay Drive   59601

By Appointment
(406) 475-3564

Collection:	General stock.
# of Vols:	3,000
Specialties:	Western Americana.
Services:	Appraisals, search service, accepts want lists, occasional catalog, mail order.
Credit Cards:	No
Owner:	Margaret Summers
Year Estab:	1976

OK Books/Bedrock Gallery
2 North Last Chance Gulch Street   59601

By Appointment
(406)449-5135
Fax: (406) 449-5135
E-mail: bedrock@interloc.com

Collection:	Specialty
# of Vols:	6,000
Specialties:	Modern first editions; Montana literature.
Services:	Appraisals, search service, accepts want lists, mail order.
Credit Cards:	No
Owner:	Bill Borneman
Year Estab:	1990

Richard Van Nice - Books   **Open Shop**
216 East Lyndale Avenue   59601   Fax: (406) 449-0131   (406) 449-0131
                                                      E-mail: vanmt@aol.com

Collection:	General stock.
# of Vols:	18,000
Hours:	Mon-Fri 8-6. Sat & Sun 8-5.
Services:	Appraisals, search service, mail order.
Travel:	Hwy 12 (East Lyndale) runs through city. The shop is between Montana and Last Chance Gulch in a converted house.
Credit Cards:	Yes
Year Estab:	1985

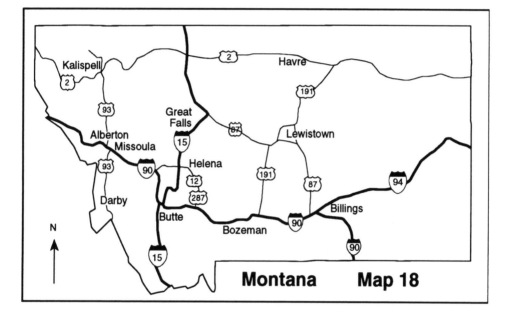

Kalispell

Blacktail Mountain Books   **Open Shop**
42 1st Avenue West   59901   (406) 257-5573

Collection:	General stock of hardcover and paperback.
# of Vols:	50,000
Hours:	Mon-Sat 10-5:30. Other times by appointment.
Services:	Appraisals, search service, accepts want lists, mail order.
Travel:	Downtown
Credit Cards:	Yes
Owner:	Jim Handcock
Year Estab:	1979
Comments:	Stock is evenly divided between hardcover and paperback.

Club Algiers - Old Books   **Open Shop**
1443 6th Avenue West   59901   (406) 257-2665

Collection:	General stock of hardcover and paperback and ephemera.
# of Vols:	5,000+
Specialties:	Western Americana; Montana; children's; metaphysics.
Hours:	Mon-Sat 11-6. Other times by appointment.
Services:	Appraisals, search service, accepts want lists.
Travel:	From Missoula off Hwy 93, turn left at 11th St West and proceed to 6th Ave, then turn left and proceed to end of block. Look for signs.
Credit Cards:	Yes
Owner:	Bonnie Germain
Year Estab:	1994
Comments:	The owner, who has been in the book business for 35 years, also sponsors a series of literary events in the shop which is in her home.

Lewistown

Poor Man's Books & Coffee   **Open Shop**
413 West Main Street   59457   (406) 538-4277

Collection:	General stock of hardcover and paperback.
Hours:	Mon-Sat 6am-3pm.
Comments:	Stock is evenly divided between hardcover and paperback.

Livingston

Gateway Books   **Open Shop**
111 West Callender Street   59047   (406) 222-8070
                                    Fax: (406) 222-8070

Collection:	Specialty. Mostly new.
Specialties:	Eastern philosophy; new age; self help; psychology.
Hours:	Mon & Sat 11-4. Tue-Fri 10-5.
Services:	Mail order.
Travel:	Livingston exit off I-90.
Credit Cards:	No
Owner:	A. Joseph & Ellen Ray
Year Estab:	1991

Gateway Books   **Open Shop**
111 West Callender Street   59047   (406) 222-8070

Collection:	General stock of mostly paperback.
# of Vols:	11,000
Hours:	Tue-Fri 10-5. Sat & Mon 11-4.

O'Byrne's Bookstore   **Open Shop**
113 West Park Street   59047   (406) 222-9362

Collection:	General stock of mostly hardcover.
# of Vols:	10,000

Specialties:	Western Americana; mystery; fishing.
Hours:	Mon-Sat 9-5.
Services:	Search service, mail order.
Travel:	Livingston exit off I-90. Proceed for about two miles to downtown.
Owner:	Bill O'Byrne
Year Estab:	1994

Missoula

The Book Exchange   **Open Shop**
2335 Brooks Street   59801   (406) 728-6342
                                                                      Fax: (406) 728-6390

Collection:	General stock of used and new paperback and hardcover.
Hours:	Mon-Sat 9-9. Sun 10-5.
Travel:	Orange St exit off I-90. Proceed south on Orange then right on Brooks. Shop is in Trempers Shopping Center.
Credit Cards:	Yes
Year Estab:	1979
Comments:	Stock is approximately 70% used, 80% of which is paperback.

Book Rack   **Open Shop**
2115 South Avenue West   59801   (406) 543-1910

Collection:	General stock of mostly paperback.
# of Vols:	20,000
Hours:	Mon-Fri 10-7. Sat 10-4. Sun 12-4.

Ron's Roost   **Open Shop**
541 South Higgins Avenue   59801   (406) 549-0587

Collection:	General stock of paperback and hardcover.
# of Vols:	30,000
Hours:	Mon-Sat 9-7. Sun 12-6.
Travel:	Higgins Ave is major north/south thoroughfare in town.
Year Estab:	1980's
Comments:	Stock is approximately 65% paperback.

Sidneys Used Books   **Open Shop**
518 South 4th West   59801   (406) 543-5343

Collection:	General stock of hardcover and paperback.
# of Vols:	10,000
Hours:	Mon-Sat 12-5.
Services:	Search service, accepts want lists, catalog.
Travel:	Orange St exit off I-90. Proceed south on Orange to 4th St.
Credit Cards:	No
Owner:	Carol Stem
Year Estab:	1979
Comments:	Stock is evenly divided between hardcover and paperback.

Red Lodge

Broadway Book Store   **Open Shop**
13 South Broadway Avenue   59068   (406) 446-2742

Collection:	General stock of new and mostly paperback used.
# of Vols:	5,000+ (used)
Hours:	Mon-Sat 10-6. Sun 12-4.

Stevensville

Rocky Mountain House Books   **Open Shop**
3972 Highway 93N, Ste F   59870   (406) 777-5425
                                                       Fax: (406) 777-5425

Collection:	Specialty used and new.
Specialties:	Western Americana; Montana; Pacific Northwest; Native Americans; Custer; outlaws and lawmen.
Hours:	Mon-Fri 10-4, except closed Wed. Sat & Sun 10-3.
Services:	Appraisals, catalog, accepts want lists.
Travel:	Hwy 93 exit off I-90. Proceed south on Hwy 93 for about 30 miles. Shop is in High Mountain Business Mall.
Credit Cards:	Yes
Owner:	Jim Dullenty
Year Estab:	1985
Comments:	Stock is approximately 70% used.

Adventures West
(406) 222-1402
221 South 10th Livingston 59047

Collection:	Specialty
# of Vols:	500-1,000
Specialties:	Western Americana.
Services:	Accepts want lists.
Credit Cards:	No
Owner:	Fred Shellenberg
Year Estab:	1991

Geoscience Books
(406) 721-7379
502 West Alder Street Missoula 59802 E-mail: geoscibk@ism.net

Collection:	Specialty
# of Vols:	30,000
Specialties:	Geology and related sciences; paleontology; mineralogy; gemology.
Services:	Search service, accepts want lists, catalog.
Credit Cards:	Yes
Owner:	Michael Cohan
Year Estab:	1989

Just Good Books
(406) 388-6918
PO Box 232 Belgrade 59714 Fax: 4063887435
E-mail: books@imt.net

Collection:	Specialty
# of Vols:	3,000-6,000
Specialties:	Hunting; fishing (signed first editions and out of print titles).
Services:	Catalog, search service, accepts want lists.
Credit Cards:	Yes
Owner:	Tom Pappas
Year Estab:	1995
Comments:	Call for hours for possible future open shop.

Log Cabin Books
(406) 837-4477
PO Box 108 Bigfork 59911

Collection:	General stock.
# of Vols:	10,000
Specialties:	Western Americana.
Services:	Appraisals, search service, catalog, accepts want lists.
Credit Cards:	No
Owner:	Joe Eslick
Year Estab:	1983

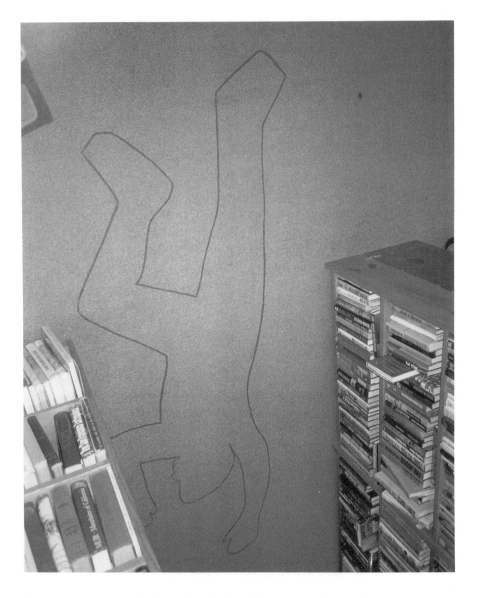

Do you think we finally found the mystery section?

Nebraska

Alphabetical Listing By Dealers

Alphabetical Listing By Location

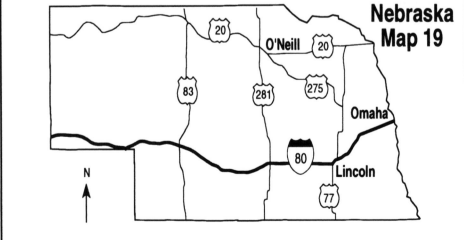

Nebraska Map 19

Grand Island

Aisle Land Books   **Open Shop**
1007 West 2nd Street   68801   (308) 384-5575

Collection:	General stock of mostly paperback.
# of Vols:	60,000
Hours:	Mon-Sat 10:30-5:30.

La Vista

Polly's Books   **Open Shop**
7101 South 84th Street   68128   (402) 331-2274

Collection:	General stock of mostly used paperback.
# of Vols:	20,000
Hours:	Mon-Fri 10-6. Sat 10-5. Sun 12:30-4:30.

Lincoln

A Novel Idea   **Open Shop**
118 North 14th Street   68508   (402) 475-8663

Collection:	General stock of paperback and hardcover.
# of Vols:	50,000
Hours:	Mon-Sat 10-6, except Thu till 9. (No evening hours in winter.) Sun 1-5.
Services:	Accepts want lists.
Travel:	From I-80, head south into downtown. Left on "O" St, then left on 14th St. Shop is just ahead on right.
Credit Cards:	No
Owner:	Cinnamon Dokken
Year Estab:	1991
Comments:	Located in the heart of downtown, this bi-level shop carries a combination of hardcover and paperback books (about a 60/40 ratio) in mixed condition. The sections are clearly labeled and the shop offers a generous selection of "more modern subjects." We didn't spot any rare items but plenty of "oldies" were on hand.

Bluestem Books   **Open Shop**
712 "O" Street   68508   (402) 435-7120

Collection:	General stock of hardcover and paperback.
# of Vols:	30,000
Specialties:	Nebraska; Western Americana; aviation; military; history; scholarly.
Hours:	Mon-Sat 10-5.
Services:	Accepts want lists, mail order.
Travel:	Downtown Lincoln exit off I-80. Proceed east on Hwy 34 to downtown then sharp right at "O" St. Shop is under the "O" St viaduct.
Credit Cards:	Yes
Owner:	Scott & Pat Wendt
Year Estab:	1975

Comments: Our very first visit for the Central States Guide (after two days on the road and a 1,350 mile journey) was to a shop most used book people would be pleased to find in their own neighborhood. This shop has "something for everyone." The majority of the books we saw were in good condition, fairly priced and easy to locate. Don't leave too soon or without checking some of the titles behind glass, or at least asking the owner about a particular volume you may not initially spot as more rare books (priced accordingly) are also on hand. The shop offers a good selection of titles in most areas and the shelves are nicely labeled.

Estuary Bookstore   **By Appointment**
128 North 13th Street, #408   68508   (402) 475-7323

Collection: Specialty
# of Vols: 10-12,000
Specialties: Literature; Nebraska literature; Irish literature; fine art; performing arts; children's.
Services: Appraisals, search service, catalog, accepts want lists.
Credit Cards: Yes
Owner: Norman Geske
Year Estab: 1989

Wordsmith Books & Art   **By Appointment**
PO Box 81066   68501   (402) 423-9552

Collection: General stock.
# of Vols: 15,000
Specialties: Nebraska history and authors; Great Plains.
Services: Appraisals
Owner: Francis Moal
Year Estab: 1982

North Platte

The Book Exchange   **Antique Mall**
At Antique Mini Mall & Flea Market   (308) 534-8476
507 North Jeffers Street 69101

Collection: General stock of mostly paperback.
# of Vols: 5,000

O'Neill

Book Warehouse   **Open Shop**
120 West Douglas 68763   (402) 336-3640

Collection: General stock.
# of Vols: 25,000
Hours: Mon-Fri 9-5. Sat 10-3.
Credit Cards: Yes
Owner: Barbara Sanders
Year Estab: 1988

Omaha

Addiction to Books   **Open Shop**
5104 South 108th Street 68127   (402) 331-2929

Collection:	General stock of paperback and hardcover.
# of Vols:	18,000
Hours:	Mon-Thu 11-7 Fri 11-5. Sat 10-5.
Travel:	108th St exit off I-680. Proceed south on 108th St to Q St. Shop is in Empire State Park Shopping Center.
Owner:	Michael Novotny
Year Estab:	1996
Comments:	A new shop (formerly owned and operated by another Omaha book dealer) just getting started when we visited the city. Unfortunately, the shop was not open on the day we were in town. We were advised by the new owner that approximately 70% of the stock was paperback.

Adventures in Bookselling   **Open Shop**
2945 North 108th Street 68164   (402) 491-3131

Collection:	General stock of paperback and hardcover.
# of Vols:	100,000+
Hours:	Mon-Sat 11-7. Sun 12-5.
Services:	Accepts want lists.
Travel:	Maple St exit off I-680. If northbound, turn left, cross over interstate and continue on Maple. If southbound, turn right on Maple. Shop is in Maple 108 Shopping Center.
Credit Cards:	No
Owner:	David Osborn
Year Estab:	1988
Comments:	When we hear about a shop boasting upwards of 100,000 volumes, we're anxious to visit. While the stock here may well meet the 100,000 criteria, the vast majority of the titles on display are paperback (which is not to suggest that the shop is bereft of hardcover items.) The books are attractively displayed, the establishment is "child friendly" and, in addition to books, you may also purchase comics, CDs and videos.

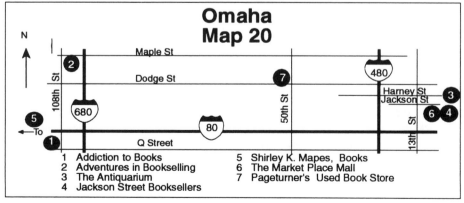

Omaha Map 20

1 Addiction to Books
2 Adventures in Bookselling
3 The Antiquarium
4 Jackson Street Booksellers
5 Shirley K. Mapes, Books
6 The Market Place Mall
7 Pageturner's Used Book Store

The Antiquarium   **Open Shop**
1215 Harney Street   68102   (402) 341-8077

Collection:	General stock of hardcover and paperback.
# of Vols:	100,000+
Hours:	Mon-Thu 11:30-8. Fri & Sat 11:30-midnight. Sun 2-6.
Services:	Appraisals
Travel:	14th St exit off I-480. Proceed south on 14th St, then left on Harney. Shop is just after the first light in Old Market area.
Credit Cards:	Yes
Owner:	Tom Rudloff & Judy Rudloff
Year Estab:	1969
Comments:	A sign at the entrance of this tri-level shop reads, "This is the largest bookshop in Nebraska." We have no doubt that the above statement is accurate in terms of the number of volumes. As for the quality of the collection, we suggest you judge for yourself. While the books are organized and shelved according to category and most are hardcover, the books are not in uniformly good condition. The selection is, however, broad enough for a patient browser to find several items of interest. A lower level houses comics, CDs and magazines.

Dickey Books   **By Appointment**
2104 South 135th Avenue   68144   (402) 330-3256
                                                   E-mail: pdickey@top.net

Collection:	Specialty
# of Vols:	10,000
Specialties:	Philosophy; psychology; literary first editions.
Services:	Catalog, accepts want lists.
Credit Cards:	No
Owner:	Paul E. Dickey
Year Estab:	1981

D.N. Dupley, Book Dealer   **By Appointment**
9118 Pauline Street   68124   (402) 393-2906

Collection:	General stock.
# of Vols:	6,000
Specialties:	Nebraska
Services:	Accepts want lists, mail order.
Credit Cards:	No
Owner:	Donald Dupley
Year Estab:	1964

Jackson Street Booksellers   **Open Shop**
1119 Jackson Street   68102   (402) 341-2664

Collection:	General stock of mostly hardcover.
# of Vols:	80,000
Specialties:	Scholarly; art; philosophy; literature.

Hours:	Mon 11-6. Tue-Thu 11-7. Fri & Sat 11-8. Sun 12-5.
Services:	Appraisals, search service, accepts want lists, mail order.
Travel:	13th St exit off I-80. Proceed north on 13th St for 1½ miles to Jackson Street, then right on Jackson to 11th St. Shop is in the Old Market area.
Credit Cards:	Yes
Owner:	Carl Ashford & Amanda Lynch
Year Estab:	1992
Comments:	A class act. This is truly a shop that dedicated book people will find a pleasure to visit. Most topics are covered and in reasonable depth. The variety of titles, both common and unusual, are such that the typical browser should take care least he or she miss a valuable find.

Library of Religious Thought **By Appointment**
3901 North 54th Street   68104 (402) 453-9808

Collection:	Specialty
# of Vols:	12,000
Specialties:	Theology
Services:	Appraisals, catalog.
Credit Cards:	No
Owner:	J. Beverland
Year Estab:	1986

Shirley K. Mapes, Books **Antique Mall**
At Brass Armadillo & Meadowlark Antique Malls Mall: (402) 896-9600
10666 & 10700 Sapp Brothers Drive Home: (402) 895-3046
Mailing address: 5114 South 121th Street Omaha 68137

Collection:	General stock.
# of Vols:	4,000-5,000
Hours:	Daily 9-9.
Services:	Search service, accepts want lists, mail order.
Travel:	Exit 439 off I-80. Malls are located side by side on frontage road adjacent to intersection of I-80 and Hwy 50.
Credit Cards:	Yes
Year Estab:	1987
Comments:	Unless you're an antique mall addict who enjoys the challenge of walking down every aisle to be certain you don't miss a particular item, you may, as we do when we visit this type of establishment, long for a pair of roller blades that would allow you to traverse the aisles more swiftly, stopping only where a reasonable number of books are on display. If you have the time and don't mind other distractions, you'll find a selection of "better than average" books at these premises. The books we saw displayed by the two identified dealers (Shirley K. Mapes and CD Woods) were in mostly good condition, represented popular subjects and were reasonably priced. Other unidentified dealers also offered better than average selections: one with a display case filled with golf books and related items and another with a generous selection of children's series books in quite good condition.

Market Place Mall   **Antique Mall**
1125 Jackson   (402) 346-4930

Hours:	Tue-Thu 10-6. Fri & Sat 11-9. Sun 12-6.
Travel:	In Old Market area.

Merchant Of Venus   **Open Shop**
5119 Leavenworth Street   68106   (402) 558-9166

Collection:	Specialty. Mostly new and some used.
# of Vols:	2,000 (used)
Specialties:	Science fiction; fantasy; horror.
Hours:	Mon-Fri 10-7. Sat 10-5.
Travel:	60th St exit off I-80. Proceed north on 60th then right on Leavenworth. Shop is in strip center on right.

Pageturner's Used Book Store   **Open Shop**
5004 Dodge Street   68132   (402) 551-7971

Collection:	General stock of hardcover and paperback.
# of Vols:	25,000
Hours:	Mon-Fri 11-7. Sat 11-6. Sun 12-6.
Travel:	42nd St exit off I-80. Proceed north on 42nd St, then west on Dodge. Shop is at northwest corner of 50th & Dodge. Parking is available in the rear.
Credit Cards:	No
Owner:	Jeff Armstrong
Year Estab:	1988
Comments:	While the books in this bi-level shop were reasonably priced, the number of hardcover volumes on display (on both levels) seemed to us to be outnumbered by the paperback stock.

Paperback Exchange   **Open Shop**
4601 South 50th Street   68117   (402) 734-7733

Collection:	General stock of mostly paperback.
Hours:	Mon & Fri 10-5. Tue-Thu 10-7. Sat 9-6. Sun 12-4.

Treasure Mart   **Open Shop**
8316 Blondo Street   68134   (402) 399-8874

Collection:	General stock of mostly paperback.
# of Vols:	30,000
Hours:	Mon-Sat 11-7. Sun 12-5, except closed first Sun of every month.

The Book Barn
1583 Stable Drive   South Sioux City 68776

Collection:	General stock and ephemera.
# of Vols:	65,000
Services:	Appraisals, search service, accepts want lists (responses only with SASE).
Owner:	Darleen J. Volkert
Year Estab:	1973

DNA Books   (402) 483-2475
1850 South 50th Street   Lincoln 68506

Collection:	Specialty
# of Vols:	2,000
Specialties:	Science fiction; fantasy; horror.
Services:	Occasional catalog, search service, accepts want lists.
Credit Cards:	No
Owner:	Barry Abrahams
Year Estab:	1986

Orville J. Grady   (402) 558-6782
6602 Military Avenue   Omaha 68104

Collection:	Specialty used and new.
# of Vols:	30,000-40,000
Specialties:	Numismatics; banking history; finance and economic history.
Services:	Appraisals, search service, accepts want lists, catalog.
Credit Cards:	No
Year Estab:	1982
Comments:	Collection may also be viewed by appointment.

Lee Booksellers   (402) 467-4416
281 East Park Plaza   Lincoln 68505   Fax: (402) 467-4859

Collection:	Specialty used and new.
Specialties:	Americana; Nebraska; numismatics.
Services:	Appraisals, catalog (new only), accepts want lists.
Credit Cards:	Yes
Owner:	James L. McKee
Year Estab:	1969

Vintage Volumes
PO Box 555   Dakota City 68731

Collection:	General stock and ephemera.
# of Vols:	60,000
Services:	Appraisals, search service, accepts want lists (responses only with SASE).
Owner:	Darleen J. Volkert
Year Estab:	1980

A book person who takes her work seriously.

Nevada

Alphabetical Listing By Dealer

Alphabetical Listing By Location

Boulder City

Gallery of the Old West   **By Appointment**
707 Canyon, # 101   (702) 294-0383
Mailing address: PO Box 60927 Boulder City 89006

Collection:	Specialty books and ephemera.
# of Vols:	3,000
Specialties:	Western Americana; firearms; hunting; natural history.
Hours:	Available only winter months.
Services:	Appraisals, search service, accepts want lists, mail order.
Credit Cards:	No
Owner:	Bob Borcherdt
Year Estab:	1987
Comments:	See Bigfork, MT listing for summer address.

Carson City

Arts & Antiques   **Open Shop**
201 West King Street 89703   (702) 882-4447

Collection:	Specialty
# of Vols:	5,000
Specialties:	Military; Western Americana.
Hours:	Wed-Sat 12-5. Other times by appointment.
Services:	Accepts want lists, mail order.
Travel:	In downtown, one block west of Hwy 395 (Carson St).
Credit Cards:	No
Owner:	Bud Klette
Year Estab:	1965

Kennedy's Books   **Open Shop**
1221 South Carson Street 89701   (702) 882-9253

Collection:	General stock of mostly new and used paperback and hardcover.
# of Vols:	2,000 (used)
Hours:	Mon-Fri 10-7. Sat 10-6. Sun 11-5.
Travel:	On Hwy 395 in Carson Mall.
Credit Cards:	Yes
Owner:	Melissa Gower
Year Estab:	1977
Comments:	Used stock is approximately 75% paperback.

Thrifty Joe's   **Open Shop**
2567 North Carson Street 89701   (702) 885-7088

Collection:	General stock of paperback and hardcover.
Hours:	Mon-Thu 10-8. Fri & Sat 10-10. Sun 10-6.
Travel:	Located on Hwy 395 in Northgate Shopping Center.
Year Estab:	1995
Comments:	See comments for Reno store.

Elko

Bookstore   **Open Shop**
1372 Idaho Street   89801   (702) 738-5342

Collection: General stock of new and mostly paperback used.
# of Vols: 3,000 (used)
Hours: Mon-Fri 9-5:30. Sat 9-5.

Ely

Sack's Thrift Store   **Open Shop**
1490 Aultman Street   89301   (702) 289-3630

Collection: General stock of paperback and hardcover.
Hours: Mon-Sat 9:30-3.
Comments: Not-for-profit shop. All books are donated.

Fallon

Alphabet Soup   **Open Shop**
76 North Maine Street   89406   (702) 423-8736

Collection: General stock of hardcover and paperback.
# of Vols: 20,000
Hours: Mon-Sat 10:30-5:30.
Travel: Hwy 50 goes through town and becomes William. From William, turn
                   north on Maine.
Credit Cards: No
Owner: Judith Seibert
Year Estab: 1994
Comments: Stock is evenly divided between hardcover and paperback.

Genoa

Lock Stock & Barrel Books   **Open Shop**
2292 Main Street   (702) 782-3468
Mailing address: PO Box 381 Genoa 89411

Collection: General stock of mostly hardcover.
# of Vols: 11,000
Specialties: Western fiction; military; history.
Hours: Mon-Sat 10:30-5:30. Sun 12-5. Best to call ahead.
Services: Appraisals, search service, accepts want lists, mail order.
Travel: Genoa Lane exit off Hwy 395. Proceed toward Genoa.
Credit Cards: Yes
Owner: Dave Pearson
Year Estab: 1991

Las Vegas

Academy Fine Books   **Open Shop**
2024 East Charleston Boulevard   89104   (702) 471-6500

Collection:	General stock and ephemera.
# of Vols:	10,000
Hours:	Mon-Sun, except closed Tue, 10-4.
Services:	Appraisals, accepts want lists, mail order.
Travel:	Charleston exit off I-15. Proceed east on Charleston for about three miles to Antique Square.
Credit Cards:	No
Owner:	Gary Frick
Year Estab:	1981
Comments:	A separate shop located in the midst of several antique dealers. Heavy in vintage paperbacks with a modest collection of hardcover books, including some nice children's volumes. The books we saw were mostly older and in mixed to good condition.

Albion Book Co.   **Open Shop**
2466-G East Desert Inn Road   89120   Fax: (702) 792-9554   (702) 792-9554
                                                    E-mail: lasteam@aol.com

Collection:	General stock of mostly hardcover.
# of Vols:	100,000
Specialties:	Modern first editions; Western Americana; art.
Hours:	Daily 10-6.
Services:	Appraisals, search service.
Travel:	In Francisco Centre, just east of Eastern Ave.
Credit Cards:	Yes
Owner:	Michael Burdo & Lisa Horine
Year Estab:	1989
Comments:	A really nice shop with quality on every shelf. The hardcover books were in pristine condition and were meticulously shelved. The shop is spacious and a pleasure to browse. If your interests are in any of the specialties listed above and/or mystery, you should really enjoy your visit here although other categories were represented in generous numbers. Paperbacks were located in the rear of the shop. The shop also has a full service espresso bar. At the time of our visit, the owners were planning to open a second shop in Las Vegas and advised us that the collection in the new shop would will be similar to, although smaller, than this one.

Alpha Omega Bibles Books   **Open Shop**
5690 Boulder Highway   89122   (702) 451-8608

Collection:	Specialty new and used.
# of Vols:	8,000
Specialties:	Religion
Hours:	Mon-Sat 12-5.
Comments:	Stock is evenly divided between new and used and approximately 70% of used books are paperback.

(Las Vegas)

Amber Unicorn/Donato's Fine Books   **Open Shop**
2202 West Charleston Blvd. #2   89102   (702) 384-5838
                                                    Fax: (702) 384-4441

Collection:	General stock of hardcover and paperback.
# of Vols:	50,000
Specialties:	Cookbooks; science fiction; military; Western Americana; metaphysics; occult.
Hours:	Mon-Sat 10-7. Sun 11-7.
Services:	Appraisals, search service, catalog, accepts want lists.
Travel:	West Charleston exit off I-15. Proceed west on West Charleston for about 4/10 mile.
Credit Cards:	Yes
Owner:	Lou & Myrna Donato
Year Estab:	1981
Comments:	A nice shop with plenty of room to display hardcover books, many of which were first editions and several of which were rare and collectible. Most subjects were represented, with the specialties listed above in particularly good quantity. The shop also carries vintage and other paperbacks. Worth a visit.

Book Bazaar   **Open Shop**
3001 East Charleston Boulevard   (702) 384-4711
Mailing address: PO Box 42005 Las Vegas 89116   (800) 268-9360

Collection:	Specialty
# of Vols:	2,000+
Specialties:	Chemistry; physics; mathematics; construction and related arts; espionage; adventure.
Hours:	Mon & Wed-Sat 10-2.
Services:	Search service (all subjects), accepts want lists, mail order.

Book Mart   **Open Shop**
512 South Las Vegas Boulevard   89101   (702) 385-2841

Collection:	General stock of mostly paperback.
# of Vols:	27,000
Hours:	Mon-Sat 9-4.

Book Shoppe   **Open Shop**
2232 South Nellis, Ste G-1   89104   (702) 641-1155

Collection:	General stock of new and mostly paperback used.
# of Vols:	25,000
Hours:	Daily 10-6, except Fri & Sat till 8.

Book Stop III   **Open Shop**
1440 East Charleston Boulevard   89104   (702) 386-4858

Collection:	General stock of hardcover and paperback.

# of Vols:	35,000
Hours:	Summer: Mon-Fri 10-6. Sat 11-5. Winter Mon-Fri 10-5. Sat 11-5.
Services:	Appraisals, search service, accepts want lists, mail order.
Travel:	Charleston exit off I-15. Proceed east on Charleston to Lafayette Square Shopping Center. Shop is east of Maryland Parkway.
Credit Cards:	Yes
Owner:	Gini Segedi
Year Estab:	1973
Comments:	A mix of hardcover books and paperbacks with most of the former being of fairly recent vintage and in generally good condition. If you spend a lot of time looking at titles, you might find some that could be of interest you. Unfortunately, we didn't. Another dealer is located in the same shopping center. (See Gundy's Book World below.)

Book Traders   **Open Shop**
4180 South Sandhill Road, Ste B5   89121   (702) 454-3212

Collection:	General stock of mostly paperback.
# of Vols:	200,000
Hours:	Mon-Fri 10-9. Sat 10-6. Sun 1-6.

Bookends   **Open Shop**
3920-A West Charleston Boulevard   89102   (702) 878-9290

Collection:	General stock of paperback and hardcover.
# of Vols:	10,000
Specialties:	Mystery; fantasy.
Hours:	Mon-Sat 10-6.
Services:	Bookbinding and restoration.
Travel:	Charleston exit off I-15. Proceed west on Charleston to Village Shopping Center.
Credit Cards:	No
Owner:	Cindy West
Year Estab:	1992
Comments:	A largely paperback shop (it even has a room devoted to romance) that also carries hardcover books in mostly good condition, including a number of collectibles. We spotted a number of desirable items behind glass and in at least two cabinets.

Booklovers   **Open Shop**
3142 North Rainbow Boulevard   89108   (702) 658-8583

Collection:	General stock of paperback and hardcover.
# of Vols:	20,000
Hours:	Mon-Fri 10-7. Sat 10-6. Sun 12-5.
Travel:	Cheyenne exit off Hwy 95. Proceed east on Cheyenne to Rainbow Ridge Plaza. Shop is at intersection of Cheyenne and Rainbow Blvd.
Credit Cards:	Yes
Owner:	Pat Gallotta
Year Estab:	1994

Comments: A heavily paperback shop with a selection of hardcover fiction on the
                 top shelves of several bookcases, most of which were fairly recent best
                 sellers in good condition and, in our judgment, a bit overpriced. Other
                 hardcover books covering a range of subjects were shelved in the rear
                 of the shop.

COAS: Books   **Open Shop**
4972 South Maryland Parkway   89119   (702) 261-9577

Collection: General stock of hardcover and paperback.
# of Vols: 50,000
Specialties: Technical; sciences; anthropology; history.
Hours: Mon-Sat 11-7.
Travel: Tropicana exit off Hwy 15. Proceed east on Tropicana. Shop is at corner
                 of Tropicana and Maryland Pkwy, just east of McCarran Airport.
Credit Cards: Yes
Owner: Patrick Beckett
Year Estab: 1995
Comments: A bit larger than it may initially appear, this shop offers a balance of
                 both hardcover and paperback titles in most categories. The hardcover
                 items were in mixed condition and represented mixed vintages with
                 the majority being relatively newer. This is the kind of shop that may
                 not require a long visit but, depending on the shop's recent acquisi-
                 tions, could with luck, bring you the title you've been searching for.

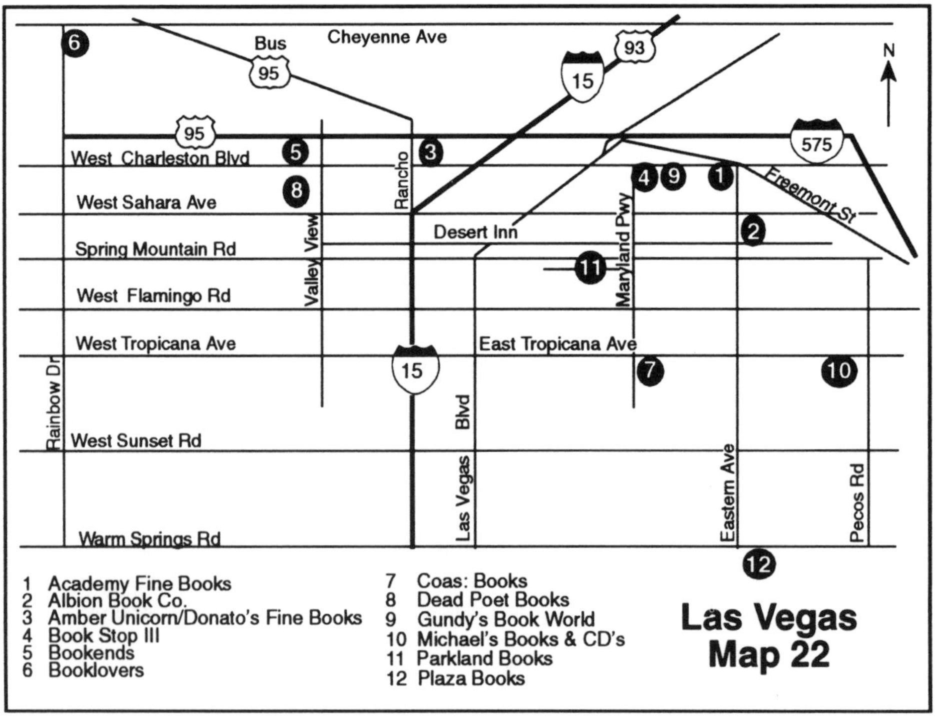

1 Academy Fine Books	7 Coas: Books
2 Albion Book Co.	8 Dead Poet Books
3 Amber Unicorn/Donato's Fine Books	9 Gundy's Book World
4 Book Stop III	10 Michael's Books & CD's
5 Bookends	11 Parkland Books
6 Booklovers	12 Plaza Books

**Las Vegas
Map 22**

Bob Coffin Books   **By Appointment**
1139 South Fifth Place   89104   Fax: (702) 598-0985   (702) 598-0982
                                                   E-mail: bcoffinb@interloc.com

Collection: Specialty books and ephemera.
Specialties: Nevada; Western Americana; mining; geology; government publica-
                  tions; maps; railroads.
Services: Appraisals, search service, catalog, accepts want lists.
Credit Cards: Yes
Year Estab: 1989

Dead Poet Books   **Open Shop**
3858 West Sahara Avenue   89102   (702) 227-4070

Collection: General stock of hardcover and paperback.
# of Vols: 12,000
Specialties: Military; metaphysics.
Hours: Mon-Sat 10-6. Sun 12-5.
Services: Accepts want lists, mail order.
Travel: Sahara exit off I-15. Proceed west on Sahara to Valley Oaks Plaza
                  shopping center.
Credit Cards: Yes
Owner: Linda & Rich Piediscalzi
Year Estab: 1992
Comments: A neat establishment with quality hardcover titles in both scholarly
                  and more mundane fields taking up the front two thirds of the shop.
                  The books we saw were in very good condition and were reasonably
                  priced. The remaining one third of the shop houses paperbacks.

Friends of Southern Nevada Libraries   **Open Shop**
3894 West Spring Mountain, #4   89102   (702) 382-3493
                                                                   ext. 254

Collection: General stock of hardcover and paperback.
Hours: Sun 1-4, the second Sunday of each month.
Travel: Between Valley View and Arville.
Comments: A not-for-profit shop operated by Friends of the Library. Entrance is by
                  membership only. The $5 membership fee can be paid at the door.

Gambler's Book Shop   **Open Shop**
630 South 11th Street   89101   (800) 522-1777   (702) 382-7555
                                                        Fax:(702) 382-7594

Collection: Specialty. Mostly new and some used.
# of Vols: 300,000
Specialties: Gambling; magic; organized crime.
Hours: Mon-Sat 9-5.
Services: Search service, catalog (new books only), accepts want lists.
Travel: One block west of Maryland Pkwy, just off Charleston Blvd.
Credit Cards: Yes
Owner: Edna Luckman

(Las Vegas)

Year Estab:	1964
Comments:	Stock of approximately 10% used, 70% of which is hardcover.

Gundy's Book World   Open Shop
1442 East Charleston Boulevard   89104   (702) 385-6043

Collection:	General stock of paperback and hardcover.
# of Vols:	20,000
Specialties:	Magazines.
Hours:	Mon-Fri 10-5:30. Sat 10-3.
Travel:	Charleston Blvd exit off I-15. Proceed east on Charleston to Lafayette Square Shopping Center.
Credit Cards:	Yes
Owner:	Sol & Elaine Levco
Year Estab:	1981
Comments:	Paperbacks clearly outnumber hardcover books here and the shop also offers "girlie" magazines for sale. The hardcover volumes we saw were in mixed condition, some average, some collectible and some just old (and not in the best condition). Another book dealer is located in the same shopping center. (See Book Stop III above.)

Michael's Books & CD's   Open Shop
3335 East Tropicana   89121   (702) 434-1699

Collection:	General stock of hardcover and paperback and CDs.
# of Vols:	30,000
Hours:	Mon-Sat 10-6. Sun 11-5.
Travel:	Tropicana exit off I-15. Proceed east on Tropicana to Pecos Rd. Shop is in Pecos Plaza.
Credit Cards:	Yes
Owner:	Michael Clark
Year Estab:	1994
Comments:	The shop offers enough hardcover items to make the collection quite respectable. The hardcover items we saw were in mixed condition and priced most reasonably. If you can search carefully, as we did, you might even find an item or two worth purchasing. As with all book searches, its often "the luck of the draw," an observation particularly appropriate in Las Vegas.

Novel Idea   Open Shop
6680 West Flamingo, #10   89103   (702) 873-2665

Collection:	General stock of mostly paperback.
Hours:	Mon-Sat 10-5:30. Sun 10:15-4.

Page After Page   Open Shop
1456 East Charleston Boulevard   89104   (702) 384-1690

Collection:	Specialty new and used.

# of Vols:	50,000 (used)
Specialties:	Science fiction; fantasy.
Hours:	Daily 9-7.
Travel:	Charleston Blvd exit off I-15. Proceed east on Charleston to Lafayette Square Shopping Center.
Owner:	Lynn Pederson
Year Estab:	1981
Comments:	This shop might have had some hardcover volumes when we visited; we just couldn't find any. (Perhaps they were stored out of sight.) The shop does have an extensive collection of comic materials and paperbacks focusing on science fiction and fantasy, including what may be some vintage titles.

Paperback Exchange   **Open Shop**
5140 West Charleston Boulevard   89102   (702) 870-5050

Collection:	General stock of mostly paperback.
# of Vols:	30,000
Hours:	Mon-Sat 10-5.

Paperback Exchange II   **Open Shop**
7150 Westcliff   89128   (702) 869-8697

Collection:	General stock of mostly paperback.
# of Vols:	20,000
Hours:	Mon-Sat 10-5.

Parkland Books   **Open Shop**
3661 South Maryland Parkway   89109   (702) 732-4474
                                            E-mail: parkland@interloc.com

Collection:	General stock of hardcover and paperback and ephemera.
# of Vols:	15,000+
Specialties:	National parks; children's; cooking; Americana.
Hours:	Mon-Sat 10-6.
Services:	Search service, mail order, accepts want lists.
Travel:	Flamingo exit off I-15. Proceed east on Flamingo to Maryland Pkwy, then left on Maryland. Shop is in Maryland Square Shopping Center.
Owner:	Marge & Ed Rothfuss
Year Estab:	1993
Comments:	A moderate sized shop that carries a mix of hardcover books, paperbacks, collectibles and yes, even some antiquarian items. The books we saw were in mixed condition, some with fairly common titles and some uncommon enough to be worthy of a second look and perhaps leading to a purchase.

Plaza Books   **Open Shop**
7380 South Eastern Avenue, Ste 102   89123   (702) 263-2692

Collection:	General stock of hardcover and paperback.
# of Vols:	20,000

Hours:	Mon-Fri 10-7. Sat & Sun 12-6.
Travel:	Hwy 215/Airport exit off I-15. Proceed on Hwy 215 to Warm Springs exit, then east on Warm Springs to Eastern. Shop is in Warm Springs Plaza.
Credit Cards:	Yes
Owner:	John Hathaway & Ann DeVere
Year Estab:	1995
Comments:	A moderate sized shop with a mix of hardcover and paperback books. A nice selection of mystery and science fiction with other subjects covered in slightly less quantity.

Reno

J. Bacon & Company   **Open Shop**
8155 South Virginia Street   89511   (702) 852-2215

Collection:	Specialty
Specialties:	Autographs; first editions; signed books; manuscripts.
Hours:	Mon-Fri 10-6. Sat 10-3.
Services:	Appraisals, catalog.
Travel:	South Virginia St exit off Hwy 395. Proceed north on Virginia.
Credit Cards:	Yes
Owner:	Jack Bacon
Year Estab:	1976

Black & White Books   **Open Shop**
1300 South Wells Avenue   89502   (702) 324-6669
                                                          Fax: (702) 324-7643

Collection:	General stock of mostly hardcover.
# of Vols:	50,000+
Hours:	Mon-Sat 10:30-7:30. Sun 12:30-6.
Services:	Appraisals, search service, accepts want lists, mail order.
Travel:	Wells Ave exit off I-80. Proceed south on Wells. Shop is at corner of Wells and Vassar.
Credit Cards:	Yes
Owner:	Lee & Ivye Johnson
Year Estab:	1994
Comments:	Quite a nice shop with a good proportion of hardcover volumes, most in fine condition and attractively displayed. Some vintage items. Many subjects represented. Certainly worth a visit.

Five Dog Books   **Open Shop**
906 Holcomb Avenue   89502   (702) 322-1917

Collection:	General stock of mostly hardcover.
# of Vols:	10,000
Specialties:	Western Americana; philosophy.
Hours:	Mon-Sat 11-4.
Services:	Appraisals, search service, accepts want lists, mail order.

Travel:	Virginia St exit off I-80. Proceed south on Virginia, then left on Center Street and proceed to Holcomb. Left on Holcomb.
Credit Cards:	No
Owner:	Manuel Esparolini
Year Estab:	1980
Comments:	Located in three or four front rooms of a private residence, this shop offers a nice selection of hardcover volumes and is particularly strong in the specialties listed above as well as "good" literature. Pleasant to visit. An affable owner.

Gambler's Bookstore   **Open Shop**
4001 South Virginia Street   89502   (702) 825-7778

Collection:	Specialty. Mostly new.
# of Vols:	100 (used)
Specialties:	Gambling; sports; horses.
Hours:	Mon-Fri 10-8. Sat 10-6. Sun 12-5.
Services:	Accepts want lists, catalog (new books only).

Fred Holabird Americana   **By Appointment**

Fax: (702) 8513432   (702) 851-0836

Collection:	General stock and ephemera.
Specialties:	Western Americana (books and documents).
Services:	Appraisals, catalog.
Year Estab:	1976
Comments:	Sells only wholesale to dealers.

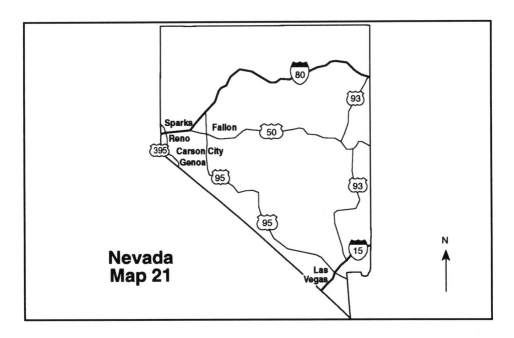

**Nevada
Map 21**

Karen Hillary Antiques & Appraisals
418 California Avenue   89509

Open Shop
(702) 322-1800

Collection:	General stock of mostly hardcover.
# of Vols:	10,000 (See Comments)
Hours:	Mon-Sat 10-4:30.
Services:	Appraisals
Travel:	Virginia St exit off I-80. Proceed south on Virginia, then right on California. Shop is between Virginia and Arlington.
Credit Cards:	Yes
Owner:	Charles Silinsky
Year Estab:	1965
Comments:	Approximately 2,000-3,000 volumes are on display at the store at any given time.

Subject Matter Books
105 Hubbard Way   89502

Open Shop
(702) 827-1225

Collection:	General stock of paperback and hardcover.
# of Vols:	5,000
Hours:	Mon-Sat 11-5.
Travel:	Just off Virginia Street, across from Peppermill casino.
Credit Cards:	No
Year Estab:	1989
Comments:	For those book people who travel by motorcycle, this is the place for you, not because the shop specializes in books dealing with motorcycles but because the owner also sells motorcycle parts from an attached room. Oh yes, the shop does carry books, both paperback and hardcover volumes, and while the number of hardcover volumes was not overly large, we did notice several interesting titles. The shop is across the street from one of Reno's premier casino hotels where, depending on your interests, you can enjoy an inexpensive meal and/or try your hand at winning enough money to buy more used books.

Thrifty Joe's
6015-C South Virginia Street   89502

Open Shop
(702) 853-6348

Collection:	General stock of paperback and hardcover, CDs and videos.
Hours:	Mon-Sat 10-8. Sun 12-6.
Services:	Yes
Travel:	Del Monte Shopping Center. Del Monte exit off Hwy 395. Proceed east on Del Monte to Del Monte Shopping Center.
Owner:	Otto Lehrack
Comments:	The name of the shop provides a clue as to what we found when we visited. Mostly paperbacks, lots of CD's and tapes, a few videos and video games and a very modest collection of hardcover books which people no doubt brought in for "trade." Unless we were misinformed, walk-ins are the sole source of the stock. This does not mean that there are no good books here. However, don't anticipate rare or collectible items.

WARC   **Open Shop**
570 Gentry Way   89502   (702) 825-1972

Collection:	General stock of paperback and hardcover.
Hours:	Daily 9-6.
Travel:	At corner of Kietzkie and Gentry. Moama exit off I-80.
Comments:	A not-for-profit shop.

Sparks

Book Gallery   **Open Shop**
1203 North Rock Boulevard   89431   (702) 356-8900
                                                          Fax: (702) 355-0946

Collection:	General stock of paperback and hardcover.
# of Vols:	150,000
Hours:	Mon-Sat 10-5. Sun 11-3.
Services:	Search service, accepts want lists, mail order.
Travel:	Rock Blvd exit off I-80. Proceed north on Rock Blvd to Ross Plaza shopping center.
Credit Cards:	No
Owner:	Geri Thornton
Year Estab:	1988
Comments:	A large store with a collection of both paperbacks and hardcover volumes in most subject areas. Easy to browse. The books were in mixed condition with few real collectibles but plenty of titles from which to select. You may also purchase comics and videos (should this be of interest to you.)

Book House   **Open Shop**
455 Greenbrae Drive   89431   (702) 331-7144

Collection:	General stock of mostly paperback.
# of Vols:	20,000
Hours:	Tue-Sat 10-6.
Travel:	Pyramid Rd exit off I-80. Proceed north on Pyramid to Greenbrae, then right on Greenbrae.
Credit Cards:	Yes
Owner:	Carolyn Zimmer
Year Estab:	1995
Comments:	A mostly paperback shop but the hardcover items on hand, although limited in number, were almost without exception in quite good condition with some interesting titles to select from. If you're the outdoor type (from guns to gardening) you could enjoy a stop here. As the owners have been contemplating a change to a "by appointment" basis, you may want to call before you travel here.

Virginia City

Buckskin & Lace   **Open Shop**
76 North C Street   (702) 847-0154
Mailing address: PO Box 860 Virginia City 89440

Collection:	Specialty. Mostly new.
Specialties:	Comstock Lode; Nevada.
Hours:	Daily 10-5.
Credit Cards:	Yes
Year Estab:	1972

Mark Twain Books   **Open Shop**
111 South C Street   (702) 847-0454
Mailing address: PO Box 449 Virginia City 89440   Fax: (702) 847-9010

Collection:	Specialty new and used books and ephemera.
Specialties:	Western Americana; Nevada; Comstock history.
Hours:	Apr-Nov: Daily 10-5. Dec-Mar: Tue-Sun 11-5.
Services:	Appraisals, accepts want lists, mail order.
Travel:	Shop is in downtown at intersection of C Street and Taylor.
Credit Cards:	Yes
Owner:	Joe & Ellie Curtis
Year Estab:	1995
Comments:	Stock is approximately 20% used.

Battle Born Books
101 South Rainbow, #28 Las Vegas 89128

Collection:	Specialty
# of Vols:	10,000
Specialties:	History; military; aviation.
Services:	Catalog, accepts want lists.
Credit Cards:	No
Owner:	Don & Kathe Swenson
Year Estab:	1989

Camelot Press
3801 Bexley Square Sparks 89434

(702) 331-0831
E-mail: huggins@pogo.scs.uar.edu

Collection:	General stock.
# of Vols:	5,000
Services:	Catalog
Credit Cards:	No
Owner:	Don Huggins
Year Estab:	1992

Renegade Books
PO Box 403   Silver Springs 89429

(702) 577-2533

Collection:	Specialty
# of Vols:	8,500
Specialties:	Nevada; modern first editions; automobiles; Western Americana.
Services:	Search service, accepts want lists, catalog.
Credit Cards:	Yes
Owner:	Tom & Lee Blomquist
Year Estab:	1970's
Comments:	Collection can be viewed by appointment.

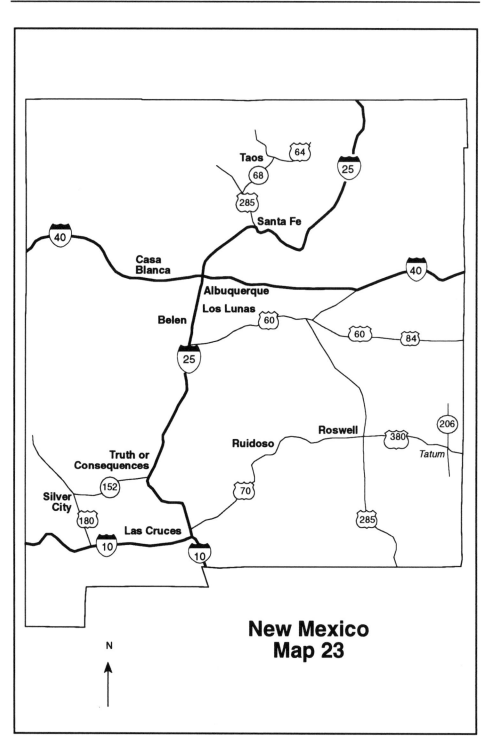

**New Mexico
Map 23**

New Mexico

Alphabetical Listing By Dealer

Alphabetical Listing By Location

Albuquerque

A Novel Idea   **Open Shop**
2805 San Mateo Boulevard NE   87110   (505) 883-6217
                                                E-mail: lcrane2240@aol.com

Collection:	General stock of hardcover and paperback.
# of Vols:	15,000
Specialties:	Technical; science.
Hours:	Tue-Sun 11-5.
Services:	Search service, accepts want lists, mail order.
Travel:	San Mateo north exit off I-40. Proceed north on San Mateo. Shop is between Menaul and Candelaria.
Credit Cards:	No
Owner:	Lisa Crane
Year Estab:	1995
Comments:	Stock is approximately 70% hardcover.

All Indian Nations Bookstore   **Open Shop**
1201 Rio Grande Boulevard NW   87104   (505) 246-8372

Collection:	Specialty new and used.
Specialties:	Native Americans.
Hours:	Mon-Sat 9-6. Sun 1:30-6.
Travel:	Exit 157A (Rio Grande Blvd) off I-40. Proceed north for one block. Shop is on west side of street.
Credit Cards:	Yes
Owner:	Victor Garcia
Year Estab:	1980

Alphaville Video   **Open Shop**
521 Central NW, Ste H   87102   (505) 242-2463

Collection:	Specialty new and used.
# of Vols:	200 (used)
Specialties:	Film
Hours:	Mon-Sat 12-9.
Travel:	On Central between 6th & 7th Streets.

Ave Maria Catholic Books & Supplies   **Open Shop**
2211 Central Avenue NW   87104   (505) 842-6288

Collection:	Specialty new and used.
# of Vols:	2,000+ (used)
Specialties:	Catholicism
Hours:	Mon-Fri 9-5. Sat 10-5.
Travel:	Between Rio Grande and Central.
Credit Cards:	Yes
Year Estab:	1986

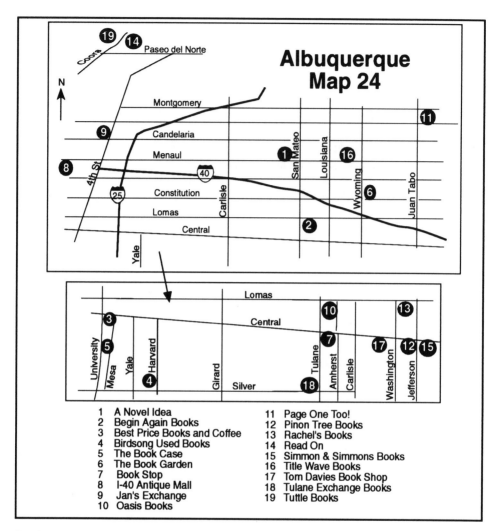

**Albuquerque
Map 24**

1   A Novel Idea
2   Begin Again Books
3   Best Price Books and Coffee
4   Birdsong Used Books
5   The Book Case
6   The Book Garden
7   Book Stop
8   I-40 Antique Mall
9   Jan's Exchange
10 Oasis Books
11 Page One Too!
12 Pinon Tree Books
13 Rachel's Books
14 Read On
15 Simmon & Simmons Books
16 Title Wave Books
17 Tom Davies Book Shop
18 Tulane Exchange Books
19 Tuttle Books

Barbara's Book Store   **Open Shop**
9800 Montgomery Boulevard NE   87111   (505) 275-1582

Collection: General stock of mostly paperback.
Hours: Mon-Sat 10-5.

Begin Again Books   **Open Shop**
5906 Lomas NE   87110   (505) 255-3757

Collection: General stock of hardcover and paperback.
# of Vols: 10,000
Hours: Wed-Sat 10:30-6.
Services: Search service, accepts want lists, mail order.
Travel: San Mateo exit off I-40. South on San Mateo then east on Lomas.
Credit Cards: Yes

Owner:	Lynn Eaves
Year Estab:	1995
Comments:	A modest sized shop displaying some nice "coffee table type books" in the front window and elsewhere with the rest of the shop carrying a mix of paperbacks and fairly recent hardcover material. While most of the books we saw were in reasonably good condition, the selection was limited.

Best Price Books and Coffee   **Open Shop**
1800 Central SE   87106   (505) 842-0624

Collection:	General stock of hardcover and paperback.
# of Vols:	1,000
Hours:	Daily 7am-11pm.
Travel:	Central Ave exit off I-25. Proceed east on Central.
Credit Cards:	Yes
Owner:	Jim Franco
Year Estab:	1991
Comments:	Stock is approximately 60% hardcover.

Birdsong Used Books & Records   **Open Shop**
139 Harvard SE   87106   (505) 268-7204

Collection:	General stock of paperback and hardcover.
# of Vols:	65,000+
Specialties:	Literature; poetry; science fiction.
Hours:	Daily, at least 11-7. Sometimes earlier, sometimes later.
Services:	Accepts want lists, mail order.
Travel:	One block east of Yale between Central and Silver.
Credit Cards:	Yes
Owner:	Brad Bumgarner-Kirby
Year Estab:	1979
Comments:	Strong in the fields identified above as well as new age literature. Hardcover items are clearly in a minority here. If you're looking for out of print titles and don't care about editions, you may find some items of interest here. But don't expect to find antiquarian or collectible hardcover titles.

Blue Eagle Book & Metaphysical Center   **Open Shop**
8334 Lomas Street NE   87110   (505) 268-3682

Collection:	Specialty new and used.
# of Vols:	3,000 (used)
Specialties:	Metaphysics
Hours:	Mon-Sat 9-9. Sun 12-5.
Travel:	On Lomas, 1½ blocks west of Wyoming.

The Book Case   **Open Shop**
109 Mesa SE   87106   (505) 247-3102

Collection:	General stock of paperback and hardcover.
# of Vols:	30,000+
Hours:	Mon-Sat 10-6. Occasional Sundays.
Travel:	Central Ave exit off I-25. Proceed east on Central, then south on Mesa.

(Albuquerque)

Credit Cards:	No
Owner:	Laura Eisner
Year Estab:	1960
Comments:	The stock is approximately 70% paperback.

The Book Garden   **Open Shop**
1502-A Wyoming, NE   87112   (505) 292-6005

Collection:	General stock of hardcover and paperback.
# of Vols:	25,000
Hours:	Mon-Sat 10-6.
Services:	Search service, accepts want lists, mail order.
Travel:	Wyoming exit off I-40. Proceed north on Wyoming for about 1½ blocks. Shop is on northeast corner of Constitution in a shopping center.
Credit Cards:	Yes
Owner:	Diane Lewis
Year Estab:	1981
Comments:	A pleasant surprise. The shop's hardcover collection almost matches its paperbacks in volume and, even though a large number of the hardcover books are of a more current vintage, there is a mix of some older volumes and a few "near collectibles." We view this as a better than average neighborhood shop.

Book Stop   **Open Shop**
3410 Central SE   87106   (505) 268-8898

Collection:	General stock of hardcover and paperback.
# of Vols:	20,000
Hours:	Mon-Sat 10-10. Sun 12-5.
Services:	Accepts want lists.
Travel:	Central exit off I-25. Proceed east on Central.
Credit Cards:	Yes
Owner:	Jerry Lane
Year Estab:	1979
Comments:	A quite good selection of scholarly books in generally good condition and reasonably priced. More than a few items (mostly behind glass) that are collectible and, in our opinion, well worth a visit.

BookMark   **By Appointment**
119 9th Street SW   87102   (505) 242-8290

Collection:	General stock.
# of Vols:	5,000
Specialties:	Western Americana; military; children's.
Services:	Accepts want lists, mail order.
Credit Cards:	Yes
Year Estab:	1994

Bookworks **Open Shop**
4022 Rio Grande Boulevard NW   87107 (505) 344-8139

Collection:	Specialty
# of Vols:	Several hundred.
Specialties:	Southwest Americana (focus on history and literature); signed limited editions, most with original artwork; letterpress books.
Hours:	Mon-Sat 9-7. Sun 9-5.
Services:	Search service, accepts want lists, mail order.
Travel:	Rio Grande Exit off I-40. Proceed north on Rio Grande for about three miles to Dietz Farm Plaza Shopping Center.
Comments:	Primarily a new book shop with a limited selection of specialty OP books.

Brotherhood of Life **Open Shop**
110 Dartmouth Drive SE   87106 (505) 255-8980

Collection:	Specialty. Mostly new.
# of Vols:	500-1,000 (used)
Specialties:	Metaphysics
Hours:	Mon-Thu 10-6. Fri 10-7. Sat 10-6. Sun 11-5.
Travel:	Between Girard and Richmond off Central.

Don's Paperback Book Exchange **Open Shop**
1013 San Mateo SE   87108 Fax: (505) 271-0079   (505) 268-0520
E-mail: don@us1.net

Collection:	General stock of mostly paperback.
# of Vols:	80,000
Hours:	Mon-Sat 10-7.

Hollingsworth's **By Appointment**
9631 Morrow NE   87112 (505) 294-4908

Collection:	Specialty books and ephemera.
# of Vols:	1,000
Specialties:	Texas; Western Americana; Southwest Americana; maps; woodblock prints from illustrated weeklies of 1800's.
Services:	Catalog
Credit Cards:	Yes
Owner:	Bob Hollingsworth
Year Estab:	1989

Hyleana Fine Books **By Appointment**
Fax: (505) 344-6678   (505) 344-3410
E-mail: hyleanab@interloc.com

Collection:	Specialty
# of Vols:	20,000
Specialties:	Latin America.
Services:	Search service, accepts want lists, mail order.
Owner:	Robert Dietz
Year Estab:	1991

(Albuquerque)

I-40 Antique Mall   **Antique Mall**
12th St & I-40   (505) 243-8011

Hours: Tue-Sun 10-6.
Travel: 6/12th St exit off I-40. Mall is along the service road.

Jan's Exchange   **Open Shop**
3719 Fourth Street NW   87107   (505) 345-2182

Collection: General stock of paperback, magazines and hardcover.
# of Vols: 300,000
Hours: Mon-Sat 10-6.
Travel: 4th St exit off I-40. Proceed north on 4th St to third light. Shop is just
                  north of Candelaria.
Credit Cards: No
Owner: Don Walsh
Year Estab: 1979
Comments: Stock is approximately 70% paperback.

Motorhead Mart   **Open Shop**
209 San Pedro NE   87108   (505) 268-6768

Collection: Specialty new and used books and magazines.
Specialties: Automobiles
Hours: Tue-Fri 11-6. Sat 11-4.
Services: Appraisals, search service, accepts want lists, mail order.
Travel: One block north of Central.
Credit Cards: Yes
Owner: Joe Abbin
Year Estab: 1994
Comments: Stock is evenly divided between new and used.

Oasis Books   **Open Shop**
625 Amherst NE   87106   (505) 268-1054

Collection: General stock of hardcover and paperback.
# of Vols: 10,000
Hours: Tue-Sat 10-6.
Travel: Carlisle exit off I-40. Proceed south on Carlisle to Lomas, right on
                  Lomas to Amherst and left on Amherst.
Credit Cards: No
Owner: Russell Wiegman
Year Estab: 1989
Comments: The majority of the books were hardcover, in good condition and
                  representing mixed vintages. We saw a nice children's section and a
                  few better books behind glass. This is the kind of shop where, while the
                  odds of picking up a truly rare item may not be great, they're a lot
                  better than playing the lottery.

Open Mind Bookstore   **Open Shop**
119 Harvard SE   87106   (505) 262-0066

Collection:	Specialty new and used.
# of Vols:	8,000 (used)
Specialties:	Metaphysics
Hours:	Mon-Fri 10-6. Sat 10-4.
Travel:	One block east of Yale.
Credit Cards:	Yes
Owner:	Rick Cramer
Year Estab:	1974

Page One Too!   **Open Shop**
11200 Montgomery, NE   87111   (505) 294-5623

Collection:	General stock of paperback and hardcover.
# of Vols:	160,000
Specialties:	Southwest Americana.
Hours:	Daily 9am-10pm.
Services:	Appraisals, search service, mail order.
Travel:	Montgomery exit off I-25 and proceed east on Montgomery. Or, Juan Tabo exit off I-40 and proceed north on Juan Tabo to Montgomery. Shop is in Eldorado Shopping Center.
Credit Cards:	Yes
Owner:	Steve & Yvette Stout
Year Estab:	1993
Comments:	One problem associated with our trips is that when we find a shop with a large selection of books, we're not always able to spend the time we should perusing the titles. While there are lots of paperbacks to choose from in this shop, true bibliophiles are encouraged to visit here since there are an equal number of shelves devoted to good quality hardcover volumes, most in very good condition. There are remainders (not necessarily a turn off) as well as older volumes, an area with vintage hardcover material and still another area labeled "rare book room" that does indeed carry some rare books (We saw a first edition Raymond Chandler in its original dust jacket and several signed volumes by other well known authors.) There are more than enough quality books here to satisfy the tastes of all but the most elite antiquarian.

Passages Bookshop & Gallery   **By Appointment**
PO Box 7877   87194   (505) 843-9133
                                                           E-mail: dca@nmia.com

Collection:	Specialty
# of Vols:	2,500
Specialties:	Art; artist's books; contemporary fine printing; photography; literature; poetry; modern first editions.
Services:	Appraisals, search service, catalog, accepts want lists.
Credit Cards:	Yes

(Albuquerque)

Owner:	David Abel
Year Estab:	1993
Comments:	We were fortunate in being able to visit this dealer prior to his switch to a "by appointment" business. What we saw were quality books in excellent condition and a fine representation in the fields of literature (especially first editions) and the fine arts. If these fields are of interest to you, a visit to this dealer could prove most satisfactory.

Piñon Tree Books   Antique Mall
At Antique Specialty Mall   (505) 268-8080
4516 Central SE   87106

Collection:	General stock.
Hours:	Mon-Sat 10-6. Sun 12-5.
Travel:	Central Ave exit off I-25. East on Central for 3½ miles.
Comments:	Typical "books in an antique mall" setup with the redeeming grace of carrying a reasonable selection of books on regional history in addition to a modest selection of titles in other areas. Located close to several other shops.

Quarto Books   By Appointment
6623 Elwood NW   87107   (505) 344-2540

Collection:	General stock.
# of Vols:	2,500
Specialties:	Books on books; bibliography; printing; art.
Services:	Appraisals, catalog.
Owner:	Paul Sternberg
Year Estab:	1978

Rachel's Books   Open Shop
532 Washington, NE   87108   (505) 260-0032

Collection:	General stock of hardcover and paperback.
# of Vols:	15,000
Specialties:	Literature; children's.
Hours:	Mon-Sat 10-5:30.
Travel:	Lomas Ave exit off I-25. East on Lomas to Washington, then south on Washington. Shop is 1/2 block ahead.
Credit Cards:	Yes
Owner:	Rachel Hess
Year Estab:	1989
Comments:	A modest sized shop with a mix of paperbacks and hardcover titles in generally good condition. Most areas are covered but few in depth. The owner, a vivacious woman will, we would almost guarantee, shake your hand before you leave the shop.

Read On   **Open Shop**
10131 Coors Road NW   87114   (505) 898-0000

Collection:	General stock of new and used hardcover and paperback.
# of Vols:	6,000 (used)
Hours:	Mon-Fri 9-7. Sat 9-5. Sun 9-4.
Services:	Search service, accepts want lists, mail order.
Travel:	Alameda exit off I-25. Proceed west on Alameda to Coors Blvd, then south on Coors Blvd for three blocks to Alameda West Shopping Center.
Credit Cards:	Yes
Owner:	Doug Jenkins
Year Estab:	1987
Comments:	Used stock is approximately 60% paperback.

Charlotte Rittenhouse, Bookseller **By Appointment**
PO Box 4422   87196 (505) 255-2479

Collection:	Specialty
# of Vols:	7,000
Specialties:	Western Americana.
Credit Cards:	No
Year Estab:	1991

Silver Wolf Books **By Appointment**
PO Box 10389   87184 (505) 898-5293
Fax: (505) 898-5293

Collection:	General stock.
# of Vols:	1,000
Specialties:	Native Americans.
Services:	Appraisals
Credit Cards:	Yes
Owner:	Bob Kanner
Year Estab:	1984

Simmons & Simmons Books **Open Shop**
4616 Central SE   87108 (505) 260-1620
E-mail: simmonsm@interloc.com

Collection:	General stock of mostly hardcover and ephemera.
# of Vols:	12,000
Specialties:	Western Americana; history; needlework; cooking.
Hours:	Mon-Sat 10-6. Sun 12-5.
Services:	Appraisals, search service, accepts want lists, occasional catalog, mail order.
Travel:	San Mateo exit off I-25. Proceed south on San Mateo to Central, then west on Central. Shop is located inside Classic Century Square.
Credit Cards:	Yes
Owner:	Melanie & Byrd Simmons
Year Estab:	1988

(Albuquerque)

Comments:	A separate (closed off) room in an antique mall with, for a change, the owner present. While many subjects are represented, the specialties above get the most attention. The books we saw were in mixed condition, some priced right, some priced more questionably. We spotted a fair share of collectibles and ephemera. If you're interested in the specialties noted above, you might enjoy a visit. The owner also displays a general stock and LPs, with an emphasis on entertainment, at the I-40 Antique Mall (see above).

Tasha's Paperback Books   **Open Shop**
2510 San Mateo Place, NE   87110   (505) 884-5491
                                                                      Fax: (505) 255-9175

Collection:	General stock of paperback and hardcover.
# of Vols:	100,000+
Hours:	Mon-Fri 11-6. Sat 10-6.
Services:	Search service, accepts want lists, mail order.
Travel:	San Mateo exit off I-40. Proceed north on San Mateo for 1/2 block and jog right into small strip center.
Credit Cards:	Yes
Owner:	Tasha Mackler
Year Estab:	1976
Comments:	"Why are we going to a shop with 'paperback' in the title," I asked Susan. Her reply was that based on past experience, shop's with similar titles have sometimes had a reasonable number of hardcover volumes. "And," she added, "the shop specializes in mystery." I must confess that I enjoyed my visit here because I have an addiction for mystery titles, particularly of the vintage variety. However, 99% of the hardcover volumes on display at this shop are either new books or part of the shop's extensive lending library. If you're a mystery fan visiting Albuquerque, we recommend you stop by. On the other hand, if you're looking for used hardcover volumes, charming as this shop is, you're less likely to find the items you're looking for.

Title Wave Books   **Open Shop**
7415 Menaul NE   87110   (505) 837-9495

Collection:	General stock of hardcover and paperback.
# of Vols:	30,000+
Specialties:	Science fiction; children's science; physics; astronomy; education; religion; home schooling.
Hours:	Mon-Sat 10-6. Sun 12-4.
Services:	Accepts want lists, mail order.
Travel:	Louisiana north exit off I-40. Proceed north on Louisiana for 3/4 mile, then east on Menaul. Shop is three blocks ahead on left.
Credit Cards:	Yes
Owner:	Cindy Heath
Year Estab:	1994

Comments: In the midst of a major renovation at the time of our visit, we observed an almost balanced mix between paperback and hardcover books with a respectable hardcover representation. Many subject areas were covered but few in depth. Most of the hardcover items we saw would be classified as reading copies.

Tom Davies Book Shop   **Open Shop**
3904B Central Avenue SE   87108   (505) 247-2072

Collection: General stock and ephemera.
# of Vols: 5,000
Specialties: Southwest Americana; manuscripts.
Hours: Mon-Sat 9-5.
Services: Appraisals, accepts want lists, mail order.
Travel: Between Carlisle and Washington.
Credit Cards: No
Owner: Eric Holmes Patterson
Year Estab: 1950's
Comments: We visited this dealer prior to his move to the above location. Based on what we saw, we would be pleased to recommend this dealer to any serious book person interested in scholarly titles in the specialty fields listed above, as well as first editions, signed copies of good literature and quality books in general. Without exception, the books we saw were in excellent condition and most reasonably priced.

Tulane Exchange Books and Music   **Open Shop**
111 Tulane SE   87106   (505) 260-0792

Collection: General stock of used hardcover and paperback and remainders.
# of Vols: 20,000 (used)
Hours: Mon-Thu 10-7. Fri & Sat 10-9. Sun 1-7.
Services: Accepts want lists.
Travel: Carlisle exit off I-40. Proceed south on Carlisle to Central then west on Central for two blocks and south on Tulane for one block.
Credit Cards: Yes
Year Estab: 1995
Comments: A large selection of quality books (with a particularly fine selection of remainders in the fields of art and photography). If you have a special interest and find your way to that section, you may well walk out of this store with a purchase or two.

Tuttle Books   **Open Shop**
5639 Paradise Boulevard NW   87114   (505) 897-7744

Collection: General stock of hardcover and paperback.
# of Vols: 25,000
Hours: Mon-Sat 10-4.
Travel: Paseo del Norte exit off I-25. Proceed west on Paseo del Norte to Golf Course Rd, then right on Golf Course and left on Paradise. Shop is in Paradise Mercado Shopping Center.

Credit Cards: No
Owner: Jean Tuttle
Year Estab: 1992
Comments: Stock is evenly divided between paperback and hardcover.

Artesia

Family Book Shelf   **Open Shop**
520 West Main Street   88210   (505) 746-9077

Collection: General stock of mostly paperback.
# of Vols: 7,000
Hours: Tue-Fri 11-5. Sat 10-2.

Belen

The Book Store   **Open Shop**
121 South Main Street   (505) 861-0314
Mailing address: 600 Bernard Belen 87002

Collection: General stock of paperback and hardcover.
# of Vols: 25,000
Hours: Tue-Fri 10-6. Sat 10-5.
Services: Accepts want lists.
Travel: Southbound on I-25: Bus I-25 exit. Northbound on I-25: Sosimo Padilla
                   exit. Proceed east to Main, then left on Main.
Credit Cards: Yes
Owner: Ray & Mary Birch
Year Estab: 1992
Comments: People do buy paperbacks. Sometimes they buy them by the dozen.
                   During our visit, several customers made purchases at this shop. In
                   addition to paperbacks, the shop does carry a modest selection of
                   hardcover books in mixed condition but few titles we believe that are
                   truly noteworthy.

Casa Blanca

The Blue-Eyed Indian Bookshop   **Open Shop**
At Exit 108 off I-40   (505) 552-6264
Mailing address: PO Box 213 Laguna 87026   (800) 514-6264

Collection: General stock of new and used hardcover and paperback.
# of Vols: 1,000 (used)
Hours: Tue-Sat 10-5.
Travel: In Casa Blanca Commercial Center, at exit 108 off I-40.
Credit Cards: Yes
Owner: Lee & Kathy Marmon
Year Estab: 1990
Comments: Used stock is evenly divided between hardcover and paperback.

Edgewood

The Book Source   **Open Shop**
Highway 333 (Old Route 66)   (505) 281-3381
Mailing address: PO Box 3720 Edgewood 87015

Collection:	General stock of mostly paperback.
Hours:	Mon-Fri 12-6:30. Sat 10:30-5:30. Sun 12-4.

Las Cruces

A Book Affair   **Open Shop**
1496 South Solano Drive 88001   (505) 522-5515

Collection:	General stock of mostly used paperback and hardcover.
# of Vols:	35,000
Specialties:	Science fiction.
Hours:	Mon-Sat 9-6. Sun 11-5.
Services:	Accepts want lists, mail order.
Travel:	Main St/U of New Mexico exit off I-10. Proceed east on University to Idaho, right on Idaho and right on Solano. Shop is at corner of Montana, on the right, in a stand alone building.
Credit Cards:	Yes
Owner:	Anne D. Grisham
Year Estab:	1990
Comments:	A mostly paperback shop that also displays back issues of *National Geographic*. Other than the specialty listed above (more in paper than hardcover) and some titles in Western Americana, we had trouble discerning anything of major interest to the traveling book person.

COAS: Books   **Open Shop**
535 South Melendres Street 88005   (505) 524-0301

Collection:	General stock of hardcover and paperback.
# of Vols:	160,000
Hours:	Mon-Sat 10-6.
Travel:	Lohman exit off I-25. Proceed west on Lohman which becomes Amador. Melendres is the last possible left turn before the railroad tracks. From I-10, take Avenida de Mesilla exit and proceed east on Mesilla, then left on Main and immediate left on Melendres
Credit Cards:	Yes
Owner:	Pat Beckett
Year Estab:	1984
Comments:	See comments on other store.

COAS: My Bookstore   **Open Shop**
317 North Main Street 88001 (800) 592-8471 (505) 524-8471
             Fax: (505) 525-1742
          E-mail: coas@huntel.com

Collection:	General stock of hardcover and paperback.

# of Vols:	200,000
Specialties:	Anthropology; archaeology; technical.
Hours:	Mon-Sat 10-6. Sun 11-5.
Travel:	Amador exit off I-10. Proceed east on Amador which becomes Lohman to Main, then left on Main. Shop is located in pedestrian mall. Use parking lots 4 and 6. From I-25, use Lohman exit. Proceed west on Lohman to Main then right on Main.
Credit Cards:	Yes
Owner:	Pat Beckett
Year Estab:	1984
Comments:	A large shop well worth visiting. Like the energizer rabbit, this is a shop that keeps going and going. We were particularly impressed by the technical section (you name it, they had it). However, the entire store offers shelf upon shelf of both common and uncommon material in almost every subject and at "bargain prices."

Evco Books   **Open Shop**
1625 South Main, Ste 6   88005   (505) 523-4032

Collection:	General stock of mostly hardcover.
# of Vols:	20,000
Specialties:	History; Southwest Americana; literature.
Hours:	Mon-Sat 9-6. Sun 11-5.
Services:	Search service, accepts want lists, mail order.
Travel:	Main St/U of New Mexico exit off I-10. Proceed straight across University onto Main St. Shop is on right in Omega Business Centre.
Credit Cards:	Yes
Owner:	Eugene Comeau
Year Estab:	1990
Comments:	A neat little shop with quality books, particularly in the specialties listed above. We saw some nice sets and good titles in other fields as well. While the stock is not huge, it has clearly been selected with care and the books are not overpriced.

Los Lunas

Book Mark   **Open Shop**
1004 Main Street SW   (505) 866-0598
Mailing address: Box 2699 Los Lunas 87031

Collection:	General stock of paperback and hardcover.
# of Vols:	35,000
Hours:	Mon-Sat 8:30-6.
Travel:	Main St exit off I-25. Proceed north on Main St for about three miles.
Credit Cards:	No
Owner:	Alberto Perez
Year Estab:	1979
Comments:	Stock is approximately 70% paperback.

Roswell

Happy Jack's Trading Post   **Open Shop**
405 East 2nd Street   88201   (505) 623-1544

Collection:	General stock of mostly paperback.
# of Vols:	20,000
Hours:	Mon-Sat 9:30-5:30.

The Turned Page II   **Open Shop**
1135 South Main   88201   (505) 625-2039

Collection:	General stock of paperback and hardcover.
# of Vols:	20,000
Hours:	Mon-Fri 10-5:30. Sat 10-4.
Travel:	Main is Hwy 285.
Credit Cards:	No
Owner:	Phyllis Sykes, Erica Sykes, Gina Price.
Year Estab:	1993
Comments:	Stock is evenly divided between paperback and hardcover.

Ruidoso

Books & Things   **Open Shop**
721 East Mechem Drive   88345   (505) 257-4976

Collection:	General stock of new and used hardcover and paperback.
# of Vols:	500-1,000 (used)
Hours:	Mon-Sat 9:30-6. Sun 12-4.
Comments:	Used stock is evenly divided between hardcover and paperback.

Santa Fe

Blue Moon Books & Video   **Open Shop**
329 Garfield Street   87501   (505) 982-3035

Collection:	General stock of paperback and hardcover.
# of Vols:	10,000-15,000
Specialties:	Metaphysics; occult; health and healing; psychology; poetry; psychedelia; women's studies.
Hours:	Tue-Sat 11-6. Mon by chance.
Services:	Accepts want lists.
Travel:	Cerrillos Rd exit off I-25. Proceed east on Cerrillos to Guadalupe, then north on Guadalupe for three blocks to Garfield. Right on Garfield.
Credit Cards:	Yes
Owner:	Carmen Blue
Year Estab:	1988
Comments:	A small, crowded but interesting shop with almost as many videos for rent (documentaries, foreign and other unusual titles) as books. The specialties listed above are represented in a respectable manner with a small alcove devoted exclusively to poetry. Literature and other subjects are on hand but in far fewer number.

(Santa Fe)

Books And More Books   **Open Shop**
1341 Cerrillos Road   87501   (505) 983-5438

Collection:	General stock of used hardcover and paperback and remainders.
# of Vols:	10,000-15,000
Specialties:	Art; photography; Southwest Americana; New Mexico; cookbooks.
Hours:	Mon-Sat 10:30-5. Sun by chance.
Travel:	From downtown, proceed south on Cerrillos. Shop is about one mile after St. Francis intersection in Kiva Shopping Center.
Credit Cards:	Yes
Owner:	Elizabeth Cook Romero & Leo Romero
Year Estab:	1987
Comments:	A nice shop with good looking books, particularly in the specialties listed above. A good selection of literature. For a change, the sign in the window that read, "Fine Used Books" was accurate.

Books Unlimited   **Open Shop**
418 Cerrillos Road   87501   (505) 982-9411
                                                                     Fax: (505) 989-8966

Collection:	General stock.
# of Vols:	5,000
Specialties:	Southwest Americana; modern first editions; Mesoamerica; art; photography.
Hours:	Mon-Sat 10-5.
Services:	Appraisals, accepts want lists, catalog.
Travel:	Cerrillos Rd exit off I-25. Proceed east on Cerrillos. Shop is four blocks south of the plaza.
Credit Cards:	Yes
Owner:	Shirley Jacobson
Year Estab:	1984
Comments:	A small shop that at the time of our visit housed the collection of five dealers. The titles we saw were quality items with more than a few "rare collectibles." This is one of those shops where one enters and is initially impressed with the volumes in one field only to discover several unusual titles in other areas of interest.

Classic Additions   **Open Shop**
215 East Palace   87501   (505) 983-2222

Collection:	Specialty new and used.
# of Vols:	300 (used)
Specialties:	Western Americana.
Hours:	Mon-Sat, except closed Wed, 10-6.
Travel:	Between Paseo de Peralta and Washington.
Credit Cards:	Yes
Year Estab:	1992

De La Peña Books   **Open Shop**
418 Cerrillos Road, #31   87501   (505) 982-9411
                                 Fax: (505) 989-8966

Collection:	General stock and ephemera.
# of Vols:	7,500
Specialties:	Mesoamerica; American Indian; Western Americana; photography; fine art; literary first editions; China; travel; maps.
Hours:	Mon-Sat 10-5. Sun by chance or appointment.
Services:	Appraisals, catalog, accepts want lists.
Travel:	See Books Unlimited above.
Credit Cards:	Yes
Year Estab:	1975
Comments:	Shares space with Books Unlimited. See comments above.

Dumont Maps & Books Of The West   **Open Shop**
301 East Palace Avenue, #1   (505) 988-1076
Mailing address: PO Box 10250 Santa Fe 87504   (505) 986-6114

Collection:	General stock and ephemera.
# of Vols:	8,000-10,000
Specialties:	Western Americana; Native Americans; exploration; maps; cartography; regional fiction; local history.
Hours:	Mon-Sat 10-6. Sun 12-5.
Services:	Catalog, accepts want lists.
Travel:	Old Pecos Trail exit off I-25. Proceed north on Old Pecos Trail to Paseo de Peralta, then right (east) to East Palace Ave. Shop is at corner of East Palace and Paseo de Peralta. Entrance and parking are on Paseo de Peralta.
Credit Cards:	Yes
Owner:	André & Carol Dumont
Year Estab:	1987
Comments:	A small, compact shop, well organized, nicely labeled and easy to browse with a rich collection of quality books in the specialties listed above. The books were in very good condition and reasonably priced.

El Colectivo Antique Center   **Antique Mall**
At De Vargas Center   (505) 820-7205
526 North Guadalupe 87501

Collection:	General stock.
# of Vols:	5,000
Hours:	Mon-Thu 10-7. Fri 10-9. Sat 10-6. Sun 12-5.
Travel:	St. Francis exit of I-25. Proceed north on St. Francis to Paseo de Peralta, then east one block on Paseo de Peralta to Guadalupe, then left on Guadalupe. Shop is in the De Vargas Center, an indoor shopping mall. Note: St. Francis crosses Paseo de Peralta twice. Take second intersection.
Comments:	There are enough books in one corner of this multi dealer antique shop to stock a small book store. The books on display (representing the

collections of three dealers at the time of our visit) consisted of some newer volumes, many older titles, and even a few "much older" items. Age does not necessarily make for a great find, though, and while the books we viewed here varied in subject matter, unless you're exceedingly lucky on the day you visit, your time might be better spent at one or more of the quality shops in Santa Fe.

Bob Fein Books   **By Appointment**
2156 Candelaro Street   87505   (505) 471-3886
                                                     Fax: (505) 471-3886

Collection:	Specialty
# of Vols:	4,000
Specialties:	Native Americans; pre Columbian art and culture; Western Americana.
Services:	Appraisals, search service, accepts want lists, catalog.
Credit Cards:	Yes
Year Estab:	1981
Comments:	Also displays at Books Unlimited in Santa Fe. See above.

Richard Fitch, Old Maps & Prints & Books   **By Appointment**
2324 Calle Halcon   87505   (505) 982-2939
                                                     Fax: (505) 982-3148

Collection:	Specialty
Specialties:	Maps (19th century and earlier of North America); cartographic references; exploration (North America).
Services:	Appraisals; search service, catalog, accepts want lists.
Credit Cards:	Yes
Year Estab:	1973

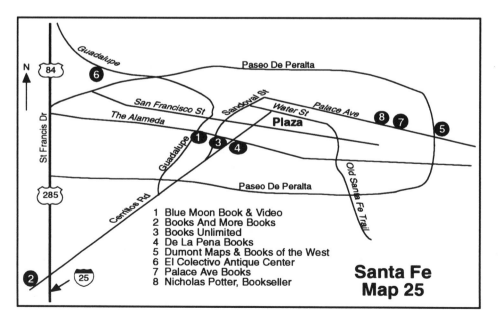

1 Blue Moon Book & Video
2 Books And More Books
3 Books Unlimited
4 De La Pena Books
5 Dumont Maps & Books of the West
6 El Colectivo Antique Center
7 Palace Ave Books
8 Nicholas Potter, Bookseller

Santa Fe Map 25

The Foliophiles Collection   **Open Shop**
129 West San Francisco Street   87501   (505) 984-8646

Collection:	Specialty
Specialties:	Manuscript leaves (from cuneiform papyrus to 20th century); incunabula; prints.
Hours:	Tue-Sat 10-5. Usually closed February.
Services:	Appraisals, mail order.
Travel:	1½ blocks west of plaza. Shop is on the second floor.
Credit Cards:	Yes
Owner:	Alfred W. Stites
Year Estab:	1993

L.E. & Mary Gay Southwest Books   **By Appointment**
1023 Tierra Drive   87505   (505) 471-2393

Collection:	Specialty
# of Vols:	4,000
Specialties:	Southwest Americana; bibliographies; books about books.
Services:	Appraisals, search service, accepts want lists, catalog.
Credit Cards:	No
Year Estab:	1949

Margolis & Moss   **By Appointment**
PO Box 2042   87504   Fax: (505) 982-3256   (505) 982-1028
                                           E-mail: mmbooks@rt.66.com

Collection:	General stock and ephemera.
# of Vols:	3,000+
Specialties:	Western Americana; illustrated; children's; photography; maps.
Services:	Appraisals, catalog.
Credit Cards:	Yes
Owner:	David Margolis & Jean Moss
Year Estab:	1979
Comments:	We visited this dealer shortly before his switch to a "by appointment" business and were fortunate enough to view a combination of truly antiquarian titles, first editions and other quality items. If the specialties above are of interest to you, a phone call to this dealer could result in a most satisfactory acquisition.

Numismatic & Philatelic Arts   **By Appointment**
PO Box 9712   87504   Fax: (505) 982-8792   (505) 982-8792
                                           E-mail: art_rubino@msn.com

Collection:	General stock of mostly used hardcover and ephemera.
# of Vols:	29,000
Specialties:	Numismatics; philately; jewelry; decorative arts; antiques; dowsing; modern first editions; literature; fine bindings; handwriting analysis.
Services:	Appraisals, search service, catalog, accepts want lists.
Credit Cards:	Yes
Owner:	Art Rubino
Year Estab:	1987

(Santa Fe)

Palace Avenue Books   **Open Shop**
209 East Palace Avenue   87501   (505) 986-0536

Collection:	General stock of mostly new books and mostly hardcover used.
# of Vols:	250-500 (used)
Specialties:	Western Americana; Native Americans.
Hours:	Mon-Sat 10:30-6.

Photo-Eye Books & Prints   **Open Shop**
376 Garcia Street   87501   (505) 988-4955

Collection:	Specialty mostly new and some used.
# of Vols:	500 (used)
Specialties:	Photography
Hours:	Mon-Sat 9-6. Summer only: Also Sun 10-5.
Services:	Appraisals, search service, accepts want lists, catalog.
Travel:	Corner of Garcia and Acequia Madre.
Owner:	Rixon G. Reed

Nicholas Potter, Bookseller   **Open Shop**
203 East Palace Avenue   87501   (505) 983-5434

Collection:	General stock and records.
# of Vols:	10,000
Specialties:	Southwest Americana; modern first editions; photography.
Hours:	Mon-Sat 10-5:30. Sun 11-4.
Services:	Accepts want lists.
Travel:	St. Francis Dr exit off I-25. Proceed north on St. Francis, then northeast on Cerrillos to the Plaza. Shop is two blocks east of the plaza.
Credit Cards:	Yes
Year Estab:	1969
Comments:	A quality shop with a strong collection in literature. Most of the books we saw were in fine condition and moderately priced. Some older volumes. Several sets with fine bindings and a healthy supply of first editions.

Santa Fe House of Books   **By Appointment**
2154 Candelaro Street   (505) 473-5161
Mailing address: PO Box 23503 Santa Fe 87502

Collection:	Specialty used and new.
# of Vols:	5,000
Specialties:	Western Americana; Southwest Americana; Native Americans.
Services:	Search service, accepts want lists, mail order.
Credit Cards:	No
Owner:	Sidney S. Margolis
Year Estab:	1978
Comments:	Stock is approximately 50% used.

William R. Talbot Antique Maps and Prints **Open Shop**
129 West San Francisco Street (505) 982-1559
Mailing address: PO Box 2757 Santa Fe 87504

Collection:	Specialty
Specialties:	Maps; prints; related books.
Hours:	Mon-Sat 10-5.
Services:	Appraisals, accepts want lists, catalog.
Travel:	Downtown
Credit Cards:	Yes
Year Estab:	1979

Carrie Vaintrub Fine Books **By Appointment**
1522 Camino de la Canada 87501 Fax: (505) 984-8953 (505) 984-8953
E-mail: 103207.1627@compuserve.com

Collection:	Specialty
Specialties:	Art; decorative arts (mostly ethnographic).
Services:	Catalog, accepts want lists.
Year Estab:	1995

Silver City

O'Keefe's Bookshop **Open Shop**
102 West Broadway 88061 (505) 388-3313

Collection:	General stock.
# of Vols:	5,000
Hours:	Tue-Sat 10-5:30.
Services:	Accepts want lists.
Credit Cards:	No
Owner:	Dennis O'Keefe
Year Estab:	1986

Taos

Dream Weaver Gallery & Coffee House **Open Shop**
228-C Paseo del Pueblo Norte 87571 (505) 758-2725

Collection:	General stock of used and new hardcover and paperback.
Hours:	Summer: Daily 8am-9pm. Winter: Daily 8-5.
Travel:	On main strip in town, in Garcia Plaza.
Comments:	Stock is approximately 75% used, most of which is hardcover.

Mystery Ink Bookshop **Open Shop**
121 Camino De La Placita 87571 (505) 751-1092

Collection:	Specialty paperback and hardcover.
Specialties:	Mystery.
Hours:	Nov-Feb: Mon-Fri 10-5. Sat 11-5. Remainder of year: Mon-Fri 10-6. Sat 11-5.
Services:	Accepts want lists, mail order.

Travel:	Camino De La Placita exit off Hwy 68. Proceed south on Hwy 68
Credit Cards:	Yes
Owner:	Thu Trang & John Pitts
Year Estab:	1994
Comments:	Stock if approximately 60% paperback.

G. Robinson Old Prints and Maps

124-D Bent Street   87571

Open Shop
(505) 758-2278
Fax: (505) 758-1606

Collection:	Specialty
Specialties:	Maps and prints from 15th-19th century.
Hours:	Mon-Sat 9:30-5:30.
Services:	Appraisals, search service, catalog.
Travel:	From Pueblo Rd in downtown, turn west on Bent St.
Credit Cards:	Yes
Owner:	George Robinson
Year Estab:	1978

Taos Book Shop

122-D Kit Carson Road   87571

Open Shop
(505) 758-3733
Fax: (505) 776-8497

Collection:	General stock of new and used books.
# of Vols:	14,000+
Specialties:	Southwest Americana; Western Americana.
Hours:	Daily 10-5, except 9-6 during summer.
Services:	Appraisals, search service, catalog, accepts want lists.
Travel:	Kit Carson Rd is Hwy 64.
Credit Cards:	Yes
Owner:	Deborah Sherman
Year Estab:	1947
Comments:	The stock is approximately 35% used, most of which is hardcover.

Tatum

C.H. Peaden's Books

PO Box 846   88267

By Appointment
(505) 398-8940

Collection:	General stock.
# of Vols:	15,000
Year Estab:	1960's

Truth or Consequences

Books & Things

205 South Foch Street   87901

Open Shop
(505) 894-6223

Collection:	General of mostly paperback.
# of Vols:	20,000
Hours:	Mon-Sat 9-4:30.

Xochis Bookstore & Gallery   **Open Shop**
430 Broadway 87901   (505) 894-7685

Collection:	General stock of hardcover and paperback.
# of Vols:	15,000
Hours:	Mon-Sat 10-7.
Services:	Search service, accepts want lists.
Credit Cards:	No
Owner:	Stan Sokolow
Year Estab:	1995

Mail Order Dealers

Abacus Books   (505) 471-2460
PO Box 6872 Santa Fe 87502

Collection:	General stock.
# of Vols:	1,500+
Specialties:	Books about books; language.
Owner:	Robert F. Kadlec
Year Estab:	1970

Buffalo Medicine Books   (505) 722-2904
Box 1762 Gallup 87305

Collection:	Specialty
# of Vols:	20,000
Specialties:	Ethnic literature (including Native American and Hispanic American); mystery.
Services:	Appraisals, search service, accepts want lists, catalog.
Credit Cards:	Yes
Owner:	Ernie Bulow
Year Estab:	1966

Casa di Libri   (505) 248-1502
1907 Silver SE, #B Albuquerque 87106   E-mail: casamuse@interloc.com

Collection:	Specialty
# of Vols:	1,000
Specialties:	Music; art; Latin America; Western Americana; books about books.
Services:	Catalog
Credit Cards:	Yes
Owner:	Troy Michael & Suzanne Casa
Year Estab:	1995

Curiouser & Curiouser   (505) 988-5840
PO Box 274 Santa Fe 87504

Collection:	Specialty
Specialties:	Children's
Services:	Catalog

Credit Cards: No
Owner: Susan Steinman
Year Estab: 1986

Mellon Books   (505) 867-1712
02 Sunrise Drive Placitas 87043

Collection: Specialty
# of Vols: 2,000
Specialties: Heredity; eugenics; genetics.
Services: Catalog, accepts want lists.
Credit Cards: No
Owner: Charles Mellon
Year Estab: 1993.

John Randall   (505) 256-7172
113-E Girard SE Albuquerque 87106

Collection: Specialty
# of Vols: 1,000
Specialties: Native American literature; Chicano literature; Latin American litera-
                  ture.
Services: Accepts want lists.
Credit Cards: No
Year Estab: 1996

Skullduggery House Books   (505) 434-6641
PO Box 1851 Alamogordo 88311   Fax: (505) 437-5704

Collection: Specialty
# of Vols: 4,500
Specialties: Mystery
Services: Appraisals, catalog, accepts want lists.
Credit Cards: No
Owner: James & Sharon Smith
Year Estab: 1990

D. Turpen Books Of Mexico And The West   (505) 292-5446
PO Box 13045 Albuquerque 87192   Fax: (505) 292-5446
                                              E-mail: dturpen@rt66.com

Collection: Specialty
# of Vols: 10,000
Specialties: Western Americana; Mexico. All non fiction.
Services: Appraisals, accepts want lists, catalog.
Credit Cards: Yes
Owner: Donald C. Turpen
Year Estab: 1991.
Comments: Collection may also be viewed by appointment.

North Dakota

Alphabetical Listing By Dealer

Alphabetical Listing By Location

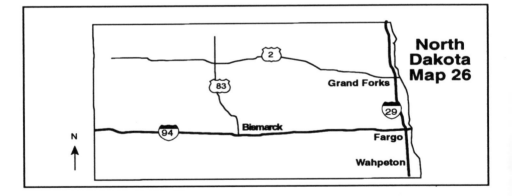

Bismarck

Owl Bookstore   **Open Shop**
1107 South 12th Street   58504   (701) 258-3003

Collection:	General stock of mostly paperback.
# of Vols:	24,000
Hours:	Mon-Fri 10-5:30. Sat 11-4.

Used Book Store   **Open Shop**
223 North 18th Street   58501   (701) 258-2227

Collection:	General stock of paperback and hardcover.
Hours:	Mon-Fri 10-5:30. Sat 10-5.
Travel:	Exit 161 off I-94. Proceed south for about 1½ miles to Main Ave. Right on Main, then right on 26th St, right on Broadway, left on 18th St.
Credit Cards:	No
Owner:	Sharon & Ron Jesz
Year Estab:	1981
Comments:	Stock is approximately 70% paperback.

Fargo

Ernie's Book Store   **Open Shop**
5 South 8th Street   58103   (701) 232-9843

Collection:	General stock of mostly paperback.
# of Vols:	12,000
Hours:	Mon-Sat 12-4:30.

Fargo Antique Mall   **Antique Mall**
14 Roberts Street   58102   (701) 235-1145

Hours:	Mon-Sat 10-5:30.
Travel:	Main Ave exit off I-94. Proceed east on Main to S. 8th St, then north on 8th St to NP Ave, east on NP Ave to Roberts and north on Roberts.

Duane Johnson, Bookseller To Town & Gown   **Open Shop**
506 Broadway   58102   (701) 232-0178

Collection:	General stock of hardcover and paperback.
# of Vols:	150,000+
Hours:	Daily 8-8.
Services:	Appraisals, search service, accepts want lists, occasional catalog, mail order.
Travel:	12th Ave north exit off I-29. Proceed east on 12th Ave to Broadway (6th St), then south on Broadway. Shop is about seven blocks ahead.
Credit Cards:	No
Year Estab:	1982
Comments:	Stock is evenly divided between hardcover and paperback. Large additional stock is in storage.

Allen J. Petersen, Books   **By Appointment**
809 20th Street South   58103   (701) 280-0538

Collection:	General stock.
Specialties:	North Dakota; hunting; Western Americana.
Services:	Appraisals, search service, accepts want lists, mail order.
Credit Cards:	No
Year Estab:	1982
Comments:	Also displays at the Fargo Antique Mall in Fargo (see above) and the Stillwater Book Center in Stillwater, MN.

Grand Forks

Book Fair   **Open Shop**
212 Demers Avenue   58201   (701) 775-6491

Collection:	General stock of mostly paperback.
# of Vols:	20,000
Hours:	Mon-Fri 10-5:30. Sat 10-5.

Dr. Eliot's Twice Sold Tales   **Open Shop**
115B North 3rd Street   (701) 775-8830
Mailing address: PO Box 5691 Grand Forks 58206   (800) 592-8830

Collection:	General stock of paperback, hardcover and ephemera.
# of Vols:	32,000
Hours:	Mon-Sat 10:30-5:30.
Services:	Search service, mail order.
Travel:	Gateway Dr exit off I-29. Follow directions to City Center Mall then turn north on 3rd St for 1½ blocks. Shop is downstairs.
Credit Cards:	Yes
Owner:	William G. Gard
Year Estab:	1993
Comments:	Stock is approximately 60% paperback.

Minot

Paperback Book Exchange   **Open Shop**
16 West Central   58703   (701) 852-5007

Collection:	General stock of mostly paperback.
Hours:	Mon-Sat 10-5.

Stanley

Books Now & Then   **By Appointment**
PO Box 337   58784   (701) 628-2084
                                                            Fax: (701) 628-2084

Collection:	Specialty hardcover and paperback.
# of Vols:	3,000+

Specialties:	Evangelical Christian (from serious theological to popular and contemporary).
Services:	Catalog, accepts want lists.
Credit Cards:	No
Owner:	Janis M. & Dennis Patrick
Year Estab:	1990
Comments:	Stock is approximately 50% hardcover.

Valley City

Eagles Nest Book Store   **Open Shop**
248 North Central Avenue   58072   (701) 845-1519

Collection:	General stock of mostly paperback.
Hours:	Mon-Sat 10-5:30.
Comments:	A not-for-profit shop selling donated and trade-in books.

Wahpeton

BDS Books   **Open Shop**
108 North 4th Street   58075   (701) 642-3231

Collection:	General stock of hardcover and paperback.
# of Vols:	60,000
Hours:	Mon-Sun 10-6, except Thu till 9.
Travel:	Wahpeton exit (Hwy 13) off I-29. Proceed east on Hwy 13 to downtown where Hwy 13 becomes Dakota Ave. Shop is at corner of Dakota and 4th St.
Owner:	Brad Stephenson
Year Estab:	1995
Comments:	Stock is approximately 60% hardcover.

Mail Order Dealers

Pandora's Books   (204) 324-8548
PO Box 54   Neche 58265   Fax: (204) 324-1628
                                                 E-mail: jgthiess@MTS.net

Collection:	Specialty paperback and hardcover.
# of Vols:	200,000
Specialties:	Science fiction; fantasy; horror; mystery; westerns, books about books.
Services:	Accepts want lists, catalog.
Credit Cards:	Yes
Owner:	J. Grant Thiessen
Year Estab:	1973

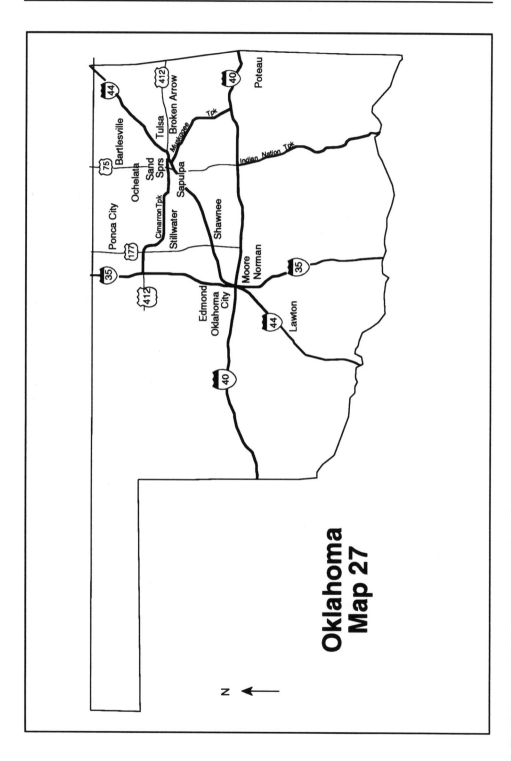

Oklahoma
Map 27

Oklahoma

Alphabetical Listing by Dealer

Alphabetical Listing By Location

Ada

Web Comic Books **Open Shop**
120 East Main Street   74820-5602   405-332-4606

Collection:	General stock of mostly paperback.
# of Vols:	9,000
Hours:	Mon-Sat 9-6.

Bartlesville

Winn's Books Plus **Open Shop**
110 East Frank Phillips Boulevard   74003   (918) 336-2727

Collection:	General stock of mostly hardcover.
# of Vols:	4,000
Specialties:	Local history.
Hours:	Mon-Fri 10-6. Sat 10-3.
Travel:	Frank Phillips Blvd exit off Hwy 75. Proceed west on Frank Phillips for about three to four miles to downtown.
Credit Cards:	Yes
Owner:	Mary R. Winn
Year Estab:	1996

Bixby

The Old Library **Open Shop**
15024-F South Memorial   74008   (918) 366-9898

Collection:	General stock of mostly paperback.
# of Vols:	20,000
Hours:	Mon-Wed 10-5. Thu-Sat 10-7.

Broken Arrow

Lighthouse Christian Bookstore **Open Shop**
1430 West Kenosha Street   74012   (918) 258-1770

Collection:	Specialty. Mostly new with limited used section.
Specialties:	Religion (Christianity)
Hours:	Mon-Fri 9am-9pm, except Wed till 6. Sat 9-8.
Credit Cards:	Yes
Owner:	Virginia Michaelis

Paperbacks Plus **Open Shop**
732 West New Orleans, #136   74012   (918) 455-1422

Collection:	General stock mostly used paperback and hardcover and remainders.
# of Vols:	35,000 (used hardcover)
Specialties:	Used hardcover is primarily non fiction..
Hours:	Mon-Fri 10-6, except Thu till 8. Sat 10-5.

Travel:	161st E. Ave exit off Hwy 51 (Broken Arrow Fwy). Proceed south on Elm to 101st St (West New Orleans). Right on New Orleans and immediate right into Vandever Acres Shopping Center.
Owner:	Chris Christensen
Year Estab:	1984
Comments:	One of those shops that upon first impression can be discouraging unless you're willing to explore. While the vast majority of the stock is paperback, there are hardcover titles in most fields and the shop has more than its share of collectibles if the browser is blessed with a keen eye. Unfortunately, a number of the hardcover books are not all in the best condition, but then prices aren't all that high either.

Edmond

Archives   **Open Shop**
1914 East 2nd Street   73034   (405) 348-6800
                                                          E-mail: archives@telepath.com

Collection:	General stock of hardcover and paperback.
# of Vols:	30,000
Specialties:	Religion; comics (collectible).
Hours:	Mon-Sat 10-6.
Services:	Appraisals, search service, accepts want lists, mail order.
Travel:	2nd St exit off I-35. Proceed west on 2nd St. Shop is on left in Oxford Pointe strip center.
Credit Cards:	Yes
Owner:	Wayne Stephens
Comments:	About one third of this shop's stock is devoted to comics, collectible comics and related materials, with the remaining two thirds divided between paperbacks and a reasonable enough number of hardcover volumes in most areas to make a stop for the "casual" collector appropriate. However, if you're looking for a rare volume, you might be better off inquiring by phone than making a trip. The owner operates two similar shops in nearby Moore and Norman.

Book Haven   **Open Shop**
364 South Kelly Avenue   73003   (405) 348-2901

Collection:	General stock of paperback and hardcover.
# of Vols:	15,000
Hours:	Mon-Sat 10-7.
Travel:	2nd St exit off I-35. Proceed west on 2nd St, which becomes Edmond Rd, for about 4½ miles. Shop is in Kelly West Shopping Center on southeast corner of Edmond and Kelly.
Credit Cards:	Yes
Owner:	Ladonna Self & Dolores Holz
Year Estab:	1994

Comments: A selection of comic books, a larger selection of paperbacks and a modest selection of fairly recent hardcover volumes in mixed condition. Most of the hardcover volumes looked like they either came from someone's attic or were book club discards.

Kingston

Book Inn **Open Shop**
Highway 70N (405) 564-2197
Mailing address: PO Box 308 Kingston

Collection: General stock of mostly paperback.
# of Vols: 20,000
Hours: Winter: Mon-Sat 8-4. Summer: Mon-Sat 9-5.

Lawton

The Lawton Book Stall **Open Shop**
1832 NW 52nd Street 73501 (405) 248-3111

Collection: General stock of paperback and hardcover.
# of Vols: 20,000
Hours: Mon-Sat 10-8. Sun 12-6.
Travel: Hwy 62 exit off I-44. Proceed west on Hwy 62 to 52nd St, then south on 52nd St for about 3/4 of a mile. Shop is on west side of street in Regency Square.
Credit Cards: No
Year Estab: 1980

Midwest City

Book Rack **Open Shop**
1717 South Air Depot Boulevard 73110 (405) 737-3781

Collection: General stock of mostly paperback.
Hours: Mon-Sat 10-6. Sun 1-6.

Moore

Archives **Open Shop**
1224 North Eastern 73160 (405) 799-0609

Collection: General stock of hardcover and paperback.
# of Vols: 30,000
Specialties: Religion; comics (collectible).
Hours: Mon-Sat 10-6.
Services: Appraisals, search service, accepts want lists, mail order.
Travel: One and one half miles from I-35. Call for directions.
Credit Cards: Yes
Owner: Wayne Stephens
Comments: See comments for Edmond shop.

Muskogee

Paperbacks   **Open Shop**
701 Eastside Boulevard 74403   (918) 682-4249

Collection: General stock of mostly paperback.
Hours: Wed-Sat 11-5:30.

Norman

Archives   **Open Shop**
614 North Porter Avenue 73071   (405) 360-6866

Collection: General stock of hardcover and paperback.
# of Vols: 30,000
Specialties: Religion; comics (collectible).
Hours: Mon-Sat 10-6.
Services: Appraisals, search service, accepts want lists, mail order.
Travel: One and one half miles from I-35. Call for directions.
Credit Cards: Yes
Owner: Wayne Stephens
Year Estab: 1988
Comments: See comments for Edmond shop.

Ball's Books   **Open Shop**
920 West Main Street 73069   (405) 364-4803

Collection: General stock of paperback and hardcover.
# of Vols: 17,000
Hours: Tue-Sat 11-8. Sun 12-6.
Travel: Main St (Norman) exit off I-35. Proceed east on Main. Shop is in a strip
center on south side of street.
Credit Cards: No
Year Estab: 1995
Comments: Stock is approximately 65% paperback.

Book Barn   **Open Shop**
1221 West Lindsey Street 73069   (405) 447-6049

Collection: General stock of mostly paperback.
# of Vols: 10,000
Hours: Mon-Sat 10-8. Sun 1-6.
Travel: Lindsey St exit off I-35. Proceed east on Lindsey for about three miles.
Shop is on left in a small strip center.
Credit Cards: Yes
Owner: Coetta Helton
Year Estab: 1993
Comments: The stock is approximately 85% paperback (some new but most used)
and a sparse selection of used hardcover volumes, mostly located along
the shop's exterior walls and mixed with new books.

The Book Stall   **Open Shop**
300 West Gray Street, Ste. 108   73069   (405) 329-6787

Collection:	General stock of paperback and hardcover.
# of Vols:	66,000
Hours:	Mon-Sat 10-9. Sun 1-9.
Services:	Appraisals, search service, accepts want lists, mail order.
Travel:	Main St exit off I-35. Proceed east on Main to Webster St, then north on Webster to Gray. Shop is one short block from Main, on the left, in a small shopping center on the southwest corner of Gray and Webster.
Credit Cards:	No
Owner:	Dale C. Hall
Year Estab:	1972
Comments:	The shop carries a large selection of paperbacks, a modest selection of hardcover books (some of which could indeed be of collectible interest), comics and even a small section of adult magazines.

Ochelata

Media Futures Bookstore   **Open Shop**
Route 1, Box 630   74051   (918) 333-3695

Collection:	General stock of hardcover and paperback.
# of Vols:	10,000
Hours:	Thu-Sat 9-5. Sun 1-5. Other times by chance or appointment.
Travel:	Proceeding south on Hwy 75 from Bartlesville, turn east on Road 24 and proceed for 1½ miles. (Road 24 is the same as Route 1).
Credit Cards:	No
Owner:	Gene & Farah Winn
Year Estab:	1986

Oklahoma City

Abalache Book & Antique Shop   **Open Shop**
311 South Klein Avenue   73108   (405) 235-3288

Collection:	General stock.
# of Vols:	35,000+
Specialties:	Oklahoma; Western Americana.
Hours:	Tue-Sat 10-4:45. Sun 12-4:45
Services:	Appraisals, accepts want lists, mail order.
Travel:	Western Ave exit off I-40. Proceed south on Western for 1½ blocks, then right on Exchange (where three streets come together). Shop is two blocks ahead in former Farmer's Market building, a complex of antique shops.
Credit Cards:	No
Owner:	Jim Edwards
Year Estab:	1956

(Oklahoma City)

Comments:	This stand alone book shop in a large building that houses a multi dealer antique mall carries a nice selection of older hardcover books many of which meet the definition of "collectible" intermixed with antiques. The owner, a friendly gentleman, is more than accommodating.

Adrian's Rare Books & Collectibles   **Open Shop**
5219 North Western   73118   (405) 848-1911

Collection:	General stock.
# of Vols:	50,000
Hours:	Mon-Sat 11-5.
Travel:	Western Ave exit off I-44. Proceed south on Western. Shop is between I-44 and 50th St.
Credit Cards:	Yes
Owner:	Adrian Pluess
Year Estab:	1996

Aladdin Book Shoppe   **Open Shop**
5040 North May   73112   (405) 942-2665

Collection:	General stock.
# of Vols:	45,000+
Specialties:	Oklahoma; Southwest Americana.
Hours:	Mon-Sat 10-5:30.
Services:	Appraisals, mail order.
Travel:	From I-40, take I-44 north to 50th St exit. Turn right (east) and proceed to May Ave (first major intersection). Proceed south on May, then left into Mayfair Village Shopping Center.
Credit Cards:	Yes
Owner:	Saundra Shuler
Comments:	If you're anywhere within 50 (No, make that 150) miles of this shop, head for it! Whether or not you make a purchase, you'll certainly appreciate the quality and selection of the volumes on hand. The shop is well organized, easy to browse and offers a healthy selection of titles in most subject areas.

Arrowhead Supply   **Open Shop**
330 SW 28th Street   73109   (405) 634-7128

Collection:	Specialty. Mostly new and some used.
Specialties:	Gemology; Native Americans.
Hours:	Call for hours.

Backnumbers   **Open Shop**
1116 NW 51   73118   (405) 840-0039

Collection:	General stock.
# of Vols:	500
Hours:	Tue-Fri 11-5. Sat 10-5.
Comments:	Shop also sells antiques.

Bell Book & Candle
4849 SE 44th Street   73135

Open Shop
(405) 672-6361

Collection:	General stock of mostly paperback.
# of Vols:	40,000
Hours:	Mon-Sat 10-6:30.

Book Nook
8401 North Rockwell   73132

Open Shop
(405) 722-0213

Collection:	General stock of mostly paperback.
Hours:	Mon-Sat 10-6:30.

Book Rack
2605 North MacArthur Boulevard   73127

Open Shop
(405) 787-9890

Collection:	General stock of mostly used paperback.
Hours:	Mon-Sat 10-6. Sun 1-6.

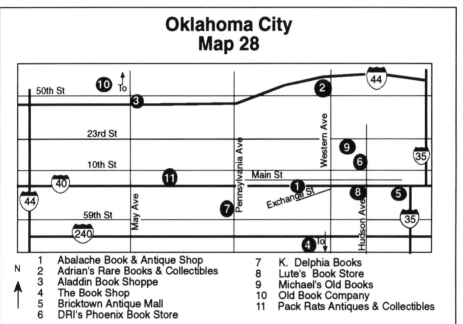

Oklahoma City Map 28

1	Abalache Book & Antique Shop
2	Adrian's Rare Books & Collectibles
3	Aladdin Book Shoppe
4	The Book Shop
5	Bricktown Antique Mall
6	DRI's Phoenix Book Store
7	K. Delphia Books
8	Lute's Book Store
9	Michael's Old Books
10	Old Book Company
11	Pack Rats Antiques & Collectibles

The Book Shop
11809 South Western   73170

Open Shop
(405) 692-2555
Fax: (405) 691-5116

Collection:	General stock of mostly used paperback and hardcover.
# of Vols:	30,000
Hours:	Mon-Sat 10-7.
Services:	Appraisals, search service, accepts want lists, mail order.
Travel:	NW 12th St exit off I-35. Proceed west on NW 12th St for about two miles where NW 12th becomes SW 119th. The shop is on the northwest corner of 119th & Western in Greenway Plaza.

(Oklahoma City)

Credit Cards:	Yes
Owner:	Michael & June Myers
Year Estab:	1973
Comments:	A neat shop with a modest number of used hardcover volumes, mostly of a fairly recent vintage, and a much larger collection of paperback titles.

Book Trader   **Open Shop**
4530 NW 50th Street   73122   (405) 787-7171

Collection:	General stock of mostly paperback.
Hours:	Mon-Sat 9:30-6.

Books 'N Tees   **Open Shop**
4615 SE 29th Street   73115   (405) 677-7763

Collection:	General stock of paperback and hardcover.
# of Vols:	25,000
Hours:	Mon-Sat 10-6.
Year Estab:	1982
Comments:	Stock is approximately 80% paperback.

Bricktown Antiques   **Antique Mall**
100 East Main Street   73104   (405) 235-2803

Hours:	Mon-Sat 10-6. Sun 12-5.
Travel:	In downtown Bricktown area, near intersection of I-40 and I-35.
Comments:	At the time of our visit, at least two dealers had booths on the second floor (an elevator is available) of this multi dealer antique mall, plus one or two other non book dealers had more limited selections of used books. If you're not rushed for time, a stop here could turn out to be a pleasant distraction.

DRI's Phoenix Book Store   **Open Shop**
805 North Hudson   73102   (405) 552-2604
                                                               Fax: (405) 236-3421

Collection:	General stock of mostly used hardcover.
# of Vols:	75,000
Specialties:	Western Americana; Oklahoma; Native Americans; self help; metaphysics; occult; hunting; fishing.
Hours:	Mon-Fri 9-6. Sat 9-5. Sun 1-5.
Services:	Search service, accepts want lists, mail order.
Travel:	Walker St exit off I-40. Proceed north on Walker to 8th St, then right on 8th and right on Hudson.
Credit Cards:	No
Owner:	Larry Sheck, Buyer
Year Estab:	1991
Comments:	Unfortunately we were unable to visit this non profit shop which was recommended to us by several local dealers.

K Delphia Books   **Open Shop**
5735 South Pennsylvania Avenue   73119   (405) 685-0284

Collection:	General stock of paperback and hardcover.
# of Vols:	12,000+
Hours:	Mon-Sat 11-5.
Travel:	59th St exit off I-44. Proceed east on 59th St to Pennsylvania, then left on Pennsylvania. Shop is just ahead in a strip center.
Credit Cards:	No
Owner:	Wayne & Kathleen Blanchard
Year Estab:	1994
Comments:	At the time of our visit, signs in the shop's window indicated that one could buy art, reference, regional, entertainment and home improvement titles inside the store. No doubt one could, but the majority of the books one would be able to select from would be paperback titles. The hardcover items we saw were recent, common or just plain older books.

Lute's Book Store   **Open Shop**
404 West Main Street   73102   (405) 232-2621

Collection:	General stock of hardcover and paperback.
# of Vols:	10,000
Hours:	Mon-Sat 10-5.
Travel:	Walker exit off I-40. Proceed north on Walker to Main St, then right on Main. Shop is one block ahead.
Credit Cards:	No
Year Estab:	1963
Comments:	A larger selection of used hardcover books than one might initially anticipate from the shop's front window. Most of the books were older and in mixed condition and some of the titles had seen better days. If you're a patient browser, however, there is a reasonable chance that you might find some titles here that have been eluding you. The owner, a gregarious octogenarian, is considering the sale of his business. Interested?

Melvin Marcher, Bookseller   **By Appointment**
6204 North Vermont   73112   (405) 946-6270

Collection:	Specialty
# of Vols:	5,000
Specialties:	Natural history; hunting; fishing; firearms; Americana.
Services:	Catalog, accepts want lists.
Credit Cards:	No
Year Estab:	1971

Michael's Old Books   **Open Shop**
928 NW 23rd Street   73106   (405) 525-0123

Collection:	General stock of hardcover and paperback.
# of Vols:	40,000+

(Oklahoma City)

Hours:	Mon-Sat 10-5 OR Mon-Thu 10-2:30. Fri & Sat 10-5. (See comments)
Travel:	East 23rd St exit off I-35. Proceed west on East 23rd.
Year Estab:	1986
Comments:	When we arrived at this shop on a Wednesday afternoon, the sign on the door read, "Closed" and the posted hours we saw were different from those given to use by the owner several weeks earlier in a phone conversation. If you want to try your luck at visiting here, we strongly urge you to phone ahead so that your trip (unlike ours) is not in vain.

Oklahoma Heritage Book Center
By Appointment

1500 North Robinson   73103
(405) 232-7338

Collection:	Specialty new and used.
# of Vols:	500
Specialties:	Oklahoma
Services:	Monthly lists.
Credit Cards:	Yes
Year Estab:	1976

Old Book Company
Open Shop

10449 North May Avenue   73120
(405) 752-4400

Collection:	General stock of hardcover and paperback.
# of Vols:	20,000-25,000
Hours:	Mon-Sat 11-6.
Services:	Appraisals, accepts want lists, mail order.
Travel:	Heffner Ave exit off I-35. Proceed west on Heffner to May Ave, then south on May. Shop is two blocks ahead, on right, in Village Park Shopping Center.
Credit Cards:	Yes
Owner:	Bob Cowden
Year Estab:	1986
Comments:	While a few sections were labeled and some titles matched the labels, elsewhere the books appeared to be shelved with a rhyme and reason that eluded us. However, if you're patient and wish to spend the time perusing this shop, you may find some titles (both fiction and non fiction) of interest. Most of the volumes we saw were in rather mixed condition. The stock was evenly divided between hardcover and paperback.

Pack Rats Antiques & Collectibles
Open Shop

2712 NW 10th Street   73107
(405) 942-4744

Collection:	General stock.
# of Vols:	3,000-4,000
Hours:	Mon-Sat 10-5. Sun 12-5.
Services:	Appraisals, accepts want lists, mail order.

Travel:	NW 10th exit off I-44. Proceed east on NW 10th. On south side of street between May and Miller.
Credit Cards:	No
Owner:	Ed Schnell & Gaylord Fisher
Year Estab:	1981

Trader Jim's   **Open Shop**
1221 SW 59th Street   73109   (405) 631-5638

Collection:	General stock of mostly paperback.
Hours:	Mon-Sat 10-6.

Ponca City

The Book House   **Open Shop**
114 North 3rd Street   74601   (405) 762-0377

Collection:	General stock of used paperback and hardcover and new books.
# of Vols:	30,000 (used)
Hours:	Mon-Fri 9-6. Sat 9-5.
Travel:	Hwy 60 exit off I-35. Proceed east on Hwy 60 to Ponca City, then north on 3rd St.
Comments:	Used stock is approximately 80% paperback.

Brace Books & More   **Open Shop**
2205 North 14th Street   74601   (405) 765-5173

Collection:	General stock new and used paperback and hardcover.
# of Vols:	15,000 (used)
Hours:	Mon-Fri 10-8. Sat 10-6. Sun 1-5.
Credit Cards:	Yes
Owner:	Jerry Brace
Year Estab:	1983
Comments:	Used stock is approximately 75% paperback.

Poteau

Bookmart   **Open Shop**
105 South McKenna   74953   (918) 647-5356

Collection:	General stock of paperback and hardcover.
Hours:	Tue-Sat 10-6.
Services:	Accepts want lists.
Travel:	Dewey Ave exit off Hwy 271/59. Proceed east on Dewey then right at first light. Shop is just ahead on left.
Credit Cards:	No
Owner:	Linda Day
Year Estab:	1993
Comments:	Stock is approximately 75% paperback.

Pryor

Book Exchange
3 North Adair Street   74361

Collection:	General stock of mostly used paperbacks.
# of Vols:	10,000-15,000 (used)
Hours:	Mon-Sat 10-5.

Sand Springs

Rod's Books and Relics
10 East Second Street   74063

Open Shop
(918) 245-9052

Collection:	General stock of hardcover and paperback.
# of Vols:	3,000
Hours:	Mon-Sat 12-5. Best to call ahead.
Travel:	Downtown exit off Hwy 64. Continue on 2nd St to heart of downtown.
Comments:	Stock is evenly divided between hardcover and paperback. Note: telephone is located in the adjoining antique shop.

Sapulpa

The Book Place
24 East Dewey   74066

Open Shop
(918) 224-5595

Collection:	General stock of paperback and hardcover.
# of Vols:	75,000 (used)
Hours:	Mon-Fri 9-6. Sat 9-5.
Travel:	On old Hwy 66.
Comments:	Stock is approximately 75% paperback.

Shawnee

Bibliotech
123 East Main Street   74801

Open Shop
(405) 275-9494
Fax: (405) 878-0649

Collection:	General stock of paperback and hardcover and comics.
# of Vols:	10,000
Hours:	Mon-Sat 10-6. Sun 1-5.
Services:	Accepts want lists, mail order.
Travel:	Kickapoo exit off I-40. Proceed south on Kickapoo, then left on Main. Shop is at corner of Main and Union.
Credit Cards:	Yes
Owner:	Randy Grizzle
Year Estab:	1994
Comments:	Stock is approximately 75% paperback.

Book Barn   **Open Shop**
413 West MacArthur Street   74801   (405) 273-2244

Collection:	General stock of paperback and hardcover.
Hours:	Mon-Sat 10-8. Sun 1-6.
Travel:	Kickapoo exit off I-40. Proceed south on Kickapoo to MacArthur St, then left on MacArthur.
Credit Cards:	Yes
Owner:	Coetta Helton
Year Estab:	1994
Comments:	See comments for Norman store.

Oklahoma Book Mine   **Open Shop**
1500 North Kickapoo   74801   (405) 273-6233

Collection:	General stock.
# of Vols:	6,000
Specialties:	First editions; Americana; Native Americans; literature; John Steinbeck.
Hours:	Tue-Sat 10-8. Sun 1-5.
Services:	Appraisals, search service, accepts want lists.
Travel:	Kickapoo exit off I-40. Proceed south on Kickapoo for about two miles. Shop is in a strip mall at corner of Independence.
Credit Cards:	Yes
Year Estab:	1993

Shawnee Book Stall   **Open Shop**
1510 North Kickapoo, A-14   74801   (405) 275-5714

Collection:	General stock of paperback and hardcover.
# of Vols:	22,000
Hours:	Mon-Sat 9:30am-8:30pm. Sun 1-6.
Services:	Search service, accepts want lists, mail order.
Travel:	Independence exit off Hwy 177. Proceed east on Independence to Kickapoo Plaza Shopping Center which is after the light at Pottenger/ Airport Dr.
Credit Cards:	No
Year Estab:	1976
Comments:	Stock is approximately 75% paperback.

Stillwater

Caravan Used Books Annex   **Open Shop**
519 West University Avenue   74074   (405) 372-6228

Collection:	General stock of hardcover and paperback.
# of Vols:	5,000
Hours:	Mon-Sat, except closed Wed, 1-5.
Travel:	Knoblock St exit off Hwy 51. Proceed north on Knoblock to university campus, then turn right on University.
Credit Cards:	No

Owner:	Peter Thomas
Comments:	Stock is evenly divided between hardcover and paperback.
Year Estab:	1971

Tahlequah

Rock'n RR Books   **Open Shop**
110 West Allen Road   74464   (918) 456-3437

Collection:	General stock of mostly paperback and records.
# of Vols:	60,000
Hours:	Mon-Sat 11-6:30.

Tulsa

BiblioMania   **Open Shop**
12929-H East 21st Street   74134   (918) 438-9889

Collection:	Specialty new and used.
Specialties:	Home schooling; bibles; religion.
Hours:	Tue-Fri 10-6. Sat 10-5.
Travel:	129th E Ave exit off I-44 or I-244. Proceed south to 21st St. Shop is in Family Plaza Shopping Center.
Credit Cards:	Yes
Owner:	Helen Stockinger
Year Estab:	1992
Comments:	Stock is about evenly divided between new and used books. Most used books are home schooling volumes..

The Book Cellar   **Open Shop**
3151 P South 129th East Avenue   74134   (918) 663-0136

Collection:	General stock of paperback and hardcover.
# of Vols:	16,000
Hours:	Tue-Fri 10-6. Sat 10-5. Sun 12-3.
Travel:	31st St exit off Hwy 169. Proceed east on 31st St for 1½ miles to 129th Ave. Shop is in Briarglenn Square.
Credit Cards:	Yes
Year Estab:	1995
Comments:	Stock is approximately 70% paperback.

Bookland   **Open Shop**
2208 East 61st Street   74136   (918) 747-0773

Collection:	General stock of paperback and hardcover.
# of Vols:	12,000
Hours:	Mon-Sat 10-6.
Travel:	Lewis exit off I-44. Proceed south on Lewis to 61st St, then west on 61st St. Shop is one block ahead, on south side, in a small strip center.
Owner:	Sandra Davis
Year Estab:	1988
Comments:	Stock is approximately 70% paperback.

Books, Inc.   **Open Shop**
2442-C East 15th Street   74104   Fax:(918) 743-0631   (918) 743-8666
                                       E-mail: TULSABKS@interloc.com

Collection:	General stock of mostly hardcover.
# of Vols:	15,000+
Specialties:	Modern literary first editions; mystery first editions.
Hours:	Mon-Fri 10:30-6. Sat 11-5.
Services:	Appraisals, search service, catalog, accepts want lists.
Travel:	15th St exit off Hwy 51 (Broken Arrow Fwy). Proceed east on 15th St. From I-44, Harvard exit. Proceed north on Harvard to 15th, then west on 15th.
Credit Cards:	No
Owner:	Gary Himes
Year Estab:	1995
Comments:	Nestled inbetween two other shops on the same street but several blocks apart, is another "quality used book dealer" whose carpets (the kind one sinks into) helps you to feel that the volumes you are viewing have the same plush quality. Most of the books we saw were in excellent condition, fairly priced (if you know your authors and the desirability of certain editions). The mystery section was particularly enticing as was the selection of vintage paperbacks. At the time of our visit, the shop had only been in business for 15 months but its second floor was already in full bloom and an additional expansion was on the horizon. If you're planning a trip to Tulsa and your time is limited, you can easily spend a full half day or more just at the three shops on 15th Street (see the First Edition Book Shop and Oak Tree Books below).

Dusty Bookworm   **Open Shop**
3711 South Harvard Avenue   74135   (918) 742-7131
                                       E-mail: nkemp@tulsa.com

Collection:	General stock of paperback and hardcover.
# of Vols:	50,000
Hours:	Mon-Sat 10-6, except Fri till 8.
Services:	Accepts want lists.
Travel:	Harvard exit off I-44. Proceed north on Harvard for 1½ miles. Shop is on right between 41st & 36th Streets.
Credit Cards:	Yes
Owner:	Nan Kemp
Year Estab:	1989
Comments:	Not necessarily the typical "mostly paperback" used book shop although it is certainly true that a majority of the stock here leans heavily in the paper direction. The store does offer a reasonable collection of hardcover books for the average reader. If your tastes are above average, however, you're not likely to find a rare item here (unless, that is, you're good at selecting lottery numbers.)

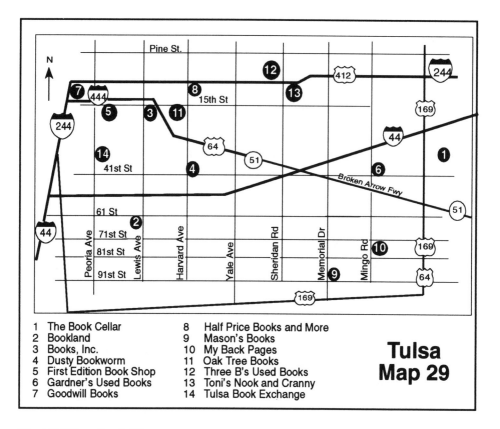

1   The Book Cellar   8   Half Price Books and More
2   Bookland   9   Mason's Books
3   Books, Inc.   10 My Back Pages
4   Dusty Bookworm   11 Oak Tree Books
5   First Edition Book Shop   12 Three B's Used Books
6   Gardner's Used Books   13 Toni's Nook and Cranny
7   Goodwill Books   14 Tulsa Book Exchange

Tulsa
Map 29

First Edition Book Shop   **Open Shop**
1502 East 15th Street   74120   (800) 539-1967   (918) 582-1967
                                                   Fax: (918) 583-9538
                                        E-mail: 1stedbks@interloc.com

Collection: General stock.
# of Vols: 100,000
Specialties: Western Americana; Native Americans; art.
Hours: Mon-Sat 9:30-5:30.
Services: Appraisals, search service, accepts want lists, mail order.
Travel: Peoria exit off I-44. Proceed north on Peoria to 15th St. Right on 15th St
                 and proceed four blocks. Shop is on south side.
Credit Cards: Yes
Owner: Della McCulloch
Year Estab: 1981
Comments: Like the other two shops on 15th Street (but a lot larger), this shop also
                 carries a fine selection of quality hardcover used volumes. The shop is
                 well organized if occasionally crowded but worth the time it may take
                 to view titles you may have been searching for for quite a while. Most
                 subjects are available with many in plentiful supply.

Gardner's Used Books & Comics   **Open Shop**
4419 South Mingo   74146   (918) 627-7323
                                                          Fax: (918) 250-8828

Collection:	General stock of paperback and hardcover.
# of Vols:	500,000
Specialties:	History; mystery; westerns; science fiction; cookbooks; religion.
Hours:	Mon-Fri 10-8. Sat 8-8. Sun 12-5.
Services:	Search service.
Travel:	Hwy 51 exit off I-44, then east on Hwy 51 to Mingo and south on Mingo to 41st St.
Credit Cards:	Yes
Owner:	Richard C. Gardner
Year Estab:	1991
Comments:	We didn't count them, but after walking around this shop, down one aisle after another, we wouldn't take issue with the owner's estimate of the number of volumes in his shop. While the majority of the items on hand are paperback, and even though the shop also sells records, CDs, comic books and magazines, the number of hardcover volumes, in mixed condition, could fill a respectable sized book store that the average book person would not mind visiting. The age of the books we saw varied from vintage to recent best sellers with a strong emphasis on fiction and mysteries but lots to select from in other areas. We have no doubt that depending on your taste and the time you're willing to spend here, you could walk out with several items of interest.

Goodwill Books   **Open Shop**
416 South Main   74103   (918) 582-2640

Collection:	General stock of paperback and hardcover.
# of Vols:	30,000
Hours:	Mon-Fri 10-4.
Travel:	In downtown between Boulder & Boston and 4th & 6th. Take Boulder exit off I-244. Proceed north on Boulder then right on 4th. Shop is in a pedestrian mall.

Half Price Books and More   **Open Shop**
1130 South Harvard Avenue   74112   (918) 587-7799

Collection:	General stock of paperback and hardcover.
# of Vols:	40,000
Hours:	Mon-Fri 10-6. Sat 10-5.
Travel:	Harvard exit off Hwy 51. Proceed north on Harvard. Shop is between 11th & 12th Sts.
Credit Cards:	Yes
Owner:	Joe Alpers
Year Estab:	1994
Comments:	Stock is approximately 75% paperback.

(Tulsa)

Mason's Books   **Open Shop**
8933 South Memorial Square, 91   74133   (918) 250-1755

Collection:	General stock of paperback and hardcover.
# of Vols:	8,000-10,000
Hours:	Mon-Sat 10-9. Sun 12-6.
Travel:	Memorial Dr exit off Hwy 169. Proceed north on Memorial to 91st St. Shop is in shopping center at northeast corner of Memorial and 91st St.
Comments:	Stock is approximately 75% paperback.

My Back Pages   **Open Shop**
7141 South Mingo   (918) 254-2526
Mailing address: 1924 South Utica, Ste 700 Tulsa 74104   Fax: (918) 747-2965

Collection:	General stock and ephemera.
# of Vols:	10,000
Specialties:	Children's; illustrated; science fiction; mystery; nostalgia; pulps; Western Americana; movie memorabilia.
Hours:	Tue-Sat 11-6. Other times by appointment.
Services:	Appraisals, search service, accepts want lists, mail order.
Travel:	Located at intersection of 71st St and S. Mingo. From Hwy 169, take 71st St exit and proceed west to East Pointe Shopping Center.
Credit Cards:	Yes
Owner:	John A. McMahan
Year Estab:	1970
Comments:	If you happen to be a nostalgia freak (one of us confesses to being so addicted) you'll find this shop well worth a visit. The vintage hardcover mysteries and selection of pulp magazines offer wonderful temptations. The shop's other stock, while modest in size, offers the browser interesting selections, depending on one's tastes. Don't look for bargains.

Mystery Book Company   **Open Shop**
3747 South Harvard   74135   (918) 744-4082
                                                               Fax: (918) 744-1783

Collection:	Specialty new and used.
Specialties:	Mystery
Hours:	Mon-Sat 10-6. Sun 1-5.
Travel:	Harvard exit off I-44. Proceed north on Harvard. Shop is on east side of street, between 31st and 36th Sts in a strip mall.
Year Estab:	1996

Oak Tree Books   **Open Shop**
2812 East 15th Street   74104   (918) 745-0002
                                                               Fax: (918) 745-0002

Collection:	General stock of mostly hardcover.
# of Vols:	25,000

Specialties: Western Americana; Native Americans.
Hours: Mon-Sat 10-6.
Services: Search service, accepts want lists, catalog.
Travel: 15th St exit off Hwy 51 (Broken Arrow Expy). Proceed east on 15th St for four blocks. From I-44, Harvard exit. Proceed north on Harvard to 15th, then west on 15th for about eight blocks. Shop is in a small strip center.
Credit Cards: Yes
Owner: Charles Curtsinger & Scott Dingman
Year Estab: 1993
Comments: A modest sized shop where the collection of books is far from modest. The shop offers a reasonable number of titles in most categories with the books themselves being well selected. This is a shop we would certainly recommend to collectors with discriminating tastes.

Peace of Mind Bookstore
1401 East 15th Street   74120

Open Shop
(918) 583-1090

Collection: Specialty used and new hardcover and paperback.
Specialties: Comparative religion; alchemy; astrology; Druids; divination; Egypt; mythology; Kabbalah; UFOs; Masons; martial arts; theosophy.
Hours: Mon-Sat 11-7. Sun 12-6.
Services: Appraisals, search service, accepts want lists, mail order.
Travel: Utica Ave exit off I-244. Proceed south on Utica to 15th St, then right on 15th St. Shop is about 1/2 mile ahead on north side.
Credit Cards: Yes
Comments: Stock is approximately 60% used, 65% of which is hardcover.

L.A. Robbins
PO Box 1331   74101

By Appointment
(918) 437-7975

Collection: Specialty
Specialties: Pulps
Services: Search service, accepts want lists, mail order.
Credit Cards: No

Three B's Used Books
838 North Sheridan   74115

Open Shop
(918) 836-8900

Collection: General stock of hardcover and paperback.
# of Vols: 50,000+
Specialties: Western Americana; literary first editions; Oklahoma.
Hours: Mon-Sat 9-6.
Services: Appraisals, accepts want lists.
Travel: Sheridan exit off I-244. Proceed north on Sheridan for about four blocks. Shop is on left, 1/4 mile north of Hwy 244 in Airway strip center.
Credit Cards: Yes
Owner: C.C. & Barbara Webster
Year Estab: 1970

Comments: A mom and pop operation with lots of older hardcover books in mixed condition. While a number of the books here have seen better days, if your interest is in vintage titles and/or more recent best sellers, there's certainly a chance that you may find that item here. Plenty of paperbacks, some collectibles and even a selection of comics.

Toni's Nook and Cranny   **Open Shop**
5 South Sheridan   74112   (918) 838-0288

Collection: General stock of paperback and hardcover.
# of Vols: 40,000
Hours: Mon-Fri 10-6. Sat 10-5.
Travel: Admiral Sheridan exit off I-44. Proceed south on Admiral Sheridan. Shop is in a small strip center.
Credit Cards: Yes
Owner: Chris Edwards
Year Estab: 1987
Comments: Stock is approximately 70% paperback.

Tulsa Book Exchange   **Open Shop**
3749 Peoria   74105   (918) 742-2007

Collection: General stock of hardcover and paperback.
# of Vols: 14,000 (hardcover)
Hours: Mon-Fri 10-7. Sat 10-5:30.
Travel: Peoria exit off Hwy 44. Proceed north on Peoria to 38th.
Credit Cards: Yes
Owner: David McIlnay
Year Estab: 1995

Ron Bever Books
(405) 478-0215

Route 3, Box 243B   Edmond 73013   E-mail: 76531.1027@compuserve.com

Collection:	General stock.
# of Vols:	15,000
Specialties:	Stock market; commodities; Wall Street; Oklahoma; Oklahoma University Press; religion.
Services:	Appraisals, search service, catalog, accepts want lists.
Credit Cards:	No
Year Estab:	1977

L.D. Dick Books
(918) 337-5547

PO Box 3711   Bartlesville 74006   E-mail: 102651.223@compuserve.com

Collection:	Specialty. Primarily paperback.
# of Vols:	20,000
Specialties:	Science fiction; herpetology; herbs; country dancing.
Services:	Catalog, accepts want lists.
Credit Cards:	No
Year Estab:	1981

The Oklahoma Bookman
(405) 354-3619

1107 Foreman Road, NE Yukon 73099

Collection:	Specialty
# of Vols:	3,000
Specialties:	Natural history; Oklahoma University Press.
Services:	Appraisals, search service, accepts want lists.
Credit Cards:	No
Owner:	D.R. (Ted) Goulden
Year Estab:	1987

Territorial Bookman
(918) 481-0436

8437 South Toledo Avenue   Oklahoma City 74137

Collection:	Specialty
# of Vols:	5,000
Specialties:	Civil War; Western Americana; black military history.
Services:	Appraisals, search service, accepts want lists, catalog.
Credit Cards:	No
Owner:	Robert Norris
Year Estab:	1976

If you start them reading at a young age, they'll be readers all their lives.

South Dakota

Alphabetical Listing By Dealer

Alphabetical Listing By Location

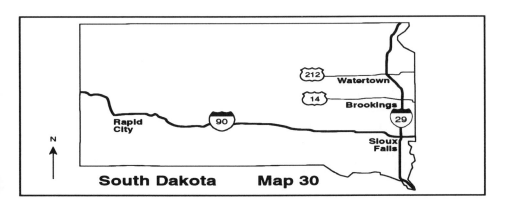

N

South Dakota   Map 30

Brookings

Yellowed Pages

Open Shop

420 Fourth Street   57006

(605) 692-2665

Collection:	General stock of paperback and hardcover, records and ephemera.
# of Vols:	50,000
Specialties:	Mystery; science fiction; local history; classics.
Hours:	Mon-Sat 10-5:30.
Services:	Search service, accepts want lists.
Travel:	Proceed west on 6th St to Main, then south on Main for two blocks.
Credit Cards:	No
Owner:	Jim Skulstad
Year Estab:	1989
Comments:	Stock is approximately 65% paperback. Dealer operates a second shop in Watertown. See below.

Mitchell

Jim McLaird

By Appointment

2430 West 23rd Avenue   57301

(605) 996-5838

Collection:	Specialty
# of Vols:	2,000+
Specialties:	Western Americana; Northern Plains region.
Services:	Accepts want lists, mail order.
Credit Cards:	No
Year Estab:	1976

Piedmont

Antiques & Art

Open Shop

HC 80, Box 793-25   57769

(605) 347-5016

Fax: (605) 347-7513

Collection:	Specialty
# of Vols:	8,000
Specialties:	Western Americana; Native Americans; cowboys; firearms; military.
Hours:	Daily 9-5.
Services:	Appraisals, search service, accepts want lists, catalog.
Travel:	Exit 40 off I-90. Shop is adjacent to highway on Tilford Rd.
Credit Cards:	Yes
Owner:	James & Peggy Aplan
Year Estab:	1956

Rapid City

Everybody's Bookstore   **Open Shop**
515 6th Street   57701   (605) 341-3224

Collection:	General stock of hardcover and paperback.
Specialties:	Black Hills, Western Americana; Native Americans.
Hours:	Mon-Sat 9:30-5:30.
Travel:	In downtown, 2½ blocks south of Hwy 44 (Omaha St) and two blocks east of Hwy 16 (8th St/Mt. Rushmore Rd).
Credit Cards:	Yes
Owner:	Kevin & Lori Speirs
Year Estab:	1992

Storyteller   **Open Shop**
520 6th Street   57701   (605) 348-7242

Collection:	Specialty. Mostly used paperback.
# of Vols:	5,000
Specialties:	Science fiction; horror; fantasy.
Hours:	Mon-Sat 10-7. Sun 1-7.
Credit Cards:	Yes
Owner:	Brian Bade
Year Estab:	1990

Sioux Falls

The Book Shop In Sioux Falls   **Open Shop**
**   (605) 336-8384

Collection:	General stock of hardcover and paperback.
# of Vols:	25,000
Specialties:	South Dakota; Sioux (Lakota/Dakota) Indians.
Hours:	Mon-Sat 10-5:30.
Travel:	Downtown
Credit Cards:	Yes
Owner:	Kay Coddington, Katherine Ann Talley, Nancy Veglahn
Year Estab:	1988
Comments:	Stock is evenly divided between hardcover and paperback.

** As we went to press, we were advised by the owners that they had lost their lease and were in the process of searching for a new location in downtown Sioux Falls. They're hoping to keep the same phone number.

Kolbe's Books & Things   **Open Shop**
1301 South Duluth   57105   (605) 332-9662

Collection:	Specialty books and ephemera.
# of Vols:	3,000
Specialties:	Dakota; Western Americana.
Hours:	Mon-Fri 1:30-5. Mornings and weekends by chance or appointment.

Travel:	Minnesota exit off I-90. Proceed south on Minnesota, then west on 21st Street. Shop is at corner of 21st and South Duluth.
Credit Cards:	No
Owner:	Robert Kolbe
Year Estab:	1972

Watertown

Yellowed Pages   **Open Shop**
10 East Kemp   57201   (605) 886-3640

Collection:	General stock of paperback, hardcover, records and ephemera.
# of Vols:	50,000+
Hours:	Mon-Sat 10-5:30.
Services:	Search service, accepts want lists.
Travel:	Hwy 212 to Hwy 81, then north on Hwy 81 to Kemp Ave. West on Kemp. Shop is between Maple and Broadway.
Credit Cards:	No
Owner:	Jim Skulstad
Year Estab:	1994
Comments:	Stock is approximately 65% paperback. Dealer operates a second shop in Brookings. See above.

Mail Order Dealers

The Cache!
Route 1, Box 178J   Hot Springs 57747

Collection:	General stock of mostly hardcover.
# of Vols:	5,000-7,000
Specialties:	Zane Grey; Western Americana; cookbooks;; children's; westerns.
Services:	Search service, accepts want lists.
Credit Cards:	No
Owner:	Martha Anderson
Year Estab:	1973
Comments:	At the time we went to press, the dealer was in the process of relocating here from Colorado and did not as yet have a telephone number.

Tennessee

Alphabetical Listing By Dealer

Alphabetical Listing By Location

Antioch

Book Gallery   **Open Shop**
5326-A Mountain View Road   37013   (615) 731-1900

Collection:	General stock of mostly new and some used paperback and hardcover.
# of Vols:	100,000
Hours:	Mon-Sat 10-9. Sun 1-5.
Services:	Accepts want lists, mail order.
Travel:	Exit 60 off I-24. Proceed east on Hickory Hollow Pkwy for about 1/4 mile to Mountain View Rd, then left on Mountain View. Shop is on left in Bell Forge Square Shopping Center.
Credit Cards:	Yes
Owner:	Joy Mann
Year Estab:	1994
Comments:	One's initial impression upon entering this shop is that all of the stock is new; it was hard indeed to find a hardcover book without a dust jacket. In many cases, used and new books were intershelved and if there were many older volumes, we failed to spot them. Prices of books were easy to identify as stickers were affixed to the dust jackets. The shop also displays several shelves of Easton Press volumes, most reasonably priced. If you're looking for a title recently out of print, there's a good chance that you might find it here. If you're looking for a rare or collectible volume, we don't think you'll be quite as lucky.

Bell Buckle

Bell Buckle Book Store   **Open Shop**
6 Railroad Square   (615) 389-9328
Mailing address: PO Box 296   Bell Buckle   37020

Collection:	General stock.
# of Vols:	12,000
Specialties:	Civil War; children's; first editions.
Hours:	Mon 10:30-2. Wed-Sat 10:30-4:30. Sun 12-4:30.
Services:	Appraisals, search service, accepts want lists, mail order.
Travel:	Exit 97 off I-24. Proceed west on Hwy 64 to Hwy 82, then right on Hwy 82 to Bell Buckle. Shop is on the square.
Credit Cards:	Yes
Owner:	Freida Meyers & Marty Mouton
Year Estab:	1978
Comments:	We're sorry we didn't get a chance to visit this shop. Books aside, we were told that the town has been preserved as a quaint old railroad community.

The Livery Stable Antique Mall   **Antique Mall**
107 Main Street   (615) 389-6354

Hours:	Mon-Sat 10-5. Sun 1-5
Travel:	Located one block off the square.

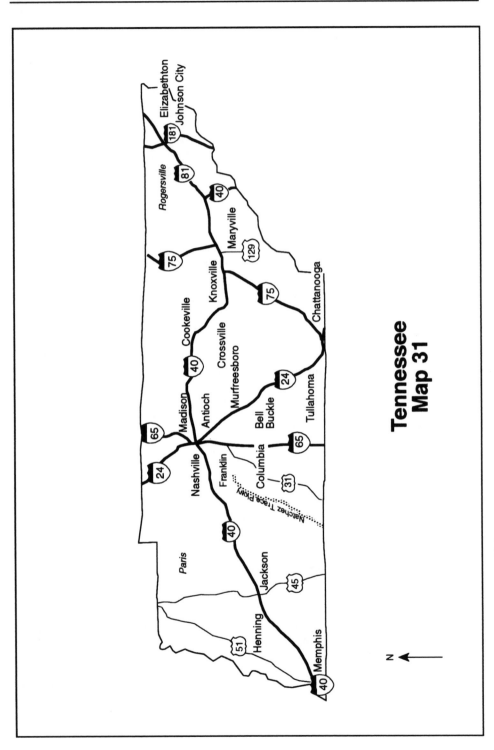

Tennessee
Map 31

Chattanooga

All Books Crabtree   **Open Shop**
410 Broad Street   (423) 266-0501
Mailing address: PO Box 366 Signal Mountain 37377
E-mail: allbooks@interloc.com

Collection:	General stock of mostly hardcover.
# of Vols:	50,000+
Specialties:	Local history; Civil War; art; natural history.
Hours:	Mon-Sat 10-6.
Services:	Appraisals, search service, accepts want lists, mail order, book binding.
Travel:	Exit 4 (4th St exit) off Hwy 27. Proceed on 4th St to Broad St, then right on Broad (second right).
Credit Cards:	Yes
Owner:	Polly Henry
Year Estab:	1989
Comments:	Our readers will be more fortunate than we were in that their visit to this shop will be at the owner's new more spacious location in the heart of downtown Chattanooga rather than the Signal Mountain location we visited shortly before the move took place. During our visit, we had the pleasure of meeting an enthusiastic proprietor whose pride in her books was evident as she showed us around the shop introducing us to some of her favorite sections. While we fully realize that the books on display during our visit may not be the ones you'll see when you visit, experience suggests that the owner's buying practices should continue to provide you with an assortment of fine titles in generally very good condition, not only in the specialties listed above, but also in other areas. If we were planning a return trip to Tennessee soon, we would certainly pay this owner a second visit. Let us know if after your visit, the new shop has lived up to our expectations.

BLK Books   **Open Shop**
6503 Slater Road, Ste. G   37412   (423) 855-8898

Collection:	General stock.
# of Vols:	25,000
Specialties:	Tennessee; regional; military; art; illustrated; modern first editions.
Hours:	Tue-Sat 10-6. Sun 1-6.
Services:	Appraisals, accepts want lists, mail order.
Travel:	Exit 1 (East Ridge) off I-75. Proceed west on Hwy 41 (Ringgold Rd) for one block, then right on Mack Smith. Proceed for about 100 yards then turn right into shopping center parking lot. Shop is at the other end of the lot.
Credit Cards:	Yes
Owner:	William N. Kirchner
Year Estab:	1990

Comments: A strictly hardcover shop with interesting titles, particularly, but not re-
                 stricted to the subjects listed above as specialties. Most of the books we
                 saw were in good to very good condition. While the shop had a modest
                 selection of books in the areas of popular cultures, its selections in non
                 fiction and literature were quite good. Several items behind glass were
                 worthy of note. Certainly worth a visit for the serious collector.

The Book Company   .   **Open Shop**
1920 South Kelly   (423) 622-1805
Mailing address: 526 South Crest Chattanooga 37404

Collection: General stock of hardcover and paperback.
# of Vols: 75,000
Hours: Thu-Sun 10-5.
Services: Accepts want lists, mail order.
Travel: Exit 181A exit off I-24. Proceed north on 4th Ave (which is Kelly) to
                 20th St. Shop is on right on the site of a flea market.
Credit Cards: No
Owner: Charlyn Harless
Year Estab: 1978
Comments: The majority of the books are displayed in what appears to be two
                 quasi permanent shed-like rooms on the site of a weekend flea market.
                 Additional books (mostly paperback) are located outdoors in front of
                 the "sheds." Most subjects were represented although few in large
                 numbers. If condition is not important to you, you might be able to
                 pick up an item or two of interest here. Our olfactory senses may not
                 have been properly attuned at the time of our visit for we sensed a kind
                 of mustiness in the air. Whether this was due to the July heat or the
                 condition of some of the books we were unable to determine. Visitors
                 are advised that the sheds are not air conditioned in the summer or
                 heated in the winter.

East Town Antique Mall   **Antique Mall**
6503 Slater Road   37412   (423) 899-5498

Hours: Mon-Fri 9-6. Sat 9-8. Sun 10-6.
Travel: See BLK Books above. Mall is in same strip center.

McKay Used Books and CDs   **Open Shop**
6401 Lee Highway   37421   (423) 892-0067

Collection: General stock of paperback and hardcover.
Hours: Mon-Thu 9-9. Fri & Sat 9am-10pm. Sun 12-8.
Travel: Hwy 75 north off I-24. Proceed north on Hwy 75 to Hwy 153, then north
                 on Hwy 153 to Lee Hwy exit. Turn right off exit. Shop is in shopping
                 center immediately on left.
Credit Cards: Yes
Owner: Anne Jacobson
Comments: See comments for Knoxville store.

Cleveland

The Book Shelf   **By Appointment**
3765 Hillsdale Drive, NE   37312   (423) 472-8408

Collection:	Specialty
# of Vols:	2,000
Specialties:	Tennessee (history and authors); Alabama (history and authors); southern history.
Services:	Search service, catalog.
Credit Cards:	No
Owner:	William R. Snell
Year Estab:	1974

Columbia

Franklin's Old Book Shop   **Open Shop**
39 Public Square   38401   Fax: (615) 540-0520   (615) 540-0520
                                            E-mail: franklin@interloc.com

Collection:	General stock and ephemera.
# of Vols:	6,000
Specialties:	Religion; World War II; presidents; espionage.
Hours:	Wed-Sat 10-6.
Services:	Appraisals, search service, accepts want lists.
Travel:	One block off Hwy 31, on the courthouse square.
Credit Cards:	Yes
Owner:	Ed & Carolyn Franklin
Year Estab:	1987

Cookeville

The Bargain Book & Stained Glass   **Open Shop**
216 West Spring Street   38501   (615) 526-8131

Collection:	General stock of paperback and hardcover, records, and CD's.
# of Vols:	100,000
Hours:	Mon-Fri 9-6. Sat 9-5.
Travel:	Burgess Falls Rd (Hwy 135) exit off I-40. Proceed south on Hwy 135 into Cookeville for approximately 2½ miles. Right on Spring St. Shop is just ahead.
Credit Cards:	Yes
Owner:	Lee & Lana Fruchey & Susan White
Year Estab:	1984
Comments:	Stock is approximately 75% paperback.

Book Barn   **Open Shop**
501 East Broad   38501   (615) 526-5979

Collection:	General stock of mostly paperback.
Hours:	Tue-Fri 9:30-5:30. Sat 10-5.

Crossville

Book Cellar   **Open Shop**
81 Cumberland Plaza   38555   (615) 456-2285

Collection: General stock of mostly paperback.
# of Vols: 40,000
Hours: Mon-Fri 9-6. Sat 9-5.

Jim Genovese Books   **Antique Mall**
At Antique Village Mall, Genesis Road   Mall: (615) 484-8664
Mailing address: PO Box 3444 38502   Bus: (615) 456-2368

Collection: General stock.
# of Vols: 5,000
Specialties: U.S. Marine Corps.
Hours: Mon-Sat 9:30-6. Sun 1-5.
Services: Search service, accepts want lists.
Travel: Exit 320 off I-40. Mall is at northwest corner.
Year Estab: 1988

Elizabethton

Blommin' Bookshelf   **Open Shop**
428 East E Street   37643   (423) 542-0771

Collection: General stock of hardcover and paperback.
# of Vols: 30,000+
Specialties: History; children's; old fiction.
Hours: Tue-Fri 10-5. Sat 10-4.
Services: Search service, accepts want lists, mail order.
Travel: Johnson City exit off I-81. Proceed southeast on I-181 to exit 31
                   (Elizabethton), the east on Hwy 67 to Elizabethton. Right on Pine St,
                   then right at second stop sign on E Street. Shop is one left.
Credit Cards: Yes
Owner: Jackie DeFoor
Year Estab: 1974
Comments: A good sized collection in crowded conditions and some double shelv-
                   ing. The books were of mixed vintage and in mixed condition with the
                   majority of the books we saw a bit older. There is organization, al-
                   though it may take the browser some time to determine just how it
                   works. If there's a title you've been searching for, the chances of
                   finding it here are far better than winning the state lottery.

Franklin

Antiquaria Books   **By Appointment**
PO Box 1226   37065   (615) 370-4971
                                                    E-mail: tune5bob@interloc.com

Collection: General stock.

# of Vols:	5,000
Specialties:	Southern Americana; Civil War; military; Western Americana.
Services:	Search service, occasional catalog, accepts want lists, mail order.
Credit Cards:	Yes
Owner:	Bob Tune
Year Estab:	1976

Halls

Murray Hudson - Antiquarian Books & Maps　　　　　　**Open Shop**
109 South Church Street　　　　　　　　　　(800) 748-9946　(901) 836-9057
Mailing address: PO Box 163 Halls 38040　　　　　　　Fax: (901) 836-9017

Collection:	Specialty books and ephemera.
# of Vols:	5,000+
Specialties:	Americana; atlases; geographies; exploration; travel; maps; globes; prints.
Hours:	Mon-Sat 9-5. Other times by appointment.
Services:	Catalog
Travel:	Two miles east on Hwy 88, off Hwy 51.
Credit Cards:	No
Year Estab:	1979

Henning

Henning Book Store　　　　　　　　　　　　　　　**Open Shop**
130 North Main Street　38041　　　　　　　　　　　　　(901) 738-5697

Collection:	General stock of paperback and hardcover.
# of Vols:	5,000 (hardcover)
Hours:	Mon-Wed, Fri & Sat 10-5.
Travel:	Henning exit off Hwy 51. Proceed north on Old Hwy 51 which becomes Main St.
Credit Cards:	No
Owner:	Anita Harber
Year Estab:	1993

Hermitage
(See Map 33, page 324)

J.S. Crouch Bookseller　　　　　　　　　　　　　**Open Shop**
4714 Lebanon Road　37076　　　　　　　　　　　　　(615) 316-0767
　　　　　　　　　　　　　　　　　　　E-mail: jscrouch@interloc.com

Collection:	General stock of mostly hardcover.
# of Vols:	30,000
Specialties:	Military; history; religion; philosophy.
Hours:	Mon-Sat 9-6.
Services:	Search service, accepts want lists, catalog.

Travel:	Exit 221A exit off I-40. Proceed north on Old Hickory Blvd to Andrew Jackson Pkwy, then right on Andrew Jackson to Lebanon Rd and right on Lebanon. Shop is on right in Oakwood Common Shopping Center.
Credit Cards:	Yes
Year Estab:	1995

Jackson

The Odd Volume Bookstore   **Open Shop**
132A Tucker Street   (901) 423-9490
Mailing address: PO Box 1258 Jackson 38302

E-mail: oddvolum@interloc.com

Collection:	General stock of hardcover and paperback.
# of Vols:	10,000+
Specialties:	Biography; history; occult; metaphysics; science fiction; fantasy.
Hours:	Tue-Sat 10:30-4:30. Sun 1-5. Other times by appointment.
Services:	Search service, accepts want lists.
Travel:	Exit 82A off I-40. Proceed south on North Highland Ave (Hwy 45) for about three miles. Shop is on the right, in rear of Simpson Shopping Center.
Credit Cards:	Yes
Owner:	Lloyd Russell
Year Estab:	1990
Comments:	A small store with a modest collection. Most of the hardcover volumes are older and in fair to good condition. Some collectibles, some common titles and a few "possible" hard to find items. Almost all exclusively reading copies. Reasonably priced.

Johnson City

The Book Place   **Open Shop**
420 West Walnut Street   37604   (423) 929-2665

Collection:	General stock of new and used hardcover and paperback.
# of Vols:	30,000 (used)
Hours:	Mon-Sat 9-7. Sun 9-6.
Services:	Search service, accepts want lists, mail order.
Travel:	Exit 31 off I-181. Proceed west on University to South Roan, then right on South Roan and left on Walnut.
Credit Cards:	Yes
Owner:	Gary & Marie Frank
Year Estab:	1986
Comments:	New books up front and a large room to the rear devoted to used books, the majority of which were hardcover. Most of the books we saw were reading copies in mixed condition and quite reasonably priced. A back wall labeled "old books" was accurately described. Some of the titles we saw in this section could be of interest to aficionados of true vintage literature. Unfortunately, not all of these books were in the best condition.

Moody Books   **Open Shop**
107 Broyles Drive   37601   (423) 282-6004

Collection:	General stock of new and mostly hardcover used.
# of Vols:	100,000
Specialties:	Religion.; autographs.
Hours:	Mon-Sat 9-8. Sun 1-5. Other times by appointment.
Services:	Appraisals, search service, catalog, accepts want lists.
Travel:	I-181 exit off I-40, then exit 35 off I-181. Turn left at Browns Mill which becomes Broyles. Shop is in the rear of the strip center.
Credit Cards:	Yes
Owner:	Gil & Linda Moody
Year Estab:	1975
Comments:	While this shop specializes in books dealing with religion (new as well as used), its secular stock of used books is quite respectable with a healthy selection of both fiction and non fiction volumes ranging from more recent to vintage titles. The collection is well organized and reasonably priced with most books in good condition. At the time of our visit, we noted a good selection of botanical titles.

Kingsport

Hills' Books   **By Appointment**
PO Box 1037   37662   (423) 247-8704

Collection:	Specialty
# of Vols:	30,000-40,000
Specialties:	Americana; Southern Americana; Civil War; Tennessee.
Services:	Appraisals, accepts want lists, catalog.
Owner:	Ann & Maynard Hills
Year Estab:	1960
Comments:	Also displays Abingdon Mercantile Mall in Abingdon, VA.

Knoxville

Andover Square Books   **Antique Mall**
At Kingston Pike Antique Mall
4612 Kingston Pike   (423) 693-8984
Mailing address: 805 Noragate Road Knoxville 37919

Collection:	General stock.
# of Vols:	8,000
Specialties:	Southern Americana; Tennessee.
Hours:	Mon-Sat 10-5:30. Sun 1-5:30.
Services:	Search service, catalog, accepts want lists.
Travel:	Papermill Rd exit off I-75/I-40. Proceed south on Papermill to second light, then left on Kingston Pike. Proceed about 1½ miles. Shop is on left, in antique mall in shopping center.
Credit Cards:	Yes

(Knoxville)

Owner:	G.A. & M.R. Yeomans
Year Estab:	1978
Comments:	This dealer breaks the "antique mall" pattern in that the books on display, while modest in number, represent quality. In addition to some nice titles in Tennessee history and general literature, there were several rare items including, at least at the time of our visit, a set of Thomas Wolfe first editions. Since there are at least two other book dealers on the same road, a stop here would certainly be worth your investment in time.

Bohemian Brigade Bookshop   **Open Shop**
7347 Middlebrook Pike   37909   (423) 694-8227
                                                         Fax: (423) 531-1846

Collection:	Specialty
# of Vols:	12,000+
Specialties:	Civil War; medicine; military medicine.
Hours:	Mon-Fri 10-6. Sat 10-4.
Services:	Appraisals, search service, catalog, accepts want lists.
Travel:	Exit 380 off I-40. Left on Kingston Pike, then left at first light onto Binginton (go under I-40). Proceed for about one mile, then left on Middlebrook Pike.
Credit Cards:	Yes
Owner:	Edgar G. Archer
Year Estab:	1986

Book Eddy   **Open Shop**
133 1/3 South Gay Street   37902   (423) 546-8837*   (423) 637-3339
                                           E-mail: bookeddy@interloc.com

Collection:	General stock.
# of Vols:	15,000
Hours:	Mon-Sat 11:15-3:30. Other times by chance or appointment.
Travel:	Exit 388A off I-40. Proceed on James White Pkwy to Summit Hill exit. Right on Summit Hill, then right on Gay St. Shop is on left.
Credit Cards:	Yes
Owner:	John Coleman
Year Estab:	1996
Comments:	At the time of our visit, the owner was in the process of stocking this new shop by transferring what he viewed as his more desirable titles from his existing shop a few blocks away (see Old City Book Shop below). Unless you're on a very tight schedule, we suggest you visit both locations rather than chance missing a hidden treasure at the other site. The ambience here is more typical of open shops and should be easier to browse than portions of its more cramped sister shop. We spotted some nice first editions, including one by Ayn Rand with dust jacket.

* The owner's second store. (See the Old Book Shop below.)

The Incurable Collector   **Open Shop**
5805 Kingston Pike   37919   (423) 584-4371

Collection:	General stock.
# of Vols:	2,000+
Specialties:	Fine bindings; illustrated; Civil War; bibles; first editions; children's.
Hours:	Tue-Sat 11-5.
Services:	Mail order.
Travel:	Papermill Dr exit off I-40 west. Left on Papermill and proceed to light at Northshore Dr. Left on Northshore, then left on Kingston Pike. Shop is after next light, on left, in small shopping center.
Credit Cards:	Yes
Owner:	James H. & Ann W. Delap
Year Estab:	1985
Comments:	We arrived at this shop at 2:20 on a Thursday afternoon. Sure enough, the sign at the front door confirmed the Tue-Sat 11-5 hours indicated above. However, a temporary sign read, "Gone to Lunch. Back at 3:30." Much as we would have liked to visit (a look through the front window suggested a small but quality stock), there was no way we could afford to wait for 70 minutes. Our suggestion: take the advice we failed to heed. Call ahead.

McKay Used Books and CDs   **Open Shop**
4931 Kingston Pike   37919   (423) 588-0331

Collection:	General stock of paperback and hardcover.
# of Vols:	150,000+
Hours:	Mon-Sat 9am-10pm, except Wed till 9. Sun 11-9.
Travel:	From downtown, proceed west on Cumberland Ave which becomes Kingston Pike. Shop is approximately five miles ahead, on the right.
Credit Cards:	Yes
Owner:	Anne Jacobson
Year Estab:	1984
Comments:	Upon entering this shop, one is initially impressed by its size and a quick glance at the shelves suggests that here indeed is a place that is extremely well organized and where one may find a book long sought after. Alas, after walking down several of the aisles trying to get used to the cubby-hole-like style of shelving, I must confess to becoming a bit dizzy (No, it was not the lunch I had). Each cubbyhole is carefully labeled which is a plus, and in some areas this can be most useful. However, for those old fashioned browsers (like myself) who are used to scanning books along traditional horizontal shelves, the task of looking up, down and across aisle after aisle became tiresome and I may have missed some terrific titles. Paperbacks outnumbered hardcover volumes and the quality and number of the hardcover volumes I saw were not overly impressive.

Old City Book Shop   **Open Shop**
111 East Jackson Avenue   37915   (423) 546-8837

Collection:	General stock of hardcover and paperback.

# of Vols:	50,000
Specialties:	Natural history; technology; philosophy; religion; ancient history; medieval history; children's.
Hours:	Mon-Thu 10:30-6. Fri & Sat 10:30-10:30. Sun 1-6.
Services:	Appraisals, search service, accepts want lists.
Travel:	Exit 388A off I-40. Proceed on James White Pkwy to Summit Hill exit. Right on Summit Hill, right on Central, right on Jackson. Shop is located in Jackson Avenue Market Place.
Credit Cards:	Yes
Owner:	John Coleman
Year Estab:	1991
Comments:	Located in the rear of an antique mall in Knoxville's "Old City" neighborhood, this shop displays books on three levels that become increasing more spacious as one ascends to the next level. (While the first level is limited in size and the books are tightly packed, browsers will find a comfortable couch to relax on on the third level.) The books we saw were in generally good condition with a few showing their age and were reasonably priced. We spotted several desirable titles. At the time of our visit, the owner was in the process of opening a second shop at a nearby location where he will be displaying what he views as his "better books" commanding higher prices. See Book Eddy above.

Pandora's Books   **Open Shop**
30-A Market Square   37902   (423) 524-1259

Collection:	General stock of mostly new and some used.
# of Vols:	1,000 (used)
Hours:	Mon-Thu 11-5. Fri 11-10. Sat 12-10.
Credit Cards:	Yes
Owner:	Susan Godseaux & Peggy Douglas
Year Estab:	1995
Comments:	Used stock is approximately 65% paperback.

What the Dickens! Bookseller   **Open Shop**
4409-U Chapman Highway   37920   (423) 579-9428

Collection:	General stock of mostly paperback.
# of Vols:	15,000
Hours:	Mon-Fri 10-7. Sat 10-6.

Lebanon

Bettie's Books & Things   **Open Shop**
1445D West Main Street   37087   (615) 444-6303

Collection:	General stock of mostly paperback.
# of Vols:	40,000
Hours:	Tue-Thu 9:30-5:30. Fri & Sat 9:30-7.

Madison

Book Attic   **Open Shop**
2142 North Gallatin Road   37115   (615) 859-7219

Collection:	General stock of paperback and hardcover.
# of Vols:	50,000
Hours:	Mon-Fri 9:30-6:30. Sat 10-6.
Services:	Accepts want lists, mail order.
Travel:	Northbound on I-65. Exit 95. Turn right on Conference Rd then quick left into shopping center (The Shoppes at Rivergate). Southbound on I-65. Exit 97 (Long Hollow Pike). Turn left and proceed on Long Hollow Pike for about three blocks to Conference, then left into shopping center.
Credit Cards:	Yes
Owner:	Teresa Hamlin
Year Estab:	1988
Comments:	Paperbacks take up the entire right side of the shop with hardcover books filling the shelves to the left, making this almost two separate bookstores. While many areas are represented, few are represented in substantial numbers. Despite that caveat, we were able to make at least two purchases and saw several other titles that we believe could be of interest to veteran book people, unless, that is, their interests are very specialized. This is one shop where we feel we can truly say, in the words of that popular game show, "The price is right."

The Great Escape   **Open Shop**
111B North Gallatin Road   37115   (615) 865-8052

Collection:	General stock of mostly paperback, plus CD's, comics and posters.
# of Vols:	1,000
Hours:	Mon-Sat 10-9. Sun 1-6.

Maryville

Southland Books   **Open Shop**
1634 West Broadway   37801   (423) 984-4847
                                                                   Fax: (423) 977-0700

Collection:	General stock of paperback and hardcover.
# of Vols:	40,000
Specialties:	Tennessee
Hours:	Mon-Wed 10-7. Thu-Sat 10-7:30. Sun 12-5.
Services:	Appraisals, catalog, accepts want lists, mail order.
Travel:	Hwy 129 exit off I-40. Proceed south on Hwy 129. At fork in road (Atlanta/Fontana exit) bear right onto Hwy 129 bypass. Shop is about three miles ahead, on left in Cornerstone Square Shopping Center.
Credit Cards:	Yes
Owner:	David E. Slough
Year Estab:	1975

Comments: Typical of many shopping center book stores with paperbacks down
                the middle aisles and hardcover volumes along the side and rear walls.
                The hardcover volumes we saw ranged from recent best sellers to truly
                older volumes. Prices were reasonable and we did see a few items that
                some collectors might find desirable.

Memphis

Bo Jo's Antique Mall   **Antique Mall**
3400 Summer Avenue   38112   (901) 323-2050

Hours: Mon-Sat 10-5. Sun 1-5.
Travel: Highland exit off I-240. Proceed north on Highland for one block then
                west on Summer.

The Book Adventure   **Open Shop**
3546 Walker   38111   (901) 452-6118
                                                                (901) 276-0609

Collection: General stock.
# of Vols: 5,000
Hours: Mon-Sat 11-6. Sun 12-6.
Services: Search service, accepts want lists, book repair.
Travel: See Mid-America below. Turn left on Walker. Shop is on left, 1/2 block
                ahead.
Owner: David Brown
Year Estab: 1976
Comments: At the time of our visit, this shop had been open just a brief time and it
                appeared that the dealer (who has been in business for 20 years) was
                still stocking his shelves. The majority of books we saw were in good
                condition and could best be described as being general in nature. Since
                the shop is less than a 1/2 block from a much larger store, a visit here
                would not be a waste of time. The dealer also displays at the nearby Bo
                Jo's Antique Mall (see above.)

Book Depot   **Open Shop**
2245 South Germantown Road   38138   (901) 754-2665

Collection: General stock of mostly paperback.
Hours: Mon-Sat 10-5:30. Sun 1-5.
Comments: Hardcover books are limited to cookbooks and children's.

Book Traders   **Open Shop**
6112 Quince Road   38119   (901) 683-2367

Collection: General stock of paperback and hardcover.
Hours: Mon-Sat 10-10. Sun 12-10.
Travel: Poplar exit off I-240. Proceed east on Poplar, then right on Ridgeway.
                Shop is in Balmoral Shopping Center and corner of Ridgeway and
                Quince.
Credit Cards: Yes

Owner:	John Dewey
Year Estab:	1993
Comments:	Stock is approximately 70% paperback.

Burke's Book Store   **Open Shop**
1719 Poplar Avenue   38104   (901) 278-7484
                                                                    Fax: (901) 272-2340

Collection:	General stock of used and new.
# of Vols:	25,000
Specialties:	Southern authors; first editions; fine bindings; Civil War.
Hours:	Mon-Fri 9-6, except Mon & Thu till 8. Sat 10-5. Sun 1-5.
Services:	Search service, mail order.
Travel:	Westbound on I-40. Continue on I-40 through Memphis till it becomes Sam Cooper Blvd, then Broad St. Turn left on East Parkway, then right on Poplar. Shop is between Evergreen and Belvedere. Eastbound on I-40: I-240 exit off I-40, then south on I-240 to Union St. Proceed east on Union, then left on Belvedere and right on Poplar. Shop is just ahead on right.
Credit Cards:	Yes
Owner:	Harriette M. Beeson
Year Estab:	1875
Comments:	An easy to browse shop with quality books and a good selection of local history titles broken down into many specific categories. The majority of the books we saw were in good to excellent condition. This is one of those book shops that recognized John Gresham before he became well known and therefore currently enjoys book signing visits from him. After our visit here, we can understand why.

Madison Avenue Books   **Open Shop**
1863 Madison Avenue   38104   (901) 729-2665

Collection:	General stock and ephemera.
# of Vols:	3,000-4,000
Specialties:	Civil War.
Hours:	Tue-Fri 11-6. Sat 12-6. Sun 1-5.
Services:	Appraisals, accepts want lists, search service, catalog.
Travel:	Southbound on I-240: Madison St exit. Continue on Madison to McLean Blvd. Northbound on I-240, Union St exit. Proceed east on Union, then left McLean and right on Madison. Shop is just ahead on right.
Credit Cards:	Yes
Owner:	John & Gloria Stephens
Year Estab:	1992
Comments:	A newly opened shop run by a former collector turned dealer, initially as a by appointment/book fair dealer and now with a full fledged shop. The stock is modest in size but not in quality. The emphasis is on regionalism and the Civil War with some baseball and children's titles.

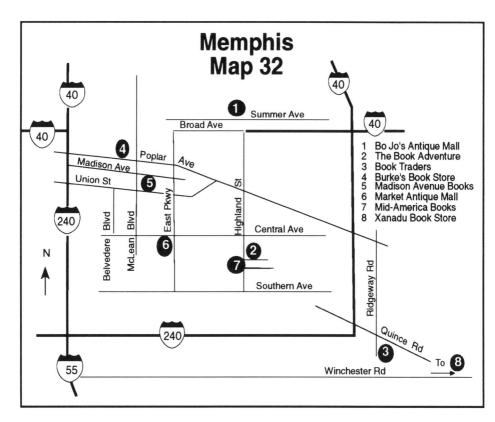

**Memphis
Map 32**

1 Bo Jo's Antique Mall
2 The Book Adventure
3 Book Traders
4 Burke's Book Store
5 Madison Avenue Books
6 Market Antique Mall
7 Mid-America Books
8 Xanadu Book Store

Market Central Antique Mall   **Antique Mall**
2215 Central   38104   (901) 278-0888

Hours: Mon-Sat 10-6. Sun 12-6.
Travel: Union St exit off I-240. Proceed east on Union. Shop is between East
                 Parkway and Cooper on south side of street.

Mid-America Books   **Open Shop**
571 South Highland   38111   (901) 452-0766

Collection: General stock of hardcover and paperback.
# of Vols: 70,000
Specialties: Science fiction; horror.
Hours: Mon-Fri 9:30-7. Sat 9:30-5. Sun 12-5.
Services: Appraisals, search service, accepts want lists, mail order.
Travel: Westbound on I-40: Highland exit. Proceed south on Highland. Eastbound
                 on I-40: I-240 south exit, then Madison St exit off I-240. Proceed east
                 on Madison to East Pkwy, then right on East Pkwy, left on Southern
                 Ave and left on Highland. Shop is just ahead on left.
Credit Cards: Yes
Owner: George Quigley
Year Estab: 1984

Comments: A good sized shop with an excellent selection of books in the specialties listed above, including both hardcover (some vintage) with dust jackets and many without. Most were quite reasonably priced. The general collection was also quite respectable. We made at least one purchase here and had we not been on a tight schedule probably would have made several others. We're hoping that the owner will quote some of the books on the want list we left.

Xanadu Book Store   **Open Shop**
7235 Winchester Road   38125   (901) 757-9885

Collection:	General stock of new and used paperback and hardcover.
Hours:	Daily 9-9.
Travel:	Riverdale exit off I-240. Proceed south on Riverdale, then east on Winchester. Shop is in shopping center between Quince and Germantown Rd.
Credit Cards:	Yes
Owner:	Beverly Lowe
Year Estab:	1988
Comments:	Stock is approximately 50% used, half of which is hardcover.

Murfreesboro

Old Book Store   **Open Shop**
1111-C Memorial Boulevard   37129   (615) 848-0817

Collection:	General stock of paperback and hardcover.
# of Vols:	25,000+
Hours:	Mon-Fri 10-6. Sat 10-5.
Travel:	Exit 78B off I-24. Proceed north on Memorial Blvd for about three miles. Shop is in a strip center.
Credit Cards:	Yes
Owner:	Clarence Smith
Year Estab:	1990
Comments:	Mostly paperbacks, plus a large number of quite reasonably priced ($18 each) Easton Press volumes for anyone interested in filling a library with impressive looking volumes, a modest number of non Easton hardcover volumes, mostly recent titles in quite good condition, a few first editions and some new books.

P. H. Duck's Book Stop   **Open Shop**
310 West Castle Street   37129   (615) 893-0690

Collection:	General stock of paperback and hardcover.
# of Vols:	75,000
Hours:	Tue & Wed 10-6. Thu-Fri 10-8. Sat 10-6. Sun 1-6.
Travel:	Exit 81 off I-24. Proceed north on Church St (Hwy 231). When one car length BEFORE third light, turn left on West Castle.
Credit Cards:	No
Owner:	Darlene McDonnell
Year Estab:	1987

Comments: If neatness is important to you, you may not feel comfortable visiting
                  here. The stock consists primarily of comics, paperbacks, Star Wars
                  paraphernalia and other such intriguing items and about 2,000-3,000
                  hardcover volumes of little distinction, all protected by a covey of cats.

Turbo's Discount Paperbacks   **Open Shop**
110 North Baird Lane   37130   (615) 895-7563

Collection: General stock of mostly paperback.
Hours: Mon-Fri 11-6. Sat 12-5.

Nashville

Best Books   **Open Shop**
211 Donelson Pike   37214   (615) 883-9193

Collection: Specialty. Mostly new and some used.
Specialties: Mormons
Hours: Tue-Sat 12-7. Other times by appointment.
Services: Search service, accepts want lists.
Travel: Exit 216C exit off I-40. Proceed north on Donelson Pike for 1½ miles.
                  Shop is in Cameron office complex.
Credit Cards: Yes
Owner: Richard Simpkins
Year Estab: 1995

Bodacious Books   **Open Shop**
5133 Harding Road, Ste. A6   37205   (615) 356-2065

Collection: General stock.
# of Vols: 32,000
Specialties: Natural history; gardening; architecture; mystery.
Hours: Mon-Sat 10-6. Sun 1-6.
Services: Search service, accepts want lists, mail order.
Travel: West End exit off I-440. Proceed west on West End (which becomes
                  Harding) for four miles. Shop is on left in Bella Meade Shopping
                  Center.
Credit Cards: Yes
Owner: Charles May & Carolyn Householder
Year Estab: 1995

Book Discoveries   **Open Shop**
2800 Bransford Avenue   37204   (615) 298-4800

Collection: General stock.
# of Vols: 15,000
Specialties: Art; children's; cookbooks; gardening; history; literature; religion.
Hours: Tue-Fri 10-5. Sat 10-4.
Services: Search service, mail order.
Travel: Exit 79 off I-65. Proceed east on Armory Dr to Powell, then north on
                  Powell which becomes Bransford.

Credit Cards:	Yes
Owner:	Geneva M. Henderson
Year Estab:	1992
Comments:	Each room of this former residence is filled with interesting titles representing, in strength, all of the specialties listed above as well as more general subjects. We were impressed by the variety of the titles and the condition of most of the books. Whether or not the shop's specialties are of interest to you, we feel certain that most serious book people would appreciate a visit here.

Book Shop Maybe   **Open Shop**
3736 Old Hickory Boulevard   37209   (615) 352-4801

Collection:	General stock of mostly paperback.
Hours:	Mon-Sat, except closed Wed, 10-6. Sun 1-5.

Bookman   **Open Shop**
1724 21st Avenue South   37212   (615) 383-6555

Collection:	General stock of mostly hardcover and ephemera.
# of Vols:	45,000
Specialties:	Mystery; science fiction; history; modern first editions.
Hours:	Mon-Fri 10-6. Sat 10-4. Sun 10-2.
Services:	Appraisals, accepts want lists, mail order.
Travel:	21st Ave/Hillsboro exit off I-440. Proceed north on 21st Ave South. Shop is just south of Blackmore/Wedgewood.
Credit Cards:	Yes
Owner:	Larry & Saralee Woods
Year Estab:	1995
Comments:	This shop's solution to running out of space is to double shelve books throughout the entire store. Where paperbacks make up the front layer, it's possible to see the hardcover titles standing behind them. This is not always the case, however, and if the browser is in a hurry, a winning title that has been back shelved could be easily overlooked. The books, representing mixed vintages and in mixed condition (with the majority being "okay") are worth viewing if you have the time and patience.

Books at Cummins Station   **Open Shop**
209 10th Avenue South, Ste 211   37203   (615) 259-2254
       Fax: (615) 259-2254

Collection:	General stock of mostly used hardcover and paperback.
# of Vols:	8,000
Hours:	Mon-Sat 12-6.
Travel:	From 1-40, exit 209A (Demonbreun St). Proceed east on Demonbreun to 10th Ave, then south on 10th.
Credit Cards:	Yes
Owner:	Brock Mehler
Year Estab:	1996
Comments:	Stock is evenly divided between hardcover and paperback.

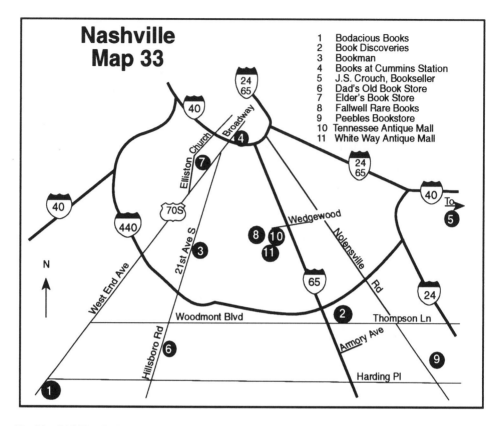

Nashville Map 33

1 Bodacious Books
2 Book Discoveries
3 Bookman
4 Books at Cummins Station
5 J.S. Crouch, Bookseller
6 Dad's Old Book Store
7 Elder's Book Store
8 Fallwell Rare Books
9 Peebles Bookstore
10 Tennessee Antique Mall
11 White Way Antique Mall

Dad's Old Book Store   **Open Shop**
4004 Hillsboro Road   37215   (615) 298-5880
                                                       Fax: (615) 298-2822

Collection:	General stock.
# of Vols:	50,000
Specialties:	Civil War; southern history; autographs; manuscripts; first editions; fine bindings.
Hours:	Mon-Sat 10-6. Sun 12-5.
Services:	Appraisals, catalog, accepts want lists.
Travel:	Hillsboro exit off I-440. Proceed south on Hillsboro for about one mile, then turn left into driveway for Green Hills Court, a strip center. (The shops are perpendicular to the street.) The shop is 1½ blocks passed Hillsboro High School.
Credit Cards:	Yes
Owner:	Ed Penney
Year Estab:	1980
Comments:	A book person's bookshop. While the shop is not huge, it does have a very nice selection of quality titles in most areas and is delightfully decorated with framed autographs and photographs (for sale) of well known personalities in the world of entertainment and public affairs.

Several signed firsts, many books falling legitimately into the antiquarian category and lots inbetween. A pleasure to browse and even more fun it you walk away with a find (though you may spend a bit more than you had anticipated.)

Elder's Book Store   **Open Shop**
2115 Elliston Place   37203   (615) 327-1867

Collection:	General stock of mostly used hardcover.
# of Vols:	50,000-60,000
Specialties:	Civil War; Tennessee; southern fiction; genealogy.
Hours:	Mon-Fri 9-5. Sat 9-2.
Services:	Appraisals, search service.
Travel:	Church St exit off I-40. Proceed west on Church for nine blocks where Church joins Elliston at 22nd Ave North.
Credit Cards:	Yes
Owner:	Charles Elder
Year Estab:	1968
Comments:	This long established shop has a fine selection of good books. (Translation: some rare, many hard to find, plenty of collectibles and a number of truly antiquarian volumes.) Most of the titles we saw, with the exception of children's, fall into the more serious or scholarly category. Lots of books of local interest. We did see a number of books on the shelves which were not priced and wondered if this was just happenstance.

Fallwell Rare Books   **Antique Mall**
At Antique Merchants   (615) 269-8728
2015 8th Avenue   37204

Collection:	General stock.
# of Vols:	12,000
Specialties:	Literature; history; Tennessee; Kentucky.
Hours:	Mon-Sat 10-5. Sun 1-5.
Services:	Appraisals, mail order.
Travel:	Wedgewood exit off I-65. West on Wedgewood, then south on 8th St.
Owner:	Marshall Fallwell, Jr.
Year Estab:	1985

The Great Escape   **Open Shop**
1925 Broadway   37203   (615) 327-0646

Collection:	General stock of mostly paperback, plus CD's, comics and posters.
# of Vols:	1,000
Hours:	Mon-Sat 10-90. Sun 1-6.

Mostly Mysteries   **Antique Mall**
At Green Hills Antique Mall   (615) 298-1436
4108 Hillsboro Road   37215   E-mail: emery_K@NSTI01.NSTI.TEC.TN.US

Collection:	Specialty paperback and hardcover.

Specialties:	Mystery.
Hours:	Mon-Sat 10-5:30. Sun 1-5.
Services:	Mail order.
Travel:	Hillsboro exit off I-440 exit. Proceed south on Hillsboro for about three miles. Shop is on the left.
Owner:	Kathy Emery
Year Estab:	1994
Comments:	Stock is approximately 70% paperback.

Peebles Bookstore   **Open Shop**
360 Elysian Field Road   37211   (615) 832-1577

Collection:	General stock of paperback and hardcover.
# of Vols:	25,000
Hours:	Mon-Fri 10-6. Sat 10-4:30.
Travel:	From intersection of Harding Pl and Nolensville Rd, proceed four blocks north on Nolensville to Elysian Fields Rd.
Credit Cards:	No
Owner:	Roddie Peebles
Year Estab:	1988
Comments:	Stock is approximately 75% paperback.

Tennessee Antique Mall   **Antique Mall**
654 Wedgewood Avenue   37203   (615) 259-4077

Hours:	Mon-Sat 10-6. Sun 1-6.
Travel:	Wedgewood exit off I-65. Proceed east on Wedgewood for 1½ blocks.

White Way Antique Mall   **Antique Mall**
1200 Villa Place   37212   (615) 327-1098

Hours:	Mon-Sat 10-5. Sun 1-5.
Travel:	Wedgewood exit off I-65. Proceed west on Edgewood to Villa Place, right on Villa Place.

Oak Ridge

Mr. K's Used Books and CD's   **Open Shop**
374 South Illinois Avenue   37830   (423) 483-8659

Collection:	General stock of mostly paperback.
# of Vols:	20,000
Hours:	Mon-Sat 9-9. Sun 12-8.

Paris

First Folio   **By Appointment**
1206 Brentwood   38242   (901) 644-9940
                                                         Fax: (901) 644-9940

Collection:	General stock.
# of Vols:	7,000

Specialties:	Books on books; bibliography; private press; fine bindings; illustrated.
Services:	Appraisals, catalog, accepts want lists.
Credit Cards:	Yes
Owner:	Dennis R. Melhouse & Dennis I. Hatman
Year Estab:	1985

Rogersville

Tennessee Books and Autographs   **By Appointment**
109 South Church Street   (423) 921-9017
Mailing address: PO Box 637 Rogersville 37857   Fax: (423) 921-9017

Collection:	General stock and ephemera.
# of Vols:	10,000
Specialties:	Tennessee; Americana; historical autographs; Civil War.
Services:	Appraisals, catalog, accepts want lists.
Credit Cards:	No
Owner:	George E. Webb, Jr.
Year Estab:	1978

Tullahoma

Barclay Books   **Open Shop**
106 South Jackson Street   (615) 455-8882
Mailing address: PO Box 357 Tullahoma 37388

Collection:	General stock.
# of Vols:	7,500
Specialties:	Aviation; The South; religion; women's studies.
Hours:	Mon-Fri 9-1 & 1:30-5.
Services:	Search service, accepts want lists, mail order.
Travel:	Located on Hwy 55.
Credit Cards:	No
Owner:	Angela Barclay Arnold
Year Estab:	1985
Comments:	A most pleasant little shop in a quiet little town not too far off the interstate where the number of books on display may be modest but the owner is a real delight. The kind of place where, because it may not be visited too often, could well hold a hidden treasure. The books we saw were in generally good condition, of mixed vintage and quite reasonably priced. Many subject areas were represented.

R. R. Allen Books   (423) 584-4487
5300 Bluefield Road Knoxville 37921

Collection:	Specialty
# of Vols:	2,500
Specialties:	Tennessee; unusual books of a general nature.
Services:	Catalog
Owner:	Ronald Allen
Year Estab:	1961

Black Kat Books   (615) 597-1270
PO Box 271 Smithville 37166   Fax: (615) 597-1270

Collection:	Specialty
# of Vols:	4,000+
Specialties:	Occult; metaphysics; herbalism; homeopathy.
Services:	Appraisals, search service, catalog, accepts want lists.
Credit Cards:	No
Owner:	Sandi Wakefield
Year Estab:	1993

Susan Davis, Bookseller   (901) 362-1423
6629 Knight Arnold #4 Memphis 38115

Collection:	Specialty
# of Vols:	600
Specialties:	Literary first editions (old and new).
Services:	Appraisals, catalog.
Credit Cards:	No
Year Estab:	1994

Donaldson's Books   (423) 687-8872
600 Inskip Road, #A-202 Knoxville 37912

Collection:	General stock and some ephemera.
# of Vols:	3,000
Specialties:	Children's; illustrated; literature; natural history; Americana.
Services:	Accepts want lists.
Credit Cards:	No
Year Estab:	1977

Emeritus Books   (423) 637-4868
PO Box 11421 Knoxville 37919   E-mail: EmeritusBK@aol.com

Collection:	Specialty
# of Vols:	2,000
Specialties:	Books about books; history of science; history of technology.
Services:	Search service, accepts want lists, mail order.
Credit Cards:	No
Owner:	Gerald Lundeen
Year Estab:	1995

George's Books & Autographs (901) 685-8995
4444 Walnut Grove Road Memphis 38117

Collection:	Specialty
Specialties:	Signed books.
Services:	Accepts want lists.
Owner:	George Whitworth
Year Estab:	1986

Liber III (615) 454-2219
1310 Melrose Tullahoma 37388

Collection:	General stock of new and used hardcover and paperback.
# of Vols:	5,000
Specialties:	New Age.
Services:	Search service, accepts want lists.
Owner:	R.T. Gault
Year Estab:	1968

McGee's First Varieties (615) 373-5318
8012 Brooks Chapel Road, Ste. 247 Brentwood 37027
E-mail: bibliopole@aol.com

Collection:	Specialty
# of Vols:	2,000-5,000
Specialties:	Modern fiction; science fiction; mystery (all first editions).
Services:	Appraisals, search service, catalog, accepts want lists.
Credit Cards:	No
Owner:	Tom McGee
Year Estab:	1994

Olde Book Place (423) 926-2691
PO Box 1261 Johnson City 37605

Collection:	General stock of hardcover and paperback.
# of Vols	5,000
Services:	Accepts want lists.
Owner:	Arthur & Judy Blevins
Year Estab:	1991.
Comments:	Stock is approximately 75% hardcover. Collection can also be viewed by appointment.

R & R Books (423) 569-8506
Route 3, Box 593 Oneida 37841

Collection:	General stock.
# of Vols:	1,000
Services:	Accepts want lists, search service.
Credit Cards:	No
Owner:	Ron Wilson
Year Estab:	1996
Comments:	Calls in evening only.

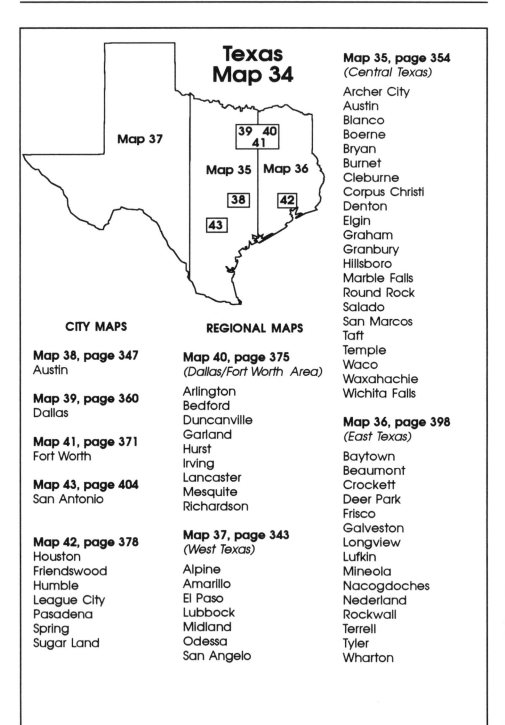

Texas
Map 34

Map 37

39 40
41

Map 35 | Map 36

38 42

43

Texas

Alphabetical Listing By Dealer

Alphabetical Listing By Location

Abilene

Classic Books on Pine
157 Pine Street   79601

Open Shop
(915) 675-6667
Fax: (915) 671-1399

Collection:	General stock of mostly new books.
# of Vols:	7,000
Hours:	Mon-Sat 10-5.
Comments:	Approximately 5% of stock is used.

Alpine
(Map 37, page 343)

Front Street Books
608 East Holland Avenue   79830

Open Shop
(915) 837-3360
Fax: (915) 837-1126

Collection:	General stock of new and used paperback and hardcover.
# of Vols:	20,000+
Specialties:	Texas; ranching; Native Americans.
Hours:	Mon-Sat 9-6. Sun 1-6.
Services:	Mail order.
Travel:	Hwy 90 eastbound. Shop is located in downtown.
Credit Cards:	Yes
Owner:	John M. & Jean E. Hardy
Year Estab:	1995
Comments:	Stock is evenly divided between new and used. Used stock is approximately 65% paperback.

Amarillo
(Map 37, page 343)

Bookland
1948 Civic Circle   79109

Open Shop
(806) 358-9442

Collection:	General stock of paperback and hardcover.
# of Vols:	40,000+
Specialties:	Texas
Hours:	Mon-Sat 9:30-6.
Travel:	Georgia exit off I-40. Shop is at southeast corner of I-40 and Georgia in Wolflin Square Shopping Center.
Credit Cards:	No
Owner:	Don Sanders
Year Estab:	1990
Comments:	The majority of the stock here is paperback and the hardcover books we saw were a mixed breed of recent fiction, some sets and a few unusual items in generally mixed condition. If you're on a tight schedule, consider the above observations.

Donna's Book Stop
3019 West 6th Avenue   79106

Open Shop
(806) 379-8940

Collection:	General stock of mostly paperback.
# of Vols:	20,000
Hours:	Mon-Fri 10-6. Sat 10-5
Travel:	Georgia exit off I-40. North on Georgia to 6th Ave, then west on W. 6th.
Credit Cards:	Yes
Owner:	Donna Fortenberry
Year Estab:	1989
Comments:	The vast majority of the books here are paperbacks with only a small (perhaps a few hundred) hardcover volumes of recent vintage. Not a shop for the serious book person.

Magazine Book Exchange
3009 West 6th Avenue   79106

Open Shop
(806) 372-8041

Collection:	General stock of mostly paperback.
Specialties:	Magazines
Hours:	Mon-Sat 10-5.

One More Time
112 South Western Street   79106

Open Shop
(806) 355-5052

Collection:	General stock.
# of Vols:	5,000
Specialties:	Western Americana; Southwestern Americana; Civil War.
Hours:	Mon-Sat 10-5:30.
Services:	Appraisals, search service, accepts want lists, mail order, lists.
Travel:	Western St exit off I-40. Proceed north on Western.
Credit Cards:	No
Owner:	E.P. Taylor
Year Estab:	1993

Rae's Pages
701-C South Georgia   79106

Open Shop
Fax: (806) 372-3378   (806) 372-7880
E-mail: sgerik@arn.net

Collection:	General stock of paperback and hardcover.
# of Vols:	10,000
Hours:	Mon-Fri 10-6. Sat 9-5.
Travel:	At corner of 7th St.
Credit Cards:	Yes
Owner:	Santos Tenorio
Year Estab:	1982
Comments:	With (we regret to say) few "real" book dealers in this community, this establishment, while not necessarily rich in stock, did carry more hardcover volumes (even a few unusual and better titles) than the other shops we visited. The majority of the stock consisted of paperbacks and comics, but a book person could spend a short time here viewing the store's limited hardcover collection.

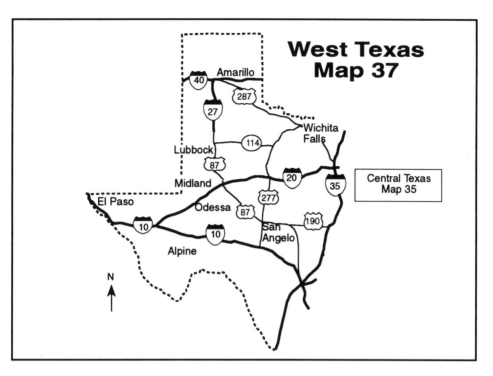

Stuarts's Jack and Jill   **Open Shop**
4006 South Washington Street   79110   (806) 355-1811

Collection: General stock of mostly paperback.
Hours: Mon 12-5:30. Tue-Fri 10:15-5:30. Sat 10:15-5.

Time And Again   **By Appointment**
3201 West 6th Avenue   79106   (806) 371-0271

Collection: General stock and ephemera.
# of Vols: 7,000
Specialties: Texas; Western Americana.
Services: Appraisals, search service, accepts want lists, mail order.
Owner: Doris Welch Reid
Year Estab: 1978

The Word Shoppe   **Open Shop**
2624 Wolfin Avenue   79109   (806) 359-8202

Collection: Specialty paperback and hardcover.
# of Vols: 35,000
Specialties: Religion, with an emphasis on Protestant Evangelical.
Hours: Mon-Sat 10-6.
Services: Appraisals, accepts want lists, mail order.
Travel: Georgia St exit off I-40. Proceed south on Georgia, then left on Wolfin.
Credit Cards: Yes

Owner:	Linda Green
Year Estab:	1993
Comments:	Stock is approximately 55% paperback.

Archer City
(Map 35, page 354)

Booked Up
216 South Center Street   76351

Open Shop
(817) 574-2511
Fax: (817) 574-4245

Collection:	General stock.
# of Vols:	500,000+
Hours:	Mon-Sat 10-5.
Services:	Accepts want lists, mail order.
Travel:	Hwy 174 exit off Hwy 287. Continue on Hwy 174 (which becomes Hwy 25) into Archer City. Turn left at blinking light onto Center St. (Note: the above address is one of three Booked Up locations on Center St. At the time of our visit, "216" was the main shop.
Credit Cards:	Yes
Owner:	Larry McMurtry
Year Estab:	1988
Comments:	If you have ever dreamed of being locked in a bookshop overnight (or better yet, over a weekend), this is probably as good a place as any to dream about. I could not understand why during our visit the shop was not overflowing with voracious buyers. Books here are carefully selected (whoever is doing the buying for this establishment deserves high praise), meticulously organized, are in good condition and are reasonably priced. There are rows upon rows upon rows of titles to peruse. Once you have examined all of the shelves in one building, walk across the street and begin again in a second building. (By the time this book is in print, a third building just a short distance down the street should be open for visitors.) The staff we met were friendly, helpful and as courteous as one might expect to find. If we had a spare weekend once or twice a year, we would fly down here and spend it winding our way in and out of the rows upon rows of bookcases.

Arlington
(Map 40, page 375)

Half Price Books, Records, Magazines
2211 South Cooper   76013

Open Shop
(817) 860-5247

Collection:	General stock of hardcover and paperback and remainders.
Hours:	Mon-Sat 9am-10pm. Sun 11-8.
Travel:	Cooper St exit off I-20. Proceed north on Cooper to Pioneer Pkwy. Shop is in Kroger Shopping Center.

John Marston's Book Shop   **Open Shop**
2131 North Collins, Suite 401   76011   Fax: (817) 861-8930   (817) 861-1070
                                          E-mail: marstonsb@aol.com

Collection:	General stock of hardcover and paperback and CDs.
# of Vols:	35,000
Specialties:	Modern first editions; literature; history; religion; military; movies; music.
Hours:	Mon-Sat 10-9. Sun 11-7.
Services:	Appraisals, search service, accepts want lists, mail order.
Travel:	Hwy 157 exit off I-30. Proceed north on Hwy 157 (Collins) for three blocks. Shop is on right in Seville Common Shopping Center.
Credit Cards:	Yes
Owner:	John Marston Sladden
Year Estab:	1989
Comments:	A better than average store with a mix of paperbacks (approximately 60% of the stock), new books and an ample supply of hardcover volumes, mostly recent editions and in good condition.

ProTech   **Open Shop**
253 Lincoln Square   76011   (817) 548-8324

Collection:	Specialty. Mostly new and limited used.
Specialties:	Computers; mathematics; science; engineering.
Hours:	Mon-Sat 9-9. Sun 12-6.

Athens

Pea Picker Book Store   **Open Shop**
108 West Tyler Street   75751   (903) 675-3488

Collection:	General stock mostly used paperback.
# of Vols:	500+ (used hardcover)
Hours:	Mon-Sat, except closed Wed, 10-5.

Austin

Adventures in Crime & Space Books   **Open Shop**
609A West 6th Street   78701   (512) 473-2665
                                          E-mail: acs@eden.com

Collection:	Specialty new and used paperback and hardcover.
# of Vols:	40,000
Specialties:	Science fiction; fantasy; horror; mystery; espionage; graphic novels; fantasy art; signed.
Hours:	Mon-Thu 11-8. Fri & Sat 11-9. Sun 11-7.
Services:	Appraisals, search service, catalog, accepts want lists.
Travel:	6th St exit off I-35. Proceed west on 6th St for 13 blocks.
Credit Cards:	Yes
Owner:	Willie Siros, Scott Cupp & Lisa Greene
Year Estab:	1994

Comments: While the majority of the used items in this shop are paperback, there are
                 enough hardcover books, both recent and vintage, to make this a worth-
                 while stop if the specialties are of interest to you. Then again, as the stock
                 is computerized, a call could save you a trip unless you like to browse.

Apollinaire's Bookstore   **Open Shop**
2118 Guadalupe   78705   (512) 495-9093

Collection: Specialty hardcover and paperback.
# of Vols: 5,000
Specialties: Literature; history; philosophy; scholarly.
Hours: Mon-Sat 12-6.
Services: Appraisals, search service, accepts want lists, mail order.
Travel: 26th St exit off I-35. Proceed west on 26th St, then left (south) on
                 Guadalupe.
Credit Cards: Yes
Owner: David Ray
Year Estab: 1990
Comments: Stock is evenly divided between hardcover and paperback

Asylum Books   **Open Shop**
2906 San Gabriel   78705   (512) 479-0015
                                                      E-mail: asylumbks@aol.com

Collection: General stock of mostly hardcover.
# of Vols: 8,500
Specialties: Modern literature; mystery; military; children's series.
Hours: Tue-Sat 10-7:30. Sun 12-6. Monday by appointment or chance (after-
                 noons, most likely).
Services: Appraisals, search service, catalog, accepts want lists.
Travel: Martin Luther King Blvd exit off I-35. Proceed west on Martin Luther
                 King, then right on Lamar, right on 29th, then sharp left. Shop is the
                 second building on left.
Credit Cards: Yes
Owner: Lissa Allspach & Bob Wolfkill
Year Estab: 1993
Comments: A nice selection of hardcover books, most of which were in very good
                 condition. Mixed vintage. Reasonably priced.

Austin Books   **Open Shop**
5002 North Lamar   78751   (512) 454-4197

Collection: Specialty new and used.
Specialties: Science fiction; fantasy.
Hours: Mon-Fri 11-7. Sat 10-7.
Travel: 51st St exit off I-35. Proceed west on 51st St which dead ends at Lamar.
                 Turn left on Lamar.
Credit Cards: Yes
Year Estab: 1978
Comments: Stock is approximately 50% used.

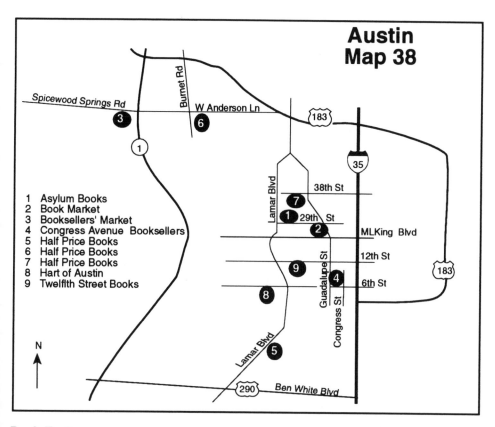

Austin Map 38

1 Asylum Books
2 Book Market
3 Booksellers' Market
4 Congress Avenue Booksellers
5 Half Price Books
6 Half Price Books
7 Half Price Books
8 Hart of Austin
9 Twelflth Street Books

Book Exchange
7411 Burnet Road   78757

Open Shop
(512) 454-6139

Collection:	General stock new and mostly paperback used.
# of Vols:	50,000 (used)
Hours:	Mon-Sat 10-6. Sun 1-5.

Book Garage
5304 Evans Avenue   78751

Open Shop
(512) 453-8618

Collection:	General stock mostly paperback.
# of Vols:	5,000
Hours:	Wed-Sat 10-6. Sun 12-6.

Book Market
In Dobi Mall
21st & Guadalupe
Mailing address: PO Box 142147 Austin 78714

Open Shop
(512) 499-8708
Fax: (512) 499-8708
E-mail: mvinson@io.com

Collection:	General stock.
# of Vols:	15,000
Specialties:	Scholarly; American literature; Texas; Civil War; philosophy; literary criticism.

(Austin)

Hours:	Mon-Thu 10-8. Fri & Sat 10-10.
Services:	Appraisals, search service, accepts want lists, occasional catalog, mail order.
Travel:	Martin Luther King Blvd exit off I-35. Proceed west on Martin Luther King for about 3/4 mile, then right on Guadalupe. Shop is two blocks ahead on right.
Credit Cards:	Yes
Owner:	Michael Vinson
Year Estab:	1991

Booksellers' Mall   **Open Shop**
8650 Spicewood Springs Road, Ste 133   78759   (512) 331-6099

Collection:	General stock of primarily hardcover.
Hours:	Mon-Fri 10-8. Sat 10-6. Sun 12-6.
Travel:	At corner of Hwy 183 (Research Blvd) and Spicewood Springs Rd. Shop is in Spicewood at 183 Shops shopping center.
Credit Cards:	No
Owner:	E. Schunck, President
Year Estab:	1993
Comments:	A group shop with 8-10 dealers.

Congress Avenue Booksellers   **Open Shop**
716 Congress Avenue   78701   (512) 478-1157

Collection:	General stock of mostly new books and some used paperback.
# of Vols:	10,000
Hours:	Mon-Fri 7:45-7. Sat & Sun 9-5.
Services:	Search service, accepts want lists, mail order.
Travel:	6th St exit off I-35. Proceed west on 6th and right on Congress. Shop is between 6th & 7th Sts.
Credit Cards:	Yes
Owner:	Jim Cochran
Year Estab:	1976
Comments:	Primarily a new book store. During our visit, we were shown one aisle (both sides) of used books, most of which appeared to be of quite recent vintage. If you're looking for any kind of selection of used items, you would do better elsewhere.

Alan & Mary Culpin, Booksellers   **By Appointment**
3606 Chalkstone Cove   78730   (512) 502-9041
                                                    E-mail: culpinbk@ont.com

Collection:	Specialty books and ephemera.
# of Vols:	2,000
Specialties:	Children's; illustrated; Texas; military; Civil War; cookbooks; fore-edge paintings.

Services: Appraisals, search service, catalog.
Credit Cards: Yes
Year Estab: 1976

Curio Corner Books   **Open Shop**
7201 Hart Lane 78731   (512) 342-1667

Collection: General stock.
# of Vols: 15,000+
Specialties: Children's; cookbooks; modern first editions.
Hours: Call for hours.
Services: Search service.
Credit Cards: No
Owner: Jerry Schmidt
Comments: This dealer was in the process of moving from Oklahoma City to Austin
at the time of publication. Call for shop location and hours.

Half Price Books, Records, Magazines   **Open Shop**
3110 Guadalupe 78229   (512) 451-4463

Collection: General stock of hardcover, paperback and remainders.
Hours: Mon-Sat 10-10. Sun 12-9.
Travel: 38th St exit off I-35. Proceed west to Guadalupe, then left on Guadalupe.
Shop is six blocks ahead on right. From MOPAC (Loop 1), take 35th St
exit. Proceed east to Guadalupe, then turn right.

Half Price Books, Records, Magazines   **Open Shop**
2929 South Lamar 78704   (512) 443-3138

Collection: General stock of hardcover, paperback and remainders.
Hours: Mon-Sat 10-10. Sun 12-9.
Travel: Ben White Blvd (Hwy 290/71) exit off I-35. Proceed west on Ben
White to Lamar Blvd, then north on Lamar to Corners Shopping Center.

Half Price Books, Records, Magazines   **Open Shop**
8868 Research Boulevard 78758   (512) 454-3664

Collection: General stock of hardcover, paperback and remainders.
Hours: Mon-Sat 10-10. Sun 12-9.
Travel: Hwy 183 exit off I-35. Proceed west on Hwy 183 and exit at Burnet Rd,
circling back under Hwy 183 to eastbound access road. Shop is about
one half mile ahead on south side of access road.

Hart of Austin Books   **Antique Mall**
At Antique & Decorative Arts Center   (512) 477-8962
1009 West 6th Street
Mailing address: 2508 Galewood Place Austin 78703

Collection: General stock.
# of Vols: 30,000
Specialties: Texas; Western Americana; children's; illustrated; fine bindings; literature.

(Austin)

Hours:	Mon-Sat 10-6. Sun 1-5.
Services:	Appraisals, accepts want lists, mail order.
Travel:	6th St exit off I-35. Proceed west on 6th. From Loop 1, proceed east on 5th, then left on Baylor for one block. Parking is available in the rear.
Credit Cards:	Yes
Owner:	Patricia Hart
Year Estab:	1992
Comments:	Located in an upscale antique mall, the books in this rather small booth fit in with the mall's general "flavor" in that they were higher priced items. While we saw a variety of titles, some of which may have been quite desirable (some first editions), the overall selection was rather limited. The owner may indeed have the number of books shown above, but only a fraction of that number was on display during our visit.

Kids n Cats   **Open Shop**
5732 Burnet Road   78756   (512) 458-6369

Collection:	General stock of mostly paperback.
Hours:	Mon-Sat 11-6.

Libby's New & Used Book Store   **Open Shop**
7212 Cameron Road   78752   (512) 451-0024

Collection:	General stock of mostly used paperback.
# of Vols:	45,000
Hours:	Mon-Sat 9:30-6:30.

Mac Donnell Rare Books   **By Appointment**
9307 Glenlake Drive   78730   (512) 345-4139

Collection:	Specialty books and ephemera.
# of Vols:	3,000
Specialties:	Literary first editions (19th & 20th century English and American).
Services:	Appraisals, catalog, accepts want lists.
Credit Cards:	No
Owner:	Kevin Mac Donnell
Year Estab:	1986

Mysteries & More   **Open Shop**
11139 North IH35, #176   78753   Fax: (512) 339-1695   (512) 837-6768
                                                        E-mail: mystrymore@aol.com

Collection:	Specialty. Primarily used paperback.
# of Vols:	28,000
Specialties:	Mystery; horror; science fiction; adventure; true crime; westerns.
Hours:	Tue-Fri 10-7. Sat 10-5. Sun 12-5.
Services:	Search service, catalog, accepts want lists.
Travel:	Southeast corner of Broker Lane and I-35 North.
Credit Cards:	Yes

Owner:	Elmer & Jan Grape
Year Estab:	1990
Comments:	Stock is approximately 90% used, 85% of which is paperback.

Poor Richard's Books   **By Appointment**
PO Box 5876   78763   (512) 346-4056
E-mail: poorrich@interloc.com

Collection:	General stock.
# of Vols:	3,000
Specialties:	Modern first editions; mystery; World War II; sailing.
Services:	Search service, accepts want lists, mail order.
Credit Cards:	No
Owner:	Richard Bobbitt
Year Estab:	1994

ProTech   **Open Shop**
12444 Research Boulevard   78759   (512) 258-1400

Collection:	Specialty. Mostly new and some used.
# of Vols:	500-1,000 (used)
Specialties:	Computers; mathematics; engineering; science.
Hours:	Mon-Sat 9-9. Sun 12-6.

Dorothy Sloan Rare Books   **By Appointment**
PO Box 49670   78765   (512) 477-8442

Collection:	General stock.
# of Vols:	3,000
Specialties:	Mexican American War; Americana.
Services:	Appraisals, search service, accepts want lists, catalog.
Credit Cards:	Yes
Year Estab:	1981

Texas Independence Emporium   **By Appointment**
8600 Appalachian   78759   (512) 346-2542

Collection:	General stock.
# of Vols:	20,000
Specialties:	Texas, Native Americans; Western Americana; exploration; cartography.
Services:	Mail order.
Credit Cards:	No
Owner:	Joe Tyson
Year Estab:	1953
Comments:	Fiction section limited to pre-1930 works.

12th Street Books   **Open Shop**
827 West 12th Street   78701   (512) 499-8828

Collection:	General stock of paperback and hardcover.
# of Vols:	15,000

Hours:	Mon-Fri 8-7. Sat 10-6.
Travel:	15th St exit off I-35. Proceed west on 15th, then south on West Ave and west on 12th. Shop is 1/2 block ahead.
Credit Cards:	Yes
Owner:	Mike Hale
Year Estab:	1993
Comments:	Surrounded by two or three used college textbook shops, this store offers a general collection that is modest in size but interesting in terms of titles. A visit here should not take very long. The shop also has a coffee bar.

Ray S. Walton Rare Books   **By Appointment**
11109 Henge Drive   78759   (512) 250-5416

Collection:	Specialty
# of Vols:	2,000
Specialties:	Western Americana.
Services:	Appraisals, accepts want lists, catalog.
Credit Cards:	No
Year Estab:	1968

Bay City

Rainbows End Books   **Open Shop**
2510 Avenue F   77414   (409) 245-5333

Collection:	General stock of mostly paperback.
Hours:	Mon-Fri 9-5:30. Sat 10-4.

Baytown
(Map 36, page 398)

Book Barn   **Open Shop**
222 East Texas Avenue   77520   (281) 428-1645

Collection:	General stock of paperback and hardcover.
# of Vols:	50,000
Hours:	Mon-Sat 9:30-5.
Travel:	N. Main exit off I-10. Proceed south on N. Main for two to three miles, then left on Texas.
Credit Cards:	Yes
Owner:	Darlene Haley
Year Estab:	1984
Comments:	Stock is approximately 75% paperback.

Beaumont
(Map 36, page 398)

The Book Gallery   **Open Shop**
2402 North Street   77702   (409) 835-2665

Collection:	General stock of mostly hardcover.

# of Vols:	15,000
Specialties:	Texas; modern first editions; theater.
Hours:	Mon-Fri 9:30-5:30. Sat 9:30-4.
Travel:	Calder exit off I-10. Proceed east on Calder, then north on 8th St. Shop is at corner of North and 8th.
Credit Cards:	Yes
Owner:	George Anderson & Trent Jenkins
Year Estab:	1988
Comments:	Located in a former private residence, the rooms in this shop are filled with books in generally good condition. Most of the selections are hardcover with some paperbacks and trade editions intershelved. The specialties listed above are represented in reasonable quantity and the books we saw were fairly priced. A neat shop. Pleasant to browse.

The Bookseller   **Flea Market**
At King Mart Flea Market   Home: (409) 892-8144
2651 South 11th Street
Mailing address: 3715 Acorn Circuit Beaumont 77703

Collection:	General stock of mostly hardcover.
# of Vols:	25,000
Specialties:	Texas; military; religion; gardening; biography.
Hours:	Thu-Sun 10-6.
Services:	Appraisals, accepts want lists, mail order.
Travel:	From I-10 take Hwy 90 toward town (College St). Right on 11th St.
Owner:	Carl B. Rush
Year Estab:	1981

Red B4 Books   **Open Shop**
3875 Calder Avenue   77706   (409) 838-2789

Collection:	General stock of mostly paperback.
# of Vols:	15,000
Hours:	Mon-Sat 10-6.
Travel:	Calder exit off I-10. Proceed north on Calder. Shop is in 23rd St. Plaza Shopping Center
Comments:	Primarily a paperback shop with a scattering of mostly newer hardcover volumes, including book club editions. Not what we would call a book lover's paradise.

Bedford
(Map 40, page 375)

Half Price Books, Records, Magazines   **Open Shop**
713 Harwood Drive   76021   (817) 581-9888

Collection:	General stock of hardcover, paperback and remainders.
Hours:	Mon-Sat 9am-10pm. Sun 11-8.
Travel:	Brown Trail exit off Hwy 183/121. Proceed north to Harwood, then right on Harwood. Shop is on left in Harwood Village North.

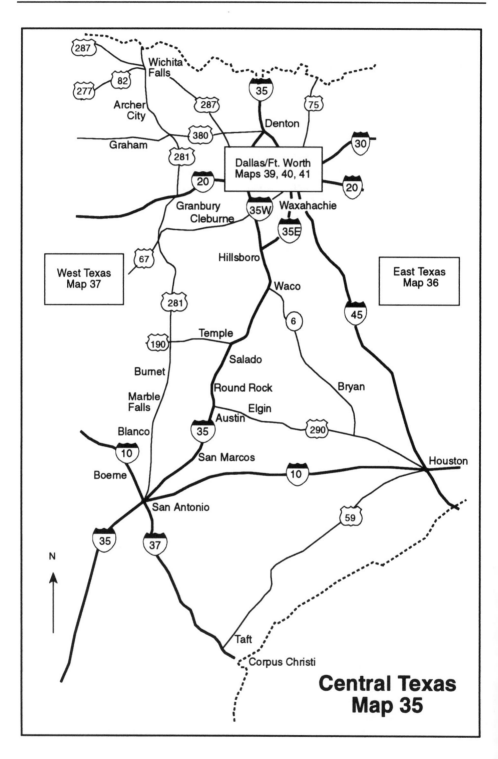

West Texas
Map 37

East Texas
Map 36

Central Texas
Map 35

Big Spring

The Bookworm   **Open Shop**
1001 South Lancaster   79720   (915) 263-4554

Collection:	General stock of mostly paperback.
# of Vols:	100,000
Hours:	Mon-Fri 10-5.

Blanco
(Map 35, page 354)

Maggie Lambeth   **Open Shop**
At Gandalff's Goldwerkes   Fax: (210) 833-5169   Home: (210) 833-5252
309 Main   78606   Store: (210) 833-4560

Collection:	General stock and ephemera.
# of Vols:	8,000
Specialties:	Texas; Native Americans; Southwest Americana; Mexico; E.S. Curtis photogravuers.
Hours:	Thu & Fri 10-5. Sat 10-4:30. (See Comments)
Services:	Appraisals, search service, catalog, accepts want lists.
Travel:	From Austin, proceed west on Hwy 290, then south (left) on Hwy 281.
Credit Cards:	Yes
Year Estab:	1975
Comments:	Also available on a by appointment basis at home location.

Boerne
(Map 35, page 354)

Book Mark   **Open Shop**
133 South Main Street   78006   (210) 249-3490

Collection:	General stock.
# of Vols:	3,000+
Specialties:	Texas; first editions.
Hours:	Tue-Sat 10-5. Sun 12-5
Services:	Accepts want lists, mail order.
Travel:	Boerne exit off I-10. Follow signs into town.
Credit Cards:	Yes
Owner:	Doris Davies
Year Estab:	1981

Brackettville

Ben E. Pingenot Rare Books   **By Appointment**
22 Colony Row, Fort Clark Springs   78832   (210) 563-2195

Collection:	Specialty
Specialties:	Texas; Western Americana.
Services:	Appraisals, accepts want lists, catalog.
Year Estab:	1986

Bryan
(Map 35, page 354)

Half Price Books, Records, Magazines   **Open Shop**
3828 South Texas Avenue   77802   (409) 846-2738

Collection:	General stock of hardcover, paperback and remainders.
Hours:	Mon-Sat 10-9. Sun 12-9.
Travel:	Hwy 6 becomes Texas Ave. From Hwy 21, turn south on Texas Ave.

Buffalo

Cypress Book Co.   **By Appointment**
PO Box 535   75831   (903) 322-3621

Collection:	Specialty. Mostly used.
# of Vols:	2,000
Specialties:	Texas
Services:	Search service, accepts want lists, catalog.
Credit Cards:	Yes
Owner:	Anne Jordan
Year Estab:	1976

Burnet
(Map 35, page 354)

Books Plus   **Open Shop**
600 East Polk Street   (512) 756-2551
Mailing address: 1207 Sherrard Burnet 78611

Collection:	General stock of paperback and hardcover.
# of Vols:	60,000
Hours:	Mon-Sat 9-6.
Travel:	Hwy 29 exit off I-35. Proceed west on Hwy 29. Shop is on Hwy 29.
Owner:	Gina Baker
Year Estab:	1993
Comments:	Stock is approximately 75% paperback.

Canyon

Branding Iron Gallery   **By Appointment**
1408 4th Avenue   79015   (806) 655-1167

Collection:	Specialty
# of Vols:	1,000
Specialties:	Texas; Western Americana.
Services:	Accepts want lists, mail order.
Owner:	John R. Henry
Year Estab:	1993

Cleburne
(Map 35, page 354)

Bill's Books
116 South Main
Mailing address: PO Box 592 Cleburne 76031

Open Shop
(817) 645-7591

Collection:	General stock of paperback and hardcover.
# of Vols:	200,000
Hours:	Mon-Sat 9-6.
Travel:	Burleson exit off I-35W. Proceed south on Hwy 174 which merges into Hwy 171 for about 10 miles to Cleburne where Hwy 171 becomes Main.
Credit Cards:	No
Year Estab:	1980
Comments:	If your car is on Hwy 171 and you're in the town of Cleburne during the hours that this shop is open, feel free to drop in. What you'll view is a shop that has thousands of paperbacks shelved in rather narrow aisles as well as thousands of hardcover items in very mixed condition and difficult to view. If new shelves have not been constructed by the time of your arrival, you may also see a mountain of hardcover books in a corner of the store with no rational way of determining what may be in the middle of the mound. The owner assures us, however, that since he has already checked the titles before the books became part of the mountain, there is not likely to be a Hemingway first edition hidden there.

Conroe

Canada's Book Store
517 East Davis Street 77301

Open Shop
(409) 756-6344

Collection:	General stock of mostly paperback.
# of Vols:	50,000
Hours:	Mon-Fri 10-5. Sat 12-3.

Gates Book Exchange
515 Lilly Boulevard 77301

Open Shop
(409) 788-2030

Collection:	General stock of mostly paperback.
# of Vols:	100,000+
Hours:	Mon-Sat, except closed Wed, 10-4:30.

Corpus Christi
(Map 35, page 354)

Half Price Books, Records, Magazines
5425 South Padre Island Dr, #185 78411

Open Shop
(512) 991-4494

Collection:	General stock of hardcover, paperback and remainders.
Hours:	Mon-Sat 9:30am-10pm. Sun 11-9.
Travel:	Staples exit off South Padre Island Dr. Shop is in Moore Plaza at southwest corner of the intersection.

Crockett
(Map 36, page 398)

Sassy Bookworm   **Open Shop**
1027 South 4th Street   75835   (409) 544-8686

Collection: General stock of mostly paperback.
# of Vols: 65,000
Hours: Mon-Fri 10-5. Sat 10-3.
Comments: Word has it that despite the preponderance of paperbacks, the shop is
                   "worth a visit" if you're in the area.

Crosby

Bear's 1/2 Price Books   **Open Shop**
6115 FM 2100   77532   (281) 328-8035

Collection: General stock of mostly paperback.
# of Vols: 80,000
Hours: Tue-Fri 12-6. Sat 12-5.

Dallas

Aldredge Book Store   **Open Shop**
2909 Maple Avenue   75201   (214) 871-3333

Collection: General stock.
# of Vols: 12,000
Hours: Mon-Sat 10-6. Sun by chance.
Services: Catalog
Travel: Oak Lawn exit off I-35. Proceed north (right if northbound) on Oak
                   Lawn, then east on Maple. Shop is between Oak Lawn and McKinney.
Credit Cards: Yes
Owner: Dick Bosse
Year Estab: 1947
Comments: This shop proves the old adage that good things come in small pack-
                   ages (although the shop is not so very small). If there was a paperback
                   book anywhere we did not spot it. What we did see were books in good
                   condition representing many subject areas. Whether or not you find a
                   title you've been looking for, you should enjoy browsing here as the
                   collection is top notch and the prices are right.

Antiquarian of Dallas   **Open Shop**
2609 Routh Street   75201   (214) 754-0705

Collection: General stock.
# of Vols: 2,000+
Hours: Mon-Sat 11-5.
Services: Appraisals, accepts want lists, mail order.
Travel: Oak Lawn exit off I-35. Proceed north on Oak Lawn, east on Maple, left
                   on McKinney and left on Routh.
Credit Cards: Yes

Owner: George Chamberlain
Year Estab: 1989

Battarbee's Books   **Antique Mall**
At Forestwood Antique Mall   Mall: (972) 661-0001
5333 Forest Lane 75244   Home: (214) 357-3400

Collection:	General stock and ephemera.
# of Vols:	10,000
Specialties:	Hunting; wildlife; nature; fishing; Africa; Theodore Roosevelt; Livingston; Stanley; Rowland Ward; Daniel Boone; Davey Crockett.
Hours:	Mon-Wed 10-6. Thu-Sat 10-8. Sun 12-6.
Services:	Search service, accepts want lists, mail order.
Travel:	See David Grossblatt, Bookseller below.
Credit Cards:	Yes
Owner:	Larry Battarbee
Year Estab:	1994
Comments:	If you're into hunting, wildlife, nature or any of the specialties listed above, you should be impressed both by the quality and range of the volumes on display at this location. One could easily fill an entire library on the subject by making just a single stop here.

Campbell's Book Store   **Antique Mall**
Mailing address: 13402 Bayard Circle Dallas 75243   Home: (972) 644-6810

Collection:	General stock.
Owner:	Jo Ellison
Comments:	Displays at Forestwood Antique Mall (see above) and Knox Street Antique Mall (see below).

Roger & Lorraine Carroll   **By Appointment**
5310 Live Oak 75206   (214) 827-3214

Collection:	General stock.
# of Vols:	3,000
Specialties:	Children's; children's series (boys) prior to 1940; illustrated.
Year Estab:	1980

Classic Trains And Hobbies   **Open Shop**
11110 Petal Street 75238   (214) 349-7573
                                        Fax: (214) 349-1267

Collection:	Specialty new and used.
Specialties:	Railroad and model trains.
Hours:	Mon-Fri 10-6. Sat 10-5.
Services:	Appraisals, search service, lists, accepts want lists.
Travel:	Exit 13 (Jupiter/Kingsley) off I-635. Go north on Jupiter for 1/2 mile to Petal, then left on Petal. Shop is in Northeast Dallas Business Park.
Credit Cards:	Yes
Owner:	Bill Harris
Year Estab:	1974
Comments:	Stock is approximately 40% used.

Dallas Books & Antiques   **Antique Mall**
At Unlimited Limited Antique Mall   (972) 490-4085
15201 Midway Road   75244

Hours: Daily 10-6.
Travel: Midway exit off I-635. Proceed north on Midway to Beltline.

The Englishman's Antiques   **Open Shop**
15304 Midway Road   75244   (972) 980-0107

Collection: General stock.
# of Vols: 1,000-2,000
Hours: Mon-Sat 10:30-5:30. Sun 12:30-5:30.
Travel: Midway Rd exit off I-635. Proceed north on Midway for two blocks.
Credit Cards: Yes
Owner: Anthony Clingly
Year Estab: 1984
Comments: Shop also sells antiques.

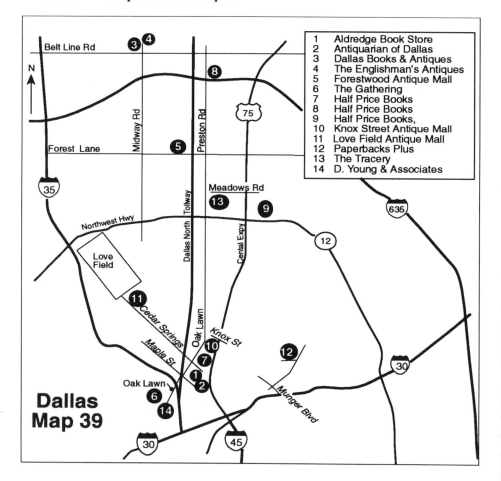

1	Aldredge Book Store
2	Antiquarian of Dallas
3	Dallas Books & Antiques
4	The Englishman's Antiques
5	Forestwood Antique Mall
6	The Gathering
7	Half Price Books
8	Half Price Books
9	Half Price Books,
10	Knox Street Antique Mall
11	Love Field Antique Mall
12	Paperbacks Plus
13	The Tracery
14	D. Young & Associates

Dallas
Map 39

The Gathering **Antique Mall**
1515 Turtle Creek Boulevard (214) 741-4888

Hours: Mon-Sat 9-6.
Travel: At Oak Lawn and Turtle Creek.

Greenway Books **Antique Mall**
At Love Field Antique Mall Mall: (214) 357-6500
6500 Cedar Springs Road Home: (214) 352-0706
Mailing address: PO Box 9062 Dallas 75209 Fax: (214)352- 5121

Collection: General stock.
# of Vols: 3,000+
Hours: Mon-Sat 10-7. Sun 10-5.
Services: Search service.
Travel: Across from Love Field Airport.
Credit Cards: Yes
Owner: Gail Glick
Year Estab: 1987
Comments: A departure from the typical antique mall, we were happy to find four dealers (Greenway Books, plus three other dealers) who displayed in a single area at the rear of this mall and whose quality books, including many first editions (most in quite good condition), making a stop here well worth your while. We purchased on unusual item by a most collectible author at an excellent price.

David Grossblatt, Bookseller **Antique Mall**
At Forestwood Antique Mall Mall (972) 661-0001
Mailing address: PO Box 720035 Dallas 75372 Home: (214) 823-7542

Collection: General stock and ephemera.
# of Vols: 10,000
Specialties: Western Americana; Texas; Civil War, children's; art; illustrated; fine bindings; literature.
Hours: Mon-Wed 10-6. Thu-Sat 10-8. Sun 12-6.
Services: Appraisals, catalog, accepts want lists.
Travel: Northbound on Dallas Tollway: Forest exit. Proceed west on Forest. Shop is on right. Southbound on tollway: Galleria/Inwood exit. Proceed on service road to Inwood and Forest, then east on Forest. Shop is on left.
Credit Cards: Yes
Year Estab: 1973
Comments: Strong in all of the areas described above. The books we saw were hardly the typical antique mall titles. Rather, they represented a healthy selection of books that should overcome the antique "mall-a-phobia" you may have acquired.

Half Price Books, Records, Magazines **Open Shop**
4234 Oak Lawn 75219 (214) 526-8440

Collection: General stock of hardcover and paperback and remainders.

(Dallas)

Hours:	Mon-Sat 10-10. Sun 12-7.
Travel:	Oak Lawn exit off I-35. Proceed east on Oak Lawn for one mile to Plaza Shopping Center.

Half Price Books, Records, Magazines   **Open Shop**
13388 Preston Road   75240   (972) 701-8055

Collection:	General stock of hardcover and paperback and remainders.
Hours:	Mon-Thu 9:30-9. Fri & Sat 9:30-10. Sun 12-7.
Travel:	Preston Rd exit off I-635. Proceed north for one block. Shop is on right.

Half Price Books, Records, Magazines   **Open Shop**
5915 East Northwest Highway   75231   (214) 363-8374

Collection:	General stock of hardcover and paperback and remainders.
# of Vols:	200,000+
Hours:	Daily 9:30am-10pm.
Travel:	Northwest Hwy exit off I-75. Proceed east on Northwest Hwy to Shady Brook. Left on Shady Brook. Shop is at northeast corner of the intersection.
Comments:	Since we like to visit at least one of the Half Price Book stores located in each of the regions this chain serves, we're glad we had the opportunity to visit this Dallas location which also serves as the chain's flagship store. As with all Half Price locations, this store offers plenty of remainders (about half the stock) but we also saw a sufficient number of older hardcover books (several of which we would certainly classify as hard-to-find) to make the shop an interesting stop for all but the stodgiest of antiquarians.

History Merchant   **Open Shop**
2723 Routh Street   75201   (214) 742-5487

Collection:	Specialty used and new.
Specialties:	History; British and American history; World War II; Winston Churchill.
Hours:	Wed-Sat 10-4:30. Other times by appointment.
Services:	Search service, mail order.
Travel:	Between McKinney & Cedar Springs.
Credit Cards:	Yes
Year Estab:	1987

Craig Hokenson   **By Appointment**
PO Box 820171   75382   (214) 349-2007

Collection:	Specialty
# of Vols:	5,000
Specialties:	Modern first editions; mystery (first editions).
Services:	Appraisals, accepts want lists, catalog.
Year Estab:	1990

Knox Street Antique Mall **Antique Mall**
3319 Knox Street (214) 521-8888

Hours: Mon-Wed 10-6. Thu-Sat 10-8. Sun 12-6.
Travel: Knox/Henderson exit off Hwy 75 (Central Hwy). Proceed west on Knox for about four blocks.

Bob Lakin Books & Collectibles **By Appointment**
3021 Lavita Lane   75234 (972) 247-3291

Collection: Specialty
# of Vols: 3,500
Specialties: Signed; modern fiction; children's illustrated; Oz; mystery; movies; science fiction.
Services: Search service, catalog, accepts want lists.
Credit Cards: No
Year Estab: 1981

Lotus Books and Gems **Open Shop**
17630 Davenport Road, #101   75252 (972) 713-7660

Collection: Specialty new and used paperback and hardcover.
# of Vols: 2,000
Specialties: Spirituality; self help; holistic.
Hours: Mon-Sat 12-8. Sun 12-6.
Travel: Preston Rd exit off I-635. Proceed north on Preston, east on McCallum, north on Davenport.
Credit Cards: Yes
Owner: Delsie Price
Year Estab: 1994
Comments: Stock is evenly divided between new and used.

John R. Mara Law Books **Open Shop**
5628 Richmond Avenue   75206 (214) 821-1979

Collection: Specialty new and used.
Specialties: Law
Hours: Mon-Fri 9-5.
Services: Lists, search service, accepts want lists.

Paperbacks Plus **Open Shop**
6115 La Vista Drive   75214 (214) 827-4860
E-mail: luckydog@dal.cleaf.com

Collection: General stock of hardcover and paperback, CDs, records and comics.
# of Vols: 50,000+
Hours: Mon-Sat 9-9. Sun 11-7.
Services: Accepts want lists and requests, preferably using form on web page for Lucky Dog Books (http://www.cleaf.com/~luckydog).
Travel: Munger Ave exit off I-30. Proceed north on Munger, then right on Columbia and left on La Vista.
Credit Cards: Yes

(Dallas)

Owner:	John & Marquetta Tilton
Year Estab:	1974
Comments:	Being more interested in the "Plus" of the shop's title, we spent little time in the two romance rooms (exclusively paperback), but liked the two children's rooms (mixed hardcover and paperback), got a stiff neck looking at the selection of the hardcover used items on the top shelves of the mystery and science fiction sections and strolled rapidly through the rest of the shop which displayed hardcover volumes, including some older titles, in several non fiction areas. If you're in the neighborhood, a stop would be appropriate. If you have to drive a distance, you might want to call ahead to see if the titles you're seeking are likely to be on hand. The shop also sponsors literary events.

ProTech   **Open Shop**
5455 Belt Line Rd, 2nd Fl.   75240   (972) 239-8324

Collection:	Specialty. Mostly new and limited used.
Specialties:	Computers; mathematics; engineering; science.
Hours:	Mon-Sat 9-9. Sun 12-6.

Tom's Books   **Open Shop**
10218 East Northwest Highway   75238   (214) 342-8045

Collection:	General stock of mostly paperback.
# of Vols:	50,000-60,000
Hours:	Mon-Sat 9:30-6:30.

The Tracery   **Open Shop**
6027 Glendora   (214) 361-5269
Mailing address: PO Box 670236 Dallas 75367

Collection:	General stock.
# of Vols:	9,000
Specialties:	Christmas; World War II; first editions; children's.
Hours:	Daily 9-6. But best to call ahead.
Services:	Search service, accepts want lists, mail order.
Travel:	Meadow Rd exit off Hwy 75. Proceed west on Meadow to Preston Rd, then left on Preston for one block, then east on Glendora. Shop is in the owner's home.
Credit Cards:	No
Owner:	Onnie & Julie Clem
Year Estab:	1990

D. Young & Associates   **Open Shop**
At Dallas Design Center   Fax: (214) 742-2666   (214) 742-2665
1025 North Stemmons   75207   E-mail: youngbks@/.net

Collection:	General stock.
# of Vols:	10,000+

Specialties:	Fine bindings.
Hours:	Mon-Fri 9-4:30. Other times by appointment.
Services:	Search service, accepts want lists, mail order.
Travel:	Oak Lawn exit off I-35. Proceed west on Oak Lawn for one block to Hi Line, then south on Hi Line to I-35 access road. Follow access road to Dallas Design Center.
Credit Cards:	No
Owner:	Dorothy & Don Young
Year Estab:	1985

Deer Park
(Map 36, page 398)

The Dusty Cover   **Open Shop**
8317 Spencer Highway   77536   (281) 476-0580

Collection:	General stock of used and new paperbacks and hardcover.
# of Vols:	30,000 (used)
Hours:	Mon-Thu 10-8. Fri & Sat 10-6. Sun 12-5.
Travel:	Underwood exit off Hwy 225. Proceed south on Underwood to Spencer Hwy, then right on Spencer. Shop is on right in San Jacinto Shopping Center.
Credit Cards:	Yes
Owner:	Edith Schultz
Year Estab:	1994
Comments:	Used stock is approximately 75% paperback.

Pauline's Bookstore   **Open Shop**
1617 Center   77536   (281) 479-7300

Collection:	General stock of mostly used paperback.
Hours:	Tue-Sat 10-6.

Denton
(Map 35, page 354)

Recycled Books   **Open Shop**
200 North Locust Street   76201   (817) 566-5688

Collection:	General stock of hardcover and paperback, records & CDs.
# of Vols:	150,000
Hours:	Daily 9-9.
Travel:	Fort Worth exit off I-35E. Proceed north on Fort Worth, then right on Hickory. Shop is downtown, on northeast corner of the square.
Credit Cards:	Yes
Owner:	Don Foster
Year Estab:	1983
Comments:	You may thank Susan if you're fortunate (as was I) to have the opportunity to visit this fabulous bookstore. Since our road travels begin rather early and end rather late in the day, I was a bit grumpy when told

by a clerk at 8:45am that the store would not open until 9am (they were pledged to adhere to store's "no early admittance" policy, due in part, we were told, to the fact that "this is Texas where people can carry guns"). Miffed by this experience, but pleased that Susan coaxed me into the store after she had visited it briefly, I'm happy to say that this is indeed one of those establishments "not to be missed" no matter how far you may have to drive to get there. The books, almost universally in good condition, are quite nicely displayed. Every subject is covered in great depth with labels and subheadings. The books are meticulously shelved and the titles represent a wide scope, from the more common (of which we saw a few) to the more interesting (of which we saw many). The lower level covers an area equal in size to the main level and a mezzanine is also quite large. If there is anything else I can say to tempt you to visit this store I would certainly do so but perhaps the best plug I can give this shop is that I walked out with several volumes, all quite reasonably priced, and had we had additional time, I could easily have filled my trunk. P.S. Don't miss some of the titles behind the locked glass cases.

Treasure Aisles   **Open Shop**
1220 West Hickory Street   76201   (817) 484-6161

Collection:	General stock of paperback and hardcover.
# of Vols:	10,000
Hours:	Mon-Fri 10-6. Sat 10-4.
Travel:	Exit 466B (Ave D) off I-35. Proceed north on Ave D for one block, then east on Eagle for one block, north on Ave C for 6 blocks and right on Hickory.
Credit Cards:	Yes
Owner:	Kennedy Poyser
Year Estab:	1991
Comments:	Stock is approximately 70% paperback.

Duncanville
(Map 40, page 375)

Bill's Books   **Open Shop**
658 Big Stone Gap Road   75137   (972) 298-3996

Collection:	General stock of mostly used paperback.
# of Vols:	40,000
Hours:	Mon-Sat 10:30-6:30.

Duncanville Books & Dolls   **Open Shop**
101 West Camp Wisdom Rd, #J   75116   (972) 298-7546

Collection:	General stock of paperback and hardcover.
# of Vols:	45,000
Hours:	Mon-Sat 10-6. Sun 12-6.
Travel:	I-20 westbound: Main St exit. Proceed south on Main for one block then

right on Camp Wisdom Rd (just after the railroad tracks). I-20 eastbound: Duncanville Rd exit. Proceed south (right) on Duncanville Rd to dead end then left at Camp Wisdom (just before railroad tracks).

Credit Cards:	Yes
Owner:	Jerry Hoffmann
Year Estab:	1966
Comments:	If you have a soft heart, a grandchild or young daughter, it would be best to wear blinders when visiting here as one half of the shop is devoted to the sale of collectible quality special edition dolls. The rest of the shop displays paperbacks, comics and a fair sampling of hardcover volumes in most categories. We found the books to be reasonably priced and had no trouble making a small purchase. Your own tastes and needs will determine your own experience here.

El Paso
(Map 37, page 343)

Book Basket   **Open Shop**
9828 Montana, Ste O   79925   (915) 598-1287

Collection:	General stock of mostly paperback.
# of Vols:	40,000
Hours:	Mon-Fri 10-6. Sat 9-5.

Book Gallery   **Open Shop**
2800 East Yandell Drive   79903   (915) 562-4528

Collection:	General stock of mostly used.
# of Vols:	100,000
Specialties:	Western Americana; military.
Hours:	Mon-Fri 9:30-5:30. Sat 9:30-5. Closed Sun & Mon in summer.
Services:	Appraisals, search service, accepts want lists.
Travel:	Piedras exit off I-10. Proceed north on Piedras to Yandell. Left on Yandell. Shop is immediately on left.
Credit Cards:	Yes
Owner:	George Skanse
Year Estab:	1964
Comments:	Located on the same premises as a gift shop (owned by the same owner), this shop has a good sized collection of older hardcover volumes. Perhaps we were not there long enough to spot any antiquarian or rare books, or perhaps they just alluded us.

The Book Rack   **Open Shop**
10780 Pebble Hills Boulevard   79935   (915) 598-2279

Collection:	General stock of mostly paperback.
# of Vols:	40,000
Hours:	Mon-Fri 10-7. Sat 9-6.

BOOKS...at the Pass of the North
PO Box 4904   79914

By Appointment
(915) 757-1681
E-mail: 76270.255@compuserve.com

Collection:	Specialty
# of Vols:	1,500
Specialties:	Texas; Southwest Americana; military; Carl Hertzog; Tom Lea.
Services:	Search service, catalog, accepts want lists.
Credit Cards:	Yes
Owner:	J.G. McDaniel
Year Estab:	1988

Bookworm Exchange
3355 North Yarbrough Drive   79925

Open Shop
(915) 598-8123

Collection:	General stock of mostly paperback.
# of Vols:	50,000+
Hours:	Mon-Sat 10-7.

Clark's Paperback Exchange
5412 Will Ruth Avenue   79924

Open Shop
(915) 755-6767

Collection:	General stock of mostly paperback.
# of Vols:	70,000+
Hours:	Tue-Sat 9-5.

West Side Paperback Exchange
6110G North Mesa Street   79912

Open Shop
(915) 584-8478

Collection:	General stock of mostly paperback.
# of Vols:	60,000
Hours:	Tue-Sat 10-6.

Elgin
(Map 35, page 354)

ABC Depot Books
201 North Main   78621

Open Shop
(512) 285-9332

Collection:	General stock of paperback and hardcover.
# of Vols:	15,000
Hours:	Wed & Thu 10-5. Fri 10-7. Sat 10-2.
Travel:	Hwy 290 to Elgin, then continue on Loop 109 which becomes Main St.
Owner:	Teri & Damon Daughtry
Year Estab:	1982
Comments:	Stock is approximately 70% paperback.

Euless

The Stevensons
316 Sage Lane   76039

By Appointment
(817) 354-8903

Collection:	Specialty

Specialties:	Boy and girl scouting; Ernest Thompson Seton.
Services:	Appraisals, catalog.
Credit Cards:	Yes
Owner:	James G. Stevenson
Year Estab:	1972

Farmers Branch

Book Haven   **Open Shop**
12895 Josey Lane   75234   (972) 241-5114

Collection:	General stock of mostly paperback.
# of Vols:	30,000
Hours:	Mon-Sat 10-7.

Fort Worth

Barber's Book Store   **Open Shop**
215 West 8th Street   76102   (817) 335-5469
                                                                                   Fax: (817) 332-5319

Collection:	General stock.
# of Vols:	75,000
Specialties:	Texas; illustrated; fine bindings.
Hours:	Wed-Sat 10-5. Mon & Tue by chance. Best to call ahead.
Services:	Appraisals, search service, accepts want lists, mail order.
Travel:	Downtown exit off I-30. Proceed on Commerce St to 8th St, then left on 8th. Shop is in central business district.
Credit Cards:	Yes
Owner:	Brian A. Perkins
Year Estab:	1925
Comments:	If you enjoy browsing the shelves for older and/or rare titles, plan to spend some extra time here as the shop has lots of crevices, aisles, crannies and even a few nooks. Shelves are nicely labeled with some unusual categories, e.g., "crazy journalists." A fun place to visit with an excellent selection in the specialties listed above and some glass encased shelves waiting for the right antiquarian to make a purchase. If your interests take you to more mundane and popular subjects, ask the owner about his shop a few blocks away where he displays such items.

The Book Collector   **By Appointment**
2704 Ryan Ave   76110   (817) 927-7595

Collection:	Specialty
# of Vols:	5,000
Specialties:	Anthropology; Native Americans; Mexico; Latin America; mystery; chess.
Services:	Catalog, accepts want lists.
Credit Cards:	No
Owner:	Michael Utt
Year Estab:	1995

Book Shoppe

Open Shop

1822 West Berry Street   76110

(817) 926-8208

Collection:	General stock of paperback and hardcover.
# of Vols:	30,000+
Hours:	Mon-Sat 10-5:30.
Travel:	Berry St exit off I-35W. Proceed west on Berry. Shop is just before Cleburne on north side of street.
Credit Cards:	No
Owner:	Joyce Taylor
Year Estab:	1984
Comments:	Stock is approximately 75% paperback.

John S. Burns - Books

Antique Mall

At The Antique Colony

Mall: (817) 731-7252

7200 Camp Bowie Boulevard

Home: (817) 531-8873

Mailing address: 2514 North Hughes Ave. Fort Worth 76103

Collection:	General stock and ephemera.
# of Vols:	5,000
Specialties:	Children's; Texas; Southwest Americana; poetry; drama; fiction.
Hours:	Mon-Sat 10-6. Sun 12-6.
Services:	Appraisals, search service.
Travel:	Between I-20 and I-30 at the traffic circle in west Fort Worth.
Credit Cards:	Yes
Year Estab:	1990

Half Price Book Barn

Open Shop

1001 Hemphill Street   76104

(817) 335-3902

Collection:	General stock of hardcover and paperback.
# of Vols:	12,000
Hours:	Mon, Thu, Fri 10:30-5:15.
Travel:	Rosedale exit off I-35. Proceed west on Rosedale to Hemphill, then right on Hemphill. Shop is between Rosedale and Pennsylvania.
Credit Cards:	No
Owner:	Sam & Jean Rance
Year Estab:	1960's
Comments:	Unfortunately, this shop was closed on the day we visited Ft. Worth. We were advised by the owner that the stock is evenly divided between hardcover and paperback.

Half Price Books, Records, Magazines

Open Shop

6912 Ridgmar Meadow Road   76116

(817) 732-4111

Collection:	General stock of hardcover, paperback and remainders.
Hours:	Mon-Sat 9am-10pm. Sun 11-8.
Travel:	Green Oaks exit off Hwy 30. Proceed north on Green Oaks for about one mile then left into Ridgmar Town Square Shopping Center.

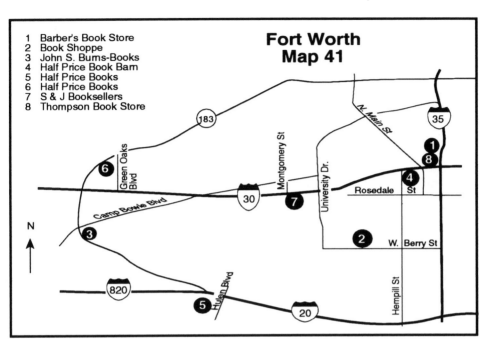

Fort Worth
Map 41

1 Barber's Book Store
2 Book Shoppe
3 John S. Burns-Books
4 Half Price Book Barn
5 Half Price Books
6 Half Price Books
7 S & J Booksellers
8 Thompson Book Store

Half Price Books, Records, Magazines
5246 South Hulen Street   76132

Open Shop
(817) 294-1166

Collection:	General stock of hardcover, paperback and remainders.
Hours:	Mon-Sat 9am-10pm. Sun 11-8.
Travel:	Hulen St exit off I-20. Proceed south on Hulen to Hulen Fashion Center.

Russell Light Books And Art
PO Box 17725   76102

By Appointment
(817) 738-9407

Collection:	General stock.
Specialties:	Fine bindings; fore-edge, illustrated; Winston Churchill.
Comments:	Displays at the following Dallas locations: Knox Street Antique Mall, The Gathering, Aldredge Book Shop and The History Merchant. See individual listings.

Omnibooks by Mail
3728 Potomac Avenue   76107

By Appointment
(817) 732-4202
E-mail: omnibook@interloc.com

Collection:	Specialty
# of Vols:	5,000
Specialties:	Literary first editions; Texas; golf.
Services:	Appraisals, search service (first editions), catalog, accepts want lists, consignment sales.
Owner:	Ken Hobbs
Year Estab:	1990

S & J Booksellers   **Antique Mall**
At Montgomery Street Antique Mall   Mall: (817) 735-9685
2601 Montgomery Street   Home: (817) 282-1470
Mailing address: 1717 Acorn Lane Hurst 76054

Collection:	General stock.
# of Vols:	3,000
Services:	Search service, accepts want lists, mail order.
Travel:	Montgomery St exit off I-30. Mall is at the exit, on the southeast corner
Owner:	Susan & John Koskelin
Year Estab:	1991
Comments:	Additional books can be viewed by appointment.

Thompson Book Store   **Open Shop**
900 Houston Street   76102   (817) 877-0500

Collection:	General stock of paperback and hardcover.
# of Vols:	300,000
Hours:	Mon-Fri 9-5. Sat 10-4.
Services:	Accepts want lists, mail order.
Travel:	Downtown exit off I-35. Proceed south to 6th St to Houston, then left on Houston. Shop is two blocks ahead. From I-30, see Barber's Book Store above.
Credit Cards:	No
Owner:	Eddie Eaves
Year Estab:	1936
Comments:	Paperbacks abound in this shop although there are some hardcover books on display. Most of the hardcover items we saw were of fairly recent vintage and with few exceptions did not appear to offer an exciting challenge to the ever alert book hunter. HOWEVER, since there is a "class act" book shop less than one block away, you really can't go wrong stopping here on the chance that you might find an item of interest.

Fredericksburg

Lone Star Books   **Open Shop**
Route 2, Box 104   78624   (210) 997-6495

Collection:	General stock of mostly paperback.
Hours:	Tue-Sat 10-6.

Friendswood
(Map 42, page 378)

Jem Books   **Open Shop**
3224 FM 528   77546   Fax: (281) 996-9918 (281) 996-9918
                                                  E-mail: jembooks@interloc.com

Collection:	General stock of mostly used paperback and hardcover.
# of Vols:	20,000

Hours:	Mon-Sat 10-7.
Services:	Search service, accepts want lists, mail order.
Travel:	FM 528 exit off I-45. Proceed west on FM 528. Shop is on right in a shopping center.
Credit Cards:	Yes
Owner:	Jack & Elizabeth Mantoura
Year Estab:	1994
Comments:	An attractive shop, well organized and labeled with a good balance between hardcover and paperback books and at least two glass cases displaying collectible items. The hardcover items were of mixed vintage with an emphasis on more recent volumes.

Frisco
(Map 36, page 398)

Main Place Antiques   **Antique Mall**
6990 Main Street   (972) 335-3300
Mailing address: PO Box 1818 Frisco 75034

Hours:	Tue-Sat 10-5. Sun 1-5.
Travel:	Located on FM 720, between Preston Rd and North Dallas Tollway.

Galveston
(Map 36, page 398)

Books et Cetera   **Open Shop**
1820 45th Street   77550   (409) 762-1422

Collection:	General stock of mostly used paperback.
# of Vols:	25,000
Hours:	Mon-Sat 10-6. Sun 12-5.

Galveston Bookshop   **Open Shop**
514 23rd Street   77550   (409) 765-6919

Collection:	General stock of paperback and hardcover.
# of Vols:	20,000
Hours:	Mon-Sat 10-5:30. Sun 12-4.
Services:	Accepts want lists, mail order.
Travel:	I-45 ends and becomes Broadway. Continue on Broadway to 23rd St, then left on 23rd St.
Credit Cards:	No
Owner:	John Kemmerly
Year Estab:	1991
Comments:	Although we saw some hardcover volumes here (a mix of newer items in dust jackets and some older volumes along a side wall), more than 85%-90% of the shop's stock is paperback, neatly shelved, but unfortunately of less interest to us.

Novel Ideas   **Open Shop**
1816 Market Street   77550   (409) 763-3844

Collection:	General stock of used and new hardcover and paperback.
# of Vols:	15,000 (used)
Hours:	Mon-Sat 10-6. Sun 12-6.
Travel:	See Galveston Book Shop. Proceed east on 19th St, then right on Market St. Shop is just ahead.
Credit Cards:	Yes
Owner:	Larry Beebe
Year Estab:	1996
Comments:	Open only a month at the time of our visit, the shop was still in the process of settling in. We saw a combination of new and used items which included a mix of some paperbacks, hardcover items, textbooks, a second level devoted to used magazines, LPs and CDs and a coffee bar under construction. With two other used book dealers in town, if you're in the Galveston area, we suggest you visit all three.

Yesterday's Books   **Open Shop**
101 21st Street   (409) 762-6608
Mailing address: PO Box 8187 Galveston 77553

Collection:	General stock.
# of Vols:	10,000
Hours:	Daily 10-5.
Services:	Search service, accepts want lists.
Travel:	See Galveston Book Shop. Turn left on 21st St.
Credit Cards:	No
Owner:	Louise Nichols
Year Estab:	1992
Comments:	A neat little shop located inside a renovated warehouse building turned mini mall in the heart of Galveston's historic Strand district. The shop offers a modest collection of primarily hardcover items covering interesting subjects but not in sufficient depth to really search for a specific item in a particular field. However, as the owner does an extensive search business, you might wish to contact her to determine if she has, or can locate, a title you're looking for.

Garland

(Map 40, page 375)

Books Etc   **Open Shop**
3420 Broadway Boulevard, #103   75043   (972) 278-9023

Collection:	General stock of mostly paperback.
# of Vols:	8,000
Hours:	Tue-Sat 10-6.

Books N Stuff   **Open Shop**
513 West State Street   75040   (972) 271-3418

Collection: General stock of mostly used and new paperback.
# of Vols: 30,000
Hours: Mon-Fri 9:30-5:30. Sat 9:30-5.

Half Price Books, Records, Magazines   **Open Shop**
1560 Northwest Highway   75041   (972) 681-3348

Collection: General stock of hardcover, paperback and remainders.
Hours: Mon-Sat 10-9. Sun 12-6.
Travel: Northwest Hwy exit off I-635. Proceed east on Northwest Hwy for about
                   one mile to Saturn Rd. Shop is on right in East Gate Shopping Center.

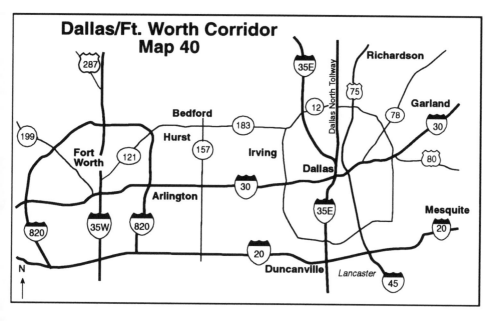

Graham
(Map 35, page 354)

Pratt's Books   **Open Shop**
502 Oak Street   76450   (817) 549-5341

Collection: General stock.
# of Vols: 17,000
Specialties: Texas; history.
Hours: Tue-Fri 11-5. Sat by chance or appointment.
Services: Search service, accepts want lists.
Travel: In downtown on the square.
Credit Cards: No
Owner: Rozella Pratt

Year Estab: 1984
Comments: A quiet little shop in a quiet little town with a most respectable collection of hardcover books dealing with Texas history as well as a nice sampling of other more general subjects. The majority of the books we saw were in good condition, with a couple of shelves of what the owner refers to as "oldies."

Granbury
(Map 35, page 354)

Book Nook   **Open Shop**
1424 East Highway 377   76048   (817) 279-7555

Collection: General stock of mostly used paperback.
# of Vols: 20,000
Hours: Mon-Fri 10-6. Sat 10-5.

Log Cabin Books   **Open Shop**
119 East Ridge Street   76048   (817) 573-1208

Collection: General stock.
# of Vols: 2,500
Hours: Tue-Sun 10-4.
Travel: On Hwy 377. Downtown, on the square.
Owner: Mary Downs
Year Estab: 1981

Highlands

Bev's Books   **Open Shop**
509 North Main Street   77562   713-426-5233

Collection: General stock mostly paperback.
# of Vols: 20,000
Hours: Tue-Fri 12-7. Sat 10-6.

Hillsboro
(Map 35, page 354)

The Book Cellar   **Antique Mall**
At Franklin Street Antique Mall   (817) 582-9740
55 West Franklin   76645

Collection: Specialty
Specialties: History; Texas.
Hours: Mon-Sat 10-5. Sun 1-5.

Hillsboro Antique Mall   **Antique Mall**
114 South Waco Street   76645   (817) 582-8330

Hours: Mon-Sat 10-5. Sun 1-5.
Travel: Exit 368A off I-35.
Comments: If you like antique malls, there are lots more in Hillsboro.

Houston

A Book Buyers Shop
1305 South Shepherd   77019

Open Shop
(713) 529-1059
Fax: (713) 529-5769

Collection:	General stock.
# of Vols:	22,000
Specialties:	Texas; Civil War; chess; religion.
Hours:	Mon-Sat 10-6. Sun 12-6.
Services:	Appraisals, catalog.
Travel:	Shepherd/Greenbriar exit off Hwy 59. Proceed north on Shepherd. Shop is on the right in a stand alone building.
Credit Cards:	Yes
Owner:	Christine Doby
Year Estab:	1975
Comments:	A bi-level shop with a very nice selection of books, most in good condition. While most subjects were represented, we observed a particularly strong history section. We saw lots of first editions, vintage items, some oddities and some antiquarian items. As is always the case, with turnover, one never knows what you'll find but we think this is a shop worth visiting.

Accents, Etc.
At Trademart Antique Mall
2121 Sam Houston Tollway North
Mailing address: 5434 Coral Ridge Road Houston 77069

Antique Mall
(713) 465-8971

Collection:	Specialty
# of Vols:	3,000
Specialties:	Fine bindings published before 1900.
Hours:	Fri-Sun 10-6.
Travel:	See O/P Book Store below.
Owner:	Ben Phillips
Comments:	Additional books may be viewed by appointment.

Affordable Books
7999 Hansen, #328   77061

By Appointment
(713) 944-4006
Fax: (713) 944-4006

Collection:	General stock of paperback and hardcover.
# of Vols:	50,000
Services:	Appraisals, search service, accepts want lists, catalog.
Credit Cards:	Yes
Owner:	Bob Thiery
Year Estab:	1982
Comments:	Stock is approximately 65% paperback.

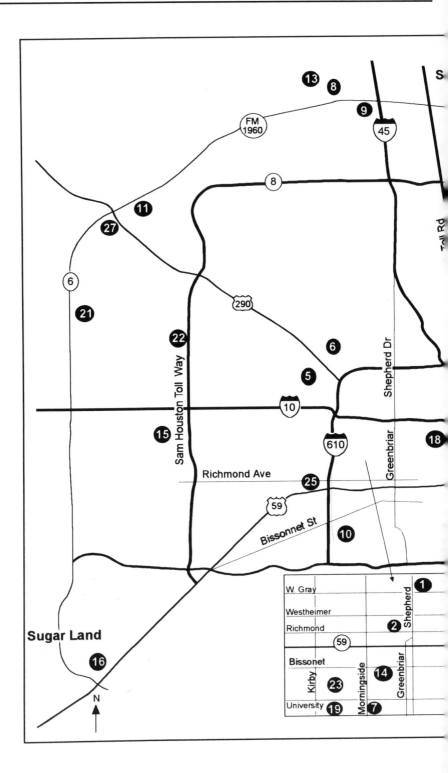

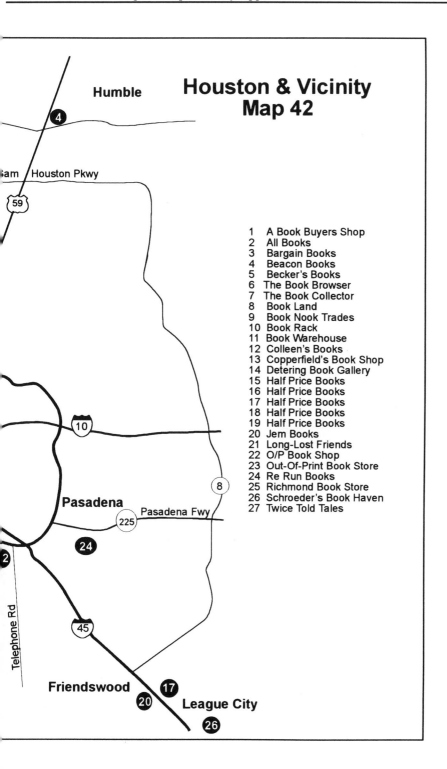

Humble

Houston & Vicinity
Map 42

Sam Houston Pkwy

59

1 A Book Buyers Shop
2 All Books
3 Bargain Books
4 Beacon Books
5 Becker's Books
6 The Book Browser
7 The Book Collector
8 Book Land
9 Book Nook Trades
10 Book Rack
11 Book Warehouse
12 Colleen's Books
13 Copperfield's Book Shop
14 Detering Book Gallery
15 Half Price Books
16 Half Price Books
17 Half Price Books
18 Half Price Books
19 Half Price Books
20 Jem Books
21 Long-Lost Friends
22 O/P Book Shop
23 Out-Of-Print Book Store
24 Re Run Books
25 Richmond Book Store
26 Schroeder's Book Haven
27 Twice Told Tales

10

8

Pasadena

225 Pasadena Fwy

24

2

Telephone Rd

45

Friendswood

17

20 League City

26

(Houston)

All Books   **Open Shop**
2126 Richmond   77098   (713) 522-6722

Collection:	General stock.
# of Vols:	20,000
Specialties:	Mushrooms and fungi; natural history; children's; art; history; modern fiction.
Hours:	Mon 11-4. Tue-Sat 11-6.
Services:	Accepts want lists, mail order.
Travel:	Shepherd/Greenbriar exit off Hwy 59. Proceed north on Shepherd, then left on Richmond. Shop is just ahead on right.
Credit Cards:	Yes
Owner:	Van & Susan Metzler
Year Estab:	1988
Comments:	A small but quality shop with books that have been well cared for. In addition to a section of classical fiction, another of mainstream fiction and a healthy selection of history titles, we spotted several items of scholarly interest. If you're looking for cookbooks or light paperback reading, this shop may not be your cup of tea.

Armchair Adventures   **By Appointment**
7230 Redding   77036   (713) 988-2515
                                                            Fax: (713) 270-8919

Collection:	General stock.
# of Vols:	25,000
Specialties:	Hunting; guns; military; mountaineering; fishing; architecture; natural history.
Credit Cards:	No
Owner:	Ralph Hutzler

Becker's Books   **Open Shop**
7405 Westview   77055   Fax: (713) 465-3037   (713) 957-8088
                                            E-mail: msmilagro@aol.com

Collection:	General stock of mostly hardcover and ephemera.
# of Vols:	60,000
Specialties:	Texas; biography; history.
Hours:	Daily 11-7.
Services:	Search service, accepts want lists.
Travel:	Wirt Rd exit off I-10. Proceed north on Wirt then right on Westview. Shop is about three blocks ahead on right in a former private home.
Credit Cards:	Yes
Owner:	Dan & Ann Becker
Year Estab:	1994
Comments:	Two stand alone buildings (one behind the other) house an interesting collection of hardcover and paperback books as well as a collection of ephemera. Plenty of nooks and crannies where long lost treasures may be

hidden. Unless your schedule is very tight, a stop here should be most rewarding, particularly for nostalgia buffs. We saw lots of material on Texas, as well as a number of bound leather sets. This is the kind of place you will either like very much or want to get out of quickly. We liked it.

The Book Browser   **Open Shop**
5608 Pinemont   77092   (713) 680-1870

Collection:	General stock of paperback and hardcover.
# of Vols:	50,000 (hardcover); 100,000 (paperback)
Specialties:	Mystery; science fiction; cookbooks.
Hours:	Tue-Sun 10-6, except Fri till 2am.
Services:	Appraisals, search service, accepts want lists, mail order, catalog in planning stage.
Travel:	Antoine exit off Hwy 290. Proceed north on Antoine, then right on Pinemont. Shop is just ahead.
Credit Cards:	Yes
Owner:	Russell Law
Year Estab:	1978
Comments:	A large store with a large selection of paperbacks (including some vintage titles) as well as comics. If you walk around the shop, however, you'll find a number of bookcases and alcoves devoted to hardcover titles in most fields of interest. The books we saw were of mixed vintage and in mixed condition and the selection was reasonable enough (depending on the tightness of your schedule) to consider a visit. The shop also carries some ephemera and collectibles.

The Book Collector   **Open Shop**
2347 University Boulevard   77005   (713) 661-2665
                                                               Fax: (713) 661-2697

Collection:	General stock.
# of Vols:	38,000
Specialties:	Fine bindings; first editions; children's; Napoleon; Civil War.
Hours:	Mon-Sat 10-6. Sun 12-5.
Services:	Appraisals, search service, accepts want lists, mail order.
Travel:	In Rice University village at corner of Morningside.
Credit Cards:	Yes
Owner:	James & Carol Taylor
Year Estab:	1989
Comments:	You don't have to be an Anglophile to enjoy a visit to this shop-although it certainly would help. The owner is pleased to report that through his contacts in Great Britain, he is able to acquire almost any book of interest that comes from that part of the world and his shop certainly has that flavor. The shop also offers miniature soldiers and other *object d'art* designed to "create a mood." In addition to first editions and British literature and history, the shop also carries, if you're willing to squeeze into narrow aisles and around display tables, a more general collection. Prices reflect the shop's ambience.

(Houston)

Book Nook Trades   **Open Shop**
221-D FM 1960 West   77090   (281) 587-0873

Collection:	General stock of paperback and hardcover.
# of Vols:	40,000-50,000
Hours:	Mon-Sat 10-7.
Travel:	FM 1960 exit off I-45. Shop is at southwest corner of FM 1960 and I-45 in Cypress Station Shopping Center.
Credit Cards:	No
Owner:	Virginia L. Perryman
Year Estab:	1993
Comments:	A nice neighborhood shop that offers the community a mostly paperback collection and some hardcover items, mostly of recent vintage. Lots of children's items.

Book Rack   **Open Shop**
4024 Bellaire   77025   (713) 666-9511

Collection:	General stock of paperback and hardcover.
# of Vols:	5,000 (hardcover)
Hours:	Tue Sat 10-7. Sun 1-7.
Travel:	Bellaire exit off I-610. Proceed east on Bellaire for one mile. Shop is in shopping center at northwest corner of Bellaire and Wesleyan.

The Book Scene   **Open Shop**
2202 Ella Boulevard   77008   (713) 869-6117

Collection:	General stock of mostly paperback.
# of Vols:	20,000
Hours:	Tue-Sat 11-6.

Book Warehouse   **Open Shop**
8825 Solon, Ste E-1   77064   (281) 469-5879

Collection:	General stock of hardcover and paperback.
# of Vols:	150,000
Hours:	Mon-Sat 10-7. Sun 12-5.
Services:	Appraisals, accepts want lists, mail order.
Travel:	FM 1960 exit off Hwy 290. Proceed west on FM 1960 for about 4½ miles, then right on Solon. Shop is at end of street.
Credit Cards:	Yes
Owner:	Pat Garrett
Year Estab:	1990
Comments:	While the shop calls itself a warehouse, it's physical appearance and setting is not as stark as the name implies. The bi-level shop contains a mix of paperbacks, mostly on the first floor, and mixed vintage hardcover items in generally good condition on the upper level. Although we saw a few titles that might fall into the collectible category, and that were priced quite reasonably, we suspect that most of the shop's business comes from the first floor.

Colleen's Books   **Open Shop**
6880-C Telephone   77061   (713) 641-1753

Collection:	General stock and ephemera.
# of Vols:	100,000
Specialties:	Texas
Hours:	Mon-Wed & Fri & Sat 10-4.
Services:	Appraisals, search service, catalog, accepts want lists.
Travel:	Airport Blvd exit off I-45. Proceed west on Airport to Telephone Rd, then right on Telephone. Shop is two blocks ahead on left.
Credit Cards:	Yes
Owner:	Colleen Urbanek
Year Estab:	1971
Comments:	Now that I've made my purchases, I don't mind if the rest of the world discovers this shop. One can find best sellers and recent books almost anywhere (and this shop has its fair share). But, this shop is particularly strong in vintage titles in almost every field—and the prices are right. The shop is well labeled and the owner has a delicious sense of humor. P.S. Try to arrive during the owner's anniversary month and enjoy a discount based on the number of years she's been in business (25 years and 25% off when we visited).

Detering Book Gallery   **Open Shop**
2311 Bissonnet   77005   Fax: (713) 529-0309   (713) 526-6974
E-mail: dbg@hti.net

Collection:	General stock.
Specialties:	Fine bindings; press books; modern first editions; sets; illustrated; fine printing.
Hours:	Daily 10-6.
Services:	Search service, catalog, accepts want lists.
Travel:	Shepherd/Greenbriar exit off Hwy 59. Proceed south on Greenbrier to Bissonnet, then right on Bissonnet.
Credit Cards:	Yes
Owner:	Herman E. Detering III
Year Estab:	1976
Comments:	The decision to call this bi-level establishment a "gallery" is, we believe, most appropriate for the shop does have a kind of museum-like quality. The books we saw were almost universally in very fine condition and beautifully displayed. The rare book area on the second floor displayed first editions, leather bound sets, etc. If you truly love books and enjoy seeing and purchasing quality books, you'll want to visit here.

K.L. Givens Books   **Antique Mall**
At Heirlooms Etc. Antique Mall   Mall: (281) 496-1926
1706 Highway 6 South   77077   Home: (281) 531-0686

Collection:	General stock.
# of Vols:	700

(Houston)

Specialties:	Children's; fine bindings; illustrated.
Hours:	Mon-Sat 10-6. Sun 12-5.
Travel:	Hwy 6 exit off I-10. Proceed south on Hwy 6. Shop is on west side of street just past Briarforest.

Half Price Books, Records, Magazines   **Open Shop**
11920 Westheimer   77077   (281) 558-4968

Collection:	General stock of hardcover, paperback and remainders.
Hours:	Mon-Sat 9am-10pm. Sun 9am-8pm.
Travel:	Dairy Ashford exit off I-10. Proceed south on Dairy Ashford to Westheimer, then east on Westheimer to Kirkwood. Shop is in Kirkwood Westheimer Shopping Center.

Half Price Books, Records, Magazines   **Open Shop**
18111 Egret Bay Boulevard   77058   (281) 335-1283

Collection:	General stock of hardcover, paperback and remainders.
Hours:	Mon-Fri 7:30am-10pm. Sat 9am-10pm. Sun 10am-8pm.
Travel:	NASA Rd exit off I-45. Proceed east on NASA Rd for about one mile to Egret Bay Blvd. Right on Egret Bay. Shop is on the left.

Half Price Books, Records, Magazines   **Open Shop**
2537 University Boulevard   77005   (713) 524-6635

Collection:	General stock of hardcover, paperback and remainders.
Hours:	Mon-Sat 9am-10pm. Sun 9am-8pm.
Travel:	Kirby exit off Hwy 59S. Proceed south on Kirby. Left at fifth light onto University. Shop is just ahead on right.

Half Price Books, Records, Magazines   **Open Shop**
2410 Waugh Drive   77006   (713) 520-1084

Collection:	General stock of hardcover, paperback and remainders.
Hours:	Mon-Sat 10-9. Sun 10-8.
Travel:	Allen Pkwy exit off Hwy 45. Proceed on Allen to Studemont/Montrose. Left on Studemont/Montrose, then right on Hyde Park. Shop is at intersection of Hyde and Waugh.

Long-Lost Friends   **Open Shop**
4934 Highway 6 North   77084   (281) 859-4788
                                                            Fax: (281) 859-7806

Collection:	General stock of paperback and hardcover.
# of Vols:	50,000
Specialties:	Children's; science fiction.
Hours:	Mon-Sat 10-6, except Wed till 8. Sun 12-6.
Services:	Search service, accepts want lists, mail order.
Travel:	East side of Hwy 6, four miles north of I-10 in Bear Creek Square Shopping Center.

Credit Cards:	Yes
Owner:	Tom White
Year Estab:	1992
Comments:	We had mixed feelings about this shop. In one sense, we observed a larger number of paperbacks than hardcover books. On the other hand, we recognized that among the hardcover selections (the largest proportion of which were of fairly recent vintage) there were some "oldies but goodies" including a dozen or so mysteries (which we assume were purchased from the same source) by William Le Queux, an author not commonly seen and desirable to collectors of vintage mysteries. Apparently, the owner had the same observation for those books, as well as other similarly collectible titles, were priced accordingly.

Mc Laren Books   **By Appointment**
10935 Creektree   77070   (281) 469-1484

Collection:	General stock and ephemera.
Specialties:	Texas; Western Americana.
Services:	Catalog, accepts want lists.
Credit Cards:	No
Owner:	G. Alan Mc Laren
Year Estab:	1975

Mordida Books   **By Appointment**
PO Box 79322   77279   (713) 467-4280
         Fax: (713) 467-4182

Collection:	Specialty
# of Vols:	12,000
Specialties:	Mystery; spy; first editions.
Services:	Appraisals, search service, catalog, accepts want lists.
Credit Cards:	Yes
Owner:	Dick Wilson
Year Estab:	1987

Murder By The Book   **Open Shop**
2342 Bissonnet   77005   (713) 524-8597

Collection:	Specialty new and used hardcover and paperback.
# of Vols:	10,000 (used)
Specialties:	Mystery
Hours:	Mon-Sat 10-6. Sun 12-5.
Services:	Appraisals, search service, accepts want lists, mail order.
Travel:	Kirby exit off Hwy 59. Proceed south on Kirby to Bissonnet, then left on Bissonnet.
Credit Cards:	Yes
Owner:	Martha Farrington
Year Estab:	1980
Comments:	Stock is approximately 50% used, 50% of which is hardcover.

(Houston)

O/P Book Shop   **Open Shop**
At Trademart Antique Mall   (713) 973-8006
2121 Sam Houston Tollway North   77043

Collection:	General stock.
# of Vols:	5,000
Specialties:	Oz; children's.
Hours:	Fri-Sun 10-6.
Travel:	From Hwy 10, exit at Beltway 8, then Hammerly exit off Beltway. Do turnaround and look for antique mall.
Credit Cards:	Yes
Owner:	Jim Ryberg
Year Estab:	1976

Out-Of-Print Book Store   **Open Shop**
2450 Times Boulevard   77005   (713) 526-8616

Collection:	General stock.
# of Vols:	5,000-10,000
Specialties:	Oz; Texas; children's series.
Hours:	Mon-Sat 10-6.
Travel:	Kirby exit off Hwy 59. South on Kirby, left on Times Blvd.
Credit Cards:	Yes
Owner:	Jim Ryberg
Year Estab:	1976

Paperback Trader   **Open Shop**
10904 Scarsdale Boulevard, #270   77089   (281) 481-3425

Collection:	General stock of mostly paperback.
# of Vols:	70,000
Hours:	Mon-Fri 11-7. Sat 12-6.

Paperbacks Etc   **Open Shop**
3210 South Shepherd Drive   77098   (713) 521-1020

Collection:	General stock of mostly paperback.
# of Vols:	25,000
Hours:	Mon-Sat 11-5:30.

Richmond Book Store   **Open Shop**
6423 Richmond Avenue   77057   (713) 952-5845
                                                                              Fax: (713) 952-5845

Collection:	General stock of paperback and hardcover.
# of Vols:	62,000
Specialties:	Texas; Civil War; military; religion; new age; history; magazines.
Hours:	Mon-Sat 11-7. Sun 11-5.
Services:	Search service, accepts want lists, mail order.

Travel:	Hillcroft exit off Hwy 59. Proceed north on Hillcroft to Richmond then right on Richmond. Shop is in a small shopping center.
Credit Cards:	Yes
Owner:	Conrad "Pat" Harness
Year Estab:	1990
Comments:	The shop offers a healthy supply paperbacks, magazines (e.g., *National Geographic* and *Playboy*) and far fewer hardcover items. The hardcover titles we did see represented a mix of recent publications and older volumes, most of which appeared to be reading copies. While we did see some interesting titles, with the exception of the specialties listed above, there was little consistency in terms of numbers.

Third Planet   **Open Shop**
2718 SW Freeway   77098   Fax: (713) 528-1067   (713) 528-1067
                                                    E-mail: 3planet@third-planet.com

Collection:	Specialty used and new.
# of Vols:	10,000 (used)
Specialties:	Science fiction; fantasy; horror; mystery.
Hours:	Mon-Wed & Sat 10-7. Thu & Fri 10-8. Sun 12-6.
Services:	Appraisals, accepts want lists, mail order.
Travel:	Kirby exit off Hwy 59. Shop is on the north side of the freeway, on the feeder road.
Credit Cards:	Yes
Year Estab:	1976
Comments:	Approximately 90% of the used stock is paperback. The hardcover used books are mostly first editions.

Twice Told Tales   **Open Shop**
8648 Highway 6 North   77095   (281) 463-4961
                                                    E-mail: twictold@interloc.com

Collection:	General stock of paperback and hardcover.
# of Vols:	75,000+
Hours:	Tue-Sun 10-6.
Services:	Search service, accepts want lists.
Travel:	Located on east side of Hwy 6, one mile south of Hwy 290, between Huffmeister and West.
Credit Cards:	Yes
Owner:	Karen Comeau, Georgann Francis, Christine Kovach
Year Estab:	1985
Comments:	A nice sized shop with a large selection of paperbacks and a reasonable selection of hardcover volumes (in some cases intershelved with paperbacks). The hardcover volumes we saw represented both older and more recent titles. Most were in good condition and were reasonably priced. A careful perusal of the shelves also revealed a fair share of collectibles.

Humble
(Map 42, page 378)

Beacon Books   **Open Shop**
1315 East 1st Street, #E   77338   (281) 446-9663

Collection:	General stock of paperback and hardcover and sheet music.
# of Vols:	20,000+
Specialties:	Religion (Christianity); history; home schooling; engineering; children's.
Hours:	Tue-Sat 10-6.
Services:	Accepts want lists, mail order.
Travel:	Humble/FM 1960 exit off Hwy 59. Proceed east on 1st St for about 1½ miles. Turn left into Artesian Plaza, a small shopping area.
Credit Cards:	Yes
Owner:	John & Fran Morris
Year Estab:	1992
Comments:	A small shop with a mix of paperback and hardcover volumes and an emphasis on the specialties listed above. However, other subjects are represented, particularly mystery and general fiction. The books were in mixed condition and of mixed vintage. Many book club editions and reading copies.

Ye Olde Book & Gift Shoppe   **Open Shop**
407 East Main Street   77338   (281) 446-0564

Collection:	General stock of mostly paperback.
# of Vols:	90,000
Hours:	Mon-Sat 9:30-5.

Hurst
(Map 40, page 375)

Book Trader   **Open Shop**
181C Hurstview Drive   76054   (817) 581-8899

Collection:	General stock of paperback and hardcover.
Hours:	Mon-Thu 9-7. Fri & Sat 9-6.
Services:	Search service, accepts want lists, mail order.
Travel:	Norwood exit off Hwy 183. Proceed north on Norwood, then west on Harwood and north on Hurstview. Shop is in small strip center on left.
Credit Cards:	No
Owner:	Marie Trichka
Comments:	Stock is approximately 75% paperback.

Irving
(Map 40, page 375)

Half Price Books, Records, Magazines   **Open Shop**
3913 West Airport Freeway, #104   75062   (972) 659-0634

Collection:	General stock of hardcover, paperback and remainders.

Hours:	Mon-Thu 9:30-9:30. Fri & Sat 9:30am-10pm. Sun 12-7.
Travel:	Irving/183 exit off I-35. Proceed west, then take Beltline North exit and stay on service road. Store is between Beltline and Esters Rd.

ProTech   **Open Shop**
4030 Belt Line Road   75038   (972) 258-8324

Collection:	Specialty. Mostly new and limited used.
Specialties:	Computers; mathematics; engineering; science.
Hours:	Mon-Sat 9-9. Sun 12-6.

Jacksonville

Little White Barn   **Open Shop**
223 North Bolton Street   75766   (903) 586-1091

Collection:	General stock of mostly paperback.
# of Vols:	80,000
Hours:	Wed-Sat 9-5, except till 3 on Sat.

Katy

Katy Budget Books   **Open Shop**
2347 Fry Road   77449   (281) 578-7770

Collection:	General stock of mostly used paperback.
# of Vols:	100,000
Hours:	Mon-Fri 9-7. Sat 10-8. Sun 12-5.

Kaufman

Lone Star Autographs   **By Appointment**
PO Box 500   75142   (972) 932-6050
                                 Fax: (972) 932-7742

Collection:	Specialty
Specialties:	Autographs; signed books (especially of presidents and first ladies).
Owner:	Larry Vnzalik & Michael Minor
Year Estab:	1982

Kileen

Book Exchange   **Open Shop**
106A East Beeline Lane   76548   (817) 690-2443

Collection:	General stock of mostly paperback.
Hours:	Mon-Sat 10:30-6:30.

La Marque

Books & Treasures   **Open Shop**
1101 Bayou Road   77568   (409) 935-7200

Collection:	General stock of mostly paperback.

# of Vols:	50,000
Hours:	Mon-Sat 10-5:30.

La Porte

Peggy's Book Shop   **Open Shop**
9635 Spencer Highway   77571   (281) 478-4848

Collection:	General stock of mostly used paperback.
# of Vols:	50,000-60,000
Hours:	Mon-Sat 10-8.

Lancaster
(Map 40, page 375)

Book Shelf   **Open Shop**
306 West Pleasant Run Road   75146   (972) 227-1461

Collection:	General stock of mostly paperback.
# of Vols:	30,000
Hours:	Mon-Sat 10:30-5:30.

Justin Books   **By Appointment**
286 Creekwood Drive   75146   (972) 227-3523
                                                    Fax: (972) 218-5878
                                            E-mail: justinbk@interloc.com

Collection:	General stock.
# of Vols:	10,000
Specialties:	Children's series; signed; modern first editions; mystery; Texas; genealogy; business; *Gone With The Wind*; cookbooks; southern literature.
Services:	Appraisals, search service, accepts want lists, mail order.
Credit Cards:	Yes
Owner:	Bonnie Justin
Year Estab:	1972

Laredo

Traveller Books   **By Appointment**
PO Box 970   78040   (210) 722-6762
                                                    Fax: (210) 726-8335

Collection:	Specialty books and ephemera.
# of Vols:	2,000+
Specialties:	Confederacy; Texas; Virginia; autographs.
Services:	Search service, catalog, accepts want lists.
Credit Cards:	No
Owner:	John & Cecilia Keck
Year Estab:	1984

League City
(Map 42, page 378)

Schroeder's Book Haven
104 Michigan Avenue   77573

Open Shop
(281) 332-5226
Fax: (281) 332-1695
E-mail: schroedr@interloc.com

Collection:	General stock of mostly used books and ephemera.
# of Vols:	25,000
Specialties:	Texas; Western Americana.
Hours:	Tue-Sat 10-6, except Thu 12-8.
Services:	Search service, catalog, accept want lists.
Travel:	FM 518 exit off I-45. Proceed east on FM 518 for about two miles. After crossing railroad tracks, take second left. Shop is on corner of FM 518 and Michigan.
Credit Cards:	Yes
Owner:	Faye Schroeder, Owner. Bert Schroeder, Manager
Year Estab:	1967
Comments:	An attractive shop with a combination of used and new books and with a strong bent towards Texana. Unfortunately, most subject areas were limited in terms of volume. Fortunately, intershelved with most books were a few finer older editions which could prove of interest to the visiting bibliophile.

Lewisville

Paperback Trader
1112 West Main   75067

Open Shop
(972) 219-8400

Collection:	General stock of mostly paperback.
Hours:	Mon-Fri 10-6, except Thu till 8. Sat 10-5. Sun 12-4.

Longview
(Map 36, page 398)

Bookmark
1905 West Loop 281   75604

Open Shop
(903) 297-5800

Collection:	General stock mostly used paperback and hardcover.
# of Vols:	20,000
Hours:	Mon-Sat 9:30-5.
Travel:	In Park Place Shopping Center.
Credit Cards:	Yes
Owner:	Julie Foreman
Year Estab:	1991
Comments:	Stock is approximately 80% used, 65% of which is paperback.

Lubbock
(Map 37, page 343)

Book Alley   **Open Shop**
3424 34th Street   79410   (806) 795-8744

Collection: General stock of hardcover and paperback.
# of Vols: 50,000
Hours: Mon-Sat 12-5:45. Sun 1-5.
Travel: 34th St exit off I-27. Proceed west on 34th.
Comments: One of the challenges involved in attempting to visit open shops in a
                  state as large as Texas is working out a feasible itinerary for a day's
                  worth of book hunting. Unfortunately, this establishment had a noon
                  opening, which, because of our travel schedule, forced us to bypass
                  Lubbock. The next time we visit Texas we'll try to correct this over-
                  sight. Suffice to say that the information provided above comes from
                  the shop's owner.

Lu's Book Stop   **Open Shop**
2425 34th Street   79411   (806) 797-6994

Collection: General stock of mostly paperback.
# of Vols: 60,000
Hours: Mon-Sat 11-6.

Lukfin
(Map 36, page 398)

A First Edition Bookshop   **Open Shop**
117 Cotton Square   75904   (409) 639-1187

Collection: General stock of mostly used hardcover and paperback.
# of Vols: 5,000+
Hours: Mon-Sat 10-6.
Services: Search service, accepts want lists, mail order.
Travel: Downtown, across from the library.
Credit Cards: Yes
Owner: Terry Todd & Mark Hopson
Year Estab: 1994
Comments: We're not certain whether or not it's a good idea for a used book store to be
                  located across from a large public library; we suppose that the local read-
                  ing public will have to make that choice. At the time of our visit, the shop
                  had a mix of paperback and hardcover items, including a number of older
                  volumes which were popular in their time, as well as the usual classics, a
                  selection of book club editions, science fiction, etc. We regret to advise
                  that if you're on the main highway, veering from it to visit here may not
                  bring you the satisfaction you might hope for.

Read Books
511 South Timberland Drive   75901

Open Shop
(409) 639-9686

Collection:	General stock mostly used paperback and new.
# of Vols:	10,000 (used)
Hours:	Mon-Sat 10-6.

Marble Falls
(Map 35, page 354)

Bargain Books
1612B North Highway 281   78654

Open Shop
(210) 693-5628

Collection:	General stock of paperback and hardcover.
# of Vols:	45,000
Hours:	Mon-Sat 10-5:30.
Travel:	On Hwy 281.
Credit Cards:	No
Owner:	Mac McLeod
Year Estab:	1995
Comments:	Stock is approximately 65% paperback.

Crandall's Corner
700 4th Street Village   78654

Open Shop
(210) 693-8426

Collection:	General stock of paperback and hardcover.
# of Vols:	15,000
Hours:	Mon-Fri 9-5. Sat 9-12.
Travel:	4th St exit off Hwy 281. Proceed east on 4th.
Credit Cards:	Yes
Owner:	Bill & Cindy Prather
Year Estab:	1979
Comments:	Stock is approximately 80% paperback.

McKinney

Commons Book Store
317 North Tennessee Street   75069

Open Shop
(972) 542-2219

Collection:	General stock of mostly paperback.
# of Vols:	30,000
Hours:	Mon-Thu 11-5. Fri 12-5.

Mesquite
(Map 40, page 375)

Half Price Books, Records, Magazines
1645 Town East Boulevard, #584   75150

Open Shop
(972) 686-0233

Collection:	General stock of hardcover, paperback and remainders.
Hours:	Mon-Sat 9:30am-10pm. Sun 12-7.

Travel:	Town East Blvd exit off Hwy 635. Proceed east on Town East to Emporium East Blvd. Shop is on the left in Market East Shopping Center.

Paperbacks Plus   **Open Shop**
108 East Davis Street   75149   (972)285-8661
E-mail: luckydog@dal.cleaf.com

Collection:	General stock of hardcover and paperback, CD's, records and comics.
# of Vols:	50,000+
Hours:	Mon-Sat 9-9. Sun 11-7.
Services:	Accepts want lists and requests, preferably using form on web page: http://www.cleaf.com/~luckydog.
Travel:	Galloway exit off Hwy 80. Proceed south on Galloway to Davis. Shop is at corner. From I-35, Military Pkwy exit. Proceed east on Military which becomes Davis.
Credit Cards:	Yes
Owner:	John & Marquetta Tilton
Comments:	See comments for Dallas store.

Midland
(Map 37, page 343)

Miz B's Used Books   **Open Shop**
2505 West Ohio   79701   (915) 682-5618

Collection:	General stock of paperback and hardcover.
# of Vols:	400,000
Hours:	Mon-Fri 9:30-6. Sat 10-5:30.
Services:	Accepts want lists, mail order.
Travel:	Midkiff Ave exit off I-20. Proceed north on Midkiff to Ohio, the east on Ohio.
Credit Cards:	Yes
Owner:	Sherry Dummer
Year Estab:	1971
Comments:	A fairly large shop with a substantial collection of paperbacks. The shop does offer some hardcover volumes, however, and in some sections they are labeled and sorted. In other areas, though, the hardcover books are mixed to the point where it becomes fascinating to wonder how they happened to arrive on a particular shelf. Actually, we saw several titles that would certainly fit the "collectible" category. The good news is that they were priced quite reasonably. The bad news is that many of them were not in the best condition.

Words & Music   **Open Shop**
At Tradearama   (915) 684-8129
617 East Illinois   79701

Collection:	General stock of hardcover and paperback.
# of Vols:	15,000
Hours:	Wed-Sat 9-5.

Travel:	LaMesa Rd exit off I-20. Proceed north on LaMesa to Front St, then left on Illinois. Shop is two blocks ahead in rear of the Tradearama building.
Credit Cards:	No
Year Estab:	1984
Comments:	Located in a rear corner of a flea market building, this shop offers paperbacks, a generous supply of Reader's Digest Condensed Books, some videos and a few thousand hardcover volumes in mixed condition, of mixed vintage and of very mixed interest levels (but not ours).

Yesterday's News Antiques   **Open Shop**
3712-C West Wall Street   79703   (915) 689-6373

Collection:	General stock.
# of Vols:	200-500
Hours:	Mon-Sat 11-6.
Travel:	On Business Loop 80.
Owner:	Tina M. Howard
Year Estab:	1993
Comments:	Primarily an antiques shop with a small used book section.

Miles

Dark Destiny Books   **Open Shop**
101 North Robinson Street   76861   Fax: (915) 468-6703   (915) 468-3381
E-mail: darkdestny@aol.com

Collection:	Specialty new and used paperback and hardcover.
# of Vols:	2,000+
Specialties:	Horror, including British horror and Texas horror; Texas mystery authors; magazines.
Hours:	Mon-Sat 10-6. Sun 1-6.
Services:	Appraisals, search service, catalog, accepts want lists.
Travel:	From San Angelo, proceed north on Hwy 67, then left on Robinson (at yellow caution light).
Credit Cards:	No
Owner:	Jeff McGuire
Year Estab:	1991
Comments:	Stock is approximately 40% used, 40% of which is hardcover.

Mineola
(Map 36, page 398)

Books Etc   **Open Shop**
103 South Johnson Street   75773   (903) 569-2828

Collection:	General stock mostly used hardcover and paperback.
# of Vols:	200,000
Hours:	Tue-Sat 9-5.
Travel:	Tyler exit off I-20. Proceed north on Hwy 69 to Mineola.

Credit Cards:	No
Year Estab:	1990
Comments:	Unfortunately, on both our outbound and return trip through Texas we found ourselves in east Texas on the two days this shop is normally closed. We're advised by the owner that the stock is about evenly mixed between hardcover and paperback. If, unlike us, your schedule brings you to Mineola on the right day of the week and you get to visit this shop, let us know what you found.

Nacogdoches
(Map 36, page 398)

A Novel Idea Bookstore   **Open Shop**
4201 North Street   75961   (409) 569-2116

Collection:	General stock of mostly paperback.
# of Vols:	28,000
Hours:	Mon- Fri 10-6. Sat 10-4.

View From Orbit Books & Computers   **Open Shop**
905 East Main Street   75961   Fax: (409) 569-0992   (409) 564-5818
E-mail: jomayhar@postoffice.tcac.com

Collection:	General stock of paperback and hardcover.
# of Vols:	50,000+
Hours:	Mon-Fri 8:30-5. Sat 8:30-4.
Services:	Accepts want lists.
Travel:	From Hwy 59 in downtown Nacogdoches, proceed east on Hwy 21. Shop is located at corner of Hwy 21 (East Main) & University Dr.
Credit Cards:	Yes
Owner:	Joe & Ardath Mayhar
Year Estab:	1984
Comments:	A combination used book dealer and computer service center (one can rent computers and printer time here as well as learn basic computer skills.) Based on that information, we thought we would see a modern (or at least a well organized) book dealer. Instead, what we saw were lots of paperbacks (some on shelves and some on the floor) and a mixed collection of hardcover books, many with common titles and the one or two by desirable authors in less than the best condition and, we think, overpriced.

Nederland
(Map 36, page 398)

Betty's Books   **Open Shop**
2111 Nederland Avenue   77627   (409) 724-7202

Collection:	General stock of paperback and hardcover.
# of Vols:	30,000
Hours:	Tue-Sat 10-5:30.

Year Estab: 1986
Comments: Stock is approximately 60% paperback.

New Braunfels

Prime Source Open Shop
1661 South Seguin Avenue   78130 (210) 625-6981

Collection: General stock of mostly paperback.
Hours: Fri-Sun 10-6.

Odessa
(Map 37, page 343)

Double Read Open Shop
4233 North Dixie Boulevard   79762 (915) 363-0621

Collection: General stock of mostly paperback.
# of Vols: 35,000
Hours: Mon-Sat 10-6.

Heavenly Treasures Open Shop
1123 East 42nd Street   79762 (915) 367-3636

Collection: Specialty new and used hardcover and paperback.
# of Vols: 500+ (used)
Specialties: Religion (Christian).
Hours: Mon-Sat 10-6.
Travel: John Ben Shepherd Pkwy exit of I-20. Proceed north on John Ben Shepherd to 42nd St, then west on 42nd St.
Credit Cards: Yes
Owner: Keith & Kelli Eddings
Year Estab: 1993

Ye Old Bookworm Open Shop
517 North Grant Avenue   79761 (800) 239-2908 (915) 333-9913
E-mail: bookworm@interloc.com

Collection: General stock of paperback and hardcover.
# of Vols: 70,000+
Hours: Mon-Sat 9:30-5:30. Other times by appointment.
Services: Search service, catalog, accepts want lists.
Travel: Exit 116 off I-20. Proceed north on Hwy 385 for 1.7 miles to downtown.
Credit Cards: Yes
Owner: Dorthy Bennett
Year Estab: 1991
Comments: A very neat little shop run by a charming couple, which, we are sure, serves its community quite well. In addition to a large number of paperbacks, hardcover fiction titles are displayed on the upper shelves in the front of the shop while most of the non fiction hardcover items are in a separate room to the rear of the shop. While we were unable to spot any truly rare items here, your eyes may be sharper than ours.

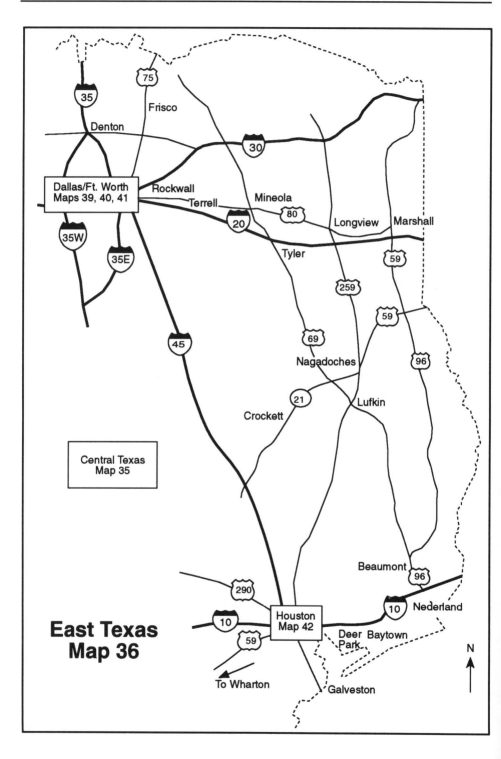

Frisco

Denton

Dallas/Ft. Worth
Maps 39, 40, 41   Rockwall

Terrell   Mineola

Longview   Marshall

Tyler

Nagadoches

Crockett   Lufkin

Central Texas
Map 35

Beaumont

290

Houston
Map 42   Nederland

East Texas
Map 36   Deer Baytown
                    Park

To Wharton   Galveston

N

Paris

Books Galore and More
1505 20th NE   75460

Collection:	General stock of mostly paperback.
# of Vols:	30,000
Hours:	Mon-Sat 10-5.

Pasadena
(Map 42, page 378)

Re Run Books
115 West Southmore Avenue   77502

Collection:	General stock of paperback and hardcover.
# of Vols:	65,000+
Specialties:	Military; Texas; children's; modern first editions; religion.
Hours:	Daily 9-6:30.
Travel:	Shaver/Main exit off Hwy 225 (Pasadena Fwy). Proceed south on Shaver for about one mile then right on Southmore. Shop is just ahead on left.
Credit Cards:	Yes
Owner:	Jack Sherrell
Year Estab:	1987
Comments:	A fair sized shop with a balance of hardcover and paperback items. For a change, we didn't see the familiar pattern of hardcover and paperback books displayed in different parts of the shop. While most of the hardcover items we saw appeared to be reading copies of fairly recent publications, we did spot a fair number of more vintage items, in addition to some first editions. We even made a purchase.

Plano

Bookcase
1301 Custer Road, Ste. 243   75075

Collection:	General stock of mostly paperback.
Hours:	Mon-Fri 10-6. Sat 10-5.

Richardson
(Map 40, page 375)

Book Tree
702 University Village   75081

Collection:	General stock of paperback and hardcover.
# of Vols:	20,000
Specialties:	Mystery
Hours:	Mon-Sat 10-6. Sun 11-5.

Travel:	Two miles east of North Central Expy on Beltline Rd at Plano Rd. Shop is on left, in Tom Thumb Shopping Center.
Credit Cards:	Yes
Owner:	Barry & Terry Phillips
Year Estab:	1987
Comments:	While not huge in size, the shop does carry a very nice selection of quality hardcover books and is particularly strong in its specialty with nice vintage editions as well as more modern titles. We spotted several rare items, some behind glass. A comfortable store to visit and most reasonably priced.

Half Price Books, Records, Magazines   **Open Shop**
2100 Alamo Road   75080   (972) 234-4286

Collection:	General stock of hardcover, paperback and remainders.
Hours:	Mon-Sat 9:30am-10pm. Sun 11-8.
Travel:	Campbell Rd exit off I-75. Store is on northwest corner of Central and Campbell.

Rockwall
(Map 36, page 398)

Roma's Preread Books   **Open Shop**
555 East I-30   75087   (972) 771-6344

Collection:	General stock of used and new paperback and hardcover.
# of Vols:	10,000 (used)
Hours:	Mon-Thu 10-7. Fri & Sat 10-8.
Travel:	At intersection of I-30 and Hwy 740.
Owner:	Roma Faith
Comments:	Stock is approximately 75% used, 75% of which is paperback.

Round Rock
(Map 35, page 354)

Book Shop   **Open Shop**
2120 North Mays   78664   (512) 244-9193

Collection:	General stock of new and used paperback and hardcover.
# of Vols:	10,000 (used)
Hours:	Mon-Thu 10-6. Fri & Sat 10-8. Sun 12-5.
Travel:	Exit 254 off I-35. Proceed on access road to Rock Creek Shopping Center.
Credit Cards:	Yes
Owner:	Bob & Mark Shirey
Year Estab:	1989
Comments:	Used stock is approximately 75% paperback.

Salado
(Map 35, page 354)

Fletcher's Books   **Open Shop**
Corner of Main Street & Salado Plaza   76571   (817) 947-5414
Mailing address: PO Box 65 Salado 76571

Collection:	General stock used hardcover and new.
# of Vols:	20,000 (used)
Specialties:	Texas
Hours:	Daily 8:30-6:30.
Services:	Search service, accepts want lists.
Travel:	Salado exit off I-35. Shop is just off exit.
Credit Cards:	Yes
Owner:	Tyler Fletcher
Year Estab:	1926

San Angelo
(Map 37, page 343)

The Book Porch   **Open Shop**
4129 Ben Ficklin Road   76903   (915) 659-8600

Collection:	General stock of hardcover and paperback.
# of Vols:	5,000
Specialties:	Texas; Western Americana; magazines (western, treasure and Civil War).
Hours:	Wed-Sat 11-6. Other times by appointment.
Services:	Search service, catalog, accepts want lists.
Travel:	Ben Ficklin Rd exit off Hwy 87. Proceed west on Ben Ficklin.
Credit Cards:	No
Owner:	Felton Cochran
Year Estab:	1995
Comments:	Located in a private residence, the collection here is modest in size but well representative of Texas history (particularly in terms of magazines). Other subjects are on hand but not in depth. The books we saw were quite reasonably priced.

Cottage Book Shoppe   **Open Shop**
1705-07 West Beauregard Avenue   76901   (915) 653-6244

Collection:	General stock of paperback and hardcover.
# of Vols:	10,000+
Hours:	Mon-Sat 10:30-6.
Credit Cards:	No
Owner:	Virginia Hall
Year Estab:	1990
Comments:	We arrived at this shop at 12:30pm, having been previously advised that the shop opened at 10:30. What we found was a closed shop and an intriguing series of signs on the window: one sign announced a 10:30

opening, another read, "Open Come In" and a third gave the shop's hours as: "Open 12:30-6." Since we decided not to wait (who knows what time the shop would eventually open), all we could do was look through the front window which was decorated profusely with an assortment of dolls and stuffed animals (the owner also owns an adjoining neddlecraft shop, also closed at the time of our visit.) The store appeared to be fairly large and certainly has a selection of hardcover books, not merely along the side walls but also in the center of the shop. Sorry we can't be more helpful. Perhaps one of our readers can provide us with additional information that we can include in a future Supplement.

Ye Ole Fantastique Book Shoppe   **Open Shop**
1218 West Beauregard   76901   (915) 653-1031

Collection:	General stock of hardcover and paperback.
# of Vols:	70,000
Specialties:	Texas; religion; World War I & II.
Hours:	Mon-Sat 10-6.
Services:	Appraisals
Travel:	Beauregard exit off Hwy 87 (Bryant Blvd). Proceed west on Beauregard.
Credit Cards:	No
Owner:	Charles Hall
Year Estab:	1968
Comments:	Not much to see from the outside and you may even be turned off by the sign on the door that reads, "No one under 18 allowed without parents." However, this is a legitimate used book shop that offers, in addition to a substantial supply of paperbacks, a large number of hardcover volumes in mixed condition and displayed in a maze of room after room after room. While we saw many reading copies and books that were not in the best condition, we also spotted some interesting historical volumes that could be just what some university library or scholar has been looking for. Unfortunately, the shop is not well organized and browsers will need a sharp eye to spot titles in the subject areas they're looking for.

San Antonio

All Points of View   **By Appointment**
PO Box 321   78292   (210) 732-6660

Collection:	Specialty new and used.
# of Vols:	5,000-10,000
Specialties:	Sociology; Marxism; black studies.
Services:	Accepts want lists, occasional catalog.
Credit Cards:	No
Owner:	John W. Stanford
Year Estab:	1960's
Comments:	Stock is approximately 30% used.

Antiquarian Book Mart   **Open Shop**
3127 Broadway   78209   (210) 828-4885
                                                              (210) 828-7433

Collection:	General stock of hardcover and paperback.
# of Vols:	300,000
Hours:	Mon-Sat 10-6.
Services:	Appraisals
Travel:	Mulberry Ave exit off Hwy 281. Proceed west on Mulberry to Broadway then left (north) on Broadway for two blocks. Shop is on left. Parking is available in rear.
Credit Cards:	Yes
Owner:	Dr. Frank Kellel, Jr., owner. Robert F. & Keven L Kellel, managers
Year Estab:	1967
Comments:	While the shop does carry paperbacks, its main thrust is hardcover books in most subject areas, with an emphasis on religion and children's. The books we saw were in generally good condition and ranged from early titles to some more recent volumes. We were impressed by the range and scope of many of the titles, more than a few not frequently seen. Considering the shop's location immediately adjacent to one used store, a few blocks away from another and immediately in front of the Antiquarian Book Mart Annex that offers quality titles (see below) we believe a stop here is well worth your investment in time.

Antiquarian Book Mart Annex   **Open Shop**
3132 Avenue B   78209   (210) 828-7433

Collection:	General stock.
# of Vols:	30,000+
Specialties:	Literature; humanities; fine press; Americana; military; Texas; Southwest Americana.
Hours:	Fri & Sat 12-4. Other times by appointment.
Services:	Appraisals
Travel:	See above. Shop is located in a stand alone building in the rear parking lot of the Antiquarian Book Mart.
Credit Cards:	Yes
Owner:	Dr. Frank Kellel, Jr.
Year Estab:	1967
Comments:	While this shop was technically closed at the time of our visit, the owner's son, who manages the adjoining book store, was kind enough to allow us to visit. Traveling book people who identify themselves and would like to visit this shop during "off" hours may be equally privileged. The books here reflect the owner's careful effort to carry quality titles, particularly in the specialties listed above. Each of the shop's four rooms was nicely labeled and easy to browse and the books were reasonably priced. If your interests fall into any of the categories listed above, you're more than likely to leave this shop with a smile on your face. A "New Arrivals" section is located on the second floor.

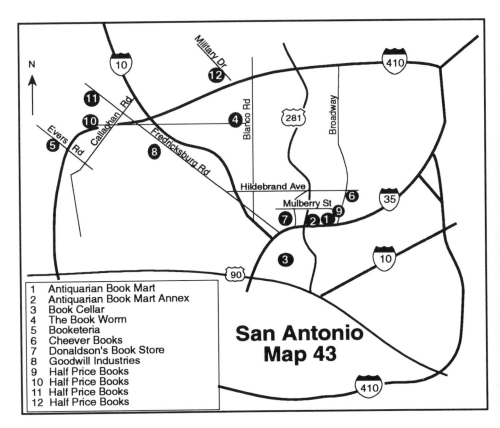

1   Antiquarian Book Mart
2   Antiquarian Book Mart Annex
3   Book Cellar
4   The Book Worm
5   Booketeria
6   Cheever Books
7   Donaldson's Book Store
8   Goodwill Industries
9   Half Price Books
10 Half Price Books
11 Half Price Books
12 Half Price Books

San Antonio Map 43

Book Cellar
210 West Market Street   78205

Open Shop
(210) 227-9519

Collection:	General stock of paperback and hardcover.
# of Vols:	100,000
Hours:	Tue-Sat 11-3.
Travel:	Downtown, at corner of Presa and Market in basement of Hertzberg Circus Museum.
Comments:	Operated by Friends of the Library. All books are donated.

Book Den
449 McCarty   78216

Open Shop
(210) 525-8033

Collection:	General stock of mostly paperback.
# of Vols:	10,000
Hours:	Mon-Sat 9:30-6.

Book Exchange
6025 Tezel Road, #104   78250

Open Shop
(210) 680-4552

Collection:	General stock of mostly paperback.
Hours:	Mon-Sat 10-6.

Book Peddler
5528 Walzem Road   78218

Open Shop
(210) 656-0839

Collection:	General stock of mostly paperback.
# of Vols:	25,000
Hours:	Tue-Sat 9:30-5.

The Book Worm
4707 Blanco Road   78212

Open Shop
(210) 342-4258

Collection:	General stock of hardcover and paperback.
# of Vols:	150,000
Specialties:	Cookbooks; art; military; mystery; children's; nature.
Hours:	Mon-Sat 10-5:30.
Services:	Appraisals, search service, accepts want lists, mail order.
Travel:	Blanco Rd exit off 410 loop. Proceed south on Blanco. Shop is on the right in a small strip center.
Credit Cards:	No
Owner:	Patricia Corn & Sharon Atchley
Year Estab:	1979
Comments:	A good sized shop with a mix of paperback and hardcover titles. Mostly reading copies in mixed condition. Of the specialties listed above, we felt that the shop was particularly strong in vintage hardcover mysteries (the numbers were solid and selection wide.)

Booketeria
5530 Evers Road   78238

Open Shop
(210) 680-8555

Collection:	General stock of hardcover and paperback.
# of Vols:	35,000
Specialties:	Military; Texas; cookbooks.
Hours:	Tue-Sat 9:30-5:30.
Services:	Accepts want lists, mail order.
Travel:	Evers Rd exit off Loop 410. Proceed west on Evers for 1/4 mile. Shop is on left in Crestview Plaza, a small strip center.
Credit Cards:	Yes
Owner:	Paul Harwell
Year Estab:	1977
Comments:	A modest collection with a balance between paperback and hardcover titles. The store is larger than initially appears with a back room devoted exclusively to hardcover books. The books we saw were of mixed vintage and in mixed condition with the specialties listed above well represented. Other areas were represented in less depth.

Cheever Books
140 Carnahan Street   78209

Open Shop
(210) 824-2665

Collection:	General stock of hardcover and paperback.
# of Vols:	50,000
Specialties:	Texas; regional history; Western Americana; history.

(San Antonio)

Hours:	Mon-Sat 10-8. Sun 12-8.
Services:	Search service, accepts want lists.
Travel:	Hildebrand exit off Hwy 281. Proceed east on Hildebrand to Broadway, right on Broadway and left on Carnahan. Shop is across from the Witte Museum behind a fast food outlet.
Credit Cards:	Yes
Owner:	Cece Cheever, owner. John Peace, manager.
Year Estab:	1986
Comments:	An easy to overlook shop (because of its location immediately behind a fast food restaurant) which, in our view, should not be overlooked. In addition to paperbacks, the shop has a nice selection of hardcover volumes in many subject areas, particularly in the specialties listed above. One can meander through several small rooms and in each one locate books of interest. The volumes that we saw were in generally good condition.

Donaldson's Book Store   Open Shop
2421 North St. Mary's Street   78212   210-732-0496

Collection:	General stock of hardcover and paperback.
# of Vols:	250,000
Specialties:	Texana, Western Americana; Civil War; World War II.
Hours:	Tue-Sat 9-3.
Travel:	St. Mary's St exit off Hwy 281. Proceed south on St. Marys to Ashby.
Comments:	Stock is evenly divided between hardcover and paperback.

Goodwill Industries   Open Shop
3401 Fredericksburg Road   78201   (210) 736-1373

Collection:	General stock of hardcover and paperback.
Hours:	Mon-Sat 10-9. Sun 12-6.

The Great Exchange   Open Shop
4137 Naco Perrin, #2   78217   (210) 656-8891

Collection:	General stock of mostly paperback used and new.
# of Vols:	75,000+
Hours:	Mon-Fri 10-6, except Thu till 7. Sat 10-5. (Same for all stores)
Travel:	Perrin Beitel exit off Loop 410. Proceed north on Perrin Beitel for about 2½ miles. After main post office, turn west on Naco Perrin.
Credit Cards:	Yes
Owner:	Yolanda Grau & Marilyn McKenzie
Year Estab:	1979
Comments:	We visited the flagship shop in this six store chain (all located in San Antonio) and found it to be overwhelmingly stocked with paperbacks and hardcover books, most commonly seen elsewhere, accounting for perhaps 10% of the titles. The shop itself was spacious and easy to browse. Since the chain's other locations (see below) are substantially smaller, you can judge for yourself the wisdom of visiting any of them.

Other Great Exchange Locations

1242 Austin Highway	(210) 822-8128
15062 San Pedro	(210) 490-9698
8454 Fredericksburg	(210) 615-0257
8407 Bandera Road	(210) 543-0870
6900 San Pedro	(210) 824-8181

Half Price Books, Records, Magazines   **Open Shop**
3207 Broadway   78209   (210) 822-4597

Collection: General stock of hardcover, paperback and remainders.
Hours: Mon-Sat 9:30-9. Sun 12-8.
Travel: Mulberry exit off Hwy 281. Proceed east on Mulberry to Broadway, then turn left on Broadway. Parking is available in rear.

Half Price Books, Records, Magazines   **Open Shop**
4919 Northwest Loop 410   78229   (210) 647-1103

Collection: General stock of hardcover, paperback and remainders.
Hours: Mon-Sat 9:30am-9pm. Sun 12-8.
Travel: Summit Pkwy exit off Loop 410. Proceed north on Summit Pkwy for about 1/2 mile. Shop is in Loehmann's Village shopping center.

Half Price Books, Records, Magazines   **Open Shop**
2106 Northwest Military Highway   78213   (210) 349-1429

Collection: General stock of hardcover, paperback and remainders.
Hours: Mon-Sat 9:30-9. Sun 11-8.
Travel: Castle Hills exit off Loop 410. Stay to right at fork on NW Military Hwy. Shop is 1/4 mile ahead on left just before West Ave.

Half Price Books, Records, Magazines   **Open Shop**
7959 Fredericksburg Road, #137   78229   (210 692-8868

Collection: General stock of hardcover, paperback and remainders.
Hours: Mon-Sat 9:30-9. Sun 12-8.
Travel: Fredericksburg exit off Loop 410. Proceed north on Fredericksburg to Medical Dr. Shop is in the Oak Hills Shopping Center.

JJ's Book Store   **Open Shop**
6924 Military Drive West   78227   (210) 674-0910

Collection: General stock of mostly paperback.
Hours: Mon 10-6. Tue-Sat 10-7.

San Marcos
(Map 35, page 354)

Tangram Bookstore   **Open Shop**
316 North LBJ Drive   78666   (512) 392-0002

Collection: General stock of paperback and hardcover.
# of Vols: 6,000

Hours:	Mon-Fri 8:30-5. Sat 9-5.
Credit Cards:	No
Comments:	Stock is approximately 75% paperback.

Sherman

Book Rack   **Open Shop**
220 Sunset Boulevard, Ste C6   75092   (903) 893-7372

| *Collection:* | General stock mostly paperback used and some new books. |
| *Hours:* | Mon-Sat 9:30-5:30. |

Spring
(Map 42, page 378)

Bargain Books   **Open Shop**
22776 Cypresswood Drive   77373   Fax: (281) 821-1790   (281) 821-8336
                                              E-mail: trader_ed@i-link.net

Collection:	General stock of paperback and hardcover.
# of Vols:	6,000 (hardcover)
Specialties:	Science fiction; fantasy.
Hours:	Mon-Sat 11-7. After hours and Sun by appointment.
Travel:	From either Hwy 59 or I-45, exit at FM 1960, then from FM 1960, turn north on Cypresswood. Shop is two miles north in a shopping center.
Credit Cards:	No
Owner:	Ed Currie
Year Estab:	1989
Comments:	Stock is approximately 80% paperback.

Book Land   **Open Shop**
7135 Louetta, Ste U   77379   (281) 376-4058

Collection:	General stock of paperback and hardcover.
# of Vols:	100,000
Specialties:	History; Texas; science fiction.
Hours:	Mon-Sat 10-7. Sun 12-6.
Services:	Appraisals, search service, accepts want lists, mail order.
Travel:	Louetta exit off I-45. Proceed west on Louetta for about 4½ miles. Shop is in a small strip center set back from the street and behind two fast food shops.
Credit Cards:	Yes
Year Estab:	1994
Comments:	Wanna buy books cheap? On the day we visited this shop, the owner was offering books for 2/99¢, 3/99¢ or 5/99¢ depending upon which outside rack the books were displayed on. Inside, the store is dominated by paperbacks with a number of alcoves displaying hardcover books, most of which were of fairly recent vintage and in reasonably good condition.

Copperfield's Book Shop **Open Shop**
8220 Louetta Road   77379 (281) 376-7323

Collection:	General stock mostly used paperback and hardcover.
# of Vols:	30,000+
Hours:	Mon-Sat 10-9. Sun 1-6.
Travel:	FM 1960 exit off I-290. Proceed north on FM 1960 to Champion Forest Drive. Left on Champion, then right on Louetta.
Credit Cards:	Yes
Owner:	Paul Schamerhorn
Year Estab:	1992
Comments:	Clean, neat, nicely carpeted and easy to browse. The shop offers a mix of new and used paperbacks and hardcover titles, mostly intershelved. Few volumes (at least as far as we could see) that would fall into the truly rare or collectible category, although this observation obviously depends on the owner's periodic purchases and could change by the time of your visit.

Sugar Land
(Map 42, page 378)

Half Price Books, Records, Magazines **Open Shop**
3203 Highway 6 South   77478 (281) 265-0900

Collection:	General stock of hardcover, paperback and remainders.
Hours:	Mon-Sat 10-10. Sun 10-8.
Travel:	One mile south of intersection of Hwy 59 & Hwy 6. Take Hwy 6 to Williams Trace Blvd. Shop is in High and Square Shopping Center.

Sulphur Springs

Vivian's Main Street Book Shop **Open Shop**
230 Main Street   75482 (903) 885-2665

Collection:	General stock of mostly paperback.
# of Vols:	40,000

Taft
(Map 35, page 354)

Collectors Market **Open Shop**
113 Green Avenue   78390 (512) 528-3353

Collection:	General stock of hardcover and paperback and ephemera,
# of Vols:	20,000
Hours:	Thu-Sun 10-6.
Travel:	In downtown.
Services:	Accepts want lists.
Credit Cards:	Yes
Owner:	Ken Kruse
Year Estab:	1977
Comments:	Stock is evenly divided between hardcover and paperback.

Temple
(Map 35, page 354)

Book Cellar   **Open Shop**
3 West Central   76501   (817) 773-7545

Collection: General stock of paperback and hardcover.
# of Vols: 35,000
Specialties: Texas
Hours: Mon-Sat 9:30-5.
Travel: Central exit off I-35. Proceed east on Central to Main. Look for stair-
                   way at corner of Central and Main. Shop is below street level.
Credit Cards: Yes
Owner: Bob Jones
Year Estab: 1980
Comments: At least half or more of the stock on display is paperback. At the time
                   of our visit, the hardcover stock was strong in mystery, science fiction
                   and Texas while other areas offered a hit or miss selection of titles that
                   ranged from book club editions to a three volume set of the papers of
                   Woodrow Wilson. This is one of those shops that may not immediately
                   impress but could have just the item you want, though not necessarily
                   in the best of condition.

Terrell
(Map 36, page 398)

Books and Crannies   **Open Shop**
305 West Moore Avenue   75160   (972) 563-5481

Collection: General stock of mostly used paperback and hardcover.
Hours: Tue-Fri 10-5:30. Sat 10-4.
Travel: In downtown.
Comments: Stock is approximately 80% used, 75% of which is paperback.

Tomball

The Bookmart   **Open Shop**
28105 Tomball Parkway, #105   77375   (281) 351-0255

Collection: General stock of mostly paperback.
# of Vols: 10,000
Hours: Tue-Sat 10-6.

Tyler
(Map 36, page 398)

The Book Inn   **Open Shop**
520-A East Front Street   75702   (903) 593-6391

Collection: General stock of mostly used paperback.
Hours: Mon-Sat 9-5.

Hurley's Books   **Open Shop**
107 South Bonner   75702   (903) 592-9038

Collection:	General stock of mostly paperback.
# of Vols:	30,000
Hours:	Mon-Fri 9:30-5. Sat 9:30-3.

Pea Picker Book Store   **Open Shop**
2803 University Boulevard   75701   (903) 566-9014

Collection:	General stock of mostly paperback.
Hours:	Mon-Sat 9:30-5:30.

Timeless Books & Music   **Open Shop**
4129 South Broadway Avenue   75701   (903) 509-2007

Collection:	General stock of paperback and hardcover and records.
# of Vols:	50,000
Hours:	Mon-Sat 10-7.
Travel:	Tyler (Hwy 69) exit off I-20. Proceed south on Hwy 69 into Tyler. Hwy 69 becomes Broadway in downtown. Shop is about four miles after downtown square.
Credit Cards:	Yes
Owner:	Gary Pendley
Year Estab:	1995
Comments:	Stock is approximately 75% paperback.

Trudy's Fireside Books   **Open Shop**
117 East 8th Street   75701   (903) 593-3611

Collection:	General stock of mostly new books and some used.
# of Vols:	15,000
Hours:	Mon-Fri 9:30-7. Sat 9:30-5:30. Sun 1-6.

Universal City

B & M Book Store   **Open Shop**
115 East Wright Boulevard   78148   (210) 658-0811

Collection:	General stock of mostly paperback.
# of Vols:	20,000
Hours:	Mon-Sat 10-6.

Victoria

Maranatha Book Store   **Open Shop**
5003J John Stockbauer Drive   77904   (512) 572-0600

Collection:	General stock of mostly paperback.
# of Vols:	20,000
Hours:	Mon-Sat 10-6.

Waco
(Map 35, page 354)

Bankston's Used Books   **Open Shop**
1321 South Valley Mills Drive   76711   (817) 755-0070

Collection:	General stock of paperback and hardcover.
# of Vols:	1,000
Hours:	Mon-Sat 10:30-6.
Comments:	Stock is approximately 60% paperback. The shop is primarily a collectibles shop.

Gladys' Book Store   **Open Shop**
710 Austin Avenue   76701   (817) 754-7868
                                                            Texas only: (800) 467-7868

Collection:	General stock of hardcover and paperback, magazines and remainders.
# of Vols:	1 million
Hours:	Mon-Fri 10-5. Sat 10-3.
Travel:	4th St exit off I-35. Proceed west on 4th St, then left on Austin.
Credit Cards:	No
Owner:	Gladys Strakos
Year Estab:	1983
Comments:	The owner, a most pleasant lady, indicates that her shop holds one million volumes. Who are we to take exception to that estimate (though we would hardly be that optimistic.) If you're interested in older LPs, you might find some winners here. In terms of the book population, though, there are lots and lots and lots of paperbacks. With regard to the hardcover items, the number of volumes on hand is certainly respectable enough, but their condition, for the most part, can best be described as "old, used and worn." This does not mean that a sharp scout couldn't locate a title or two of value, but unless you fall into that category, in our judgment, you're more likely to find better pickings elsewhere.

Golden's Book Exchange   **Open Shop**
3112 Franklin Avenue   76710   (817) 754-5729

Collection:	General stock of mostly paperback.
Hours:	Mon-Sat 10-6. Sun 1:30-4:30.

Waxahachie
(Map 35, page 354)

The Lancaster Bookie   **Flea Market**
At Waxahachie Flea Market   Market: (972) 937-4277
FM Road 877   Home: (972) 227-1020
Mailing address: 539 Willow Wood Lancaster 75134

Collection:	General stock and ephemera.
# of Vols:	5,000

Hours:	Fri 4-9. Sat 10-9, Sun 10-6.
Services:	Appraisals, search service, accepts want lists, mail order.
Travel:	Exit 399A off I-35E. Proceed east on Rogers which becomes FM 877. Shop is in a flea market with permanent buildings.
Credit Cards:	No
Owner:	June Eddy
Year Estab:	1981

The Wright Collection   **By Appointment**
333 Harbin Street   75165   (972) 937-6502

Collection:	Specialty
Specialties:	Texas; Western Americana; Civil War; Mexico; mystery.
Services:	Catalog, accepts want lists.
Credit Cards:	No
Owner:	Hugh & Linda Wright
Year Estab:	1945

Wharton
(Map 36, page 398)

Friends of the Library Used Bookstore   **Open Shop**
117 South Fulton Street, Ste. 3   77488   (409) 532-4757

Collection:	General stock of paperback and hardcover.
# of Vols:	5,000-10,000
Hours:	Mon, Wed, Fri 10-2.
Travel:	At junction of Hwy 60 and Fulton St, just east of Wharton County Courthouse.

Wichita Falls
(Map 35, page 354)

Bookseller   **Open Shop**
1800 Kemp Boulevard   76309   (817) 761-4170

Collection:	General stock of mostly paperback used and new.
# of Vols:	50,000
Hours:	Mon-Sat 10-6.

Cosmic Squire Books, Records & Magazines   **Open Shop**
1519 Monroe Street   76309   (817) 322-0684

Collection:	General stock of mostly used hardcover and paperback.
# of Vols:	15,000
Specialties:	Texas; Southwest Americana; biography; music; literature.
Hours:	Mon-Sat 11-5:30. Sun by chance.
Services:	Mail order.
Travel:	Hwy 82 (Kell Blvd) exit off Hwy 281, then right on Monroe.
Credit Cards:	No

Owner: Lorraine M. McGuire
Year Estab: 1979
Comments: Located on the same street as several antique shops, one might almost associate the contents of this shop with its neighboring establishments in that its inventory is a mix of older paperbacks, hardcover volumes, reference books, magazines (lots and lots of back issues), etc. While most categories are represented, few are represented in depth.

Wimberley

Paperback Swap Shop   **Open Shop**
In Wimberley North Too Plaza   78676   (512) 847-5370
Mailing address: PO Box 1179 Wimberley 78676

Collection: General stock of mostly paperback.
Hours: Tue-Fri 10-5. Sat 10-3.

If we get rid of the piano, we'll have room for more books.

A Tale of Two Sisters (817) 540-3075
2509 Stone Hollow Drive Bedford 76021

Collection:	Specialty
# of Vols:	3,000
Specialties:	Modern first editions.
Services:	Accept want lists, catalog.
Credit Cards:	No
Owner:	Cathy Koebernick & Charlene Coffield
Year Estab:	1995

Alcott Books (713) 774-2202
5909 Darnell Houston 77074 Fax: (713) 774-2202

Collection:	Specialty
# of Vols:	4,000
Specialties:	Modern first editions; signed books; mystery; illustrated children's.
Services:	Appraisals, search service, accepts want lists, mail catalog.
Credit Cards:	No
Year Estab:	1987

Bay Tree Books Book Search Service (281) 286-4538
PO Box 890782 Houston 77289

Collection:	Specialty
# of Vols:	2,000
Specialties:	Space; anthropology.
Services:	Search service.
Credit Cards:	No
Owner:	Adelaide Socki
Year Estab:	1991

Carroll Burcham Booksellers (806) 799-0419
5546 17th Place Lubbock 79416 E-mail: burcham@interloc.com

Collection:	General stock.
# of Vols:	6,000
Specialties:	Americana, especially Texas and the West.
Services:	Search service, accepts want lists.
Credit Cards:	No
Owner:	Carroll & Nancy Burcham
Year Estab:	1991

Carousel Booksellers (903) 597-9202
2920 Fry Avenue Tyler 75701

Collection:	Specialty books and ephemera.
# of Vols:	1,000
Specialties:	Modern art and architecture; avant garde periodicals, books with original prints; prints and print makers.
Services:	Search service, catalog, accepts want lists.
Credit Cards:	No

Owner: Mike A. Hatchell
Year Estab: 1982

Adrian Crane   (972) 235-4444
8111 LBJ Freeway, Ste 1265 Dallas 75251   Fax: (972) 235-4454

Collection: Specialty
# of Vols: 1,000
Specialties: Reptiles and amphibians.
Services: Accepts want lists.
Credit Cards: No
Year Estab: 1991

Dovel O P Book Sales   (281) 334-1451
2210 Crossbrook Street League City 77573   Fax: (281) 480-2599

Collection: General stock and ephemera.
Services: Search service, accepts want lists.
Credit Cards: No
Owner: Sam Dovel
Year Estab: 1995

Early West   (409) 693-0808
PO Box 9292 College Station 77842

Collection: Specialty new and used.
# of Vols: 3,000 (used)
Specialties: Western Americana.
Services: Search service, accepts want lists, catalog.
Credit Cards: Yes
Owner: Jim & Theresa Earle
Year Estab: 1965

Elm Tree Books   (281) 497-7535
PO Box 79183 Houston 77279   E-mail: gwill@accesscomm.com

Collection: General stock.
# of Vols: 6,000
Services: Appraisals, search service, accepts want lists, occasional lists.
Credit Cards: No
Owner: George Williford
Year Estab: 1988

Finders Keepers Out Of Print Book Search   (409) 283-2643
PO Box 2189 Woodville 75979   Fax: (409) 283-3386
                                               E-mail: findkeep@interloc.com

Collection: General stock.
# of Vols   2,500
Services: Appraisals, search service (for libraries, schools and businesses only),
                  catalog, accepts want lists.
Credit Cards: No

Owner:	Judi Fouts Patrick
Year Estab:	1983

James Fowler Books (281) 444-4289
PO Box 73153 Houston 77273

Collection:	Specialty
# of Vols:	1,500-2,000
Specialties:	Aviation
Services:	Search service, accepts want lists.
Credit Cards:	No
Year Estab:	1992

G.N. Gabbard Books (903) 628-2788
602 Cannon New Boston 75570

Collection:	Specialty paperback and hardcover.
# of Vols:	3,000
Specialties:	Fantasy; science fiction; mystery; occult; scholarly.
Services:	Accepts want lists.
Credit Cards:	No
Year Estab:	1980

Geographic Enterprises (972) 289-7107
PO Box 850246 Mesquite 75185 Fax: (972) 329-7921

Collection:	Specialty
Specialties:	National Geographics.
Services:	Catalog, search service, accepts want lists.
Credit Cards:	No
Owner:	Lew Begley
Year Estab:	1964

Kenston Rare Books (214) 526-7033
PO Box 12374 Dallas 75225

Collection:	Specialty
# of Vols:	5,000
Specialties:	Texas; Western Americana.
Services:	Appraisals, search service, catalog, accepts want lists.
Credit Cards:	No
Owner:	Ken Huddleston
Year Estab:	1991

Library Books (972) 690-6949
PO Box 7240 Dallas 75209 Fax: (972) 479-1038

Collection:	Specialty
# of Vols:	35,000
Specialties:	Modern literary firsts; contemporary drama; periodicals (pre-1950); reference; newspapers (19th & 20th centuries); sports newspapers.
Services:	Search service, catalog, accepts want lists.

Credit Cards: Yes
Owner: Cameron Northouse
Year Estab: 1976

W. M. Morrison - Books   (512) 266-3381
15801 La Hacienda Austin 78734

Collection: Specialty books and ephemera.
# of Vols: 3,000
Specialties: Texas; Western Americana; reference.
Services: Appraisals, catalog.
Credit Cards: No
Owner: Richard & Shelly Morrison
Year Estab: 1951

George Owen Books   (214) 956-8280
PO Box 226901 Dallas 7522   Fax: (214) 956-8280

Collection: General stock.
# of Vols: 100,000
Specialties: Western Americana; Texas.
Services: Appraisals, search service, accepts want lists, lists.
Credit Cards: No
Year Estab: 1980

Albert L. Peters Bookseller   (817) 236-1141
PO Box 136814 Fort Worth 76136

Collection: Specialty
# of Vols: 3,000
Specialties: Americana, with emphasis on Western and Southwest Americana.
Services: Catalog, accepts want lists.
Credit Cards: No
Year Estab: 1977

G. Jay Rausch, Bookseller   (512) 949-1071
14225 SPID, Suite 10-B Corpus Christi 78418

Collection: General stock.
# of Vols: 12,000
Specialties: Scholarly
Credit Cards: Yes
Owner: G.J. & Sally Rausch
Year Estab: 1980.
Comments: Sells only to libraries.

Research Periodicals & Book Services   (281) 556-0061
PO Box 720728 Houston 77272   Fax: (281) 779-2992
                                                  E-mail: rpbs@rpbs.com

Collection: Specialty
Specialties: Periodicals (back issues of scholarly journals).

Services: Occasional catalog.
Owner: Jay Sullivan
Year Estab: 1985

Martin S. Rook, Bookseller (512) 447-9974
3402A Dolphin Drive Austin 78704 E-mail: rookbook@ix.netcom.com

Collection: General stock.
# of Vols: 5,000
Specialties: Music (classical); nautical; railroads.
Services: Search service, accepts want lists.
Credit Cards: No
Year Estab: 1995

Sacred And The Profane (281) 255-8767
PO Box 1360 Tomball 77377 E-mail: profane@cruzio.com

Collection: Specialty
# of Vols: 5,000+
Specialties: Gay and lesbian; counter culture (1960's and 1970's).
Services: Search service, accepts want lists.
Owner: Susan Fox
Year Estab: 1987

Michael S. Seiferth (210) 824-4136
106 Hiler Road San Antonio 78209 Fax: (210) 824-1564
E-mail: mseifert@texas.net

Collection: General stock.
# of Vols: 15,000
Specialties: 17th & 18th century literature and history; Oriental rugs; books on books.
Services: Appraisals, search service, accepts want lists, on-line catalog.
Credit Cards: No
Year Estab: 1972

Southern Majesty Books (512) 991-9150
6402 Meadow Circle Corpus Christi 78413

Collection: Specialty
# of Vols: 5,000+
Specialties: Southern women; modern first editions.
Services: Search service, catalog, accepts want lists.
Credit Cards: No
Owner: Mary Rose S. Hedberg-Butler
Year Estab: 1986

Tenderfoot Books (214) 942-0909
1674 Kessler Canyon Drive Dallas 75208

Collection: Specialty
# of Vols: 3,000
Specialties: Civil War; Texas.

Services: Catalog, accepts want lists.
Credit Cards: No
Owner: Clay Garrison
Year Estab: 1986.

Trackside Books   (713) 772-8107
8819 Mobud Drive Houston 77036   Fax: (713) 772-1850
                                   E-mail: trakside@interloc.com

Collection: Specialty. Mostly used and some new.
# of Vols: 10,000
Specialties: Railroads
Services: Appraisals, search service, accepts want lists, catalog.
Credit Cards: No
Owner: Larry Madole
Year Estab: 1964

Van Siclen Books   (210) 349-7913
111 Winnetka Road San Antonio 78229

Collection: Specialty new and used.
# of Vols: 500+ (used)
Specialties: Ancient Egypt.
Services: Appraisals, accepts want lists, occasional catalog.
Credit Cards: No
Owner: Charles Van Siclen
Year Estab: 1981

Wanabee Books   (281) 556-1142
3927 Summit Valley Houston 77082

Collection: Specialty
# of Vols: 2,000
Specialties: Cookbooks (pre 1940).
Services: Appraisals, accepts want lists, catalog in planning stage.
Credit Cards: No
Owner: Dorothy Adams
Year Estab: 1994

Utah

Alphabetical Listing By Dealer

Alphabetical Listing By Location

American Fork

J.L. Green
PO Box 174   84003

By Appointment
(801) 756-6717

Collection:	Specialty
# of Vols:	5,000
Specialties:	History; Western Americana.
Credit Cards:	No
Year Estab:	1966

Bountiful

Bountiful Paperback Exchange
2 North Main Street   84010

Open Shop
(801) 292-2818

Collection:	General stock of mostly paperback.
# of Vols:	600-1,000 (hardcover)
Hours:	Tue-Sat 11-5:30, except Wed & Thu till 8.
Travel:	5th South exit off I-15. Proceed east on 5th South for three lights, then left on Main. Shop is five blocks ahead.
Comments:	Used hardcover is primarily non fiction and fiction classics.

Cedar City

Book Den
58 North Main Street   84720

Open Shop
801-586-8303

Collection:	General stock of mostly paperback.
Hours:	Summer: Mon-Sat 10-6. Winter: Mon-Sat 11-6.

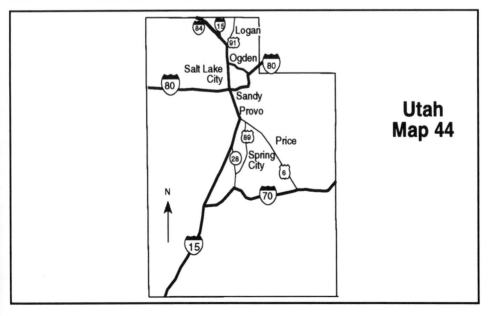

Logan

Books of Yesterday   **Open Shop**
27 North Main Street   84321   (801) 753-3838

Collection: General stock of hardcover and paperback.
Specialties: 35,000-40,000.
Hours: Mon-Thu 11-7. Fri 11-9. Sat 10-5.
Services: Search service, accepts want lists, mail order.
Travel: Hwy 89/91 exit off I-15. Hwy 89/91 becomes Main St.
Credit Cards: Yes
Owner: Sue P. Rakes
Year Estab: 1975
Comments: We drove quite a distance to reach this community and found a shop
                     with a collection of paperbacks and hardcover books, some of which
                     were labeled "collectible," and magazines. We have no doubt that the
                     shop serves the reading needs of its community quite well. There may
                     even have been some collectible or antiquarian items that we failed to
                     see (although we did spot a two volume set of the recollections of John
                     Sherman). If you happen to be near Logan, a visit here would not be a
                     total loss. On the other hand, if you're thinking of driving many miles
                     to reach this shop, consider making a phone call first to determine if
                     the shop has what you're looking for.

Orrin Schwab - Books   **By Appointment**
191 East 1000 N #1   (801) 755-9124
Mailing address: PO Box 4502 Logan 84323

Collection: General stock.
# of Vols: 4,000
Specialties: Utah; Mormans; Western Americana; military.
Services: Appraisals, search service, catalog, accepts want lists.
Credit Cards: Yes
Year Estab: 1991

Murray

Paperbacks Plus   **Open Shop**
685 West 5300 South   84123   (801) 261-8780

Collection: General stock of mostly paperback.
Hours: Mon-Sat 11-6.

Ogden

Books & Things   **Open Shop**
2438 Washington Boulevard

Collection: General stock of mostly paperback.
# of Vols: 2,000+

Hours:	Usually Mon-Sat 11-6.
Comments:	Not a shop worth driving out of one's way for, although the shop is located next to another used book dealer with a larger stock (see below). The selection of hardcover books is rather limited and their quality questionable.

The Bookshelf
2432 Washington   84401

Open Shop
(801) 621-4752
Fax: (801) 393-2815

Collection:	General stock of used and new hardcover and paperback.
# of Vols:	40,000+ (used)
Specialties:	Science fiction; fantasy.
Hours:	Mon-Sat 10-7. Sun 1-6.
Services:	Accepts want lists, mail order.
Travel:	Northbound on I-15 (from Salt Lake City): 24th St exit. Turn right and continue on Martin Luther King which becomes 24th St. Cross viaduct over railroad tracks and continue to Washington Blvd. Right on Washington. (Park north of building; owner will validate parking.)
Credit Cards:	Yes
Year Estab:	1981
Comments:	A good sized bi-level shop with a combination of new and used paperbacks and hardcover volumes, plus comics, magazines, games, CDs and videos. Considering the overall mix of the store's stock and the absence of any careful organization of the hardcover books (found mostly on the second floor), we suspect that unless your patience is greater than ours, your stop here may be a brief one.

Orem

Book Baron
355 South State Street   84058

Open Shop
(801) 225-4088

Collection:	General stock of mostly paperback.
Hours:	Mon-Sat 10-6.

Price

Crystal Dreams Bookstore & Gift Shop
29 East Main Street   84501

Open Shop
(801) 637-5510

Collection:	General stock of paperback and hardcover.
# of Vols:	3,000
Hours:	Mon-Sat 10-6.
Comments:	Stock is approximately 65% paperback.

Provo

Experienced Books   **Open Shop**
56 South Freedom Boulevard   85127   (801) 371-9293

Collection:	General stock of paperback and hardcover.
# of Vols:	6,000-8,000
Hours:	Tue-Sat 10-6.
Travel:	Center St exit off I-15. Proceed east on Center to 200 West (Freedom Blvd), then right on 200 West.
Credit Cards:	No
Owner:	Keith Clawson
Year Estab:	1996
Year Estab:	1996
Comments:	See comments for Salt Lake City shop.

Foxmoor Books   **Open Shop**
1700 North State Street   84601   (801) 375-9215

Collection:	General stock of mostly paperback.
# of Vols:	60,000-70,000
Hours:	Mon-Sat 10-7.

Grandin Book   **Open Shop**
116 West Center Street   84601   (800) 350-9363   (801) 377-1298
                                                      Fax: (801) 373-3322

Collection:	General stock of mostly hardcover.
# of Vols:	50,000
Specialties:	Emphasis on the liberal arts; Utah; Mormons.
Hours:	Mon-Sat 10-6.
Services:	Appraisals and search service (regional only), catalog, accepts want lists.
Travel:	Center St exit off I-15. Proceed east on Center St for about one mile.
Credit Cards:	Yes
Owner:	Lyndon Cook
Year Estab:	1984
Comments:	A spacious shop with books well displayed. In addition to the specialties listed above, the shop had a nice selection of military books, poetry and general literature.

Pioneer Book   **Open Shop**
**   (801) 377-1272

Collection:	General stock of hardcover and paperback.
# of Vols:	500,000
Specialties:	Religion; Mormons; children's; technical manuals; foreign language books.
Hours:	Mon-Sat 9-7.
Services:	Appraisals, mail order.

Credit Cards:	Yes
Owner:	Richard B. Horsley
Year Estab:	1980
Comments:	We had the opportunity to visit this establishment shortly before it had to vacate its former premises. At the time of our visit, we were impressed by both the size of the collection (although some sections had already been boxed in anticipation of the move) and the space available for its display. (Whether the store's new location will permit the display of as many volumes is up in the air.) We saw some new but mostly older volumes in mixed condition as well as some rare (collectible) items. The specialties listed above were well represented. While discriminating book people may pass over many of the selections here, they may also, if they possesses a keen eye, spot some worthwhile finds.

** At press time, the owner was still searching for a new 'home" and was operating out of a temporary location. We suggest you check the above phone number for the shop's current status.

Saint George

Doc's Book Loft   **Open Shop**
596 East Tabernacle, #B   84770   (801) 634-1039

Collection:	General stock of mostly paperback.
Hours:	Mon-Sat 10-6.

Salt Lake City

A Better Book   **Open Shop**
1450 South Main   84115   (801) 487-2766

Collection:	Specialty. Mostly used.
# of Vols:	5,000
Specialties:	Western Americana; Mormons.
Hours:	Mon-Sat 10-6.
Travel:	13 South exit off I-15. Proceed east on 13 South to Main then south on Main.
Credit Cards:	No
Owner:	Jeff Clark
Year Estab:	1994

Alpha Books   **Open Shop**
251 South State, #6   84111   (801) 355-2665

Collection:	Specialty
# of Vols:	2,000
Specialties:	Utah; Mormons.
Travel:	See the Serious Scholar below. The shop is located on the mezzanine.
Services:	Catalog in planning stage.
Owner:	Will Quist
Year Estab:	1995

B & W Collector Books   **By Appointment**
3466 South 700 East   84106   (801) 466-8395

Collection:	General stock.
# of Vols:	50,000
Services:	Appraisals, search service, accepts want lists.
Credit Cards:	Yes
Owner:	Sherry Black
Year Estab:	1994

Beehive Collector's Gallery   **By Appointment**
368 East Broadway   84111   (801) 533-0119

Collection:	Specialty books and ephemera.
# of Vols:	5,000
Specialties:	Mormons; Western Americana; military.
Services:	Accepts want lists, mail order.
Credit Cards:	Yes
Owner:	Nyal W. Anderson
Year Estab:	1955

Benchmark Books   **Open Shop**
3269 South Main, Ste. 250   (801) 486-3111
Mailing address: PO Box 9027 Salt Lake City 84109   Fax: (801) 4863452

Collection:	Specialty new and used.
# of Vols:	20,000 (used)
Specialties:	Mormans; Utah; Western Americana.
Hours:	Mon-Fri 10-6. Sat 10-5.
Services:	Appraisals, search service, accepts want lists, catalog.
Travel:	3300 South exit off I-15. Proceed east on 3300 South to Main, then left on Main. Shop is between State and West Temple
Credit Cards:	Yes
Owner:	Curt Bench
Year Estab:	1987

Book Shoppe   **Open Shop**
270 South State Street   84111   (801) 532-8520

Collection:	General stock.
# of Vols:	2,000-5,000
Hours:	Mon-Sat 12:30-6.
Services:	Accepts want lists.
Travel:	5th South exit off I-15. Proceed east on 5th South to State St, then north on State for two blocks.
Credit Cards:	No
Owner:	Bonnie Burt
Year Estab:	1969
Comments:	If your time is limited, "keep going" as this shop is small, its collection limited and the titles, except for Latter Day Saints (LDS) is limited.

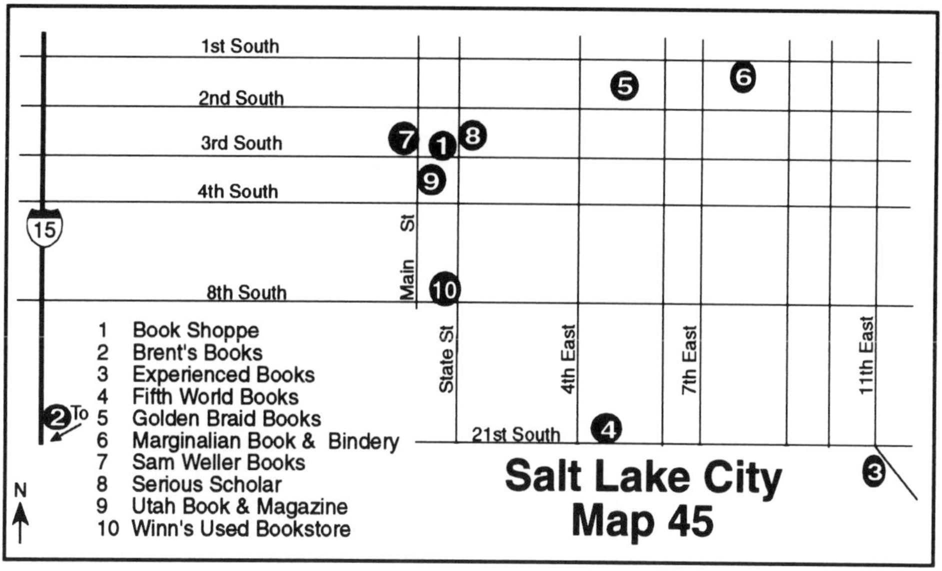

```
        1st South
        2nd South                              ❺        ❻
        3rd South              ❼ ❶ ❽
        4th South                  ❾
⑮
        8th South              ❿
```

1	Book Shoppe	
2	Brent's Books	
3	Experienced Books	
4	Fifth World Books	
5	Golden Braid Books	
6	Marginalian Book & Bindery	
7	Sam Weller Books	
8	Serious Scholar	
9	Utah Book & Magazine	
10	Winn's Used Bookstore	

Salt Lake City
Map 45

N ↑

Brent's Books   **Open Shop**
7650 South Redwood Road, #4   84084   (801) 569-2757

Collection:	General stock of paperback and hardcover.
# of Vols:	15,000
Hours:	Mon-Sat 10-6.
Travel:	7200 South exit off I-15. Proceed west on 7200 South to Redwood Rd, then south on Redwood. Shop is in Kelly Plaza.
Credit Cards:	No
Year Estab:	1994
Comments:	Stock is approximately 65% paperback.

Carpe Diem Books   **By Appointment**
PO Box 17036 84117   Fax: (801) 272-9569   (801) 278-7835
                                        E-mail: carpdiem@ix.netcom.com

Collection:	Specialty
# of Vols:	3,000
Specialties:	Western Americana; modern first editions.
Services:	Appraisals, search service, accepts want lists, catalog.
Credit Cards:	Yes
Owner:	James Bryant
Year Estab:	1994

Deseret Industries Thrift Store   **Open Shop**
743 West 700 South   (801) 579-1200

Collection:	General stock of paperback and hardcover.
Hours:	Mon-Sat 10-6.
Comments:	This is the main location for a series of not-for-profit thrift shops located throughout Utah. All books are donated.

(Salt Lake City)

Experienced Books   **Open Shop**
2150 Highland Drive   84106   (801) 467-0258

Collection:	General stock of paperback and hardcover.
# of Vols:	150,000
Hours:	Mon-Sat 10-6. Sun 1-5.
Services:	Accepts want lists.
Travel:	13th East exit off I-80. Proceed north on 13th East to 21st South, then left on 21st South. At light at bottom of hill, turn left on Highland Dr. Shop is one block ahead on right in Hyland Plaza.
Credit Cards:	No
Owner:	Keith Clawson
Year Estab:	1989
Comments:	A bi-level shop offering more paperbacks than hardcover items but with enough of the latter to tempt one to visit "just in case." While the stock is organized, one has to work to find the subject areas one is looking for. Hardly the neatest store we've visited, particularly the lower level (two to three times the size of the street level space) laid out in a series of nooks and crannies with lots of space to get lost in.

Fifth World Books   **Open Shop**
419 East 2100 South   84115   (801) 486-6437

Collection:	General stock of hardcover and paperback.
# of Vols:	20,000
Specialties:	Eastern religions; New Age; philosophy; literary criticism.
Hours:	Mon-Sat 11-5.
Services:	Accepts want lists.
Travel:	Between 400 and 500 East.
Credit Cards:	No
Owner:	Robert Firmage
Year Estab:	1990
Comments:	A serious collector should enjoy a visit to this shop. The stock is strong in literature, eastern philosophy, the occult, etc. The books we saw were varied and priced to sell.

Golden Braid Books   **Open Shop**
151 South 500 East   84102   (801) 322-1162

Collection:	General stock of mostly new and some used.
# of Vols:	500 (used)
Specialties:	Metaphysics
Hours:	Mon-Sat 10-9. Sun 10-6.

Hi Uinta Trading Co.   **By Appointment**
2600 Highland Drive   84106   (801) 466-9319

Collection:	Specialty books and related items.
# of Vols:	1,500

Specialties:	Boy scouts; Western Americana; Mormons.
Services:	Appraisals, search service, accepts want lists, catalog.
Credit Cards:	Yes
Owner:	Ted Murdock
Year Estab:	1991

Marginalian Book & Bindery   **Open Shop**
814 East 100 South   84102   (801) 322-5544

Collection:	General stock of paperback and hardcover and ephemera.
# of Vols:	25,000
Specialties:	Philosophy; anthropology; poetry; literary criticism.
Hours:	Mon-Fri 10-7. Sat & Sun 11-6.
Services:	Search service, accepts want lists, binding, restoration and repair.
Travel:	600 South exit off I-15. Left on 700 East, then right on 100 South. Shop is one block ahead on right.
Owner:	Michael Sorenson
Year Estab:	1991
Comments:	We arrived here at 3pm on a Wednesday and found a "Closed" sign on the window (despite the hours listed above which were provided by the owner). With several other book stores to visit in Salt Lake City, we would hesitate to recommend a stop here without a phone call ahead to assure yourself that you will not be wasting your time.

Sam Weller Books   **Open Shop**
254 South Main Street   84101   (801) 328-2586
                                                               (800) 333-7269

Collection:	General stock of used hardcover and paperback and new.
# of Vols:	1 million (used)
Specialties:	USGS publications; Western Americana; Mormons.
Hours:	Mon-Fri 9:30am-9pm. Sat 9:30-6.
Services:	Appraisals, search service, accepts want lists, occasional catalog.
Travel:	6th South exit off I-15. Proceed on 6th South for about two blocks to Main, then left on Main. Shop is 3½ blocks ahead. The store will validate parking in any of the surrounding parking lots.
Credit Cards:	Yes
Owner:	Tony Weller
Year Estab:	1929
Comments:	An absolute must stop if you're in the Salt Lake City area or within several hundred miles. This shop has it all. If you have no interest in new books, skip the first floor and walk up to the mezzanine where a slow paced walk around the periphery of the store will give you a chance to browse titles in many areas including religion, metaphysics, literature, plus a section displaying attractive sets and a rare book room. More general titles, in generous numbers, are located in a basement that is large, well labeled and dizzying in terms of the scope of subjects displayed as well as the quality of most of the books. Had our trunk been larger, we would have left with far more books than we purchased.

(Salt Lake City)

Ken Sanders, Books   **By Appointment**
PO Box 26707   84126   Fax: (801)467-1495   (801) 467-1490
                                                     E-mail: ken@dreamgarden.com

Collection:	Specialty
# of Vols:	10,000
Specialties:	Western Americana; modern first editions; Native Americans; LDS.
Services:	Accepts want lists, catalog.
Year Estab:	1990

Scallawagiana   **By Appointment**
PO Box 2441   84110   (801) 539-1231

Collection:	Specialty
# of Vols:	2,000+
Specialties:	Freemasonry; Utah; Mormons.
Services:	Search service, accepts want lists, catalog.
Credit Cards:	No
Owner:	Kent Walgren
Year Estab:	1980

Serious Scholar   **Open Shop**
251 South State Street   84111   (801) 328-2202

Collection:	General stock of mostly hardcover.
# of Vols:	5,000-10,000
Specialties:	Bible studies.
Hours:	Mon-Sat 12-5:30.
Services:	Accepts want lists.
Travel:	600 South exit off I-15. Proceed east on 6th South, then left on State St. Shop is in the International Mart building.
Credit Cards:	No
Owner:	Robert Harrison
Year Estab:	1992
Comments:	A limited stock in mixed condition and of mixed vintage. Located immediately adjacent to a "collectible" shop and with a another dealer in the same building (see Alpha Books above), this is an easy "three for one" visit.

Utah Book & Magazine   **Open Shop**
327 South Main Street   84111   (801) 359-4391

Collection:	General stock of paperback and hardcover.
# of Vols:	150,000 (book)
Specialties:	Magazines
Hours:	Mon-Sat 6-6.
Services:	Search service, accepts want lists, mail order.
Travel:	6th South exit off I-15. Proceed east on 6th South to Main St, then left on Main. Shop is about 1½ blocks ahead.

Owner: Peter Marshall
Year Estab: 1916
Comments: An ample collection of paperbacks along with magazines (particularly *Soldier of Fortune* and related gun magazines), comics, an adult section and some hardcover books in mixed condition and not particularly well organized. If you have patience and want to sample the atmosphere, go ahead.

Winn's Used Bookstore   **Open Shop**
724 South State   84111   (801) 532-7147

Collection: General stock of hardcover and paperback.
# of Vols: 5,000
Hours: Mon-Sat 11-5.
Credit Cards: No
Year Estab: 1983
Comments: A small, compact shop with a mix of paperbacks and hardcover books. While no areas were represented in depth, we did see some interesting regional titles. One of those shops that you can be in and out of quickly but where you may also leave with an interesting find.

Sandy

Main Street Exchange   **Open Shop**
8519 South State Street   84070   (801) 255-9669

Collection: General stock of paperback and hardcover.
# of Vols: 25,000
Hours: Tue- Fri 11-6. Sat 11-5.
Travel: 90th South exit off I-15. Proceed east on 90th South to State, then north on State for four blocks. Shop is in a former residence.
Credit Cards: Yes
Owner: Lori Oakason
Year Estab: 1992
Comments: Stock is approximately 70% paperback.

Sam Weller Books   **Open Shop**
8191 South 700 East   84070   (801) 566-0219

Collection: General stock of new and used hardcover and paperback.
# of Vols: 50,000
Hours: Mon-Fri 10-9. Sat 10-6.
Travel: Union Park exit off Hwy 215. Proceed south on Union Park, staying in far right lane. Turn right at Ft Union Blvd, then left at 900 East which becomes 700 East. The shop is between 8400 and 8000 South
Credit Cards: Yes
Owner: Tony Weller
Comments: Approximately 25% of the shop's stock is used.

Spring City

Turn of the Century Books   **Open Shop**
190 North Main Street   (801) 462-9443
Mailing address: PO Box 70 Spring City 84662   Fax: (801) 462-9411

Collection:	General stock.
# of Vols:	3,000
Specialties:	First editions; Utah; Mormons; history.
Hours:	May-Oct: Tue-Sat 11-6. Other months: by chance or appointment.
Services:	Search service, accepts want lists.
Travel:	Exit 225 off I-15. Proceed east to Mt. Pleasant, then south on Hwy 89 to Hwy 117, then southeast on Hwy 117 for four miles to Spring City. Shop is on southeast corner of Main St & 2nd North.
Credit Cards:	Yes
Owner:	Daniel J. & Helen E. Keenan
Year Estab:	1992
Comments:	Shop is located in a national historic district.

West Jordan
(See Salt Lake City)

Blackstone & Coke, Antiquarian Books
(801) 582-0869
2054 Michigan Avenue Salt Lake City 84108
E-mail: blackstn@aol.com

Collection:	Specialty books and related prints.
Specialties:	Law; early US and British history; manuscripts.
Services:	Appraisals, search service, catalog, accepts want lists, design and printing of custom bookplates.
Credit Cards:	No
Owner:	Richard King
Year Estab:	1994

Frontier Books
(801) 763-0773
PO Box 871 American Fork 84003

Collection:	General stock.
# of Vols:	10,000
Specialties:	Western Americana; LDS.
Services:	Appraisals, search service, accepts want lists, catalog.
Credit Cards:	No
Owner:	Bruce McDaniel
Year Estab:	1995

Clark J. Phelps Antiques
(801) 364-4747
390 K Street   Salt Lake City 84103

Collection:	Specialty books and ephemera.
Specialties:	Alcoholics Anonymous.
Services:	Accepts want lists, mail order.
Credit Cards:	No
Year Estab:	1974

Lynn Pulsipher
(801) 377-3046
PO Box 1111 Provo 84603

Collection:	Specialty
# of Vols:	75-100
Specialties:	LDS; Western Americana.
Services:	Catalog, search service, accepts want lists.
Year Estab:	1989

Roger Wangemann Books
(801) 225-1803
1147 East 435 North   Orem 84097

Collection:	Specialty
# of Vols:	2,500
Specialties:	LDS; Western Americana.
Year Estab:	1967

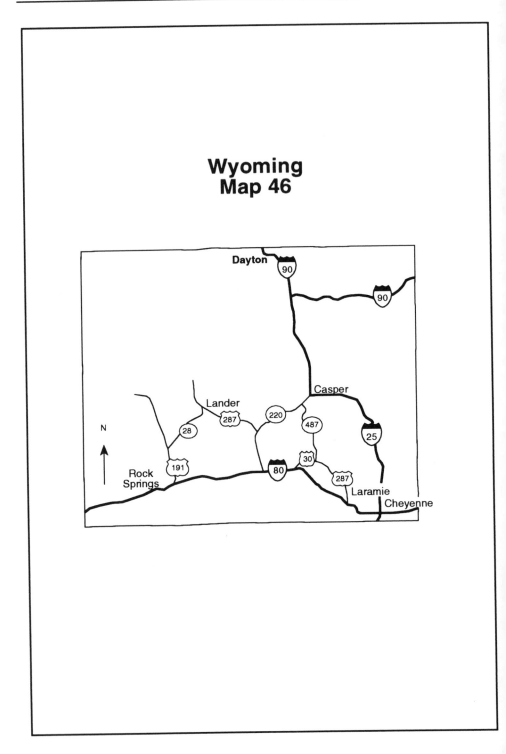

Wyoming
Map 46

Wyoming

Alphabetical Listing by Dealer

Alphabetical Listing By Location

Casper

The Book Gallery   **Open Shop**
235 East 1st Street   82601   (307) 234-4412

Collection:	General stock.
# of Vols:	2,000+
Specialties:	Early 20th century fiction; Wyoming; Western Americana; European history.
Hours:	Tue-Fri 1-5:30. Sat 10-4.
Services:	Search service.
Travel:	Center St (downtown) exit.
Credit Cards:	Yes
Owner:	Mary Lou Morrison
Year Estab:	1993

The Book Exchange   **Open Shop**
1020 East 2nd Street   (307) 237-6034

Formerly The Book Shelf, the new owner was in the process of moving into the above new location at the time we went to press. For information on stock and hours, please call the above phone number.

The Book Peddler   **Open Shop**
4270 South Poplar   82601   (307) 266-2021

Collection:	General stock of new and mostly paperback used.
Hours:	Mon-Sat 10-5.
Credit Cards:	Yes
Owner:	Carroll L. Propp
Year Estab:	1990
Comments:	Stock is approximately 40% used, 80% of which is paperback.

Cheyenne

Chiefly Books   **Open Shop**
1914 Thomes Avenue   82001   (307) 778-6101

Collection:	General stock.
# of Vols:	14,000
Specialties:	Western Americana.
Hours:	Mon-Fri 10-5:30. Sat 12-5.
Services:	Appraisals, search service, accepts want lists, mail order.
Travel:	West Lincolnway exit off I-25. Proceed east on Lincolnway to downtown, then left on Thomes. Shop is three blocks ahead on left in an old church.
Credit Cards:	Yes
Owner:	Don Patterson
Year Estab:	1994

Cody

The Jordan Gallery   **Open Shop**
1349 Sheridan Avenue   82414   Fax: (307) 527-4944   (307) 587-6689
                                              E-mail: jjordon@crib.com

Collection: Specialty books and related materials.
Specialties: First editions; Yellowstone National Park; big game hunting; fishing; Will
                  James; gambling; western autographs; outlaws; Native Americans.
Hours: Mon-Sat 9-5. Longer hours in summer.
Services: Search service, catalog, accepts want lists.
Credit Cards: Yes
Owner: Jerry Jordan
Year Estab: 1970

Wyoming Well Book Exchange   **Open Shop**
1902 Sheridan Avenue   (307) 587-4249
Mailing address: PO Box 340 Cody 82414

Collection: General stock of mostly paperback.
Hours: Mon-Sat 8-6.

Dayton

Summerhouse Books   **Open Shop**
402 Main Street   (307) 655-9714
Mailing address: PO Box 66 Dayton 82836

Collection: General stock.
# of Vols: 7,000+
Specialties: Western Americana; Wyoming.
Hours: Mon-Sat 10-5, except closed Wed in winter.
Services: Search service, catalog, accepts want lists, mail order.
Travel: Ranchester exit off I-90. Proceed on Hwy 14 for six miles to Dayton.
Credit Cards: Yes
Owner: Bonnie Switzer & Janet Wolney
Year Estab: 1976

Lander

Cabin Fever Books   **Open Shop**
163 South 5th Street   82520   (307) 332-9580

Collection: General stock of new and mostly paperback used.
# of Vols: 5,000-10,000 (used)
Hours: Mon-Sat 10-6.

Laramie

High Country Books   **Open Shop**
306 South Second Street   82070   (307) 742-5640

Collection: General stock of mostly used paperback and hardcover.

# of Vols:	21,000 (used)
Hours:	Mon-Sat 10-6. Sun 12-4.
Travel:	3rd St exit off I-80. Proceed on 3rd St toward town. Turn left on Garfield, then right on 2nd St.
Credit Cards:	Yes
Owner:	Andee Gilliam
Year Estab:	1972
Comments:	Used stock is approximately 65% paperback.

Rock Springs

Wyoming Book & Music Exchange   **Open Shop**
411 North Front Street   82901   (307) 362-0685

Collection:	General stock of paperback and hardcover and records.
# of Vols:	3,500
Hours:	Mon-Sat 10-5.
Travel:	Elk St exit off I-80. Proceed south for 1½ miles.
Services:	Appraisals
Comments:	Stock is approximately 75% paperback. The shop also sells antiques.

Mail Order Dealers

Best of the West Books   (307) 737-2222
46 Wakely Road   Sheridan 82801

Collection:	Specialty
# of Vols:	500
Specialties:	Will James; cowboys; cattle and horses.
Services:	Search service, occasional catalog.
Owner:	Lee Douglas
Year Estab:	1976

Charles Hall   (307) 634-1782
3755 Dover Road Cheyenne 82001

Collection:	Specialty
# of Vols:	6,000
Specialties:	Western Americana; military; autographs.
Services:	Appraisals, search service, accepts want lists, occasional catalog.
Year Estab:	1971

Star Valley Books   (307) 883-3070
PO Box 989 Thayne   83127   Fax: (307) 883-4070
E-mail: heidi@cyberhighway.net

Collection:	General stock.
Services:	Search service, catalog, accepts want lists.
Credit Cards:	No
Owner:	Robert L. Rozell
Year Estab:	1992

Specialty Index

The Used Book Lover's Guide Series

Your guide to over 6,000 used book dealers.

Pacific Coast Guide
1,350 dealers • 474 pp • $18.95
ISBN 0-9634112-5-X

New England Guide
750 dealers • 383 pp • $16.95
ISBN 0-9634112-4-1

Central States Guide
1,250 dealers • 465 pp • $18.95
ISBN 0-9634112-6-8

Mid-Atlantic Guide
Rev. Edition due Spring '97 • $18.95
ISBN 0-9634112-7-6

Midwest Guide
1,000 dealers • 449 pp • $17.95
ISBN 0-9634112-3-3

South Atlantic Guide
600 dealers • 336 pp • $15.95
ISBN 0-9634112-2-5

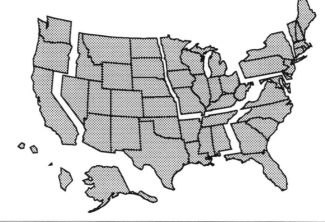

Keeping Current

As a service to our readers, we're happy to make available, at cost, Supplements for each of our guides.

The Supplements, published annually, provide our readers with additional listings as well as information concerning dealers who have either moved or gone out of business.

Much of the information in the Supplements comes to us from loyal readers who, in using our guides, have been kind enough to provide us with this valuable data based on their own book hunting experiences.

Should you wish to receive the next Supplement for the book(s) you currently own, complete the Order Form on the next page and enclose $2.50 for each Supplement, plus postage. The Supplements will be mailed as they become available.

ORDER FORM

Book Hunter Press
PO Box 193 • Yorktown Heights, NY 10598
(914) 245-6608 • Fax: (914) 245-2630

GUIDES	Price	# of Copies	Disc.	Unit Cost	Total
New England	16.95				
Mid-Atlantic *	18.95				
South Atlantic	15.95				
Midwest	17.95				
Pacific Coast	18.95				
Central States	18.95				
ANNUAL SUPPLEMENTS					
New England	2.50				
Mid-Atlantic	2.50				
South Atlantic	2.50				
Midwest	2.50				
Pacific Coast	2.50				
Central States	2.50				

* For Spring '97 Revised Edition

SPECIAL DISCOUNTS
Any combination of books
2-5 copies: 20%
6 or more copies: 40%

Subtotal
Shipping
(NYS residents only) Sales Tax
TOTAL

SHIPPING   Guides: $2.45 for single copies. Add 75¢ for each add'l. copy.
Supplements: 50¢ each.

Name_____

Company_____

Address_____

City_____ State_____ Zip_____

Phone_____

MC Card _____ Visa _____ Exp Date _____

Card # _____

Signature_____